Trends in Software-Defined Networking

TRENDS IN SOFTWARE-DEFINED NETWORKING

Jocelyn O. Padallan

ARCLER PRESS

www.arclerpress.com

Trends in Software-Defined Networking

Jocelyn O. Padallan

Arcler Press
4164 Lakeshore Road
Burlington, ON L7L 1A4
Canada
www.arclerpress.com
Email: orders@arclereducation.com

ISBN: 978-1-77956-416-0 (Hardcover)

ABOUT THE AUTHOR

Jocelyn O. Padallan is Associate Professor I from Laguna State Polytechnic University, Philippines and she is currently pursuing her Doctor in Information Technology has Master in Information Technology and Master of Arts in Education from the same University. She has passion for teaching been Instruction and College of Computer Studies - Student Council Adviser at Laguna State Polytechnic University.

TABLE OF CONTENTS

LIST OF FIGURES

LIST OF TABLES

PREFACE

Software-defined networking (SDN) represents a revolutionary shift in computer networking by fundamentally separating the control plane from the data plane. This separation enhances flexibility and scalability, enabling network administrators to manage and reconfigure network traffic dynamically and efficiently. In traditional networks, various devices such as switches, routers, hubs, and repeaters are managed with complex protocols, requiring substantial manual configuration and management. This complexity often results in limited flexibility and challenges in network tuning. SDN addresses these issues by consolidating network control into a single, centralized controller, which manages all traffic flow and configurations.

Recent trends in SDN include Network Function Virtualization (NFV) and Software-Defined Wide Area Network (SDN-WAN). NFV transforms network functions traditionally embedded in hardware into software instances that run on virtualized infrastructure, improving flexibility and reducing costs. SDN-WAN extends centralized control across wide-area networks (WANs) to cloud providers, optimizing network traffic and enhancing quality of service (QoS) through intelligent routing and resource allocation.

The centralized nature of SDN also bolsters security by allowing all traffic to pass through a single firewall, making it easier to deploy Intrusion Detection Systems (IDS) and Intrusion Prevention Systems (IPS) effectively. This centralized control supports automation in network management, such as the configuration of Virtual LANs (VLANs) and improves traceability of network changes.

A significant protocol in SDN is OpenFlow, which facilitates traffic routing among diverse switches and routers regardless of the manufacturer. OpenFlow enhances the enforcement of security policies and network management at a central level, bypassing the limitations of physical device configurations. This book consolidates the latest topics on SDN advancements, explores its challenges, and provides solutions to address these issues, offering a comprehensive resource for understanding and implementing SDN technologies.

The book *Trends in Software-Defined Networking* offers a comprehensive exploration of the latest developments in SDN, organized into 10 insightful chapters. It begins with a detailed examination of centralized and distributed control and data planes, setting the stage for understanding the core principles of SDN architecture. The second chapter examines into OpenFlow, a pivotal protocol that enables interoperability and flexible traffic routing across various network devices. Subsequent chapters focus on SDN controllers, which manage network traffic and configurations, and network programmability, which facilitates the automation of network management tasks. The book further explores data center concepts and constructs, highlighting the evolution of data center networks in the context of SDN. Network Function Virtualization (NFV) is also covered, illustrating how virtualizing network functions enhances network flexibility and efficiency. Additionally, the book discusses network topology and topological information abstraction, essential for understanding the structural dynamics of SDN environments. Building an SDN framework is addressed, providing practical guidance on implementing and integrating SDN solutions. The final chapters present use cases for bandwidth scheduling, manipulation, and calendaring, as well as for data center overlays, big data, and NFV, demonstrating the real-world applications and benefits of SDN technologies. Collectively, these chapters offer a thorough overview of current trends, challenges, and solutions in SDN, making it an invaluable resource for professionals, researchers, and students looking to deepen their understanding of this transformative field.

–Author

CHAPTER 1

CENTRALIZED AND DISTRIBUTED CONTROL AND DATA PLANES

Contents

INTRODUCTION

Software-defined networking (SDN) is a network implementation methodology that makes use of software-based controllers to interface with hardware and decide traffic routing. A network that is defined by software separates packet forwarding and network control from closed, proprietary physical hardware (e.g., routers and switches) and instead makes use of commodity hardware that can be programmed (e.g., bare metal switches) and software that adheres to standards for managing packet forwarding. The term "bare metal" describes SDN switches that are configured without an operating system or suite of networking apps preinstalled, i.e., without an abstraction layer (also known as a hypervisor) between the hardware and applications. The foundation of SDN is the separation of the switching hardware and software. End-to-end network flow visibility is made possible by the SDN technique, which also allows for fine-grained traffic path optimization and network-wide data flow control. SDN has gained a lot of traction, especially in data centers and on wide area networks (WANs).

According to software-defined networking (SDN), networks must have separate control and data planes, and an open interface clearly defines how these two planes should be divided:

i. **Control Plane (Software):** Decides the behavior of the network, including the path packets should take while traveling through it. These network traffic flows are managed by a controller located in the control plane of an SDN architecture.

ii. **Data Plane (Hardware):** Permits data to be sent from the sender to the recipient. In particular, a data plane carries out the directives from the control plane on a per-packet basis, including tasks like forwarding packets along the routes that the control plane specifies.

Disaggregation is the term used to describe the process of dividing the control and data planes, allowing different parties to be in charge of each plane. Put another way, disaggregation refers to the ability of a network operator to buy data plane hardware from a different vendor and control plane software from a different vendor.

Distributed control plane is used by all traditional networking devices, including switches and routers. Yet, a more recent networking model, i.e., A centralized control plane is used by software-defined networking, or SDN. A distributed control plane is one in which each networking device's control plane is located inside the device. To control the data plane, each device has its own control plane. A device that houses the control planes of every device is part of the centralized control plane system. This device manages the data plane operations of every networking device at the same time. We refer to this device as an SDN controller, or controller.

1.1. SDN VS. TRADITIONAL NETWORKS: REVOLUTION OR EVOLUTION

The networking industry is definitely using SDN as a buzzword. Businesses are starting to adopt software-defined networks more and more. This section will address the questions of whether this technology is a true disruptor that will eventually replace legacy networks or if it is a natural next step in the evolution of networks.

1.1.1. SDN for Enhancing Legacy Networks

This is not a revolution, but rather a step forward for networks. Examining the advantages of SDN technology or even putting it into practice does not imply dismantling the conventional network architecture. SDNs are meant to enhance current networks, not to completely replace them. From a conceptual standpoint, we can have a meaningful conversation about SDNs if we combine automation with long-standing networking concepts and solutions.

1.1.2. Separating the Control and Data Planes

Control plane and data plane separation is one of the key ideas in SDN. Of course, one could argue that this is nothing new as it has long been a standard feature of conventional network hardware. Separate control cards are used by carrier grade routers to determine routing, and a collection of line cards is used to forward traffic in accordance with the information sent by the control card. SDNs, however, use this idea in a more advanced manner. Here, a controller is seen as a distinct entity that lives remotely, gives instructions to forwarders, and makes decisions based on the network's overall state, viewing the network as a whole. The distinction lies in the criteria used to make decisions.

1.1.3. The Concept of Underlay and Overlay Networks Adopted for a New Use

Probably the second thing that comes to mind is the existence of overlay and underlay networks. However, are these networks truly novel? Considering the provider's networks, which employ a variety of transport protocols, including MPLS, is it possible to argue that the notion of isolating the transport from the transmitted data is novel? Do VPNs serve any additional functions? In fact, BGP, EVPN, VXLAN, and MPLS are among the protocols that are currently in use in data centers. Thus, ideas that have been around for a while have been adapted for a new purpose.

1.1.4. SDN Enhancing Traditional Networks

Three aspects of SDNs stand out when compared to traditional networks in a summary. Initially, the WAN made use of the concept of controlling plane and data plane separation. As a result, controllers that intelligently route traffic over the network while viewing it from a helicopter perspective were developed. Without a central brain, this whole management would not be feasible. Second, implementing underlay and overlay in DCs, along with a spine and leaf topology and the widely known EVPN and BGP protocols in conjunction with VXLAN, helped optimize data center resource utilization. By integrating an external controller to oversee both the overlay and underlay, we can effortlessly construct a robust network that maximizes resources.

Lastly, advanced virtual network creation across all computes is now possible with VMs/containers where SDN controllers have been introduced and integrated with platforms like OpenStack or Kubernetes. One excellent illustration of such a solution is tungsten fabric. Apart from the aforementioned three concerns, an additional aspect of SDNs that has not been explored is the user's capacity to configure network devices. Once more, the concept of executing custom script on the routers is not new; it has been conceivable to do this for a while. However, the concept of programming an entirely new feature and implementing it on the hardware is what we are talking about here.

1.1.5. SDN Business Benefits

As you can see, there are many advantages to implementing SDNs. It is not necessary to wait for a vendor to develop a new feature when it can be done internally or by a third party, as we have covered in the latter example. Here, a significant reduction in time-to-market (TTM) is anticipated. As demonstrated by the other cases, additional benefits include improved network resilience (leading to quality improvement) and agility in adapting to changing needs, as well as resource usage optimization (resulting in cost optimization).

1.2. EVOLUTION OF SDN

Project Ethane (Casado et al., 2007), conducted at Stanford University, established a novel architecture designed especially for business networks. It is made up of two abstraction planes: the data plane, which is made up of ethane switches with a secure communication channel to the controller and is used to enforce the controllers' decisions, and the control plane, which is made up of the centralized controller and manages the network's policies and security issues. This work shows that network management is made easier with such a split architecture. The promise demonstrated by the Ethane project prompted the creation of OpenFlow (McKeown et al., 2008); a general protocol that has made it possible for a controller to speak with network switches that have enabled OpenFlow. OpenFlow specifically gives the controller the ability to add, remove, or alter forwarding entries in the switch flow table, which in turn controls how the network behaves. One of the most popular protocols, it is currently standardized by the Open Networking Foundation (ONF). Ethane lacks general programmatic control of the network because it was designed with a specific purpose in mind. To address this, the Ethane team has developed Nox (Gude et al., 2008), a general-purpose network controller, which made use of the OpenFlow protocol. Network administrators can program the Nox controller through the Nox user interface. It is the first of the many general purpose network controllers, such as Ryu, Difane (Yu et al., 2010), etc., paving the way for software defined networks.

1.2.1. The Control Plane

All of the network's switches are managed by a single entity known as a centralized controller. It raises the issues of scalability constraints and single point of failure. It is now essential to solve these issues if SDN is to be widely used.

The success of separating the network's control and data planes is evidenced by the emergence of new applications, as the Ethane project demonstrates. But it's becoming clear that centralized controllers are not scalable as the network gets bigger. In Onix (Koponen et al., 2010), is the first controller to suggest a distributed hierarchical control plane in which local decisions about the network they have managed are made by lower tier Onix controllers. The root controller is given access to the aggregated localized data and control decisions, which allows it to make global decisions. Transferring some of the controller's workload to the switches is another way to address the scalability issue, as shown in (Yu et al., 2010). But doing so necessitates changing the switch hardware. Since it takes at least a few years to design and construct changes to the switch hardware, this approach is not commonly used. Hyperflow, a different logically centralized, physically distributed controller, was unveiled concurrently with the development of Onix (Tootoonchian & Ganjali, 2010).

In contrast to Onix, this controller distribution architecture is flat, allowing each controller to see the entire network while making local decisions. The subscribe publish paradigm is used to transmit the control events to one another. The earlier-developed Nox controller is used in its construction. They also demonstrate how scalable these architectures are by using little control channel bandwidth and leaving plenty of space for growth. While the single point of failure issue has been resolved, attention still needs to be paid to the latency caused by the inter-controller communication between the two tiers. By dividing the controller functionality among several controllers or the switches, the solutions that have been put forth up to this point have made the control plane scalable. The decision of which switch should be assigned to which controller has not been made explicitly in these works. This type of inquiry is currently referred to as the controller placement issue.

The literature mentioned above makes it clear that in order to make the control plane scalable, multiple controllers are required. Heller et al. (2012) authored the initial manuscript addressing the issue of controller placement, i.e., the number of controllers needed in a network and their optimal placement. They examine the issue of controller placement, particularly in relation to WAN topologies. The placement metric that was selected was latency. The researchers find that while a single controller suffices for moderate service level agreements, it is insufficient to manage network failure after testing their algorithms on a variety of topologies. Additionally, they draw the conclusion that, in large WAN-like networks, it is not ideal to place controllers randomly throughout the network. Instead, the location of the controllers must be carefully chosen to optimize for the given metric, such as latency, reliability, etc. Zhang et al. (2011) used metrics like valid control paths and resiliency protection to evaluate reliability when placing the controllers in addition to just distributing them. The switch and controller have dependable connectivity thanks to these metrics. In addition, the network is separated into numerous domains, resulting in a large number of edges connecting switches within each domain and a small number of edges connecting switches between domains. In order to boost reliability, these controllers are located on a switch that is a part of a domain.

Another recent study (Levin et al., 2012) has published research on the eventual and robust consistency of the controllers'-maintained network views or network state data. They also go over how the consistency type will determine how the application-level programs need to be adjusted. They demonstrate how an inconsistent global view can result in application program suboptimal performance, including routing loops. Having a consistent global perspective requires more expensive communication. This is a trade-off between two different kinds of application programs. The first is a sophisticated yet reliable application program that recognizes the possibility that the controller data is out-of-date and adjusts appropriately. The second application program is less sophisticated and more straightforward, but it ignores the possibility that the controller data is out-of-date.

Since then, a number of placement metrics, including the anticipated percentage of legitimate paths to the controller for the WAN environment, have been formally defined (Hu et al., 2012). The percentage of operational paths between the switches and the controller following a network component failure, such as a node or link failure, is known as the expected percent of valid paths. The authors suggest arranging controllers in the network in an avaricious manner. They do this by figuring out the likelihood that a networking component will fail. SDN network scalability has been achieved through the use of hierarchical multi-controller architecture (Hassas & Ganjali, 2012). Only local domain level information is maintained by lower tier controllers, while global network level information is managed by top tier controllers. Controllers at lower tiers can make local decisions (e.g., recognize mouse or elephant flows), without having to get in touch with the top controller. To get a view of the entire network, the top tier controllers in this case subscribe to the lower tier controllers.

For the links between the switches and the controller, the resilient network problem (Beheshti & Zhang, 2012) is developed, along with a metric for safeguarding resiliency. If a switch has a route to the controller other than via the routing tree of the controller, it is referred to as protected. There are two suggested algorithms for controller placement. The first algorithm chooses a placement that results in the fewest number of unprotected switches after performing a brute force search over all potential controller placements. In order to raise the switches protection metric, the second algorithm, which is heuristic based, determines the controller location of a densely connected switch.

Previous research concentrated on the location of static controllers, but Bari et al. (2013) dynamically assigned controllers in response to changes in the underlying network's state, thereby resolving the controller placement issue. In an effort to reduce flow setup time and communication overhead, the monitoring module allocates and deallocates switches to the controllers while keeping an eye on the controllers. Furthermore, Hock et al. (2014) examine how switches must be reassigned to a new controller as a result of a controller failure. When the primary controller malfunctions, they have a set of backup controllers that they utilize. In this case, a metric based on the communication delays between a switch and its primary and secondary controller is used to determine the controller placement. They demonstrate that their placement is parabolic.

The latency and load are both considered as a metric for controller placement by UlHuque et al. (2015). They have dynamically reassigned the switches to controllers in order to evenly distribute the load as the load on the switches varies. Kreutz et al. (2013) formulate two optimization problems and create an SDN failure model to explain network failures in SDN, i.e.,

Controller Placement under Comprehensive Network States (CPCNS) problem and Controller Placement under Single Link Failure (CPSLF) problem. Then, for these failure models, they have proposed the best controller placement algorithms. A specialized heuristic, which takes into account a particular set of optimization objectives, is developed by Lange et al. (2015a) and used for controller placement. Lange et al. (2015b) present POCO, a framework for Pareto-based Optimal Controller placement that provides operators for Pareto optimal placements with respect to different performance metrics. They employ a heuristic method, which is less precise but produces faster computation, for large networks.

Some time ago, Zheng et al. (2017) is built on a core-edge separated architecture, with a hybrid implementation of the control tasks. Depending on where the traffic is, the edge switches are grouped into local control groups. The network edge is frequently given coarse-grained control tasks. Only a very small number of intergroup or other fine-grained control events are under the control of the central controller. To remain lazy, the central controller continuously modifies how the edge switches are grouped. UlHuque et al. (2017) divided the network into sub-regions and determined the best location for the controller module based on a sub-region with a maximum latency bound. This allowed for the operation of the maximum number of switches while minimizing the maximum latency. Only very dynamic networks are appropriate for the resource-intensive dynamic controller placement technique.

Current research (Wang et al., 2018) on the placement of controllers in wide area networks, have divided the network using a clustering algorithm to reduce end-to-end latency. Presently, works on controller placement are focusing a wide array of networks such as wireless networks (Dvir et al., 2018), 5G networks (Liu et al., 2018), etc. Additionally, these studies develop intricate placement metrics that account for the unique features of these networks, such as increased packet loss or hidden terminal issues with 5G networks' reliability.

1.2.2. The Data Plane

In SDN, destination-based routing may cause scalability problems. Using source routing is one way to solve this issue. In this case, the switches only forward the packet based on the path of the packet, which is stored in the packet itself and carries information from the source to the destination. The lack of a central decision-making body and network-wide data makes source routing uncommon in traditional networks. Since SDN offers both of these strategies, source routing is becoming more and more common.

While Secondnet (Guo et al., 2010) is among the first works that employs port switching to perform source routing in data centers; however, it is not implemented in SDN. Instead of using the link details, port switching stores the path information using the egress port number. Because the switches are essentially stateless and the servers make the routing decisions, they demonstrate the scalability of source routing. Soliman et al. (2012) is one of the first papers to discuss source routing in SDN. They have enhanced source routing with reverse path calculation. They have added reverse path calculation to improve source routing. The ingress port number replaces the egress port number as the packet enters a switch, indicating the packet's reverse path. Additionally, they demonstrated how link failure can be managed locally, with the switch selecting a different outgoing link in accordance with the alternate link data that is stored in the switch.

Installing forwarding information on the switches is a task that source routing relieves the controller of. Although source routing resolves the scalability issue, it is not robust against link failure because the switches are not actively forwarding packets. In 2013 (Stephens et al., 2013), the researchers have focused on making source routing resilient to failure. The primary responsibilities in this case are the Plinko forwarding function, source routing, path computation on the controller, and reverse path computation using each switch's ingress port number. The final function is to store backup routes in the packet to be used in case the primary path fails. Their algorithm starts by putting source routing into practice. The switch local to the failure locates and stores a different path in case of a packet's link failure. In the event that the link fails, this data is used to forward the current packet as well as any subsequent ones. In 2013 (Ramos et al., 2013a) the authors have done extensive work on source-controlled routing. A resilient source routing algorithm has been developed as part of this work.

Here, a primary route has been calculated, and a secondary route between the source and the destination has been found and stored in the packet. In the event that the primary route is compromised, the backup route must be taken. They also make sure that nothing creates a loop. An attempt is made to limit the secondary route's length. They have further improved on this work in Ramos et al. (2013b), to support arbitrary topologies. Sci propose that latency can be reduced significantly by removing fields in packet headers that are unnecessary in the SDN environment. In 2013 (Alizadeh et al., 2013), the authors discuss scalability issues in SDN. They propose the separation of edge and core controllers. They suggest dividing controllers at the edge and core. In this case, network status collection is handled by the core controller and path installation is handled by the edge controller. Scalability can be increased with this method because the edge controller can install paths more quickly because it is not burdened with network status collection functionality. Even though Alizadeh et al. (2013) are not about source routing; instead, they offer ways to make source routing more efficient by separating path installation from status collection and making use of packet header bits that are left over.

Katta et al. (2016) use a switch that monitors congestion to determine the optimal path—rather than all paths—to the destination in order to solve the scalability issue on the data plane caused by constrained switch memory. They used the P4 programming language to program the switch data plane in order to implement this solution (Bosshart et al., 2014). Zhang et al. (2016) create a routing strategy that uses less TCAM space and is aware of switch memory. They employ subnet masks to minimize the number of entries in each table and aggregate flows between various source and destination pairs. The time required to install the lengthy flow table entries into TCAM memory is a significant barrier to the data plane's scalability. Bifulco et al. (2017) note that it is quicker to install flow rules on software and remove them from hardware, so they employ a hybrid strategy of hardware and software switches to solve this issue. Therefore, software is always the first to update the forwarding table. To increase overall throughput, entries are eventually moved to TCAM-based forwarding tables and eventually deleted from there.

A new method for determining TCP flow that is about to terminate by examining FIN packets was presented in a recent paper (Shirali-Shahreza & Ganjali, 2018). The average table occupancy is then decreased by using this information to speed up the flow rule eviction. Another new approach that has been suggested recently is the prudent use of software tables—which have a higher capacity but shorter lookup times—in combination with TCAM memory (Kentis et al., 2018). The controller placement solution is compiled in Table 1.1.

Table 1.1. *Summary of Controller Placement Solutions*

Issues Addressed	**Architecture**	**Metric**	**Domain**	**Topology**	**Component of Failure**	**References**
Onix – Hierarchical controller placement	Hierarchical	Logical groups	Enterprise	Random	None	Koponen et al. (2010)
Hyperflow – Distributed control plane	Flat	Proximity	Medium enterprise	Star	Component failure	Tootoonchian & Ganjali (2010)
Flat control plane	Flat	Reliability	Medium enterprise	Random	Node and link failure	Zhang et al. (2011)

Effect of different positions of controllers	Flat	Latency	WAN	Random	Node and link	Heller et al. (2012)
Kandoo – Offloading controller application	Hierarchical	Proximity	Data center	Tree	None	Hassas Yeganeh & Ganjali (2012)
Fast fail over mechanism	Flat	Resiliency protection	Enterprise	Tree	Switch	Beheshti & Zhang (2012)
Dynamic controller placement	Hierarchical	Flow set up time	Internet	Random	Switch	Bari et al. (2013)
Pareto optimal number of controllers	Flat	None	Internet	Random	Node and link	Hock et al. (2014)

Source: https://idr.nitk.ac.in/jspui/bitstream/123456789/14489/2/CO09P02.pdf.

1.2.3. Moving Information Between Planes

Today's larger multislot/multicard (chassis-based) distributed warding systems function internally in a way that is similar to some of the physically distributed but logically centralized control mechanisms of SDN. Here, what's interesting are the details surrounding the distribution of tables and their hardware instantiation. Examining a typical distributed switch's internal operations reveals several features and behaviors that are similar to those of an externalized control plane. Certain behaviors regarding the communication between these elements are necessary for the system to be resilient and fault tolerant, for instance, in systems where the control plane is located on an independent processor/line card and the data planes are located on other, independent line cards. If the control plane is taken off the chassis and moved farther away, it is worthwhile to look into whether or not all of these are required (i.e., either rationally or rigidly centralized).

Let's start by discussing the fundamentals of packet forwarding. Is the data plane listening for every packet it receives when the control plane instructs it to forward packets? More specifically, are there methods by which traffic can be black holed (i.e., abandoned without warning in hardware-based firewall systems that are covered by various vendors' implementations)? This is a question that needs to be asked regardless of whether the program or control entity is centralized, semi-centralized, or synchronized in some other way with other components of a distributed control network. These systems allow for data-embedded detection mechanisms for forwarding table distribution errors (e.g., table versioning) or within the mechanism of transfer (e.g., using a hash or cookie created from its contents to sign the table. These mechanisms guarantee synchronization and correctness of the distributed software versions of the table once they are programmed. Similarly, the memory driver software (partially related to the forwarding hardware) implements verification routines between the software and hardware versions of the table.

After the control plane programs the data plane, some vendors have put in place procedures to verify hardware entries post facto, or after the forwarding chip and ancillary memories have been checked for soft errors. There are related procedures to move entries, mark problematic blocks, and manage references in these situations. These hardware verification procedures are typically costly, so they are frequently used as a backdrop (a.k.a. scavenger) mechanisms. In order to achieve this, batching and bulking techniques are frequently used to optimize the transfer and memory write routines in order to minimize transaction overhead.

A secondary lookup is carried out on the outgoing slot or card that is identified in the first stage of an ingress lookup, which is carried out by certain multislot/multicard systems. Two-stage lookups may, depending on how they are used, enable an optimization that lowers the egress FIB size through a process known as localization. Under these circumstances, situations involving two-stage asynchronous loss could arise, which call for some attention and are actually hard to notice until they break. These are pertinent to the control of SDN forwarding.

1.2.4. Separating Data Plane and Control Plane

The networking industry was the first to popularize the idea of separating the control plane from the data plane. This nomenclature can be used in engineering to denote a method of dividing logical components of the system using the networking principles.

The primary goal is to divide functionality into two areas: data retrieval (Data Plane) and control (Control Plane). Developing highly available systems that continue to provide services to users even in the event that system components fail is the aim.

1.2.4.1. Data Plane

The majority of data transformations take place on the data plane. The Data Plane is designed with simplicity, regularity, and processing speed in mind. All functions and processes that forward data from one interface to another based on control plane logic are collectively referred to as the data plane.

1.2.4.2. Control Plane

The data plane is under the control of the control plane. Put simply, it encompasses all operations and procedures that choose which data transmission path to take modifications such as resource creation, saving, deletion, and updating. Any modifications are also propagated by the control plane.

When a user configures Multi-Factor Authentication (MFA), for instance, the control plane takes care of the setup, saving the TOTP or a backup MFA method to the database. This is an example of a control plane and data plane. The control plane would also handle newly created or updated events and propagate them to a database if you were utilizing an event-style architecture. This information would be retrieved from the database by the data plane.

1.2.4.3. Benefits of Separating the Data Plane and Control Plane

It makes sense and is true that the control, plane, and data planes are separated. As separation delivers no words, it can be beneficial for code development, hardware development, infrastructure integration, and control plane and data plane functions to be separate.

1. **Scalability:** Cloud providers are able to scale the control plane and data plane independently by keeping them apart. Many data plane resources can be managed by the control plane, which can scale up or down to satisfy demand. This makes it possible for cloud providers to guarantee high availability and effectively manage a range of workloads.
2. **Resilience:** Removing these planes improves the resilience of the system. The control plane is able to identify and respond to data plane failures by reallocating resources or restarting failed services. This isolation makes sure that the control plane's general management and orchestration capabilities are unaffected by problems in the data plane.
3. **Flexibility:** The development and operations teams can concentrate on their specialized tasks when there is a clear division between them. While operations teams oversee and improve the control

plane, developers can create data plane applications that function well. This assignment of duties improves agility and facilitates quicker application deployment and scaling.

4. **Security:** These regulations are applied throughout the data plane by the control plane. By ensuring uniform policy enforcement, this centralized security management lowers the possibility of configuration errors and security lapses. To prevent unwanted access to data and processes, the data plane can also employ isolation techniques.

In contemporary cloud infrastructures, the division of the control plane and data plane is a fundamental design principle. Numerous advantages come with this architectural strategy, such as security, resilience, scalability, and flexibility.

1.2.4.4. Drawbacks of Separating Control and Data Plane

In certain circumstances, the control plane and data plane architecture is a great one to use. It's simple to overengineer solutions, which expands their scope, slows down delivery, and makes them more complex. This may lengthen the time needed to comprehend the solution before making progress with it. Planning is essential when choosing the architecture of your system. You ought to be fully aware of the functional and non-functional requirements, as well as the functions of each element in your design.

1.2.4.5. Management Plane

The management plane is another plane that can be defined in addition to the data and control planes. Additional services for the Data Plane are available on the Management Plane, and they don't interfere with business operations. All of the control and monitoring functions are handled by the management plane. When creating highly available and independently scalable services, it's a great idea to adhere to the control plane and data plane architecture. But before you do, do your homework and confirm that this is the right architectural pattern to use for the solution you are creating.

1.3. DISTRIBUTED CONTROL PLANES

As our ultimate network scale problem to date, the Internet has given rise to a distributed, eventual consensus control paradigm. The model involves the cooperation of individual elements or their proxies to distribute reachability in a formation that creates a localized view of a consistent, loop-free network. Since the propagation delays of reachability updates, which are a feature of the distributed control plane model in any network larger than a small home network, create a fairly complex network graph, we refer to this model as eventual consensus. The model's intermittent nonsynchronization by design may result in less ideal forwarding paths, but it should also prevent or minimize transitory cycles, also referred to as micro-loops in the overall path. This idea is illustrated in Figure 1.1.

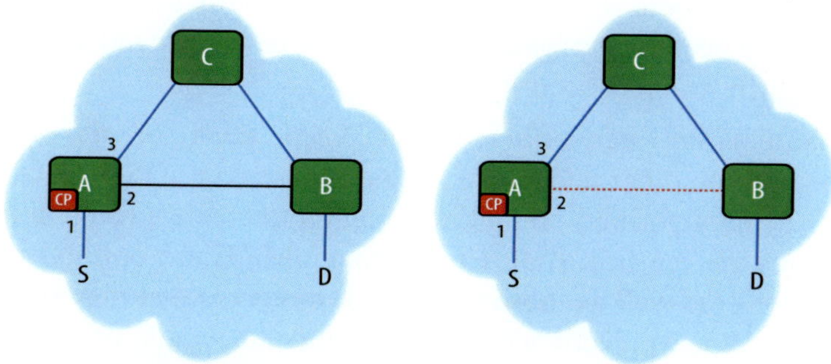

Figure 1.1. *Eventual consistency of routing state.*

Source: Thomas, D. N., & Ken, G., (2013). SDN: Software Defined Networks, O'Reilly Media, Inc. ISBN: 9781449342302.

Examine the network on the left, which is made up of three nodes (A, B, and C) and a cloud. The state of the network is inconsistent and shows a looping network at time = 0. Given that traffic is flowing between nodes A and B due to forwarding, packets may cycle in this scenario if they are transmitted. However, the connection between nodes A and B is broken at time = 1, as shown by the cloud on the right of the figure. This illustrates the idea of eventual consistency, according to which the network may experience brief periods of instability before routing message updates are shared amongst network nodes.

1.3.1. IP and MPLS

Among the models of distributed control are MPLS and IP forwarding. These forward-looking paradigms involve the exchange of reachability and route information, which subsequently leads to the programming of data plane paths to realize those paths.

A quick generalization, however, will enable a discussion of some of the relative benefits and drawbacks of this specific model and, as a result, a better comprehension of some SDN concepts regarding control and data plane distribution.

1.3.2. Creating the IP Underlay

Using an IGP is the cornerstone of the current IP control plane paradigm. Usually, a link-state protocol like OSPF or ISIS takes this form. Reachability between a connected, acyclic graph of IP forwarding elements is established via the IGP. After configuration, IGP protocols create connections with neighbors that are set up correctly and oversee control protocol sessions that share reachability data (i.e., NLRI or route state). The inherent safeguards for forming neighbor relationships and accepting protocol-related data have changed along with the awareness of infrastructure security.

The participating network elements keep track of the aggregated advertisements from other nodes in a state database (e.g., OSPF database) and use a shortest path algorithm on that information to create a reachability graph that is centered on the best routes to destinations. These optimal routes are added to the RIB (as well as those from other protocols that may be operating on the same element). Network events include the gain or loss of these relationships (neighbors) or the reachability on links where the element has a bound reachability advertisement but no neighbor relationship. These events spread through the domain by means of a distributed flooding algorithm built into the protocol definition, so that all elements speaking that specific control protocol that are still connected to one another (either directly or indirectly) eventually notice and process the event.

Using the techniques of recursion, summarization, route filtering, and compartmentalization (physical/logical), the scale of the control plane state in such networks is addressed in both the physical and logical design. The elements can be physically or logically divided into areas or other IGP hierarchies in order to address the general scale issue caused by the number of IGP neighbors supported, the number of events that can be processed, the size of the link state database or other state structure, and/or other related entities. The operator has the ability to leak specific information across area borders or, if feasible, summarize reachability information from other areas at area boundaries.

The IP control paradigm typically uses the border gateway protocol (BGP) to advertise reachability across administrative boundaries or to carry reachability data sets—notably, different address families that represent further abstractions like virtual private networks across a network without carrying it in the IGP. A peering relationship between these neighbors, like that of the IGP component of the control plane, leads to an exchange of all or any subsets of the neighbor's BGP data store. Reachability data is divided into multiple address families, which leads to this. Recursion provides more scalability and accessibility for this data in the control and data planes. As demonstrated in Figure 1.2, recursion enables the network control plane to distribute in-formation with distinct attributes unique to various protocols that link via a sequence of shared keys. In the IGP data set, for instance, this optimization permits the representation of numerous BGP NLRI through a single IP destination address (or a set, if the operator makes use of control plane protocol features that permit multiple equal cost paths to the advertising entity and/or multiple best paths to the destination). When the control plane creates the entries for the data plane, the BGP information becomes information associated with leaves off our acyclic IGP graph (FIB).

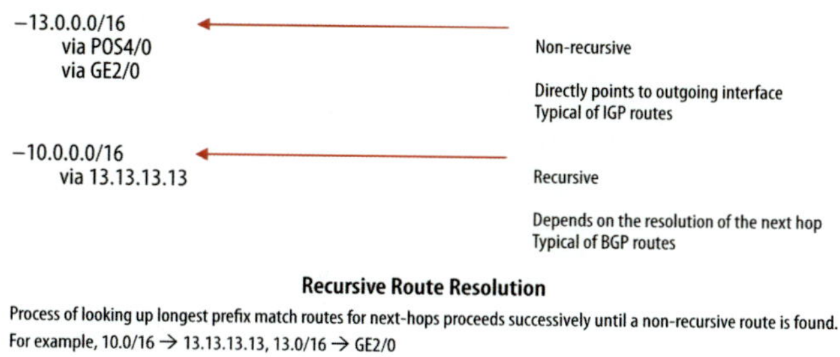

Figure 1.2. *Route recursion.*

Source: Thomas, D. N., & Ken, G., (2013). SDN: Software Defined Networks, O'Reilly Media, Inc. ISBN: 9781449342302.

The BGP prefix is finally resolved in the data plane by this recursion using the IGP "next hop" to point to a fully qualified adjacency for the layer 2 components of a forwarding entry. In the end, this forwarding entry serves as a destination MAC entry for the path's subsequent router/switch interface. Through the use of different policy tools, the operator has some additional control over the summarization and advertisement of the control state at these external boundaries. Within the IP model, both standardized and proprietary behaviors that permit local policies to govern the preference of learned reachability enable a certain level of additional, localized control over which data within the control plane data set is selected for forwarding in the data plane. By altering the characteristics of a prefix prior to re-advertisement or by locally redistributing a static route entry into a dynamic routing protocol, for instance, these tools can indirectly influence the preferences of neighbors for a specific route state. If there isn't an existing route in the RIB with a longer duration or a higher administrative preference, a non-redistributed static route may have an impact on local decisions. The protocols' rules govern prefix preference in each protocol table, and administrative preference across the tables of the various protocols governs preference in the RIB. However, the longest match of a destination prefix will ultimately determine forwarding decisions in the FIB. It is true that using policy tools in conjunction with IGP/BGP recursion can get complicated, but this is how control planes are managed in the real world. These configuration changes that could have an impact on the control and data plane outcomes can be managed centrally and pushed to the distributed elements, just like any other configuration atom in contemporary routers/switches. Some of the fundamental issues that propel SDN's popularity afflict this mechanism. That is, a very practical feature of an SDN controller is that it acts as a provisioning agent, a control point that allows inconsistent data models and CLI semantics between vendors and slow configuration commit times. In the end, one of the improvements that SDN offers is that this operational lag prevents network elements from being controlled programmatically. For numerous network administrators, control entails having the adaptability to modify the results of forwarding choices and being able to accomplish this easily (and through programming!). This can involve, for instance, optimizing the network's elasticity and efficiency in response to new information or requirements that go beyond the algorithmic definition of "best." In most implementations, there is also limited scalability with both static routes and route policies.

1.3.3. Convergence Time

Years of structure and traversal (lookup) algorithm optimization have gone into the FIB (or data plane forwarding state entries) in the IP model. According to this model, load balancing and convergence are just as crucial as the previously mentioned black holes for network designers and operators. Convergence is the amount of time that passes between when a network element introduces a change in a destination's reachability as a result of a network event and when all other relevant network elements notice and instantiate this change. The reader may already be aware of one of the components of convergence: the propagation delay of a particular update. This is typically a function of the average distance, expressed in the number of intervening nodes that must re-flood or re-advertise the update, from the site of the first change. The final stages of convergence concentrate on locally processing the update, including updating the FIB and RIB, as well as instantiation in the data plane.

Every protocol contains a unique internal timer that is used to generate different kinds of events specific to that protocol in order to optimize both the propagation/flooding mechanism and convergence processing at the protocol level. Making "hello" messages for neighbors is one example of this. Knowing the best settings for a protocol's timers in a particular network design used to be considered part of the arcana of IP networking. Most common implementations today have internalized a large portion of this as defaults for the different protocols. The way this is handled for BGP, which distributes massive amounts of data to numerous peers, is especially fascinating. In order to decrease redundant update generation processing, speed up convergence at the routing or control plane level, and improve update transmission efficiency, various vendors offer message update packing, update prioritization, peer update grouping, and other internal optimizations.

Various vendors have created event-driven reaction strategies and table organization strategies for important recursive elements of the FIB (e.g., the BGP subsequent hop). By reducing the quantity and kind of FIB modifications that follow a network event, these optimizations lessen convergence. With certain types of hardware, these optimizations allow for performance ranging from several 1,000 to over 10,000 updates per second.

1.3.4. Load Balancing

In distributed IP forwarding, load balancing progressed from packet-by-packet processing to hashes of progressively larger portions of the IP header. This happened in response to the extent to which gateway devices—such as those used for voice and other media—began to represent an increasing number of individual flows. Although there are nonequal-cost variants for specific uses, load balancing is typically applied to equal cost paths or bundled point-to-point circuits.

The computation algorithm and possible imbalances in flow size that an implementation may experience limit the actual efficiency of a load balancing algorithm. These may lead to issues with binpacking efficiency, which in turn may limit the number of bundle members or equal cost paths that the implementation can support.

1.3.5. High Availability

High Availability in the distributed IP context is provided through several mechanisms:

- Network redundancy, also known as the "two of everything" approach, allows for the failure of a link or element by providing redundant routers/switches and redundant paths in the network design.
- Using redundant route processors and switch control modules, redundancy is achieved at the element level. The redundant processors can work in either a stateless active/standby mode (which normally implies an interruption in forwarding if there is no alternative path) or through stateful mirroring of control process data (e.g., nonstop routing).

1.3.6. Creating the MPLS Overlay

When discussing SDN, MPLS is an addition to the packet header—an encapsulation that enables the IP network operator to construct logical tunnels or overlays on the network (the underlay), as Figure 1.3 illustrates.

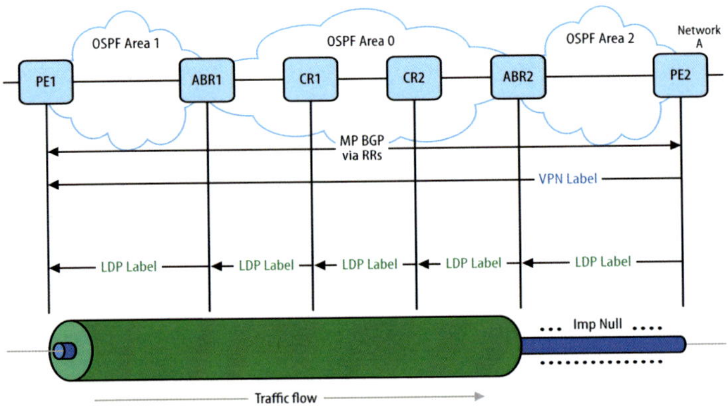

Figure 1.3. *An MPLS VPN (VRF label distribution via route reflection) over an OSPF multiarea underlay.*

Source: Thomas, D. N., & Ken, G., (2013). SDN: Software Defined Networks, O'Reilly Media, Inc. ISBN: 9781449342302.

The label itself is 24 bits, which means there are 1,048,575 labels (the labels 0 through 15 are reserved) (Figure 1.4).

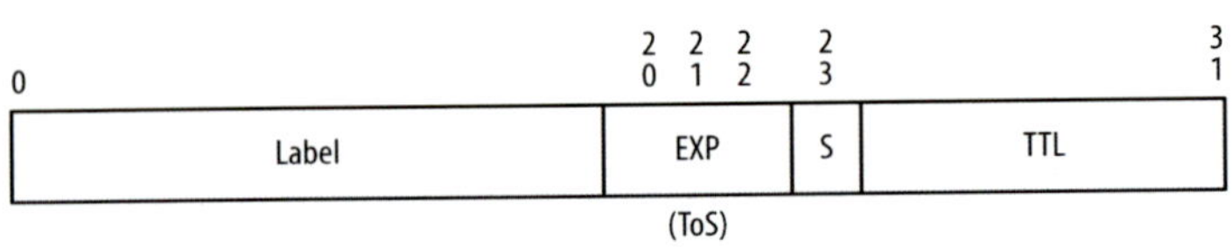

Figure 1.4. *MPLS label.*

Source: Thomas, D. N., & Ken, G., (2013). SDN: Software Defined Networks, O'Reilly Media, Inc. ISBN: 9781449342302.

Last in, first out, or LIFO order is one-way labels can be stacked. Multiple services or tunnels across a network can be created by stacking labels. These served as forerunners to the network overlays of today.

- A single label can enable an expedited lookup in the label table versus the IP forwarding table.
- Similar to the VPN, where the outer label speeds up forwarding to an element with several virtual instances (VRFs) whose discriminator is

the inner label, two labels form an abstraction that permits isolation, as seen in Figure 1.5.

- Similar to VPNs built over traffic engineering tunnels, abstractions with three or four labels allow the same forwarding through an intermediary tunnel (either protected or unprotected) (with or without fast reroute protection).

Like the IGP, many books have been written about the operation of MPLS, so we will not attempt to explain it all, but again, a general description will help with our SDN discussion going forward.

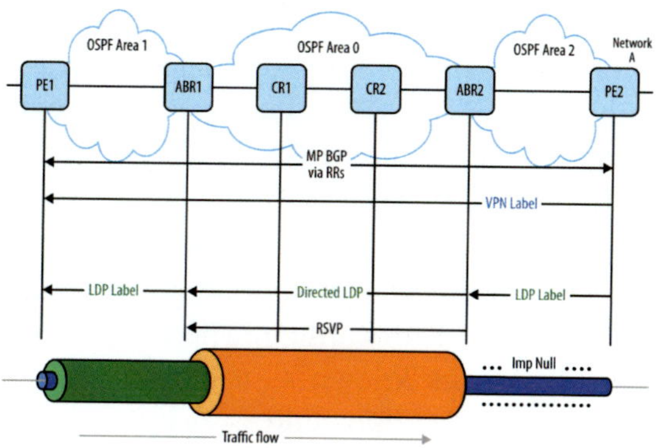

Figure 1.5. *An MPLS VPN (VRF label distribution via route reflection) over an MPLS TE core (all over an OSPF underlay).*

Source: Thomas, D. N., & Ken, G., (2013). SDN: Software Defined Networks, O'Reilly Media, Inc. ISBN: 9781449342302.

Label distribution, address binding, and label allocation are the three primary facets of MPLS operation that are configuration-controlled:

- RSVP, LDP, and BGP are possible label distribution protocols (and BGP for the labeled unicast address family). Information exchange and neighbor/session forming behaviors are features of these control protocols.
- Label allocation is typically dynamic, but in certain vendor implementations—especially when it comes to VPNs—label scale can be somewhat controlled by per-VRF or per-prefix/per-platform allocation. It is possible to order the assignment of these labels, though it is not necessary.
- Distribution of labels may occur downstream or on-demand (e.g., RSVP for traffic engineering) or LDP's default behavior, which is downstream unsolicited.

Similar to the IGP, global and local configuration can regulate some aspects of the behavior of the MPLS control plane, subject to the same restrictions mentioned earlier. This includes the capacity to manage label range, label retention policy, reserved label usage and distribution, and filter label advertisements. In addition to forward, the network element can also execute multiple push, pop, swap, push, and swap-and-push label actions. In the past, some network components lacked the capacity to support deeper label stacks or to carry out all of these functions. The data plane's forwarding behavior switches from matching the longest destination prefix match to matching the top label on the label stack when MPLS is implemented. The forwarding path will still, nevertheless, adhere to the acyclic graph that was determined for the destination prefix. By keeping extra tables and references between the IP forwarding table and the label table, this increases complexity even though it speeds up the lookup process. Additionally, MPLS increases the distributed IP control paradigm's overall complexity.

By using MPLS traffic-engineered tunnels specifically, an operator can control the tunnel's path and take advantage of network segments that aren't utilized for regular destination prefix-based forwarding. These MPLS tunnels are loaded according to a class of prefixes known as a Forwarding Equivalency Class (FEC), which determines the next hop address. A FEC can also be a collection of policies that designate particular flows or aspects of the flows' quality of service, like those that are employed in policy-based routing. Similar to the IP IGP, MPLS has improved over time, especially with regard to multipath load balancing, thanks to developments like entropy labels and sub-LSPs.

1.3.7. Replication

While specific protocols and data structures are needed for multicast replication, both MPLS and IP distributed control are equally applicable to unicast and multicast. In IP-only networks, multicast replication has a long history. It began with DVMRP, moved on to MOSPF, and finally evolved to PIM.

Multicast in the VPN context has seen recent developments in MPLS networks (MVPN). The multicast control protocols aim to prevent black holes and cycle/loops while optimizing around scale, convergence, and stability, just like their unicast relatives.

When it comes to MVPN, there are extra worries about how to balance the network's multicast state while bearing the load of packet replication on network edge elements. Similar to unicast protocols, these protocols permit a certain degree of configuration-driven control, albeit with the same drawbacks as MPLS configuration-based control and unicast IP protocols.

1.4. CENTRALIZED CONTROL PLANES

Because society has always relied on proprietary hardware, high overall network management costs have historically been caused by this. One of the expectations was that, following the successful adoption of SDN technology, this scenario would significantly alter as the trend would shift from proprietary to programmable hardware components. SDN would therefore make the network programmable, which would lower operating costs, provide a more intelligent view of the network, and permit direct network interaction between applications and the network. Therefore, SDN was predicted to lower equipment and operating costs overall and to indirectly aid in the reuse of outdated hardware components with new software solutions.

Compared to programmable hardware, proprietary hardware would have much less controllability. It was anticipated that this programmable hardware would enable businesses to manage the network as a whole with a single, centralized controller, giving them greater flexibility and authority to update and alter the code within. It was anticipated that the way networking is done would change significantly as a result of these technological advancements.

The SDN controller functions primarily by removing the network hardware's control plane and transforming it into something akin to a single point of software access and control. This controller makes it easier to install, integrate, and manage applications with greater ease and lower operating costs. It also enables network management to transition from manual to automated mode. In summary, the controllers of the SDNs were intended to replace the distributed control planes' intelligence with a centralized method of calculating network paths. This was made possible by the fact that a centralized controller can readily obtain a better overall view of network conditions than an individual router or switch, which only has a localized view. The controller would be able to effectively manage and control traffic through the network with this one view. This would undoubtedly contribute to increasing the network's overall efficiency by enhancing the functionality of each individual application that uses the network. Unfortunately, the SDN controllers—which were once thought of as network operating systems—also began to be seen as a single point of failure.

From top to bottom, the SDNs were intended to offer a far more modular level of control. Therefore, the controller could even control the flow level. This would support the creation and application of policy controls at every stage of implementation, which begins with discovery and continues with identifying packet paths, directing flow, figuring out operating expenses, preserving service quality, etc. It is necessary to perform these computations for every user and every application execution. The definition of SDN has evolved over the past year; it now encompasses any network technology that enables programmatic access to data that can be used to control a network.

1.4.1. Network Path Calculation

1.4.1.1. Centralized Network Path Calculations

The processing power and memory requirements of individual routers speed up in a policy-driven path selection scenario, wherein selecting a path through the network is more optimal from a network usage or quality-of-service perspective but less optimal from a metrics perspective. Every day, the computation of the best path gets more and more complicated. The complexity of each forwarding device could be greatly decreased if distributed control planes were removed and replaced by a controller or group of controllers. This is because the controller would take over the tasks of determining the local topology and determining the optimal path for each destination, shifting the burden from the individual boxes. Small, inexpensive, lightweight forwarding-only devices could be used in place of conventional routers by stripping the routers of this processing.

1.4.1.2. Centralized Control, Its Complexity, and Its Forwarding Issues

The placement of controllers is a crucial task in SDN architectures. Other concerns include load balancing, failure tolerance, and latency restrictions. Since there is rarely a single optimal location because at least some of these goals are in conflict, decision-makers must strike a fair balance between them. Staying away from complexity is not at all simple. It is difficult to enable the centralized controller to operate with a smaller network and scale large amounts of data. One, two, or three controllers supplying a large number of switches with forwarding information may occasionally lead to problems as well. A few instances of such scenarios are the interaction between reactive control planes and centralized computation, followed by remote responses to modifications in reachability and local topology.

The routing protocol in distributed control planes needs to find a set of loop-free paths that can go to every destination in the network before the first packet is sent across the network. In order to control the quantity and speed of state being carried in the protocol, distributed control planes frequently rely on information hiding through aggregation, since this discovery and calculation process usually involves flooding, processing, and managing a lot of information. Even with centralized route computation, some kind of information must still be hidden in order to scale the control plane. SDN control planes typically choose to switch to a reactive control plane, which means that forwarding devices only learn reachability information when they receive the first packet in a flow, as opposed to aggregation at specific topological points in the network. This has numerous disadvantages even though it does lessen the amount of forwarding state in any given device. Frequent disconnections, abrupt changes in the network's state, local cache timeouts, and cache failures are all features of reactive control planes, which are thought to be the worst-case scenario in proactive control planes. Centralized control planes always recalculate the optimal path using a sophisticated method. This is due to the fact that in the event of a local node failure, the closest controller should be notified and tasked with recalculating the path and returning the information to the impacted switches. Therefore, there aren't many quick fixes or shortcuts to these issues. This is a result of the controllers' centralized decision-making; these circumstances might not have occurred if decisions had been made by switches alone. Even though it isn't a drawback of centralized controllers, it is occasionally thought to be.

1.4.1.3. Communication and Issues Between the Controllers

The amount of work required for configuration, setup, final deployment, maintenance, troubleshooting, daily monitoring, failure probability, and other tasks was very high in the earlier distributed control planes. However, when compared to a centralized controller, all of these appeared to be very straightforward and easy. However, this is untrue; in a larger network with thousands of switches, having a single controller is not practically affordable, and there is a significant risk of unlucky failure. Therefore, it is always expected that a controller who is geographically distant will always be fully aware of how the other operates. Handling both controllers in the same way is actually not that easy. A distributed control plane needs to be made available for the communication between these two controllers.

1.4.1.4. Fingerprinting in SDN Controllers

By identifying which controller is in charge of the network, fingerprinting in SDN controllers is always a possibility (Azzouni, Braham, Nguyen, Pujolle, & Boutaba, 2016). Jagadeesan along with Mendiratta (2016) talks about how anomaly detection and analytics based on machine learning are critical for locating SDN software bugs and directing real-time network responses. All of this is due to the fact that while SDN's programmability offers great flexibility and adaptability to changing network conditions and demands, it also exposes networks to serious vulnerabilities caused by network application, control, and data plane software flaws. Cui et al. shown how to separate the planes in SDN, but this also creates new security holes in SDN networks because an adversary can fingerprint the packet-forwarding logic of the network by observing how packets are processed differently at each plane. Attacks that use fingerprinting to obtain information from packet-pair dispersion and RTT of exchanged packets are highly likely to be successful on SDN networks. These attacks are not limited to active adversaries; passive adversaries who merely keep an eye on the traffic that is exchanged with the SDN network are also capable of launching these kinds of attacks.

1.4.2. Forwarding Decisions

SDN's replacement of a few of the large, current distributed protocols was one of its main goals. It proved to be more difficult than anticipated to replace the current protocols. The amount of code needed increased significantly as the tasks grew tedious. Eventually, though, there came a time when people began to believe that their efforts were worthwhile. The network path and packed forwarding to the destination address can be found by the current routing protocol. However, they didn't really help with flow-based forwarding control, wherein independent path identification based on various applications was one of the expectations. However, a number of problems entered the picture here. The communication flow became extremely complex in order to forward each different application through the various available paths. This is a result of the quantity of nodes, quantity of applications operating on those nodes, quantity of times the connection and termination are needed, etc. The quantity of flows occurring at any given time is one of the primary problems here, and the other is the complexity of the connection setup. There may be an infinite number of communications taking place at any given time when the network is large. Here, too, setup and operating costs escalate to an extent not anticipated during SDN design. The amount of flow states anticipated during SDN design may also exceed the hardware's capacity. All of these go against SDN's development goals. Every packet header in a network hop under flow-based forwarding control is meant to be examined for path identification. This results in significant operational costs in terms of power consumption and maintenance expenses as well as hardware capacity needed to maintain the per-flow tables for each information flow.

1.4.3. Challenges and Considerations

1. **Single Point of Failure:** The centralized controller(s) can become a single point of failure. Redundancy and fault-tolerant mechanisms are crucial to ensure high availability and reliability.
2. **Latency:** Depending on the architecture and deployment, the centralized control plane could introduce latency for certain types of network operations, although this has been mitigated in modern SDN implementations.

3. **Complexity:** Implementing a centralized control plane requires careful planning and integration with existing network infrastructure. It may require changes in network architecture, hardware, and software.

1.4.4. Future Directions

1. **Hybrid Approaches:** Many networks are adopting hybrid models that combine elements of centralized and distributed control planes. This allows for flexibility and optimization based on specific network requirements.
2. **AI and Automation:** The integration of AI and machine learning into centralized control planes is expected to enhance network intelligence, automate decision-making, and improve predictive analytics for network management.
3. **5G and Edge Computing:** As networks evolve to support 5G and edge computing, centralized control planes will play a critical role in managing distributed edge resources efficiently and securely.

In summary, centralized control planes, exemplified by SDN, offer significant advantages in terms of flexibility, programmability, security, and management efficiency in modern networks. However, their deployment requires careful consideration of scalability, redundancy, latency, and integration with existing infrastructure.

REFERENCES

1. Alizadeh, M., Yang, S., Sharif, M., Katti, S., McKeown, N., Prabhakar, B., & Shenker, S. (2013). Pfabric: Minimal near-optimal datacenter transport. *In SIGCOMM* (pp. 435–446). ACM.
2. Azzouni, A., Braham, O., Nguyen, T. M. T., Pujolle, G., & Boutaba, R. (2016). Fingerprinting OpenFlow controllers: The first step to attack an SDN control plane. *In 2016 IEEE Global Communications Conference (GLOBECOM)* (pp. 1–6). IEEE.
3. Bari, M. F., Roy, A. R., Chowdhury, S. R., Zhang, Q., Zhani, M. F., Ahmed, R., & Boutaba, R. (2013). Dynamic controller provisioning in software defined networks. *In IEEE/ACM/IFIP International Conference on Network and Service Management (CNSM)*, Zurich, Switzerland.
4. Beheshti, N., & Zhang, Y. (2012). Fast failover for control traffic in software-defined networks. *In GLOBECOM* (pp. 2665–2670). IEEE.
5. Bifulco, R., Matsiuk, A., & Silvestro, A. (2017). CATENAE: A scalable service function chaining system for legacy mobile networks. *International Journal of Network Management, 27*(2), e2031. https://doi.org/10.1002/nem.2031.
6. Bosshart, P., Daly, D., Gibb, G., Izzard, M., McKeown, N., Rexford, J., Schlesinger, C., Talayco, D., Vahdat, A., Varghese, G., & Walker, D. (2014). P4: Programming protocol-independent packet processors. *SIGCOMM Computer Communication Review, 44*(3), 87–95. https://doi.org/10.1145/2656877.2656890.
7. Casado, M., Freedman, M. J., Pettit, J., Luo, J., McKeown, N., & Shenker, S. (2007). Ethane: Taking control of the enterprise. *In Proceedings of the 2007 Conference on Applications, Technologies, Architectures, and Protocols for Computer Communications (SIGCOMM 2007)* (pp. 1–12). ACM.
8. Cui, H., Karame, G. O., Klaedtke, F., & Bifulco, R. (2015). Fingerprinting software-defined networks. *In 2015 IEEE 23rd International Conference on Network Protocols (ICNP)* (pp. 453–459). IEEE.
9. Cui, H., Karame, G. O., Klaedtke, F., & Bifulco, R. (2016). On the fingerprinting of software-defined networks. *IEEE Transactions on Information Forensics and Security, 11*(10), 2160–2173. https://doi.org/10.1109/TIFS.2016.2595737.
10. Dvir, A., Haddad, Y., & Zilberman, A. (2018). Wireless controller placement problem. *In 2018 15th IEEE Annual Consumer Communications & Networking Conference (CCNC)* (pp. 1–4). IEEE.

11. Gude, N., Koponen, T., Pettit, J., Pfaff, B., Casado, M., McKeown, N., & Shenker, S. (2008). NOX: Towards an operating system for networks. *SIGCOMM Computer Communication Review, 38*(3), 105–110. https://doi.org/10.1145/1402958.1402975.
12. Guo, C., Lu, G., Wang, H. J., Yang, S., Kong, C., Sun, P., Wu, W., & Zhang, Y. (2010). SecondNet: A data center network virtualization architecture with bandwidth guarantees. *In Proceedings of the 6th International Conference on Emerging Networking Experiments and Technologies (CoNEXT '10)* (pp. 15:1–15:12). ACM.
13. Hassas Yeganeh, S., & Ganjali, Y. (2012). Kandoo: A framework for efficient and scalable offloading of control applications. *In Proceedings of the First Workshop on Hot Topics in Software Defined Networks (HotSDN 2012)* (pp. 19–24). ACM.
14. Heller, B., Sherwood, R., & McKeown, N. (2012). The controller placement problem. *Computer Communication Review, 42*(4), 473–478. https://doi.org/10.1145/2342366.2342404.
15. Hock, D., Gebert, S., Hartmann, M., Zinner, T., & Tran-Gia, P. (2014). POCO: Framework for Pareto-optimal resilient controller placement in SDN based core networks. *In Network Operations and Management Symposium (NOMS)* (pp. 1–2). IEEE.
16. Hu, Y. N., Wang, W. D., Gong, X. Y., Que, X., & Cheng, S. (2012). On the placement of controllers in software-defined networks. *The Journal of China Universities of Posts and Telecommunications, 19*(2), 92–171. https://doi.org/10.1016/j.jcup.2012.03.009.
17. Jagadeesan, L. J., & Mendiratta, V. (2016). Programming the network: Application software faults in software defined networks. *In 2016 IEEE International Symposium on Software Reliability Engineering Workshops (ISSREW)* (pp. 125–131). IEEE.
18. Katta, N., Hira, M., Kim, C., Sivaraman, A., & Rexford, J. (2016). Hula: Scalable load balancing using programmable data planes. *In Proceedings of the Symposium on SDN Research (SOSR '16)* (pp. 10:1–10:12). ACM.
19. Kentis, A. M., Pilimon, A., Soler, J., Berger, M. S., & Ruepp, S. R. (2018). A novel algorithm for flow-rule placement in SDN switches. *In 4th IEEE International Conference on Network Softwarization (NetSoft)*. IEEE.
20. Koponen, T., Casado, M., Gude, N., Stribling, J., Poutievski, L., Zhu, M., Ramanathan, R., Iwata, Y., Inoue, H., Hama, T., & Shenker, S. (2010). Onix: A distributed control platform for large-scale production networks. *In Proceedings of the 9th USENIX Conference on Operating Systems Design and Implementation (OSDI '10)* (pp. 1–6). USENIX Association.

21. Kreutz, D., Ramos, F. M., & Verissimo, P. (2013). Towards secure and dependable software-defined networks. *In Proceedings of the Second ACM SIGCOMM Workshop on Hot Topics in Software Defined Networking (HotSDN 2013)* (pp. 55–60). ACM.
22. Lange, S., Gebert, S., Spoerhase, J., Rygielski, P., Zinner, T., Kounev, S., & Tran-Gia, P. (2015a). Specialized heuristics for the controller placement problem in large scale SDN networks. *In Proceedings of the 2015 27th International Teletraffic Congress (ITC 2015)* (pp. 210–218). IEEE Computer Society.
23. Lange, S., Gebert, S., Zinner, T., Tran-Gia, P., Hock, D., Jarschel, M., & Hoffmann, M. (2015b). Heuristic approaches to the controller placement problem in large scale SDN networks. *IEEE Transactions on Network and Service Management, 12*(1), 4–17. https://doi.org/10.1109/TNSM.2015.2441510
24. Levin, D., Wundsam, A., Heller, B., Handigol, N., & Feldmann, A. (2012). Logically centralized? State distribution trade-offs in software defined networks. *In Proceedings of the First Workshop on Hot Topics in Software Defined Networks (HotSDN 2012)* (pp. 1–6). ACM.
25. Liu, J., Shi, Y., Zhao, L., Cao, Y., Sun, W., & Kato, N. (2018). Joint placement of controllers and gateways in SDN-enabled 5G-satellite integrated network. *IEEE Journal on Selected Areas in Communications, 36*(2), 221–232. https://doi.org/10.1109/JSAC.2018.2791330.
26. McKeown, N., Anderson, T., Balakrishnan, H., Parulkar, G. M., Peterson, L. L., Rexford, J., Shenker, S., & Turner, J. S. (2008). OpenFlow: Enabling innovation in campus networks. *Computer Communication Review, 38*(2), 69–74. https://doi.org/10.1145/1355734.1355746.
27. Ramos, R. M., Martinello, M., & Rothenberg, C. E. (2013a). Data center fault-tolerant routing and forwarding: An approach based on encoded paths. *In Latin-American Symposium on Dependable Computing* (pp. 104–113). IEEE.
28. Ramos, R. M., Martinello, M., & Rothenberg, C. E. (2013b). SlickFlow: Resilient source routing in data center networks unlocked by OpenFlow. *In IEEE Local Computer Networks (LCN)* (pp. 606–613). IEEE.
29. Shirali-Shahreza, S., & Ganjali, Y. (2018). Delayed installation and expedited eviction: An alternative approach to reduce flow table occupancy in SDN switches. *IEEE/ACM Transactions on Networking, 26*(4), 1547–1561. https://doi.org/10.1109/TNET.2018.2805315.
30. Soliman, M., Nandy, B., Lambadaris, I., & Ashwood-Smith, P. (2012). Source routed forwarding with software defined control: Considerations

and implications. *In Proceedings of the 2012 ACM Conference on CoNEXT Student Workshop (CoNEXT Student 2012)*. ACM.

31. Stephens, B., Cox, A. L., & Rixner, S. (2013). Plinko: Building provably resilient forwarding tables. *In Proceedings of the Twelfth ACM Workshop on Hot Topics in Networks (HotNets-XII)* (pp. 26:1–26:7). ACM.
32. Tootoonchian, A., & Ganjali, Y. (2010). HyperFlow: A distributed control plane for OpenFlow. *In Proceedings of the 2010 Internet Network Management Conference on Research on Enterprise Networking (INM/WREN '10)* (pp. 3–3). USENIX Association.
33. UlHuque, T., Si, W., Jourjon, G., & Gramoli, V. (2017). Large-scale dynamic controller placement. *IEEE Transactions on Network and Service Management (TNSM), 14*(1), 63–76. https://doi.org/10.1109/TNSM.2017.2661858.
34. Wang, G., Zhao, Y., Huang, J., & Wu, Y. (2018). An effective approach to controller placement in software defined wide area networks. *IEEE Transactions on Network and Service Management, 15*(1), 344–355. https://doi.org/10.1109/TNSM.2018.2797010.
35. Yu, M., Rexford, J., Freedman, M. J., & Wang, J. (2010). Scalable flow-based networking with DIFANE. *In Proceedings of the ACM SIGCOMM 2010 Conference (SIGCOMM '10)* (pp. 351–362). ACM.
36. Zhang, S. Q., Zhang, Q., Tizghadam, A., Park, B., Bannazadeh, H., Leon-Garcia, A., & Boutaba, R. (2016). Sector: TCAM space aware routing on SDN. *In 28th International Teletraffic Congress (ITC 28)*, Würzburg, Germany. IEEE.
37. Zhang, Y., Beheshti, N., & Tatipamula, M. (2011). On resilience of split-architecture networks. *In GLOBECOM* (pp. 1–6). IEEE.
38. Zheng, K., Wang, L., Yang, B., Sun, Y., Uhlig, S., et al. (2017). LazyCtrl: A scalable hybrid network control plane design for cloud data centers. *IEEE Transactions on Parallel and Distributed Systems, 28*(1), 115–127. https://doi.org/10.1109/TPDS.2016.2532413.

CHAPTER 2

CENTRALIZED AND DISTRIBUTED CONTROL AND DATA PLANES

Contents

INTRODUCTION

One of the earliest software-defined networking (SDN) standards is OpenFlow (OF). In order to improve its ability to adjust to shifting business needs, it first defined the communication protocol in SDN architectures. This allowed the SDN controller to communicate directly with the forwarding plane of network devices, including switches and routers, both physical and virtual (based on hypervisors). The "brains" of the SDN network are SDN controllers, which communicate with switches and routers "below" (through southbound APIs) and with applications and business logic "above" (through northbound APIs). SDN controllers have been tasked with federating between SDN controller domains using common application interfaces, such as OpenFlow and open virtual switch database (OVSDB), as more enterprises implement SDN virtual overlay networks. Any device that wishes to communicate with an SDN controller must be able to support the OpenFlow protocol in order to operate in an OF environment. By using this interface, network administrators can divide traffic, regulate flows for maximum efficiency, and begin testing new configurations and applications. The SDN controller pushes down changes to the switch/router flow-table. Hence, the protocol used in SDN to facilitate communication between the forwarding plane and control plane of the network is called Open Flow. Stated differently, Open Flow facilitates communication between the network devices and the controller by utilizing the Open Flow Interface to enable network device operations and management. It is a widely used control plane standard that facilitates communication between SDN solutions. This Layer 2 communication protocol is used in SDN to transfer data between a network switch and controller…

It is a multivendor standard for implementing SDN in networking equipment, according to the Open Networking Foundation (ONF). The OpenFlow switch's response to incoming data packets can be controlled by the OpenFlow Controller thanks to the OpenFlow protocol. The OpenFlow commands transmitted from an OpenFlow Controller to an OpenFlow switch are known as flows. Packet match fields, flow priority, different counters, packet processing instructions, flow timeouts, and a cookie make up each flow. The flows are arranged using tables. An incoming packet may be handled by flows in multiple pipelined tables before it leaves an egress port. The Forwarding Plane of the network devices is accessible through this protocol. OpenFlow is the only control plane in the switch, which makes it unique. It also withstands power outages and proactively traffic-engineers all flows and redundancies to enable the switches to perform the forwarding they are configured to perform with or without telephony. These networks are made to separate the forwarding and network control functions. This makes it possible to decouple the underlying infrastructure from applications and network services, enabling direct programmability of network control. It should be noted that the remainder of the network is unaffected by the Open Flow protocol. Not a single message would be visible in a packet capture between two switches in a network that are connected to the controller via a different port. Use of it is limited to the connection between a switch and a controller. There is no impact on the rest of the network. An OpenFlow-capable network in the real world might consist solely of OpenFlow switches or mix OpenFlow switches with conventional switches and routers. The latter kind of network is called an overlay network. While some OpenFlow applications just call for a partial OpenFlow switch deployment, others call for an OpenFlow-based network in its entirety.

2.1. OPENFLOW PROTOCOL

The most popular interface in SDN between the Data-Plane and Control-Plane Layers is the OpenFlow protocol. Stanford University proposed the OpenFlow Protocol, which made it possible to implement the idea in both software and hardware. The hardware that is already in place can be used to create new protocols and evaluate their effectiveness by using an OpenFlow protocol. The controller, or software, in SDN controls the group of switches used for traffic management. The OpenFlow protocol is used to facilitate communication between the controller and the OpenFlow switch. In addition, the switch is managed by the controller using this protocol. The SDN separates the network logic from the data forwarding devices and places it in the logically centralized distributed controllers, enabling the abstraction and centralized management of the lower-level network functionalities. However, in large-scale networks with dynamic traffic and topology conditions, this separation poses new performance and scalability issues. Numerous studies have indicated that concerns about scalability are brought about by centralization and the need to maintain global network visibility over the distributed SDN controller. The OpenFlow switch has three different kinds of tables:

i. **Flow Table:** This kind of table matches incoming packets to a particular flow and outlines the actions that must be taken on the packets.

ii. **Group Table:** Initiates various kinds of actions that impact one or more streams.

iii. **Meter Table:** Initiates various actions related to performance on a flow.

The OpenFlow Protocol provides the SDN South-Bound interface. Stated differently, this protocol serves as the communication interface between the

SDN controller (Control-Plane) and SDN switches (Data-Plane). The SDN controller can configure and manage the SDN switches thanks to this protocol. The GENI standard is compatible with the OpenFlow protocol. Because of this, a user can make slices in any way they want without having to know about the actual network infrastructure. By enabling the controller to view and modify the flow tables (forwarding rules) of the SDN Switch, an OpenFlow Protocol defines how traffic should move across the network. After comparing each incoming packet to a set of rules, the action list linked to the matched rule is carried out. An OpenFlow switch can support action lists, such as forwarding or dropping packets. In addition, an OpenFlow allows the switch to rewrite packet headers, add or remove MPLS and VLANS tags, and rewrite MAC source and destination addresses across the network.

2.1.1. Purpose

Network controllers can find out a packet's route through a network of switches thanks to OpenFlow. Switches and controllers are two different things. More advanced traffic management is possible thanks to this separation of control and forwarding than is possible with access control lists (ACLs) and routing protocols. Additionally, OpenFlow makes it possible to remotely manage switches from various vendors using a single, open protocol, even though these vendors frequently have their own proprietary interfaces and scripting languages. OpenFlow is seen by the protocol's creators as a facilitator of software-defined networking (SDN). With OpenFlow, you can add, edit, and remove packet matching rules and actions from a layer 3 switch's packet forwarding tables remotely. In this manner, the controller can make routing decisions on a regular or as-needed basis. The controller can then translate those decisions into rules and actions that have a configurable lifespan. These rules and actions are then deployed to a switch's flow table, and the matched packets are forwarded to the switch at wire speed while those rules are in effect. Packets which are unmatched by the switch can be forwarded to the controller. The controller can then decide to modify existing flow table rules on one or more switches or to deploy new rules, to prevent a structural flow of traffic between switch and controller. If it has instructed the switch to forward entire packets rather than just their header, it may even choose to forward the traffic itself. Transport Layer Security (TLS) is required according to the OpenFlow protocol, which is layered on top of Transmission Control Protocol (TCP). Controllers are expected to listen for switches wishing to establish a connection on TCP port 6653. Port 6633 was unofficially used by earlier iterations of the OpenFlow protocol. The protocol is used by certain network control plane implementations to control the network forwarding components. The primary use of OpenFlow is over a secure channel connecting the switch and controller.

2.1.2. History

The OpenFlow standard is maintained by the Open Networking Foundation (ONF), a user-led group committed to encouraging the use of software-defined networking (SDN). The first established standard communications interface between an SDN architecture's control and forwarding layers is called OpenFlow, according to ONF. OpenFlow enables direct access to and control over the virtual (hypervisor-based) and physical forwarding planes of network devices like switches and routers. The reason why modern networking devices are described as monolithic, closed, and mainframe-like is because they lack an open interface to the forwarding plane. To transfer network control from proprietary network switches to locally managed, open-source control software, a protocol such as OpenFlow is required. Several network switch and router manufacturers, such as Alcatel-Lucent, Big Switch Networks, Brocade Communications, and Radisys, have declared their intention to support OpenFlow or are shipping switches that do.

2.1.3. Development

The OpenFlow protocol was first released in version 1.1 on February 28, 2011, and the ONF was in charge of overseeing further standard development. OpenFlow version 1.2 was approved by the ONF board in December 2011 and released in February 2012. OpenFlow is currently running on version 1.5.1. On the other hand, version 1.6 is only available to ONF members and has been since September 2016. A fully featured switching solution with OpenFlow support was made available by Marvell and Larch Networks in May 2011. It was built around Marvell's networking control stack and the Prestera family of packet processors. In May 2011, Indiana University and the ONF established an SDN Interoperability Lab to evaluate the interoperability of OpenFlow and software-defined networking products from various vendors. Infoblox released LINC, an open-source software switch that is compatible with both OpenFlow versions 1.2 and 1.3. Big Switch Networks announced its OpenFlow-based SDN Suite in November of 2012, which includes a commercial controller, virtual switching, and tap monitoring applications. In February of the same year, the company released Project Floodlight, an Apache-licensed open-source OpenFlow Controller. HP announced in February 2012 that 16 of its Ethernet switch products are compliant with the standard. Google's Urs Hölzle wrote in April 2012 about how the company had completely redesigned its internal network to run under OpenFlow during the preceding two years, resulting in a significant improvement in efficiency. NEC debuted a virtual switch for Windows Server 2012 Hyper-V in January 2013. The switch is intended to enable network virtualization and OpenFlow-based software-defined networking in Microsoft environments.

2.1.4. OpenFlow Architecture

Three fundamental ideas underpin the OpenFlow architecture: (i) the network is created by the OpenFlow-Compliant switches that make up the Data-Plane; (ii) one or more OpenFlow Controllers are located on the Control-Plane; and (iii) a secure control channel connects the switches to the Control-Plane. The key components of the SDN/OpenFlow architecture are controllers and forwarding devices. As previously indicated, controllers make decisions, and forwarding devices specialize in packet forwarding. The foundation of an OpenFlow-capable forwarding device is the flow tables' pipeline. A matching rule, actions to be taken on matching packets, and counters to record matching packet statistics make up each entry in a flow table. Three key parts make up the OpenFlow architecture: switches.

An OpenFlow switch's three fundamental parts are a flow table, a communication channel, and an OpenFlow protocol. Every flow entry in a flow table has an action field associated with it (Figure 2.1). A group table, an OpenFlow channel, and multiple flow tables are all possible with an OpenFlow switch. The communication channel facilitates the transfer of commands and packets between a controller and the switch.

The OpenFlow protocol allows the OpenFlow controller to communicate with any router or switch. The OpenFlow ports on the network link the switches to one another.

They introduced a dynamic routing scheme called DIFF, which adaptively chooses routing paths for different flows according to how each one affects network resources, thereby reducing the issues of inefficient bandwidth allocation and flow-table overflow. They suggested Software-defined Adaptive Routing (STAR), an online routing system that maximizes network performance by effectively utilizing scarce flow-table resources.

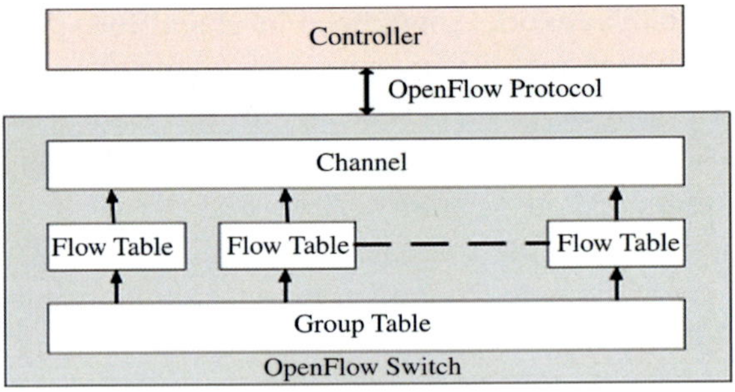

Figure 2.1. *OpenFlow model.*

Source: https://ars.els-cdn.com/content/image/1-s2.0-S2542660520301219-gr6.jpg.

2.1.4.1. Controllers

The controller maintains the flow table's flow entries and makes revisions, additions, and deletions to them. Flow-entries: flow-entries are present in every flow table. Configuring flow-entries is possible with the group table. As seen in Figure 2.2, the OpenFlow architecture basically consists of multiple pieces of switching equipment that are enabled by OpenFlow and are under the control of one or more OpenFlow controllers.

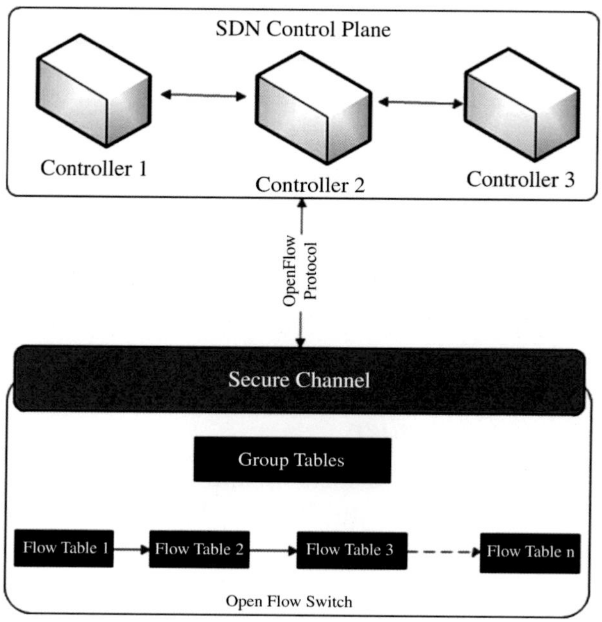

Figure 2.2. *Basic architecture of OpenFlow.*

Source: https://ars.els-cdn.com/content/image/1-s2.0-S1389128614002588-gr5.jpg.

2.1.4.2. Defining a Flow

Transmission control protocol (TCP) connections, packets arriving from the same switch port, packets with the same MAC address or IP address, and packets with the same virtual local area network (VLAN) tag are examples of flows in network traffic.

2.1.4.3. OpenFlow Switch

A group table and one or more flow tables make up an OpenFlow switch. It forwards packets and does packet lookups. Through a secure channel, the controller uses the OpenFlow protocol to control the OpenFlow-enabled switch. A set of flow entries, comprising match header fields, counters, and a set of instructions to apply to matching packets, make up each flow table in the switch.

2.1.4.4. OpenFlow Channel

The interface that links every OpenFlow switch to a controller is called an OpenFlow channel. The controller configures and controls the switch via this interface. Three different message types are supported by the OpenFlow protocol, and they are all transmitted via secure channels. These messages fall into three main categories: symmetric, asynchronous, and controller-to-switch, each with several subtypes. The controller initiates controller-to-switch messages, which are used to control or obtain information directly related to the switch's state. The switch starts asynchronous messages, which are then used to inform the controller of network events and modifications to the switch's state. Sending symmetric messages happens automatically and without request from the controller or switch. Although it can function directly over TCP, the OpenFlow channel is typically encrypted using transport layer security (TLS).

2.1.4.5. OpenFlow Controller

The controller is in charge of dispersing the necessary instructions to the network devices and keeping up with all network policies and protocols. Stated differently, the decision of what to do with packets that contain invalid flow entries rests with the OpenFlow controller. It uses the OpenFlow protocol to add and remove flow entries over the secure channel, managing the switch flow table. Network intelligence is essentially centralized by the controller. The switch needs to be able to connect to a controller via a user-specified port at an IP address that can be changed by the user but is otherwise fixed. When the switch discovers the controller's IP address, it opens a regular TLS or TCP connection with it. The OpenFlow pipeline is not used to transport traffic to or from the OpenFlow channel. As a result, before comparing incoming traffic to the flow tables, the switch must recognize it as local. The switch can connect to one or more controllers in order to establish communication. Multiple controllers increase reliability because in the event that one controller connection fails, the switch can still function in OpenFlow mode. Load balancing and quick failure recovery are made possible by the controllers' complete management of the handoff between them. The multiple controller functionality serves only to help synchronize the controller hand-offs that are carried out by the controllers as they coordinate the management of the switch among themselves. Only load balancing and controller failover are covered by the multiple controller functionality. The switch must establish a connection with each configured controller as soon as OpenFlow operation is started, and it must attempt to keep a connection with each controller at the same time. Numerous controllers have the ability to send commands from one controller to another to the switch; responses or error messages pertaining to these commands can only be sent on the controller connection that corresponds with that command. The controller usually operates on a server connected to a network.

SDN controllers can be implemented in the following three structures:

- Centralized structure;
- Distributed structure; and
- Multi-layer structure.

2.1.5. Characteristics

OpenFlow is the original software defined networking (SDN) control protocol, and it is an open-source standard that is supported by numerous vendors. It divides the forwarding plane—which handles packet routing—from the control plane, which makes decisions. The current version of the OpenFlow specification is 1.5. The Open Network Foundation looks after it. A network control protocol is called OpenFlow. OpenFlow is not used to handle network traffic. Rather, the control signals that instruct the network switches on how to route network traffic are sent by OpenFlow. Each switch in a conventional network design would have a routing table that it used to determine the best path for every packet. Most of this routing table is static, and each router's administrator would have to update it separately. An SDN controller serves as the control plane in OpenFlow. The logic and decision-making for how network traffic should move between the switches are handled by the SDN controller. To transmit messages, the SDN controller connects to every switch. Transmission Control Protocol (TCP) and Transport Layer Security (TLS) encryption are frequently used in this connection. Earlier versions used port 6633, while this one-use port 6653. The OpenFlow switches manage the network data and receive commands from the controller. The switch's flow routing table is modified by the OpenFlow commands. The flow table is the MAC address forwarding and routing tables' OpenFlow counterpart. It includes all of the instructions needed to manage network traffic on the switch.

Numerous rows of flow entries in the flow table instruct the switch on how to handle each packet. Every OSI layer of a packet, such as MAC address match, IP address match, protocol match, or port match, can be used by the flow entries. Complex rules can be created by combining these multilevel rules. Because of its degree of adaptability, every OpenFlow switch can also function as a simple firewall. Switches have the ability to forward packets to the SDN controller for inspection and the creation of a new flow rule when the packets do not match any rules. One can receive flow tables in a proactive or reactive manner. The controller forwards the flow table to every switch in a proactive delivery. Reactive mode limits the controller's output to new flow entries that the switch requests. This can enhance performance by lowering the quantity of data kept on each switch. Higher-level applications can communicate with the OpenFlow SDN controller. The business logic is contained in these higher-level apps, which are also easier for technicians to configure. After that, this is connected to the controller via a northbound interface API. The flow rules are then created by the controller.

2.1.6. Configuration

As soon as a new packet arrives, the lookup process will begin. The procedure begins in the first table and ends with a miss or a match in one of the pipeline tables. The row order in a flow table and the tables' natural sequence number are followed by the rules. The header fields of a packet received by an OpenFlow switch are compared with the entries in the flow table. The packet is handled in accordance with the actions listed in the flow table if a match is discovered. However, it encapsulates the packets in an OpenFlow Packet-In message and sends it to the controller if the received packet does not match the flow table entries. To handle the packets of the new flow, the controller can set up new forwarding rules.

Following that, the controller will instruct the switch to drop the packet or create a new entry in the flow table to accommodate the new flow. In order to learn about the existence of the switches in the network, the SDN controller initiates a protocol handshake with the SDN switch using an OpenFlow OFPT_FEATURES_REQUEST message. From the switch, it requests configuration information (including its active switch ports and corresponding MAC addresses). It forwards the data packets it receives to the controller via an OpenFlow Packet-In (OFT_PACKET_IN) message. The controller uses an OpenFlow Packet-Out (OFT_PACKET_OUT) message to send a data packet, or action list, to a switch along with instructions on what to do with it. Depending on the rules set up by a controller application, the OpenFlow Switch can be configured to function as a load balancer, firewall, router, switch, or in other capacities. In a flow table, a packet can be sent to one or more ports, encapsulated and forwarded to the controller, dropped, or sent to the standard processing pipeline. There exist various versions of the OpenFlow Protocol. New features and enhancements are added to every new version.

2.1.7. Advantages of OpenFlow

An open source SDN technology is called OpenFlow. Numerous suppliers and providers support it. Certain switches have the option to use their own internal rules or OpenFlow rules. It can be used to manage virtual switches in cloud computing in a fully virtualized network environment. OpenFlow's SDN architecture enables rapid reaction to errors and changes. It can handle extremely complex rules and is also very flexible. Consider a campus area network (CAN) with numerous buildings, switches, and two internet connections to demonstrate how to use OpenFlow. In order to reach its destination, network traffic normally travels via the closest connections. The switches can notify the controller of the status of their connection if a link between two buildings fails. The controller will then send new flow rules with a new forwarding path to the affected switches. Any traffic heading towards the internet can also be redirected over the reliable link in the event of a failure. Installing a firewall between every building, or even every floor within a building, would be costly. However, a large CAN with many different types of devices could also quickly become full of unwanted traffic. To prevent unwanted traffic from flooding the network, such as broadcast requests and Apple Bonjour, the flow rules can be configured to reject such requests.

2.2. FLOW TABLE OF SDN SWITCHES

All forwarding decisions in SDN are flow-based rather than destination-based, as in the old traditional network. Forwarding entities are called OpenFlow switches. In an OpenFlow switch, packets are handled according to a list of prioritizing entries within a flow table with a logical data structure. In OpenFlow 1.10, a flow table can hold a set of flow entries consisting of 15 field tuples: matching fields, action, statistical counter, priority, and timeout mechanism are commonly used, while some fields are optional. Matching fields are used to match packet meta data, including the ethernet type, internet protocol (IP) source and destination address, and medium access control (MAC) source and destination address. You have the option to specify exact-match or wildcard-match entries for these fields. While the latter represents multiple flows using any value indicated by an asterisk (*), the former represents a single flow. When a packet arrives, it is searched through the flowtable to see if it matches a wildcard or exact match flow. If it does, the appropriate action is performed. For each instance where the flow entry successfully matches the arriving packet, the statistical count will be increased. Priorities are assigned to wildcard matching entries; in the event that multiple packets match multiple wildcard flows, the final match with the higher priority is the match. Generally speaking, exact matches are given precedence over wildcard flows. The packet will either be dropped or forwarded to the controller if it does not match any flow. Additional actions could be routed to a particular switch port number. Every incoming packet must undergo a flow lookup. As shown in Figure 2.3, this could be accomplished with either a single flowtable or multiple flowtable pipelining up to 255 tables.

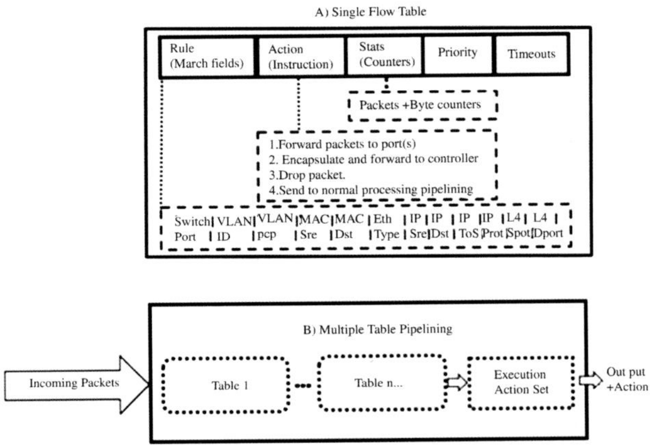

Figure 2.3. *Single vs. multiple flow table. (A) Single flow table; and (B) multiple flow table, respectively.*

Source: https://www.mdpi.com/futureinternet/futureinternet-12-00147/article_deploy/html/images/futureinternet-12-00147-g002.png.

OpenFlow 1.3 allows multiple flow table pipelining processing, which allows a packet to be processed by multiple flow tables for efficiency and flexibility reasons. The four components (matching field, action, statistic, priority, and timeout) are present in both the single and pipelining tables. Unlike the single table, the matching procedure in the pipelining tables begins at the first flow table and may move on to the following table until the matching flow entry is located. Sequential entry verification is carried out, with action typically taken at the end of the pipelining's final table. Depending on how the table-miss entry is configured, the switch will either drop the packet or send a packet-in message to the controller requesting a flow setup if there is no match. The centralized controller computes a new flow entry and sends a packet-out event to the switch instructing it to install the corresponding entry in its flowtable in the event that a packet is forwarded to it for a flow setup request. Massive flow arrivals will cause the controller to receive numerous requests for flow setup on a massive scale. A data center with 4,000 servers has the potential to receive up to 200,000 flows arrival/sec. Approximately 20 packets per flow with a flow inter-arrival time of less than 30 ms, were reported in a previous study on average flow size. These demands are very high, but the memory capacity to store forwarding entries is small. Ordinary OpenFlow switch flow tables kept their rules in ternary content addressable memory (TCAM), a unique kind of high-speed memory that allows for continuous flow entry lookup in just one clock cycle O (1). Although TCAM has a high-speed lookup capability, its memory is limited to a few 1,000 entries. Growing the TCAM size raises additional issues, including cost and the need for high power consumption.

Commodity servers that are integrated into the same switch hardware are the basis for software switches that have gained popularity recently. On a quad-core system, this kind of switch can provide a high packet processing rate of 40 Gbps along with a large flow table capacity. Comparing these switches to commodity switches, however, reveals limitations in the lookup rate. The general-purpose central processing unit (CPU) serves as the foundation for the software switch's design. Commodity switches, on the other hand, rely on application-specific integrated circuits (ASICs), which are made specifically for fast lookup. Moreover, software switches employ traditional random-access memory (RAM), which has a large storage capacity at a comparatively lower cost, to store forwarding rules.

TCAM, which aims to balance high lookup performance and matching flexibility, stores forwarding rules from OpenFlow switches. When forwarding rules are installed in software switches rather than ASICs, the OpenFlow switch's performance drops from 940 to 14 Mpbs. A flow table can be kept in CPU caches to expedite switching operations even more in software switches. These caches do, however, share the same drawbacks as the storage limitation that ASIC first introduced.

As a result, the shortage causes a number of issues, such as additional packet processing delays, update operations, and signaling overhead. Consequently, there is reason for great concern regarding the switch flowtable limitation and the frequent flow setup requests to the controller, which require further investigation, particularly in large-scale network environments like data centers and the Internet of Things.

2.2.1. Installation of Flow Table Entries

The switch flow table typically has two ways to install flow entries: reactive and proactive. Similarly, the flow table might be updated in response to certain events, like link failure or modifications to ACL rules. Two actions might be necessary in this case: deleting the outdated flow entries and installing the new entry for the alternate flow or ACL rules, respectively. An update operation of the flow table is required in this case...

2.2.1.1. Reactive Flow Table Allocation

Initially, the switch flowtable is empty while the network is booting up. As soon as a switch and controller start negotiating features, the controller will find every switch that is connected. The flowtable will be filled in two different ways. The first scenario is when the switch flowtable's first packet of flows arrives. This will result in a table-miss since the entry will not be available. By using a packet-in event, the switch executes a reactive process to handle table-misses and forwards the information to the controller for additional decision-making. The controller updates the affected switch's switch flowtable and computes the flow's correspondent entry. Reinstalling flow entries as a result of a flow modification event or flow expiration is the second scenario. For multiple flows between the switch and the controller, setting a new flow typically takes two or n messages, where n is the number of data flows. Once the rules are installed, packet transmission starts. The controller won't be consulted when processing a subsequent packet in the same flow. The processing of reactive packets is shown in Figure 2.4. Assume that three distinct packets from three distinct flows arrived at switch S1 at various times. At time t1, packet p1 arrives; at time t2, packet p2 arrives slightly after t1; and at time t3, packet p3 arrives slightly after t3. Following the arrival of packet p3, the switch looks up three times in its flowtable. As shown by arrow 1, Switch S1 buffers the three packets and creates three packet-in events to ask the controller for the corresponding flows. The controller computes the flow entries for each packet-in it receives and then sends a packet-out message back to switch S1, telling the switch to install the corresponding entries, as indicated by arrow 2. Ultimately, as message 3 illustrates, packets are queued and sent at full line rate.

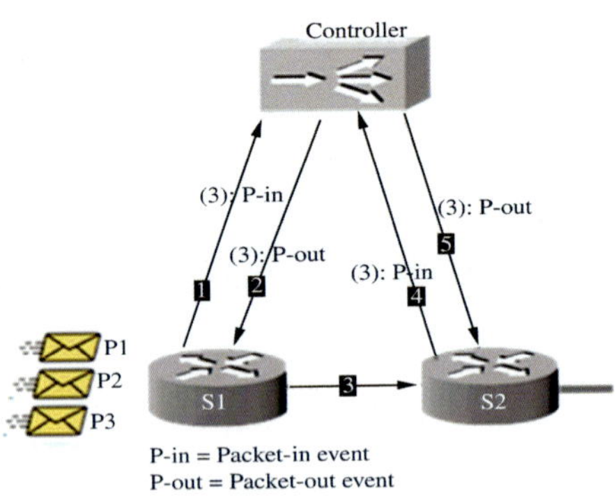

Figure 2.4. *Example of reactive entry installation.*

Source: https://www.mdpi.com/futureinternet/futureinternet-12-00147/article_deploy/html/images/futureinternet-12-00147-g003.png.

It makes intuitive sense for the two switches to exchange multiple OpenFlow messages with the controller to install flow in accordance with the current state of the network. This can quickly lead to a decline in the network's overall performance and a drop in service quality. For example, the controller should reroute all affected flows in 25 milliseconds or less in the event of a link failure. SDN real-time application is further hindered by the stringent delay needs. To prevent declining QoS, packets must be delivered to the intended destination with a guaranteed less delay. To comply with CGN's fine-grained traffic engineering delay requirement, this is required. An extended delay can worsen packet losses and traffic congestion, which can impair network performance. The results of the experiment conducted on a small-scale network consisting of 6 and 14 switches demonstrated the feasibility of meeting the carrier grade network CGN delay requirement. According to the same experiment, the amount of flow rules that must be installed or modified in the affected switch determines how long the delay will be. In the worst scenario, a topology configuration with 14 switches can take up to 300 milliseconds. Therefore, in large scale networks, it is difficult to meet the demand of the (CGN) delay budget. Furthermore, the controller and switch buffer experienced an increased processing load due to the abundance of flows. As a result, in large-scale networks, implementing a reactive approach for every flow setting might not provide the desired performance.

2.2.1.2. Proactive Flow Table Allocation

Proactive handling of incoming packets is quicker than reactive handling since the controller can set up forwarding rules before the flow arrives. The switch processes an incoming flow in accordance with the instructions specified in the flow table when the information in the packet headers matches an entry that already exists; as a result, the controller is not consulted during packet processing. For instance, as indicated by arrows 1 and 2, the controller in Figure 2.5 installed n number of flow entries ahead of time. As opposed to the reactive method, which involved exchanging n OpenFlow messages between the switch and the controller, the proactive approach involved exchanging fewer messages. The strategy reduced the controller's processing load while somewhat enhancing user QoS. The increased performance was ascribed to the absence of extra flow setup time. Crucially, even in the event that the switch loses communication with the controller, traffic flow will not be interfered with. Therefore, where flow table storage space is sufficient, a proactive approach may be preferable in order to achieve low packet processing delay with an acceptable performance. However, because of the switch memory constraint, it might not result in better performance in SDN. In the event that 200 packets from various flows arrive at the switch flow table simultaneously and the flowtable size is less than 200, there is an inevitable risk of flowtable overflow. As a result, it might cause flow that is a part of active flow to disappear. Future packets intended for an active flow require the switch to repeatedly update the flowtable for the same flow entry by triggering more packet-in events to the controller.

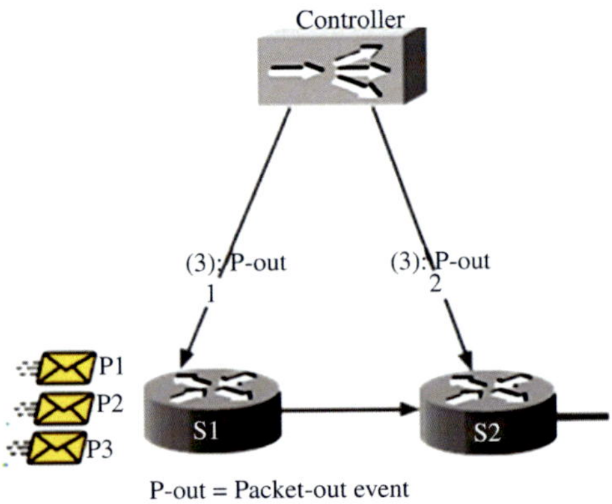

Figure 2.5. *Example of proactive entry installation.*

Source: https://www.mdpi.com/futureinternet/futureinternet-12-00147/article_deploy/html/images/futureinternet-12-00147-g004.png.

One of the difficult problems in a proactive manner has continued to be the notable increase in traffic and the tiny TCAM space gap. Large-scale networks face a greater challenge because, in the event of a failure, a vast number of backup flow entries are needed in addition to primary path flow entries to ensure the network's survival. Pushing more flow entries can quickly overload the TCAM, increasing the likelihood of overflow. Additionally, when the flowtable is fully loaded, flow entry update operations are difficult and take a long time. This is so because the number of entries in the flowtable determines how long it takes to update an entry. Thus, further research is needed to address the consumption of proactive flow entries.

2.3. OPENFLOW TABLE MEMORY MANAGEMENT

Due to its limitations, the switch flowtable is unable to hold all necessary forwarding entries. A number of suggestions were put forth to increase the limited flowtable's efficiency, as shown in Figure 2.6. Certain works employ an adaptive timeout mechanism to manage flowtable rules. Other approaches take the idea of aggregation into account when reducing the table's size. Partitioning rules and distributing across the network in a way that complies with policies based on device capacity is the subject of some work. Another way to reduce overhead switch to the controller and limit the number of concurrent forwarding rules in the switch is to use rule caching. The right flow can be installed in the switch flowtable by using machine learning techniques, which are highly effective in predicting the traffic flow pattern. The following sections go into more detail about these suggestions.

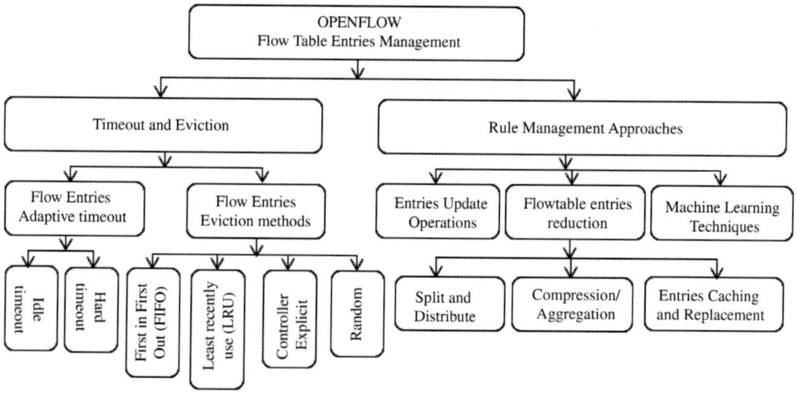

Figure 2.6. *Taxonomy of flow entries management.*

Source: https://www.mdpi.com/futureinternet/futureinternet-12-00147/article_deploy/html/images/futureinternet-12-00147-g007.png.

2.3.1. Timeout and Eviction Mechanisms

OpenFlow permitted the usage of a timeout mechanism to establish the forwarding entry's lifespan in the switch flow table, thereby resolving the issue with the switch flow table storage (TCAM). To make room for new incoming packets, an entry will be removed from the flow table if no packet matches it within the timeout period. Idle and hard timeout are the two main ways that the OpenFlow controller can currently install the timeout mechanism. Typically, the OpenFlow controller sets the flow entry's idle timeout value to a constant value in seconds for all flows.

Better performance, though, might result from using this timeout value when the packet inter-arrival time is approaching, and the flow table has enough room to hold all of the flows. Moreover, this approach could be easily implemented in a fixed network environment with little computational overhead. But given the variability of flow, as shown in Figure 2.7, a fixed value across all flows may not be able to adapt to dynamic traffic flows, particularly in a large-scale network setting. As indicated in Table 2.1, there has been a recent increase in research interest in developing a plan to extend the flow lifespan.

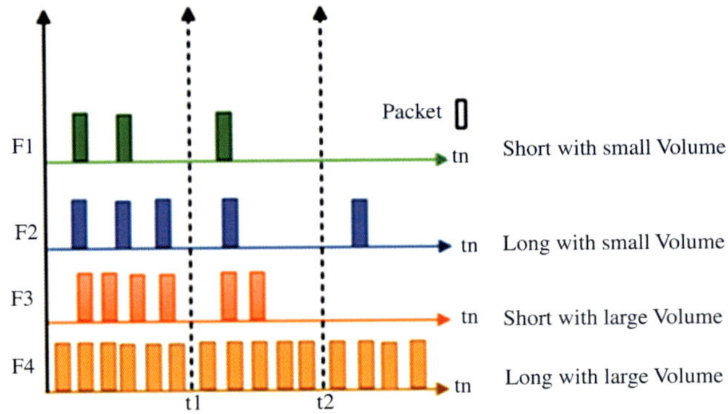

Figure 2.7. *Example of traffic flow with variability of inter arrival time.*

Source: https://www.mdpi.com/futureinternet/futureinternet-12-00147/article_deploy/html/images/futureinternet-12-00147-g008.png.

Table 2.1. *Comparison of Proposed Flow Timeout Mechanism*

Controller Placement Mode	**Method**	**Rule Eviction**	**Timeout Mode**
Reactive	Traffic feature-based idle timeout lognormal distribution.	X	Idle
Proactive	Bloom filter	Data logging using multiple bloom filters (MBF).	Idle
Reactive	Combine flow table and controller (CFC).	Idle timeout eviction	Idle
Reactive	Flow table adaptive timeout algorithm.	X	Idle
Reactive	Lognormal distribution using probability.	Random	Idle
Proactive	Flowtable vacancy and mathematical model.	Least recently used (LRU)	Idle
Reactive	Software defines adaptive routing (STAR).	LRU	Idle
Reactive	Dynamic hard timeout allocation.	LRU	Hard timeout

Proactive	Timeout calculation: idle timeout with two stage-table.	Controller randomly evict flow with no match.	Idle
Reactive	Composed of 3 modules: history flow information base (HFIB), timeout selection algorithm (TSA), and EIMC.	Entry installation and management component (EIMC).	Hard
Hybrid (reactive and proactive)	Dynamic idle and hard timeout based on traffic pattern to reduce overhead.	Based on flow packet count.	Idle and hard

Source: https://www.mdpi.com/1999-5903/12/9/147.

Assume that vt1 and vt2, respectively, are a number of packets that have been transmitted up to times t1, t2, in Figure 2.7. F1 denotes a brief flow that has few packets at both t1 and t2. F3 depicts a brief flow with a large number of packets, while F2 displays a long flow with few packets. F4 has a lengthy flow with big packets at the end. It is necessary to thus look into the viability of implementing a flow timeout strategy that can include both fixed and dynamic timeout values depending on the types of intra-flow packet inter-arrival times that are shown in Figure 2.7. Because extreme flows show variations in statistics like duration and volume, it is challenging to handle the current traffic pattern when the traditional method of applying a fixed timeout value across the flow is applied. Additionally, the effect of the timeout value on flow statistics revealed a trade-off in performance. On the other hand, a high timeout value might needlessly preserve a lot of flows for which no packet is anticipated. Regarding the brief timeout, it could cause early flow eviction, which would raise flow setup requests and reduce a long-lived flow to a smaller one. There may be more frequent evictions of consequence flows, which results in more packet-in messages being sent to the controller. This situation raises the communication overhead from the switch to the controller.

The packet inter-arrival time (PIAT) based on flow state, controller capacity, and current flowable utilization are some of the factors that affect when to set a proper timeout. Crucially, establishing an appropriate idle timeout can boost system efficiency and should be dependent on the packet inter-arrival time – a TF-idle timeout scheme that adjusts the flow entry lifecycle dynamically based on current network activity. To do this, a logarithmic normal distribution is used to estimate the traffic feature using the packet arrival distribution and interval. Given that general networks are known to undergo temporal changes accompanied by fluctuations in flow size. The technique necessitated gathering the packet arrival time statistical distribution. As a result, the controller's memory is extremely expensive. Similarly, in order to avoid displacing significant flows, flow removal should adhere to a specific protocol. TF-idle ignores flow eviction and solely concentrates on timeout settings. In addition to the timeout method, it's critical to take the flow eviction into account. In order to prevent deleting an entry that might be required in the near future, this is required. Alternatively, manage the flow entries in the flow table more effectively by employing an intelligent eviction mechanism based on data logging and the multiple bloom filters (MBF) data structure to determine when to remove a flow entry, rather than solely depending on the flow expiry period. Even so, the method went one step further and eliminated the superfluous entries. However, the system experienced an additional processing delay as a result of the encoding of some significant flow values in SRAM. In the worst scenario, the system's stability may be compromised by the variability of flow traffic patterns.

Adaptive flow table adjustment based on the percentage of active flow entries by merging controller cost and flow table. Real-time traffic monitoring is done by the algorithm. As a result, depending on various flows, the algorithm dynamically sets the idle timeout value. It's interesting to note that the algorithm might associate various timeout values with flows. Nevertheless, there is an additional computational overhead on the controller due to the computation of flow table entry costs in switch and controller computing costs. As a result, it might restrict how many switches the controller is able to manage. Additionally, getting the flow entries in real-time through message to the switch before the flow completes. Similar efforts were made to assign an appropriate idle timeout by modeling the flow as ON or OFF and analyzing the packet length and packet interval length. This necessitated some computation on the part of the switch upon packet arrival. In a similar vein, the idle timeout value is dynamically adjusted by the controller by keeping track of previous flows. When the flow arrival is uniform, the approach might be stable with a suitable idle timeout; however, if the flow shape changes to an exponential distribution, the switch may experience a significant overhead. This is because the switch calculates the resource overhead for the flow table when a packet arrives, a process that might not be possible in real-time. Furthermore, it might lessen the quantity of flows that the switch must process during the sampling period. Additionally, a packet can experience an additional processing lag. They fail to include flow eviction techniques in their work.

To install various timeout values during the sampling period, use a dynamic adaptive timeout algorithm. This is accomplished by calculating the probability of the number of flow entries that might emerge at the subsequent sampling time. After that, an idle timeout is selected based on the approximation. The controller used to alter the timeout value at each sampling interval in order to handle the dynamic nature of the traffic. As the number of flows increases, the algorithm may still be efficient with low flow arrival, but it will not perform well because it places a heavy workload on the controller and requires a large investment in processing power. Furthermore, when the timeout expires, the method removes the unused entry using a random policy. An active flow may be eliminated as a result of random flow eviction, which can significantly impair network performance by placing an additional processing burden on the controller. To count the number of active entries, a counter is set at the switch; however, it should be noted that this method could cause miscounting if duplicate SYN/FIN packets are present. Because of this, each entry is linked to a binary flag (0 or 1), which denotes an inactive state, or an active state, to prevent miscounting. Consequently, the approach could remove unnecessary entries in an intelligent manner when necessary to make room for new flows; however, it necessitates altering the OpenFlow switch flow table data structure, rendering it an unfeasible solution in terms of computation. Moreover, an LRU is used to remove an entry when the entry timeout has passed, and it is inappropriate to use an LRU in a flow-based network. Since appropriate control policies should be based on a global view of multiple rules in all switches, this algorithm replaces a single rule for each switch.

Designed a flow cache architecture with a two-stage timeout mechanism to better identify and retain important flow entries, similar to how the flow table's useful entries were preserved. At first, flow entries are kept in the main table, and the controller uses the flow entry information to compute the timeout. After that, entries are transferred to a backup table for another opportunity rather than being entirely removed due to an inactive period during which no packet is anticipated. It should be noted that in order to prevent the waste of flowtable resources, the strategy maintained the active flows and evicted transient flows. However, choosing an appropriate timeout required understanding of flow. As a result, getting old flow installation, evict, install, and packet-in in real-time is not possible. Additionally, the process of moving an entry to secondary storage for a second chance may result in an additional processing delay for a packet, which might not be ideal for applications that are sensitive to delays. Thus, it is important to set an appropriate idle timeout in order to effectively manage the valuable flow table space. It is also crucial to take into account the flow entry's deterministic life span (hard timeout) in order to maintain long-duration flows with a high number of packets within a brief inter-arrival. Unlike the idle timeout features, a dynamic hard timeout allocation is made for both predictable and unpredictable flows in order to optimize flowtable utilization. The idea is to maintain predictable flows while creating brief periods of unpredictable flow. This is accomplished by examining each packet trace to determine the type of packet arrival and then modifying the hard timeout in accordance with that analysis. An entry with a max timeout is removed using LRU when flow table utilization hits a cap. The entry-eviction scheme's inherent problem persists, despite the scheme's success in maintaining predictable flows. Since LRU is a packet-driven algorithm that can only be implemented in theory, it is not a suitable eviction algorithm for SDN. Moreover, it may not work with OpenFlow in practice and goes against one of the SDN principles, which deletes all control functions from the controller. For short live flows, IHTA takes into account the dynamic idle value; for long live flows with short packet inter-arrival times, it modifies the hard timeout value. As a result, the packet-in event is now issued to the controller much less frequently, improving communication overhead. By utilizing the built-in data collection features of OpenFlow, the shortcoming of LRU is addressed. Since flows with low packet counts are regarded as victims, eliminating them increased the efficiency of the storage that was available. It is reasonable to conclude that, without altering the SDN architecture, IHTA has, to a certain extent, decreased communication overhead and enhanced the usage of the limited flowtables.

2.3.2. Flow Rule Aggregation

Compared to destination base using conventional IP routers, SDN has been designed to support a wide range of flow-based network applications with more intricate matching patterns. The complexity stems from the forwarding rules kept in TCAM, which is a size limitation and a significant consideration when implementing OpenFlow technology. Flow entries aggregation, which lowers the number of necessary entries by combining several flow entries into one while attempting to maintain the original forwarding semantic through wildcard rules, is one alternative method for lowering TCAM demands. The linked works are summarized in Table 2.2.

Table 2.2. *Comparison of the Related Works of Flow Table Entries Reduction Mechanism*

Controller Placement Mode	Method	Goal	Use Case
Reactive	Quine-McCluskey algorithm. Hidden Markov model (HMM).	To manage the multiple flow table and reduce flow processing time.	Flowtable management
Reactive	Shrink the flow table size using binary tree aggregation.	Reduce flowtable size with fast rule updating time using aggregation technique.	Flowtable management

Reactive	Rule optimization and binary Trie aggregation.	To reduce the number of flow entries needed in the almost full-filled flow tables, while retain the original QoS.	Flowtable management
Reactive	Redundant flow entries with dynamic threshold value aggregation.	Reduce flowtable overflow problem and flow aggregation convergence time.	Flowtable management
Reactive	Flow entry compression.	Reduce flow table size by compressing matching header.	Flowtable management
Proactive	One big switch	Distribute rules via abstracted forwarding element called one big switch.	Distributed ACL and load balancer
Reactive	Flow entry compression.	To maximize the utilization of SDN switches flowtable.	Traffic engineering
Reactive	Bit and subset weaving to merge flow entries to a subset of a partition.	Reduce flowtable size with fast rule updating time using aggregation technique.	Flowtable management
Proactive	Flow entries split and distribute.	Decompose flow entries into smaller part and distribute them across forwarding element.	Distributed ACLs
Proactive	Linear optimization model.	Modeled rule allocation problem in resource-constrained OpenFlow networks with relaxing routing policy.	Traffic engineering
Proactive	Break tables into a number of smaller subtables and distributes them across network switches.	Ternary content addressable memory (TCAM) shortage problem through distributing rules.	Distributed ACLs

Source: https://www.mdpi.com/1999-5903/12/9/147.

The method reduces the number of entries that need to be stored by compressing fine-grained forwarding entries into fewer coarse-grained entries with a slightly larger matching range. It's interesting to note that OpenFlow switches or protocol don't need to be changed in order to easily implement this software solution as an optional plug-in on the OpenFlow controller. Aggregation techniques are available for farewell rules (ACL), non-prefix TCAM forwarding rules, and traditional prefix IP routing tables. However, because the aggregation technique typically fails to preserve the original semantics of the rule, updating forwarding entries or querying the traffic statistical counter by the controller presents some challenges. In addition, some OpenFlow switches might not fully support wildcard values matching fields due to the diversity of switch vendor implementation. Furthermore, in practice, many events like node failure and

QoS provisioning may result in frequent updates to flowtable rules. Because of this, an aggregation scheme needs to be flexible enough to adjust quickly and with less computation to the frequent nature of rule updates. In order to optimally aggregate rules with bit merging on the tree, the FFTA constructs optimal routing table constructor (ORTC)—based aggregation with binary search tree (BST). In order to improve execution time, the scheme constructs a BST of non-prefix flow entries by utilizing bit weaving and eliminating bit swapping. Certain rules have been found to be non-aggregatable, meaning that FFTA loses out on the chance to aggregate these flow entries. Furthermore, the network will become computationally expensive as it grows in size. An additional flow table reduction scheme is FTRS. FTRS aggregates flow entries with the same action that are headed to the same destination address while maintaining the existence of each entry at the flow path's edge. In order to do this, FTRS determined which switches—core or edge—are more likely than others to experience flow table congestion. In order to maintain fine-grained management, less significant flow entries are grouped together in the middle of the flow path while keeping entries at edge switches. After a chosen matching attribute, like the IP address, is traversed from each flow entry into a node using a binary tree (prefix tree), the number of flow entries is decreased by substituting coarse-grained nodes for the non-empty trees. FTRS has decreased flowtable consumption to some extent, but it is unable to aggregate certain kinds of flows.

In-switch dynamic flow aggregation (IDFA) mechanism as a switch application to avoid the link between the switch and the controller is a solution to the flaw in FTRS. In order to dynamically adjust and aggregate entries based on a threshold value, IDFA adds redundant flow entry insertion and verification. When compared to FTRS, IDFA was said to have a lower chance of overflow and a better aggregation convergence time. Its performance might be sufficient in a fixed network, but in large-scale networks with heavy-hitting flows, in particular, it might add unnecessary overhead. Furthermore, only a small local area network (LAN) environment is better suited for IDFA and FTRS. As an alternative, OpenFlow's 1.3 supports pipelining stages with multiple flow tables (MFT) to provide matching flexibility for entries. Using the Quine-McCluskey algorithm and pruning, the method aggregates flow entries on a regular basis. The most well-liked entries with heavy matching in probability are found using the Hidden Markov model (HMM); these entries are then added to the front-end ExTable, while the remaining entries are added to the following table. In tests, the plan decreases flow processing time and saves roughly 45% of memory space. However, because this solution necessitated a large number of entries in the front-end table, which may significantly pressurize the ExTable and potentially cause an overflow problem, the inherent architecture of Agg-ExTable is its weakness. Adopting such solutions in large-scale networks may also be difficult, particularly given the variability that flows display. By adding brief tags to the packet header that indicate the original number of bits used to store entries for OpenFlow switches, TCAM entries attempted to minimize the size of the flow entries in the flow table. This is accomplished by utilizing SDN's dynamic programming feature to route the packets based on those brief tags. For a given number of flows, the techniques have optimized the TCAM storage space while significantly lowering the TCAM power consumption. But in order to implement the solution, the packet header and flow table populating technique had to be altered. Furthermore, it is difficult to add an identifier to every incoming packet in ASIC-based storage because it is not a standard procedure. As a result, the packet processes slowly and suffers a performance penalty. Rifai and companions suggested Minnie, a two-module system made up of a routing and compression module. The flow table is set up with 1,000 rules as the maximum size. When more rules are added, Minnie activates the compression module, which compresses the rules according to their source, destination, and default values before selecting the best rule. After that, in a topology where the number of nodes increases, the flow is routed using the shortest path so as not to overload the flowtable. Minnie works to improve computation times and compression ratios, but some flows have a tendency to persist for a short while due to their variability. Minnie forgets to add a flexible timeout and an eviction mechanism to eliminate pointless entries and make room for a fresh flow. Additionally, the various compression techniques used could add another overhead that causes instability to the system.

2.3.3. Flow Rule Split and Distribute

At edge switches, endpoint policies such as firewall and load balancer rules are enforced. Several forwarding rules are always produced by these policies. A collection of rules is typically divided into tiny sub-tables and dispersed throughout the network in a way that complies with policies because there is not enough flow table space (TCAM). The goal of all distribution schemes is to reduce the quantity of entry rules required to implement policies in every switch. In this manner, optimization models that take memory constraints and rule dependencies into account are shown to determine which rules should be applied to which switches. One such scheme is Palette, which was created to share rules with individual ingress switches and then distribute them throughout the network, resulting in smaller sub-tables for each switch. They use a rainbow path coloring problem to formulate two greedy strategies for optimizing the sub-table entries. One limitation of the solution is that it does not address the issue of rule redundancy by balancing the size of each sub-table. In this sense, coloring is expanded upon to maximize the quantity of sub-tables (i.e., quantity of colors). To minimize table size, the SA algorithm can divide a large number of sub-tables. Although SSP can balance all sub-table sizes with low rule overhead compared to Palette, experimentally optimal results were obtained in small network topologies. Furthermore, regardless of the size of the topology, SA plus SSP may require little TCAM space to store rules. However, the stability of the system may be harmed by the entry of massive flows into a dynamic large-scale network.

In order to assign sub-rectangles to switches, a split model is decomposed using overlapping rectangles and linear programming (LP). However, because policy enforcement is carried out at multiple hosts after packets enter the network, it causes unwanted traffic. Moreover, distribution might not be able to guarantee practical space allocation for every switch in the network. In a related endeavor, the rule distribution problem under heterogeneous flow rule policy was examined for one big switch (OBS). In order to determine appropriate rule space allocations for each flow path in each switch, the author presents the LP base rule partition approach with two heuristics for rule allocation. As a result, only the rules that have an impact on packet traversal are installed. However, OBS uses five dimensions to represent endpoint policy rules, making table decomposition computationally unfeasible. In order to balance the quantity of rules stored along a path, the work of table decomposition and suitable allocation for heterogeneous flow tables with an effective rule distribution method. However, because of the rule dependency issue, the method might result in incorrect packet forwarding. In comparison, Nguyen et al. designed OFFICER, a linear optimization model intended to compute and apply effective forwarding rules in switch memory while considering memory and link capacity constraints. OFFICER views the network as a “Blackbox,” requiring it to adhere to endpoint policies set by the operator in order to optimize resource utilization through route adaptation. Thus, entries can generally be maximized by dividing and distributing them among data forwarding elements. To maintain the distribution of forwarding entries, however, more traffic overhead is introduced into the switches, particularly when the network topology is dynamically changing over time. Furthermore, in a large-scale network with massive flow arrivals, the distribution scheme might be a bottleneck.

2.3.4. Flow Rule Caching

By using wildcard rule caching to aggregate multiple flows and reuse entries across them, communication overhead can be significantly decreased. Furthermore, it is possible to lower the expense of updating and enforcing policies. However, in order to resolve conflicts between two or more overlapped packets, wildcard rules are typically stored with different priorities assigned.

Let p, for instance, be an N-dimensional ruleset R (R1, R2, R3, …, RN) with the following priority order: R1 > R2 > R3 > … RN. If rule R2 priority is higher than rule R1 and the match field of rule R1 overlaps at the intersection field of rule R2, then rule dependency exists. Because of this, caching R2 alone—without also caching R1—due to its high matching frequency could lead to improper packet forwarding. Therefore, to ensure proper packet forwarding, all other rules with a higher priority must be installed; it is not sufficient to just cache the requested rule in the event that no correspondent rule is available. Such circumstances necessitate additional storage overhead, which raises the flow table overflow. As Table 2.3 summarizes, this has attracted the attention of numerous researchers.

Table 2.3. *Comparison of the Related Works of Rule Caching Mechanism to Improve Flow Table Utilization*

Controller Placement Mode	**Method**	**Goal**	**Use Case**
Proactive	CacheFlow: cover-set using direct acyclic graph (DAG).	Improving the efficiency of TCAM. Allocate rules b/w TCAM & RAM to solve the rule dependency problem.	Distributed ACLs
Proactive	k-Hop neighboring set.	Improved cover-set to solve rule dependency the problem.	Distributed ACLs
Reactive	Uses DAG to solve the replacement problem.	TCAM replacement problem under rule dependency constraints.	Distributed ACLs
Mixed mode (reactive and proactive)	Mixed cover-set and partition.	Allocate rules b/w TCAM & RAM due to rule dependency problem.	Distributed ACLs
Reactive	Partition with buckets using a decision tree.	To mitigate the dependency problem by partitioning the field space into buckets and caching rules associated with the requested buckets.	Distributed ACLs
Proactive	Forest tree to install a branch of rules using dynamic programming (DP) method.	To maximize the number of rule hits, while limiting the number of cached rules.	Distributed ACLs

Reactive	Decision tree to install a chunk of rule.	Intelligent rule management scheme to reduce communication overhead.	Distributed ACLs
Reactive and proactive	Hybrid timeout	To handle rule dependencies with flexibly hybrid timeout mechanism.	Distributed ACLs
Proactive	Two-stage caching architecture called CRAFT for the flow table.	To solve rule dependency problem using two-stage cache.	Distributed ACLs
Reactive	In-switch rule caching and replacement (IRCR) replaces a rule according to the expected number of incoming matched flows.	To reduce flowtable overflow problem.	TCAM

Source: https://www.mdpi.com/1999-5903/12/9/147.

As an alternative, it can process the remaining traffic flow by depending on extra data paths. With the advent of recent technological advancements, software switching—which offers an alternative by storing a large number of rules—was included in the commodity switch. Software switches have helped to mitigate the storage limitation issue to some extent, but they are not compatible with wildcard rules that match multiple header fields. In order to handle the first packet of each flow in this scenario, the switch is forced to use sluggish user space processing. This results in a considerable delay in packet processing, making it unsuitable for some uses. In order to gain the advantages of both without having to pay for their disadvantages, another option to combine hardware and software (hybrid) switching is suggested based on the nature of the amount of traffic matching switch rule. To guarantee that the semantics of the single-switch rule table are maintained in the distributed implementation, however, a single rule table must be carefully distributed into multiple tables spanning across heterogeneous data paths. This can, in theory, provide a lot of storage space to handle increased traffic. Nevertheless, there was an extra packet processing delay when the packet was forwarded to a software switch and then copied back to the TCAM's flow table. This additional delay is significant—it is at least 20 ms. As a result, the time increases as the request for data flow increases over time.

As an alternative to hybrid switches, commodity switches that require no extra resources were suggested, and TCAM was only intended to be used for rule storage. There are two categories of rules: strict rules and others. Heavy-hitting rules were kept in the first partition, and the remaining rules were kept in the second. As a result, partitioning in TCAM only eliminates the extra packet processing lags encountered in the hybrid switch; nevertheless, it may complicate the installation and removal of rules due to potential rule dependencies brought on by wildcards. Higher priority rules frequently overlap with lower priority rules at the intersection field. The final match would have a higher priority when a packet matched with multiple overlap rules. Consequently, rule dependencies become a problem. For this reason, just caching the requested rule might result in improper packet forwarding. Such circumstances necessitate additional storage overhead, which raises the flow table overflow. Additionally, this will increase the likelihood of a cache miss and prevent the possibility of other new rules arriving. As a result, this circumstance will raise update costs and packet-in generation even more. Converting wildcard rules into fresh, non-overlapping micro/exact rules is an alternate technique. Slicing the lengthy dependency chain into non-overlap rules results in a large number of flow entries, but each rule has tens of overlapping rules. The memory of the switch flow table (TCAM) would eventually be overloaded by this. This makes the additional processing load that comes with storing and updating rules on the controller inevitable. Because of this, handling dependencies carefully is essential to preventing overloading the switch flow table memory and preventing improper packet forwarding.

Algorithms for rule caching cannot select and store the most frequently used rules at random. In order to select the most often used rule and cache it in the TCAM flow table, a suitable scheme must be created. In order to achieve this, cover-set (CS), which is based on the hybrid switch, was proposed. The state-of-the-art CS design work, CacheFlow, represented the wildcard rule dependencies problem by splicing a lengthy dependency chain using a direct acyclic graph (DAG). A limited set of new rules are produced by the CS algorithm, covering a large number of low priority rules that overlap with higher priority rules. The frequency with which the rule is being matched is indicated by the rule weight. Heavy-hitting rules are those that have a higher weight; as a result, they are cached in the TCAM flow table, and the remaining sets of lower priority rules are sent to the software switch. TCAM caches the set of related rules with the highest ACV until it is full. A lot of flow rules can be accommodated by CS to some extent, but this benefit has a price. Because there are many cover-set rules that must be stored in TCAM, CS does not increase the efficiency of TCAM; rather, it may increase the likelihood of flow table overflow as the number of long chain dependencies increases. Further packet processing delay resulted from the packet being forwarded to the software switch and then copied back to the TCAM's flow table. The inherent architectures of cover-set and similar solutions are generally the source of their weakness, as each hardware switch requires the installation of a software switch, which may necessitate rearranging network cabling and additional resources to host the software switches. Additionally, for performance-related reasons, it is challenging to calculate the ideal number of software switches required.

Furthermore, the software switch kernel memory space—which is likewise constrained—must contain forwarding rules that are dependent on the characteristics of the traffic. Additionally, the packet processing delay caused by software switches over hardware switches increases when the controller is consulted, and the missing rules are installed. In order to achieve this, more update operations will be started, which has an impact on the systems' stability.

The partition mechanism in the work of, in contrast to the cover-set, caches flow rules in TCAM without requiring extra resources. Large dependent rules are divided into subsets, with the most frequent rules going in the first partition and the less frequent one's going in the second. The most advanced partition-based wildcard rule caching technique is called CAB.

The primary concept involves segmenting the flow rule into numerous tiny logical storage units, or buckets, and using a decision tree to separate the rules. Although the design makes an effort to prevent buckets from overlapping, rules may occasionally overlap with more than one rule in a different bucket. The bucket is cached in the first stage, and all related rules are stored in the second stage. With a higher cache hit ratio in the fixed network, CAB can shorten the time it takes for packets to process requests.

As for future work, it can also recommend enhancing the scheme to handle dynamic traffic patterns. The idea behind CAB was to introduce CRAFT. Two-stage pipelining was employed in this scheme to lessen the packet processing delay that CacheFlow was experiencing.

According to test findings, CRAFT performs 30% better on average than CacheFlow in terms of hit ratio. In a similar vein, split rules using a decision tree and install them at the switch flow table reactively. Chunks are uninstalled along with their associate when they stop functioning.

Consequently, partition-based wildcard rule caching has increased TCAM flow table efficiency. But the work of frequently creating partition rules resulted in the creation of numerous sub-rules, which will take up a significant amount of switch memory. On the other hand, if rules are kept together without being divided in order to prevent fragmentation, a lot of buckets are produced. In this case, a lot of space would be wasted since a single rule might be duplicated in multiple buckets.

2.3.5. Machine Learning Techniques

It is essential to predict flow traffic patterns in order to install the appropriate flow in the switch storage and minimize large flow entries, which result in inefficient use of network resources. The primary goal is to offer a method for carrying out fine-grained network management by classifying various flow types based on the variability that flows display. Thus, flow classification helps network operators manage resource utilization and improved quality of service (QoS) provisioning more effectively. Simply put, network QoS is the service level that is agreed upon to provide users with network applications. Typically, end-to-end latency, bandwidth, jitter, and packet loss are used to measure it. In order to satisfy user demand, measuring and configuring such services must be made as easy as possible. Built-in data collection modules in OpenFlow allow for the collection of statistics on switches, ports, and flows. These statistics are used to support flow monitoring and preserve the knowledge of the global network. However, direct access to other crucial metrics like port utilization, delay, and jitters is not provided. While jitter and delay need to be measured in addition to port utilization, port utilization can be measured using statistical techniques. Thus, more intelligence must be used in order to effectively maintain QoS provisioning. In this approach, the controller uses statistical traffic flow data to extract knowledge using machine learning (ML) techniques. As a result, researchers have recently become very interested in using the global network state to apply machine learning algorithms in the field of SDN from the perspective of routing optimization, resource management, QoS quality of experiences, and traffic classification prediction (*see* Table 2.4).

Table 2.4. *Comparison of Machine Learning Related Work to Improve Flowtable Storage*

Controller Placement Mode	**Focus**	**Technique**	**Use Case**
Proactive	Flow monitoring to reduce congestion and packet loss in SDN.	Experimental validation	Routing rules
Proactive	Traffic classification.	Supervised learning	Routing rules
–	UDP flow classification	Support vector machine supervised learning method.	Routing rules
–	Elephant flow-aware traffic classification at the edge of the network.	Machine learning technique.	Traffic flow routing rules in DC.

Proactive	Learning method to detect elephant flows in SDN.	Decision tree	Routing rules
Proactive	Predict the duration of the flow entry.	Machine learning technique	Routing and distributed ACL rules.
Proactive	Predict when flow entry becomes stale.	Probability	Routing rules
Proactive	Machine learning techniques to decide the preserved flow between long-lived (elephant) and short-lived (mice).	Deep learning neural network.	Routing rules
Proactive	Classify flows into active and inactive to decide the right flow to remove intelligently.	Machine learning techniques.	Routing rules
Proactive	Q, learning approach to an efficiently select flow timeout value.	Machine learning techniques	Distributed ACL rules

Source: https://www.mdpi.com/1999-5903/12/9/147.

While different QoS categories can be used to categorize traffic flows, prediction techniques are used to forecast the expected traffic flow for the future. Deep packet inspection (DPI) is very effective and widely used for traffic flow classification due to its high classification accuracy, allowing for flexible assurance of both quality of service (QoS) and quality of experience (QoE). Nevertheless, DPI is unable to identify an application if its pattern is unavailable, and because it must verify every traffic flow, it consumes a lot of computational resources. Furthermore, it is unable to categorize internet traffic that is encrypted. It is difficult or even impossible to update patterns in large-scale networks with exponential traffic growth when such techniques are used. On the other hand, compared to a DPI-based approach, ML-based approaches recognize encrypted traffic more effectively and at a much lower CPU computation cost. Because of the network global and intelligence available at the SDN controller, machine learning (ML) remains effective in SDN despite its lower accuracy when compared to the legacy network. Therefore, in order to apply the ML technique, researchers make use of the controller intelligence. In order to effectively manage the limited storage resource and provide QoS in an adaptive manner, efforts have been made to categorize traffic flows from an alternative viewpoint. Elephant-mice flow aware and application-aware are two examples of this classification. The former focuses on distinguishing between application traffic flows that are delay-sensitive and non-sensitive. To minimize declining SDN QoS policy, such an application required immediate detection and redistribution along the network. It would be impossible to identify every application on the internet, especially in a large-scale network, given how quickly they are becoming more and more prevalent.

With regard to the latter, it concentrates on distinguishing between mice flows, which have a short lifespan and are delay-intolerant, and elephant flows, which have a long lifespan and consume a lot of bandwidth. Elephant flows naturally have a high volume, which makes them prone to filling the flowtable storage. Network operators can use this classification to optimize how the scarce network resources are used in accordance with their desired quality of service (QoS). Glick and associates use a machine learning approach to analyze flows at the network's edge based on elephant flow awareness. The controller then applies effective traffic flow optimization algorithms based on the classification results. The suggested approach was divided into two phases: the first involved measuring head packets to various mice and elephant flows, and the second stage used a decision tree to determine whether the flows were actually elephant flows or not. Even though SDN approaches can distribute resources to various flows in an efficient manner, there is a significant overhead associated with storing a large number of flow entries, particularly when memory is limited. Determining which flows between short and long live flows with a large number of packets will be retained in the flowtable and which flow entries the controller should process is therefore essential. In order to achieve the goal of reducing storage and controller overhead while maintaining stable performance, a flow between elephants and mice must be established. In order to achieve this, an ML-based system used two variations of reinforcement learning (RL): one deep RL and the other traditional RL-based algorithm. This allowed the system to use a deep learning neural network to identify the optimal flow that would preserve the flowtable between the long-lived elephants and the short-lived mice. The method, which was developed using flow entry historical data, forecasts the maximum length of time an entry can endure and determines which flow entry will ultimately fail. Similar to this, FlowMaster anticipates when a flow entry gets stale and deletes it to make room for the next flow that comes in. It's possible that this assumption made by FlowMaster—that flow arrival comes after poison distribution—is not actually required for practice.

The work of smart table entry eviction for OpenFlow switches (STEREOS) is necessary for a more intelligent flow deletion strategy. Flow entries were classified as active or inactive using an ML-based method. Based on this, intelligence is employed to determine which flow should be removed without incurring additional storage costs. In order to achieve this, they presented

HQTimer, a Q-learning basis for choosing to flow effective timeout values that enhance data plane performance. These methods can, however, perform better in small- to medium-sized networks; however, a dynamic large-scale network might necessitate a more complex training set, which would require additional storage to hold more historical data. Not only is switch storage limited, but so are resources and controller CPU.

Taking into account the controller's expertise in international networking and the features that the OpenFlow network comes with. Making the most of the features is crucial if you want to improve network resource management, traffic flow classification, QoS provision, and routing optimization. In order to forecast flows and choose which flow to maintain in the switch flowtable in the event of a large-scale network, further research work involving feature selections is necessary.

2.3.6. Challenges and Future Research Direction

Although the separation of the control plane from the data plane provided numerous network solutions, it also presented a number of network challenges, including overhead, security risks, and delays. Similar to the previous example, limited switch memory also presents a number of issues, including increased update operations and security threats, which can impair SDN performance, particularly in large-scale networks.

Several initiatives have been undertaken recently, each with a unique set of solutions for a range of use cases. The performance of SDN in large-scale, dynamic networks like Telco, where dense traffic flows are frequently generated, has not been extensively studied in research studies. It is demonstrated that in such an environment, there are a great number of flows that each contain a large number of packets at a brief time interval. Switch memory, however, is limited and cannot hold the necessary quantity of flow entries. Handling enormous flows with a lot of packets in a small switch flowtable is still a difficult research topic that needs more investigation.

2.3.6.1. Reactive and Proactive Flow Table Rule Installation

The possibilities of proactive and reactive flowtable rule allocation strategies have been covered in earlier sections. Table 2.5 provides an overview of the difficulties involved in each strategy. In order to maximize flowtable utilization and minimize overhead and packet delay, an effective allocation of flow rules should integrate both proactive and reactive strategies. To satisfy the demanding quality of service (QoS) demands of real-time applications, it is advised that re-routing rules be finished in less than 25 milliseconds (ms). Using proactive entries allocation for applications that are sensitive to delays is one method. Whereas the reactive strategy ought to help best-effort or non-delay applications. Developing a plan that takes traffic variability into account will be a fascinating field of study.

Table 2.5. *Reactive and Proactive Rule Allocation Challenges*

Issues	Reactive	Proactive
Switch flowtable TCAM resource	More storage	Space limitation
Frequent and dynamic flowtable network	Frequent	Less
Packet processing delay	High	Low
Packet losses	Proportional to the usage of flowtable: low	Proportional to the usage of flowtable. High may increase the chance of overflow, which leads to more packet losses.
TCAM update operation	Less because flows are installed on demand.	Hard with a significant delay because flow is installed in advance.
Controller overhead	Higher overhead because of the frequent controller consultation.	Less because already installed.
Switch overhead	Low	High
Scalability	Scalable for a large network.	Scalable for a small network.

Source: https://www.mdpi.com/1999-5903/12/9/147.

2.3.6.2. Intelligent Flow Table Management

Large-scale networks generate a lot of traffic flows more frequently, which necessitates the installation of matching flow rules and therefore uses a lot of storage capacity. The majority of current storage-related solutions have been tested on small-scale networks, such as those with 7–28 nodes and 7–43 links. For this reason, these figures cannot be compared to a big number of devices in a big network environment such as Internet of Things (IoT) or Telco. When it comes to resource management, machine learning (ML) techniques are highly effective (i.e., switches and controller(s) are examples of network components.

But the majority of machine learning approaches concentrate on flow monitoring and classification. Predicting traffic flow for real-time applications and best-effort traffic, as well as choosing which traffic flow to install beforehand, are the subjects of little research. Data collection is integrated into OpenFlow, storing flow-related information like packet and byte counts. This statistical data shows how frequently traffic flows. Thus, it will be interesting to come up with a plan that makes use of this built-in data collection to come up with a plan that will speed up flow matching and further reduce the amount of memory used in the flowtable by choosing frequently used flow rules to put in the flowtable—possibly with the help of fuzzy theory.

2.3.6.3. Flow Rule Update Operation

TCAM can support both exact and wildcard matching rules. Unlike exact matching, wildcard matching allows for multiple flows to be made at once, reusing entries across various flows and minimizing the number of entries and overhead associated with frequent flow setup requests. Nevertheless, TCAM's flow entry update operation is sluggish. Packets experienced severe delays as a result, particularly in large-scale networks. Failure recovery, for instance, must strictly adhere to the carrier-grade network's recovery delay requirements. In a network with lots of devices, it is therefore preferable to update rules as little as possible. The multi-switch flowtable update has not gotten as much attention as the single switch rules update. To better understand and minimize the packet processing delay primarily resulting from the update operation, an additional analytical model is needed. Leveraging various flow table pipelining features to flexibly devise a multi-switch flowtable rule update optimization scheme to further reduce the update delay will be an interesting area of research to pursue.

REFERENCES

1. Al-Fuqaha, A. L. A., Shuaib, K., Sallabi, F. M., & Qadir, J. (2018). SDN flow entry management using reinforcement. *ACM Transactions on Autonomous and Adaptive Systems (TAAS), 13*(2), 1–23. https://doi.org/10.1145/3158653.
2. Amaral, P., & Bernardo, L. (2016). Machine learning in software defined networks: Data collection and traffic classification. *In Proceedings of the 2016 IEEE 24th International Conference on Network Protocols (ICNP)* (pp. 1–5). Singapore.
3. Chao, T., & Wang, K. (2017). In-switch dynamic flow aggregation in software defined networks. *In Proceedings of the 2017 IEEE International Conference on Communications (ICC)* (pp. 1–6). IEEE.
4. Cheng, T., Wang, K., Wang, L. C., & Lee, C. W. (2018). An in-switch rule caching and replacement algorithm in software defined networks. *In Proceedings of the 2018 IEEE International Conference on Communications (ICC)* (pp. 1–6). Kansas City, MO, USA.
5. Glick, M., & Rastegarfar, H. (2017). Scheduling and control in hybrid data centers. *In Proceedings of the 2017 IEEE Photonics Society Summer Topical Meeting Series (SUM)*. San Juan, Puerto Rico.
6. Guo, Z., Liu, R., Xu, Y., Gushchin, A., Walid, A., & Chao, H. J. (2017). STAR: Preventing flow-table overflow in software-defined networks. *Computer Networks, 125*, 15–25. https://doi.org/10.1016/j.comnet.2017.01.001.
7. Huang, J., Chang, G., Wang, C., & Lin, C. (2016). Heterogeneous flow table distribution in software-defined networks. *IEEE Transactions on Emerging Topics in Computing, 4*(3), 252–261. https://doi.org/10.1109/TETC.2016.2601040.
8. Isyaku, B. (2020). IHTA: Dynamic idle-hard timeout allocation algorithm based OpenFlow switch. *In Proceedings of the 2020 IEEE 10th Symposium on Computer Applications & Industrial Electronics (ISCAIE)* (pp. 170–175). IEEE.
9. Kang, N., Liu, Z., Rexford, J., & Walker, D. (2013). Optimizing the one big switch abstraction in software-defined networks. *In Proceedings of the Ninth ACM Conference on Emerging Networking Experiments and Technologies* (Santa Barbara, CA, USA).
10. Kanizo, Y., Hay, D., Keslassy, I., & Background, A. (2013). Palette: Distributing tables in software-defined networks. *In Proceedings of the 2013 IEEE INFOCOM* (pp. 545–549). IEEE.

11. Kannan, K., & Banerjee, S. (2013). Compact TCAM: Flow entry compaction in TCAM for power aware SDN. *In International Conference on Distributed Computing and Networking* (pp. 439–440). Springer.
12. Katta, N., Alipourfard, O., Rexford, J., & Walker, D. (2014). Infinite CacheFlow in software-defined networks. *In Proceedings of the Third Workshop on Hot Topics in Software Defined Networking* (pp. 1–6). Chicago, IL, USA.
13. Kumar, S., Louis, S., Louis, S., Crowley, P., & Turner, J. (2006). Algorithms to accelerate multiple regular expressions matching for deep packet inspection. *ACM SIGCOMM Computer Communication Review, 36*(4), 339–350. https://doi.org/10.1145/1151659.1151690.
14. Leng, B., Huang, L., Qiao, C., Xu, H., & Wang, X. (2017). FTRS: A mechanism for reducing flow table entries in software defined networks. *Computer Networks, 122*, 1–15. https://doi.org/10.1016/j.comnet.2017.04.004.
15. Li, H., Guo, S., Wu, C., & Li, J. (2015). FDRC: Flow-driven rule caching optimization in software defined networking. *In Proceedings of the 2015 IEEE International Conference on Communications (ICC)* (pp. 1–6). IEEE.
16. Li, X., & Huang, Y. (2019). A flow table with two-stage timeout mechanism for SDN switches. *In Proceedings of the 2019 IEEE 21st International Conference on High Performance Computing and Communications; IEEE 17th International Conference on Smart City; IEEE 5th International Conference on Data Science and Systems (HPCC/SmartCity/DSS)* (pp. 1804–1809). IEEE.
17. Li, X., & Shao, Y. (2018). Memory compression for recursive flow classification algorithm in network packet processing devices. *In Proceedings of the 2018 IEEE 3rd Advanced Information Technology, Electronic and Automation Control Conference (IAEAC)* (pp. 1502–1505). IEEE.
18. Li, X., & Xie, W. (2017). CRAFT: A cache reduction architecture for flow tables in software-defined networks. *In Proceedings of the 2017 IEEE Symposium on Computers and Communications (ISCC)*. Heraklion, Greece.
19. Liu, Y., Tang, B., Yuan, D., Ran, J., & Hu, H. (2016). A dynamic adaptive timeout approach for SDN switch. *In Proceedings of the 2016 2nd IEEE International Conference on Computer and Communications (ICCC)* (pp. 2577–2582). IEEE.

20. Luo, S., Yu, H., & Li, L. M. (2014). Fast incremental flow table aggregation in SDN. *In Proceedings of the 2014 23rd International Conference on Computer Communication and Networks (ICCCN)* (pp. 1–8). IEEE.

21. Meiners, C. R., Liu, A. X., & Torng, E. (2012). Bit weaving: A non-prefix approach to compressing packet classifiers in TCAMs. *IEEE/ACM Transactions on Networking, 20*(2), 488–500. https://doi.org/10.1109/TNET.2011.2178337.

22. Mohan, P. M., Truong-Huu, T., & Gurusamy, M. (2017). Fault tolerance in TCAM-limited software defined networks. *Computer Networks, 116*, 47–62. https://doi.org/10.1016/j.comnet.2016.11.018.

23. Nguyen, X., Saucez, D., Barakat, C., & Turletti, T. (2015). Officer: A general optimization framework for OpenFlow rule allocation and endpoint policy enforcement. *In Proceedings of the 2015 IEEE Conference on Computer Communications (INFOCOM)*. Kowloon, Hong Kong.

24. Nguyen, X., Saucez, D., Barakat, C., & Turletti, T. (2016). Rules placement problem in OpenFlow networks: A survey. *IEEE Communications Surveys & Tutorials, 18*(2), 1273–1286. https://doi.org/10.1109/COMST.2016.2531739.

25. OpenFlow Reference Switch Specification. (2009). *Current*, 1–36. Available online: http://www.openflow.org/ (accessed on 2 August 2024).

26. Panda, A., Samal, S. S., Turuk, A. K., Panda, A., & Venkatesh, V. C. (2019). Dynamic hard timeout-based flow table management in OpenFlow enabled SDN. *In Proceedings of the 2019 International Conference on Vision Towards Emerging Trends in Communication and Networking (ViTECoN)* (pp. 1–6). IEEE.

27. Qian, S., Zhang, Q., Tizghadam, A., Park, B., Bannazadeh, H., Boutaba, R., & Leon-Garcia, A. (2017). TCAM space-efficient routing in a software defined network. *Computer Networks, 125*, 26–40. https://doi.org/10.1016/j.comnet.2017.01.010.

28. Rifai, M., Huin, N., Caillouet, C., Giroire, F., Moulierac, J., Lopez, D., & Urvoy-Keller, G. (2017). Minnie: An SDN world with few compressed forwarding rules. *Computer Networks, 121*, 185–207. https://doi.org/10.1016/j.comnet.2017.05.006.

29. Rossi, D., & Valenti, S. (2010). Fine-grained traffic classification with NetFlow data. *In Proceedings of the 6th International Wireless Communications and Mobile Computing Conference (IWCMC 2010)* (pp. 479–483). Caen, France.

30. Sheu, J., Lin, W., & Chang, G. (2018). Efficient TCAM rules distribution algorithms in software-defined networking. *IEEE Transactions on Network*

and Service Management, 15(4), 854–865. https://doi.org/10.1109/TNSM.2018.2871422.

31. Sheu, J., Wang, P., & Rb, J. (2017). Wildcard-rule caching and cache replacement algorithms in software-defined networking. *In Proceedings of the 2017 European Conference on Networks and Communications* (pp. 1–6). Oulu, Finland.
32. Sminesh, C. N., Kanaga, E. G. M., & Ranjitha, K. (2017). Flow monitoring scheme for reducing congestion and packet loss in software defined networks. *In Proceedings of the 2017 4th International Conference on Advanced Computing and Communication Systems (ICACCS)* (pp. 1–5). Coimbatore, India.
33. Tsai, T. (2016). Dynamic flow aggregation in SDNs for application-aware routing. *In Proceedings of the International Symposium on Communication Systems, Networks and Digital Signal Processing (CSNDSP)* (pp. 1–5). IEEE.
34. Wang, C., & Youn, H. Y. (2019). Entry aggregation and early match using hidden Markov model of flow table in SDN. *Sensors, 19*(10), 2341. https://doi.org/10.3390/s19102341.
35. Wang, L., Li, Q., Sinnott, R., Jiang, Y., & Wu, J. (2018). An intelligent rule management scheme for software defined networking. *Computer Networks, 144*, 77–88. https://doi.org/10.1016/j.comnet.2018.07.017.
36. Wu, J., Chen, Y., & Zheng, H. (2018). Approximation algorithms for dependency-aware rule-caching in software-defined networks. *In Proceedings of the 2018 IEEE Global Communications Conference (GLOBECOM)* (pp. 1–6). Abu Dhabi, UAE.
37. Xie, J., Yu, F. R., Huang, T., Xie, R., Liu, J., Wang, C., & Liu, Y. (2019). A survey of machine learning techniques applied to software defined networking (SDN): Research issues and challenges. *IEEE Communications Surveys & Tutorials, 21*(1), 393–430. https://doi.org/10.1109/COMST.2018.2861321.
38. Yan, B., Xu, Y., & Chao, H. J. (2018). Adaptive wildcard rule cache management for software-defined networks. *IEEE/ACM Transactions on Networking, 26*(3), 962–975. https://doi.org/10.1109/TNET.2017.2789782.
39. Yan, B., Xu, Y., Xing, H., Xi, K., & Chao, H. J. (2014). CAB: A reactive wildcard rule caching system for software-defined networks. *In Proceedings of the Third Workshop on Hot Topics in Software Defined Networking* (pp. 1–6). Chicago, IL, USA.

40. Yang, H., Riley, G. F., & Blough, D. M. (2020). STEREOS: Smart table entry eviction for OpenFlow switches. *IEEE Journal on Selected Areas in Communications, 38*(2), 377–388. https://doi.org/10.1109/JSAC.2019.2959862.

41. Yu, C. (2018). DROM: Optimizing the routing in software-defined networks with deep reinforcement learning. *IEEE Access, 6*, 64533–64539. https://doi.org/10.1109/ACCESS.2018.2874900.

42. Zarek, A., Ganjali, Y., & Lie, D. (2012). OpenFlow timeouts demystified. *University of Toronto*. Toronto, ON, Canada.

CHAPTER 3

SDN CONTROLLERS

Contents

INTRODUCTION

An application in SDN architecture that controls flow control for better network management and application performance is called a software-defined networking controller. Usually operating on a server, the SDN controller platform uses protocols to direct switches on where to send packets. SDN controllers reduce the amount of manual configuration required for individual network devices by directing traffic in accordance with forwarding policies set up by a network operator. The centralized controller operates the control plane as software rather than on network hardware. This feature makes it simpler to integrate and manage business apps and enables automated network management. Essentially, the SDN controller functions as a network's operating system (OS). In a software-defined network, the controller is the central component. It is located in the space between network applications and network devices at either end of the network. Applications and network devices cannot communicate without passing through the controller.

3.1. BASIC CONCEPT OF SOFTWARE-DEFINED NETWORKING (SDN)

More akin to cloud computing than traditional network management, software-defined networking (SDN) technology is a method of network configuration that allows for dynamic, programmatically efficient network configuration to enhance network performance and monitoring. The static architecture of conventional networks is what SDN aims to solve. SDN separates the packet forwarding (data plane) and routing (control plane) processes in an effort to consolidate network intelligence into a single network component. One or more controllers, which are regarded as the SDN network's brain and contain all of its intelligence, make up the control plane. The fundamental problem with SDN is that centralization has its own limitations in terms of security, scalability, and elasticity. Since the OpenFlow protocol's introduction in 2011, SDN has been frequently linked to it (allowing for remote communication with network plane elements to ascertain the path taken by network packets across network switches). But since 2012, the term has also been used by proprietary systems. These consist of the network virtualization platform from Nicira and the Open Network Environment from Cisco Systems. Similar technology is applied to a wide area network (WAN) by SD-WAN.

3.1.1. History

The origins of SDN principles can be found in the public switched telephone network, where the separation of the control and data planes was first implemented to streamline provisioning and management. This architecture was later adopted by data networks.

In 2004, the Internet Engineering Task Force (IETF) released a proposed interface standard called Forwarding and Control Element Separation (ForCES), which was the result of their consideration of different approaches to decouple the control and forwarding functions. Furthermore, a companion SoftRouter Architecture was proposed by the ForCES Working Group. A Path Computation Element (PCE)-Based Architecture and the Linux Netlink as an IP Services Protocol are two others early IETF standards that aimed to separate control from data.

There were two reasons these initial attempts did not catch on. One is that a lot of people on the Internet thought it was dangerous to separate control from data because there was a chance the control plane would malfunction. The second reason is that vendors were worried about increased competition as a result of standardizing application programming interfaces (APIs) between the control and data planes.

The Ethane project at Stanford University's computer sciences department is credited with pioneering the use of open-source software in split control/data plane architectures. It was Ethane's straightforward switch design that gave rise to OpenFlow. The first OpenFlow API was developed in 2008. NOX, an operating system for networks, was created in that same year.

Independent researchers submitted multiple patent applications in 2007 detailing useful uses of SDN, network operating systems, network infrastructure compute units as multi-core CPUs, and a technique for functionally based virtual network segmentation. After these applications were made available to the public in 2009, they were abandoned, leaving all of the information in the prior art.

Stanford researchers kept working on OpenFlow, setting up testbeds to assess the protocol's application in a single campus network and over the wide area network (WAN) as a backbone for connecting several campuses. A small number of research and production networks in academic settings were built using Quanta Computer whiteboxes and OpenFlow switches from NEC and Hewlett-Packard beginning around 2009.

Outside of academia, Nicira was the first to implement the co-developed OVS from Onix with NTT and Google in 2010. Google's B4 deployment in 2012 was one of note. Subsequently, Google announced the simultaneous deployment of Onix and OpenFlow in their datacenters. China Mobile is the site of another well-known large deployment. Avaya demonstrated software-defined networking at the 2014 Interop and Tech Field Day by extending automation from the data center to the end device and eliminating manual provisioning from service delivery. They did this by using OpenStack as an automated campus and shortest path bridging (IEEE 802.1aq).

3.1.2. Concept of SDN

With the ability to scale network resources in lockstep with application and data needs, software-defined networking (SDN) is helping organizations deploy apps and enable flexible delivery while lowering both CapEX and OpEX. In order to improve user experience, SDN is a cutting-edge method for designing, implementing, and managing networks that divide the forwarding process (data plane) from network control (control plane).

In terms of network flexibility and controllability, this segmentation of the network offers many advantages. Combining the benefits of system virtualization and cloud computing is made possible on the one hand, and implementing centralized intelligence that allows for clear network visibility is made possible for easier network management and maintenance, as well as improved network control and responsiveness, on the other.

The implementation, configuration, and troubleshooting of networks in conventional infrastructure necessitate the involvement of highly skilled network and system engineers, as well as the operational costs associated with provisioning and managing extensive multivendor networks. The intricacy and diversity of network components actually make maintenance exceedingly costly, and in the event that a frequent network failure occurs, the underlying infrastructure becomes less dependable, particularly if backup plans are not planned for within the infrastructure.

As SDN divides networking elements' routing and forwarding decisions (e.g., switches, and access points) from the data plane, the control plane only handles data pertaining to logical network topology, traffic routing, and other related topics, making network administration and management simpler. On the other hand, the control plane's defined configuration is followed by the data plane when it comes to orchestrating network traffic. SDN centralizes control functions into a controller that sets network policies.

A lot of controller platforms, like Beacon, OpenDayLight, and Floodlight, are open source. Network management can be accomplished on various levels (i.e., data plane, control, and application). For example, service providers can set up physical network elements on the data plane, configure and modify network policies and logical entities on the control plane, and allocate resources to customers via the application layer (Figure 3.1).

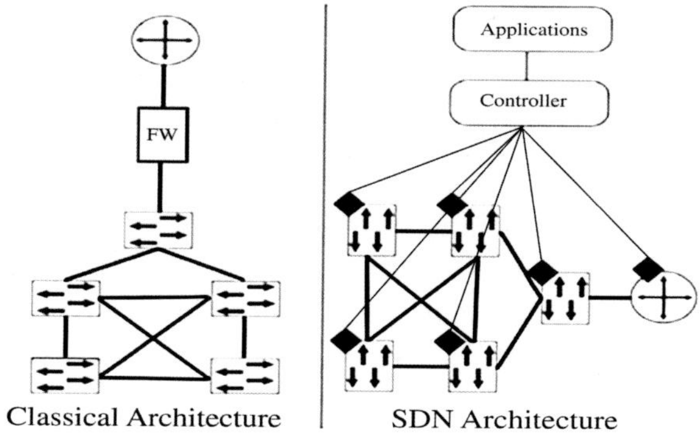

Figure 3.1. *Software-defined networking (SDN) versus classical architecture.*

Source: https://encrypted-tbn0.gstatic.com/images?q=tbn:ANd9GcTRImwwkjRRX5_kqbaupkvwB4tHybpvDVNcUg&s.

In recent years, software-defined networking has gained attention. But since the mid-1990s, this approach's concept has been developing. A true implementation of SDN has been made possible by the development of the Ethane management architecture and the OpenFlow network flow protocol. A standardized method of managing traffic and describing the way a controller interacts with network devices such as switches and routers is provided by the OpenFlow protocol. A flow table, which specifies how to handle and forward packets within the network, and an exposed OpenFlow application programming interface (API), which manages communications between switch/router and controller, make up the devices that support OpenFlow.

The Open Networking Foundation is responsible for standardizing OpenFlow. Other comparable southbound interfaces that are currently in use include SoftRouter, the Locator/ID Separation Protocol, the Path Computation Element, and the Forwarding and Control Element Separation standard set by the Internet Engineering Task Force (Table 3.1).

Table 3.1. *Software-Defined Networking versus Classical Networking*

Characteristics	SDN architecture	Classical architecture
Programmability	✓	
Centralized control	✓	
Error-prone configuration		✓
Complex network control		✓
Network flexibility	✓	

Improved performance	✓	
Easy implementation	✓	
Efficient configuration	✓	
Enhanced management	✓	

Moreover, the need for cloud services in all of their variations (e.g., SaaS, PaaS, IaaS, DaaS, UCaaS, network-as-a-service (NaaS), etc.) is sharply rising. These services present significant obstacles for service providers even though they are concentrated in data centers. The operator must adapt to the rapidly increasing demands of its clients by taking into account additional servers, network components, high quality of service, and secure architecture that complies with standards. This usually happens first and requires a significant amount of work to address new issues that arise within the core network that SDN controls and leads.

In particular, the challenges and issues that appear of paramount importance in the SDN environment are the following:

1. **Scalability:** This defines the ability of SDN to, more specifically in the control plane, handle and process an increasing workload. Scalability aims at enlarging the capacity of the SDN by implementing mechanisms such as devolving, clustering, and high processing to cope with the growing load.
2. **Reliability:** The SDN is considered reliable when it notifies of delivery failures of the data in real time. In such network, there should be a specified minimum reliability for the delivery of critical data. In today's implementations, SDN controllers must be capable of meeting real-time requirements for reliable delivery and timeliness.
3. **High Availability:** HA is an important aspect of today's services that should be available each time a customer requests a given service or resource.

Availability is usually expressed as a percentage of uptime in a given year. Unavailability of services can generally occur owing to network outages or system crashes. Network providers generally deploy backup services to offer HA by implementing redundant server hardware, server OS and network components, and so on.

4. **Elasticity:** It is the ability of SDN to dynamically adapt its capacity by scaling up or down the available resources in order to meet the variation and fluctuation of the workload. Generally, elasticity is often focused on the control plane and might be referred to as scalability.

5. **Security:** SDN security consists of protecting the information from theft or damage to the hardware and the software as well as from disruption of the services. Securing SDN encompasses physical security of the hardware, as well as preventing logical threats that may come from the network or data. SDN vulnerabilities are the entrance door to security attacks being intentional or accidental.
6. **Performance:** It refers to the amount of tasks achieved by SDN components compared with the time/resources (e.g., CPU and RAM) being used. There are many different ways to measure the performance of a network, as each network is different in nature and design. As far as SDN is concerned, the important measures are bandwidth, throughput, latency, and jitter.
7. **Resilience:** This in SDN is the capability to ensure and maintain an acceptable level of service even in case of a service, network or node failure. When an SDN element is faulty, the network should provide a continuous operational service with the same performance. In order to increase the resilience of SDN, potential challenges/risks have to be identified and addressed to protect the services.
8. **Dependability:** The dependability of SDN is strongly tied to availability and reliability terms. SDN dependability aims mainly at preventing faults and implementing fault tolerance mechanisms to guarantee service delivery even at a degraded level. In addition to HA and reliability, integrity and maintainability are also two important dependability attributes.

3.1.3. Generic Software-Defined Networking Architecture

In contrast to traditional IP networks, which have decentralized functionalities, SDN is centralized and provides network domain connections between the control and data planes within the same infrastructure. Furthermore, SDN enables backward compatibility with current standards and protocols (e.g., Ethernet, VLAN, IP, ARP, etc.).

Three layers comprise the core architecture of SDN, as shown in Figure 3.2. The application layer, which is the top layer of SDN architecture, establishes policies and provides various services like firewall, access control, IDS/IPS, quality of service, routing, proxy service, and monitoring balancer. Through the northbound API (e.g., this layer), the SDN network control management is abstracted, e.g., OpenDaylight). The control plane, which is an abstraction of the network topology, is the second layer. The controller is the primary component in charge of creating flow tables, data handling policies, abstracting network complexity, gathering data via the southbound API, and keeping an up-to-date holistic view of the network.

The southbound API communications can be deployed in two different scenarios:

- **In-Band Communication:** In this scenario, the traffic between the controller and any network device should abide by the dictated flow rules.
- **Out-of-Band Communication:** Here, the traffic does not follow flow rules. This type of deployment requires VLAN implementation to isolate the traffic flow from the communications, which depends on OpenFlow rules.

Additionally, eastbound and westbound APIs (e.g., HyperFlow), which allow several controllers to communicate control data about data plane flow. Numerous controllers based on various programming languages (Python, C/C++, Java, Ruby, etc.) are currently available.) as well as networks like Trema, NOX, Floodlight, Beacon, and Maestro. The data plane, or lowest layer, is in charge of all data operations such as fragmentation, reassembly, and forwarding. It supplies networking devices like physical and virtual switches, routers, and access points.

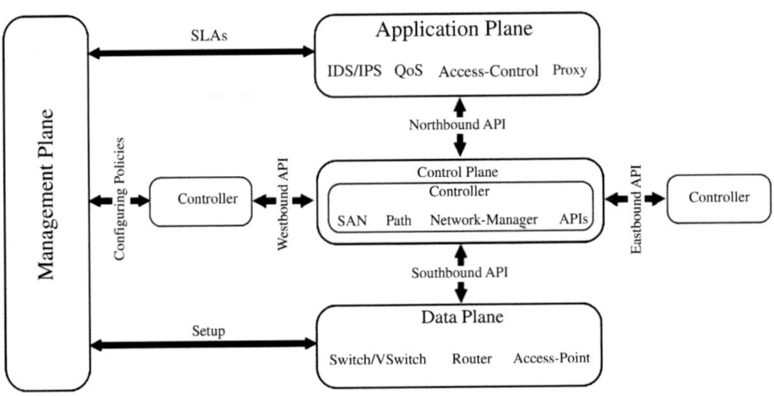

Figure 3.2. *A generic software-defined networking architecture.*

Source: https://www.researchgate.net/profile/Kamal-Benzekki/publication/313407199/figure/fig2/AS:582050350862336@1515783025114/A-generic-software-defined-networking-architecture.png.

3.1.4. Existing Network Cloud-Based Models

For improving network functionality and streamlining network management of the underlying infrastructure, such as in NaaS, there are several cloud-based model options available. An OpenFlow-based SDN model, for example, can be used to enforce network visibility globally, improve performance, and support NaaS. Users can also benefit from a wide range of dependable applications to take advantage of advanced network functions. The network virtualization model and the evolutionary model are two additional cloud-based models. SDN scalability in VLAN can be achieved by applying the network virtualization model. With this method, multiple virtual network instances can be created within a single physical infrastructure. In joint-tenant environments, this model has been introduced to address mobility across subnets and isolation. The evolutionary model provides features like configuration management, fault tolerance, and quality of service while attempting to partition the network into virtual segments (Table 3.2).

Table 3.2. *Cloud-based Models*

	Description	**Capabilities and Features**	**Limitations**
Open-Flow-based SDN Model	First designed standard interface communication protocol for SDN controllers to allow programming the forwarding tables of the network elements separation/centralization/programmability of the control plane.	Simplifying network operations Improving network availability Providing better control and performance for SDN.	OF switches support issues Compatibility issues with controller and OF switches.
Network Virtualization Model	Coexisting multiple network instances on a common physical network to facilitate network provisioning.	Addressing the scalability issues with multicasting VLAN architectures Offering multi-tenancy to the cloud.	An implementation of deep packet inspection mechanism is required to identify the individual virtual network's header by the network nodes.
Evolutionary Model	Partitioning the network into virtual communities to manage traffic and quality of service on the basis of network standards (e.g., MPLS, VXLAN) by using management interfaces.	Enhancing software control of the network Ensuring flexible virtual networks extension.	Existing interoperability issues between vendors that may not consider the implementation of some standards/protocols (Some existing solutions like OpenStack can help enabling interoperability of network devices.)

3.1.4.1. Communication Protocol

OpenFlow is used by the most popular southbound interface in SDN. The protocol that allows the controller to control switches and routers is defined in the OpenFlow specification. The OpenFlow protocol has three methods of communication: symmetric, asynchronous, and controller-to-switch. Configuring flow table configuration, handshakes, and switches is the responsibility of the controller-to-switch communication. Asynchronous communication begins with the switch that complies with OpenFlow, informing the controller through the sending of packet-in, port-status, and flow-removed messages. There is no restriction on who can start an exchange in symmetric communication. Hello and Echo are two examples of exchanged messages that are used to help identify issues with the switch-controller connection. Other messages include Set Config, Feature Request/Reply, and so forth. Depending on the security requirements and deployments, the communication between the controller and the switch can either be conducted over Transport Layer Security (TLS) or without an encryption mechanism.

3.2. SDN CONTROLLER

A key element of SDN architecture is a Software-Defined Networking (SDN) controller. Over the network elements (in the managed domain), it offers control. The Management Plane, Control Plane, and Data Plane are components of networking. For the network elements under its management, an SDN controller offers Management Plane and Control Plane functionalities. This means that an SDN controller configures (or "programs") the Data Plane (i.e., controls network elements) and manages the network elements based on network information and a set of predefined rules and policies controls the data flow across the network.

One of the main advantages of utilizing an SDN controller is that it makes network management more effective because configuration changes can be made centrally instead of needing to be made by hand for every single network component. Furthermore, an SDN controller can automate certain functions, like security and traffic control, lowering the possibility of human error and enhancing network dependability overall.

An API (Application Programming Interface), sometimes referred to as a northbound interface, is a feature that SDN controllers offer so that other systems or applications, like orchestration platforms, can communicate with the network. In these situations, an SDN controller translates the layer requirements of the application (e.g., high-level explanation of the network configuration) into a setup unique to the network elements that are supported. SDN controllers are capable of controlling software components that carry out network operations in addition to actual network hardware.

The main functions of an SDN controller include:

- Managing the flow of data in the managed network.
- Providing an API for applications and other components (e.g., orchestration platforms) to interact with the network.
- Providing visibility into the network, allowing monitoring of network performance and detection of problems.
- Automating network management tasks, such as provisioning new network elements and reconfiguring network paths.

In a software-defined network, an SDN controller is the program that serves as a strategic control point. It functions as the network's "brains" in essence. The division of a network's control and forwarding functions is known as software-defined networking, or SDN. Network function virtualization (NFV) and SDN work together to build virtual network overlays that sit on top of the actual network infrastructure.

In order to enable network administrators to oversee the network, SDN architecture depends on controllers. To deploy intelligent networks, an SDN controller controls flow control to the switches and routers "below" (via southbound APIs) and to the applications and business logic "above" (via northbound APIs). They use shared application interfaces to consolidate and mediate between various controller domains.

OpenFlow and Open Virtual Switch Database (OVSDB) are two of the most well-known protocols that SDN controllers use to communicate with the switches and routers. Many of the controller protocols that are being developed now are collaborative and open standards. For instance, the Interface to the Routing System (i2rs) working group of the Internet Engineering Task Force (IETF) created an SDN standard that allows a controller to leverage tried-and-true protocols like OSPF, MPLS, BGP, and IS-IS across a range of SDN platforms.

3.2.1. How Do SDN Controllers Work?

An SDN controller is a logically centralized entity that can also be used in hierarchical controller connections, federations of multiple controllers, and other architectures.), usually carried out as a computer program that runs on a server or group of servers.

Through its southbound interfaces, e.g., it communicates with a variety of network devices (like switches and routers) and/or software components (realizing network functions), standardized/proprietary protocols, as well as an API. A few instances of protocols are P4RT (P4Runtime – protocol-independent runtime APIs for a P4-defined or P4-described data plane), NETCONF, OpenFlow, Open vSwitch (OVS) database, and XMPP (Juniper Contrail).

3.2.1.1. Controller APIs

Through northbound interfaces, the controller can interact with applications like load balancers and firewalls. In 2013, the Open Networking Foundation (ONF) established a working group dedicated to the advancement of northbound APIs. However, the industry never agreed upon a set standard because application requirements differ so greatly from one another. Typically, the controller uses a southbound interface similar to the OpenFlow protocol to communicate with individual network devices. The controller can configure network devices and select the best network path for application traffic thanks to these southbound APIs. ONF founded OpenFlow in 2011.

3.2.2. Vendor and Open-Source SDN Controllers

On the market, there are both proprietary and open-source SDN controllers. Below are a few examples of each.

3.2.2.1. SDN Controller Vendors

Vendors that offer SDN controllers include the following:

- Cisco;
- Hewlett Packard enterprise;
- Juniper networks;
- NEC;
- Nuage networks;
- Nvidia;
- Pica8;
- VMware.

3.2.2.2. Open Source SDN Controllers

SDN controllers are also available as open-source options, including the following:

- NOX/POX;
- OpenDaylight;

- Open network operating system;
- Tungsten fabric.

3.2.2.3. SD-WAN Controllers

SDN controllers are typically utilized in networks found in data centers. However, as SDN technology advanced, the WAN proved to be a useful use case, propelling the development of software-defined WAN (SD-WAN) technology.

Following policy configurations to route WAN traffic over the most effective path, an SD-WAN controller carries out many of the same functions as an SDN controller. Compared to SDN, the SD-WAN market offers fewer noteworthy open-source options because the majority of SD-WAN controllers are usually integrated with the vendor's proprietary SD-WAN platform.

3.2.3. SDN Controller Benefits

Deployment and integration of an SDN controller into a network may bring a number of benefits:

- Provides a single, unified interface allowing network administrators and external applications (e.g., orchestration platforms) to interact (configure and manage) with the network.
- Increases the level of network automation (an SDN controller can automate network management and configuration tasks).
- Optimizes usage of resources (thanks to information covering the whole managed network domain, an SDN controller can optimize packet paths to achieve better network efficiency).
- Increases network resilience (e.g., faster reaction to changes in the network, building alternative paths).
- Possible management of physical network devices and software-based network elements.

3.2.3.1. Pros and Cons of SDN Controllers

The centralized controller can direct packets according to traffic requirements and is aware of all available network paths, which is one of the main advantages of SDN controllers. The controller can automatically alter traffic flows and alert network administrators to congested links because of its visibility into the network. Businesses can add a backup controller for redundancy by using multiple controllers. Three controllers are frequently used by open source and commercial SDN solutions. The network can function even in the event of lost connectivity or controller susceptibility thanks to this redundancy.

Securing the controller is essential to any software-defined network since it serves as a single point of failure. The entire network is accessible to the controller's owner. Thus, in order to guarantee that only authorized individuals have access, network administrators should establish security and authentication policies.

3.3. THE NEED FOR A NEW NETWORK ARCHITECTURE

The explosion of mobile devices and content, server virtualization, and the advent of cloud services are among the trends driving the networking industry to re-examine traditional network architectures. Many conventional networks are hierarchical, built with tiers of Ethernet switches arranged in a tree structure. This design made sense when client-server computing was dominant, but such a static architecture is ill-suited to the dynamic computing and storage needs of today's enterprise data centers, campuses, and carrier environments.

Some of the key computing trends driving the need for a new network paradigm include:

1. **Changing Traffic Patterns:** The enterprise data center's traffic patterns have undergone substantial modification. Today's applications access multiple databases and servers, generating a flurry of east-west machine-to-machine traffic before returning data to the end user device in the traditional north-south traffic pattern. This is in contrast to client-server applications, where the majority of the communication takes place between one client and one server. Users are pushing for access to corporate content and applications from any device, including their own, at any time, from anywhere, and they are also altering network traffic patterns in this way. Lastly, a lot of managers of enterprise data centers are thinking about a utility computing model, which could involve a public cloud, a private cloud, or a combination of the two, adding to the traffic on the wide area network.
2. **The "Consumerization of IT":** Mobile personal devices like tablets, smartphones, and laptops are being used by users more and more to access corporate networks. IT is under pressure to meet compliance requirements, safeguard corporate data and intellectual property, and allow these personal devices in a tailored way.
3. **The Rise of Cloud Services:** Both public and private cloud services have experienced unprecedented growth as a result of the enthusiastic adoption of these services by enterprises. These days,

enterprise business units want to be able to quickly and easily access infrastructure, apps, and other IT resources as needed. IT planning for cloud services is made more difficult by the need to work in an environment with stricter security, compliance, and auditing regulations as well as the possibility of overnight assumptions being altered by company reorganizations, mergers, and consolidations. Whether in a private or public cloud, self-service provisioning needs elastic scaling of network, storage, and computer resources, ideally from a shared perspective and toolkit.

4. **"Big Data" Means More Bandwidth:** Massive parallel processing on thousands of servers—all of which require direct connections to one another—is needed to handle today's big data or mega datasets. The data center is constantly in need of more network capacity due to the growth of mega datasets. The difficult challenge for operators of hyperscale data center networks is to grow the network to previously unthinkable sizes while keeping all-to-all connectivity without going bankrupt.
5. **Energy Use on Large Datacenters:** The demand for larger datacenters brought about by the emergence of the Internet of Things, cloud computing, and SaaS has increased the energy consumption of those establishments. Through the use of current routing techniques, numerous researchers have increased the energy efficiency of SDN by dynamically adjusting the network data plane to conserve energy. Additionally, research is being done on ways to increase the energy efficiency of control planes.

3.3.1. Architectural Components

The following list defines and explains the architectural components:

1. **SDN Application:** Programs that use a northbound interface (NBI) to explicitly, directly, and programmatically communicate their desired network behavior and network requirements to the SDN Controller are known as SDN Applications. Furthermore, they might use an abstracted representation of the network to inform internal decisions. One or more NBI Drivers and one or more SDN Application Logics make up an SDN Application. By exposing an additional layer of abstracted network control, SDN applications can provide one or more higher-level NBIs via the corresponding NBI agents.
2. **SDN Controller:** The SDN Applications by the SDN Controller, a logically centralized entity that is responsible for (i) translating

requirements from the SDN application layer down to the SDN Datapaths. The Control to Data-Plane Interface (CDPI) driver, the SDN Control Logic, and one or more NBI Agents make up an SDN Controller. Implementation details like the federation of multiple controllers, the hierarchical connection of controllers, communication interfaces between controllers, virtualization or slicing of network resources are neither mandated nor prohibited by the definition as a logically centralized entity.

3. **SDN Datapath:** A logical network device called the SDN Datapath offers visibility and unchallenged control over the forwarding and data processing capabilities it claims to have. The physical substrate resources may be included in full or in part by the logical representation. A CDPI agent, a collection of one or more traffic forwarding engines, and zero or more traffic processing tasks make up an SDN Datapath. Simple forwarding between the datapath's external interfaces, internal traffic processing, and termination functions are a few examples of these engines and functions. A single (physical) network element, which is an integrated physical combination of communications resources managed as a unit, may contain one or more SDN Datapaths. It is also possible to define an SDN Datapath spanning several physical network elements. This logical definition does not mandate or exclude any particular implementation details, such as data processing functionality that may involve OSI layer 4–7 operations, virtualization or slicing of the SDN Datapath, interoperability with non-SDN networking, or the management of shared physical resources.
4. **SDN Control to Data-Plane Interface (CDPI):** It is the interface defined between an SDN Controller and an SDN Datapath, which provides at least:

- Programmatic control of all forwarding operations;
- Capabilities advertisement;
- Statistics reporting; and
- Event notification. One value of SDN lies in the expectation that the CDPI is implemented in an open, vendor-neutral and interoperable way.

5. **SDN Northbound Interfaces (NBI):** These serve as interfaces between SDN Controllers and SDN Applications. They usually allow for the direct expression of network requirements and behavior as well as abstract network views. This can happen across various

functional sets (longitude) and at any level of abstraction (latitude). The expectation that these interfaces be implemented in an open, vendor-neutral, and interoperable manner is one of SDN's benefits.

3.4. SCALABILITY AND ELASTICITY

By allowing on-demand resource allocation and real-time adaptation to shifting traffic patterns, SDN promotes network elasticity. This elasticity enhances overall scalability and resource utilization by enabling networks to scale up or down swiftly and effectively in response to changing demands.

3.4.1. Scalability Challenges and Solutions

These properties make it much easier to develop control applications and enforce policies because the SDN design allows pushing all the control functionality to a centralized controller with a full network-wide view. Controllers, however, have the potential to impede network operations. The controller receives an increasing number of events and requests as the network expands, and eventually, managing all of the incoming requests presents a significant challenge. This is a widespread issue that affects all systems, not just SDN designs. The growth of network traffic may not scale with the controller's performance capabilities if the control and data planes are separated and the controller is trusted with managing the traffic over a large network, creating problems with scalability and elasticity. By dividing and sharing tasks among several controllers, several works have been proposed to reduce the workload on a single controller. These are merely workarounds for particular issues with latencies and SDNs overhead on the control plane. These scalability solution proposals, which primarily aim to reduce the overhead of the control plane by assigning part of the work to the forwarding devices, include DIFANE, DevoFlow, software-defined counters, Onix, Kandoo, HyperFlow, Maestro, and NOX-MT. Alternatively, they try to increase the throughput and latency of the controllers by implementing high-performance computing techniques like buffering, pipelining, multithreading, and parallelism. There are numerous proposals aimed at addressing the scalability problem in the control plane, while the data plane is the subject of relatively few studies (Figure 3.3). From a different angle, these works can be categorized into three kinds based on the methods employed to attain scalability: controller capacity enhancement (e.g., sophisticated processing methods), controller clusters (e.g., transferring some management tasks to the data plane and utilizing a distributed event-based control plane. A nonexhaustive list of the suggested fixes for scalability problems is shown in Table 3.3.

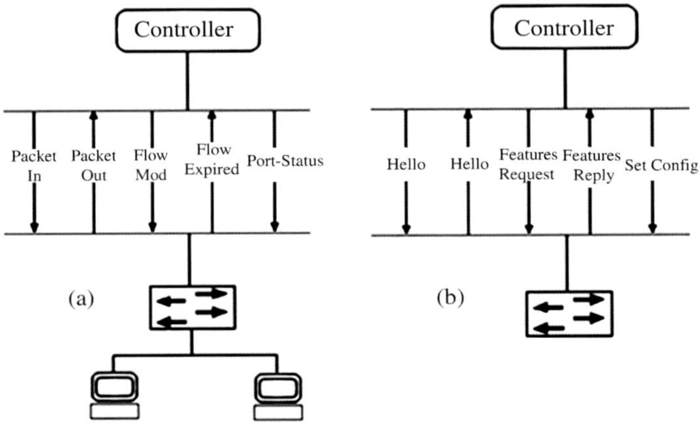

Figure 3.3. *OpenFlow exchanges.*

https://www.researchgate.net/publication/313407199/figure/fig3/AS:582050350022656@1515783025168/OpenFlow-exchanges.png

Table 3.3. *Scalability Issues, Solutions, and Challenges*

Proposal	**Main Purpose/Challenge**	**Scalability (Technique)**
HyperFlow localizes decision making to individual controllers in order to minimize the control plane response time to data plane requests.	By logically centralizing and physically distributing the network overhead across the control plane, Hyperflow provides scalability for SDN.	Clustering
ONIX platform on top of which a network control plane can be implemented as a distributed system for large-scale networks provides more general APIs for control plane implementations.	Onix allows trade-offs between scalability and consistency/ durability.	Clustering
Open Network Operating System adopts a distributed architecture for high availability and scale-out. It provides a global network view to applications, which is logically centralized even though it is physically distributed across multiple servers.	Improving scalability and performance to meet the requirements of large-scale networks.	Clustering

Pratyaastha is a new way to partition SDN application state that considers the dependencies between application state and SDN switches.	Improving the performance of the current distributed SDN control platforms by proposing a novel approach for assigning SDN switches and partitions of SDN application state to distributed controller instances.	Clustering
Kandoo is a framework that allows scalability preservation without changing switches' organization. Kandoo consists of two layers: a bottom layer grouping controllers with no knowledge of the network-wide state and a top layer containing a logically centralized controller that maintains the network-wide state.	Offloading the control applications by separating the controllers into two different roles such as a root controller and a local controller; in this way, the root controller processes rare events, and the overhead will be pushed to the local controller in order to provide scalability.	Clustering
Investigating the scalability of the SDN controller with respect to performance. Scalability is related to performance when we consider metrics such as delay, latency, and throughput.	The current Internet flow definitions have high requirements on the processing rate of the SDN controller.	Clustering
RAON implementation consists of two parts: a RAON switch and a RAON OpenFlow controller abstraction module that communicates with the RAON switch. The networks of the lower-level controllers are abstracted as big OpenFlow switches.	Solving scalability issues in OpenFlow networks by reducing complexity and increasing manageability.	Clustering
DIFANE is a distributed flow management architecture that runs a partitioning algorithm to divide the rules over switches that will handle flows instead of the controller.	Offering a scalable and efficient solution that handles the flow in the data plane by forwarding packets through intermediate switches that maintain necessary rules.	Devolving
DevoFlow aims at reducing the interactions between OF switches and controller using filtering and sampling techniques such as rule aggregation, selective local action, and approximating.	Maintaining a global visibility and providing a scalable flow management simulations for largescale networks.	Devolving
Control-message quenching is a mechanism whereby a control-message quenching switch sends only one packet-in message for each source-destination pair, which reduces unnecessary packet-in messages from the OpenFlow switch to the controller.	Enhancing the controller responsiveness and network scalability with reduced flow setup latency and higher network throughput.	Devolving

Devolving fault management to the OpenFlow switches by extending the OpenFlow protocol to support the monitoring function. OF switch emits monitoring messages without posing a processing load on the controller.	Resolving scalability limitation of the centralized fault management that is based on LLDP messages for monitoring.	Devolving
Devolving IEEE 802.1X authentication capability to data plane by inserting a legacy switch that supports IEEE 802.1X port-based authentication and placing the RADIUS server and other servers near the legacy switch to reduce authentication delays.	Improving access control and performance and reducing the high demand on the SDN controller when users attempt to authenticate against a RADIUS server.	Devolving
Maestro is a controller that has a task manager that manages incoming computations and distributes the processing to each controller instance at each core of the processor. Maestro exploits more additional throughput optimization techniques.	Improving the capacity of the controller itself by using multicores with parallel processing and multithreads for a scalable SDN.	High processing
McNettle is an extensible SDN control system implemented in Haskell that leverages the multicore facilities of the Glasgow Haskell Compiler and runtime system.	Scheduling event handlers, allocating memory, and reducing system calls in order to optimize cache usage and avoids contention on sockets and ensures that each message is processed on a single CPU core.	High processing

3.4.2. Elasticity

Elasticity is another challenge facing cloud providers to manage and adapt responsiveness of SDN demands in real time. In addition to this, cloud providers should offer more elastic access to computing and network resources. Elasticity can be seen from three dimensions as illustrated in Figure 3.4.

1. **Elastic Scalability:** Aims at ensuring the growth depending on network requirements. SDN can scale dynamically in case of high demands.
2. **Elastic Configuration:** Gives an opportunity to add, edit, and delete configuration to meet new network requirements and respond to new challenges in terms of bandwidth and throughput.
3. **Elastic Discovery:** Anticipates discoveries as well as becoming aware of possible emerging technological opportunities and threats at the right time to react and meet the new requirements and trends. The main purpose is to identify irrelevant tendencies and think of acquiring new efficient techniques/strategies that might help in improving the SDN. The observations should be made quickly, and

the action must be taken in real time to take advantage of new possible network features and/or remove potential threats by deploying novel countermeasures.

Reaching elasticity results in the best possible use of resources and SDN. Deploying, configuring, and altering an elastic SDN is straightforward and easy. In this regard, a number of works have been proposed, including distributed controller architectures that dynamically expand or contract the controller pool in response to network conditions, redistributing the traffic load among the controllers. Additional studies concentrate on SDN hierarchical techniques or load-balancing mechanisms. For example, ElastiCon, an elastic distributed controller architecture, is presented. It makes use of a dynamic adaptation of the number and locations of controllers in the SDN design to grow or shrink the controller pool based on the load of network traffic. Similar to FreeFlow, ElastiCon also takes a load-balancing mechanism for the control plane into consideration. For Follow me cloud (FMC)-based systems and mobile cloud computing, a hierarchical SDN/OpenFlow control plane is suggested. Two hierarchical levels make up the elastic control plane: a first level with a global FMC controller and a second level with multiple local FMC controllers. As the load on the global systems increases, the local FMC controllers are triggered. Table 3.4 deal directly with elasticity issues and challenges and propose solutions and enhancements.

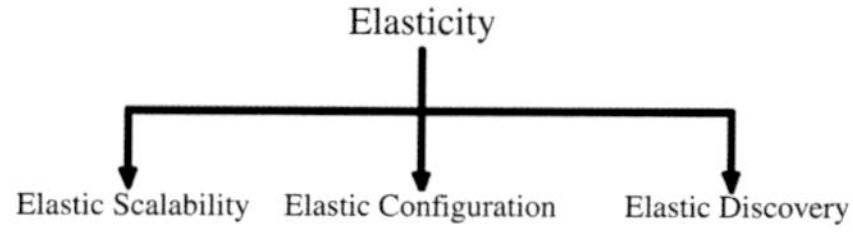

Figure 3.4. *Three dimensions of elasticity.*

Source: https://www.researchgate.net/profile/Kamal-Benzekki/publication/313407199/figure/fig4/AS:582050350862338@1515783025197/Three-dimensions-of-elasticity.png.

Table 3.4. *Elasticity Issues, Solutions, and Challenges*

Proposal	Main Purpose/Challenge	Elasticity (Technique)
ElastiCon is an elastic distributed controller architecture in which the controller pool dynamically expands or shrinks to automatically balance the load across controllers.	Addressing the load imbalance issues to offer elasticity and load-balancing equity.	Load balancing/distribution

FreeFlow (split/merge) is a system that allows transparent and balanced elasticity for stateful virtual middleboxes to have the ability to migrate flows dynamically.	Providing elasticity by the execution of virtual middleboxes.	Load balancing
Hierarchical SDN is an architectural solution that offers a new way for the forwarding and control planes. Small forwarding tables are used in the network nodes to determine paths.	Achieving elasticity and enabling more agile mechanisms for disaster recovery/fast restoration.	Hierarchical
Elastic distributed SDN controller tailored for mobile cloud computing and FMC-based systems where the SDN/OpenFlow control plane is repartitioned on a two-level hierarchical architecture: a first level with a global FMC controller and a second level with several local FMC controllers.	Ensuring elasticity with better control plane management, performance maintenance and network resources preservation.	Distribution
Pratyaastha is an elastic distributed SDN control plane that permits to efficiently assign state partitions and switches to controller instances.	Minimizing intercontroller communication and resource consumption to ensure better performances.	Distribution
A cost-saving approach for on-demand elastic network design and active flow placement in SDN environments based on generic adaptive resource control function to manage topology and control network resources dynamically and on demand.	Minimizing intercontroller communication and resource consumption to ensure better performances. Solving the underlying network design problem using the state-of-the-art integer programming.	Distribution Mixed-integer programming
Elasticity analysis of middleboxes application using NFV in SDN environment and SDN elements.	Solving elasticity or dynamic scalability issue of NFV (SDN).	(Comparison)

3.4.3. Dependability, High Availability, and Reliability

3.4.3.1. Dependability

The ability of a system to deliver dependable services in terms of availability, responsiveness, and reliability is what we refer to as dependability. If a system experiences failures with an expected probability, it can still be deemed reliable even in the event of a failure. As a result, dependability refers to the degree of confidence that can be placed in the services that a system provides.

This definition of dependability encompasses ideas related to availability and dependability. The relationships between the workloads and applications sharing the physical infrastructure are what lead to SDN's increased complexity. One of the biggest challenges facing service providers is anticipating these interactions and modifying the SDN to guarantee dependability in terms of availability and responsiveness. Identifying and allocating the necessary resources to fulfill the service level agreement (SLA) is the primary responsibility for accommodating fluctuating load and changing customer workloads. Determining the level of detail at which resources (e.g., active addition of resources (CPU cycles, cluster nodes, extra memory, increased storage capacity, and bandwidth) is crucial for long-term SLA compliance (Figure 3.5).

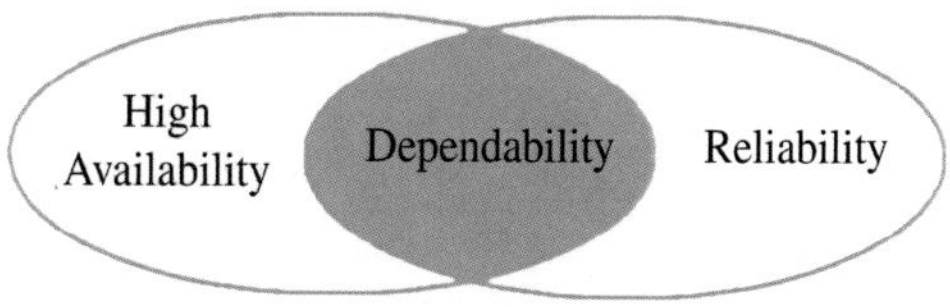

Figure 3.5. *Dependability: High availability and reliability intersection.*

Source: https://www.researchgate.net/profile/Kamal-Benzekki/publication/313407199/figure/fig5/AS:582050348277764@1515783025228/Dependability-high-availability-and-reliability-intersection.png.

Reliability remains an unresolved research issue and is a necessary condition for the implementation of SDN in real-world settings. In the vast corpus of literature addressing dependability evaluation of SDN architecture, with special attention to the control plane in various operating conditions, relatively few research works are available.

Since dependability and HA are related, the majority of proposed works address both primitives and offer a variety of solutions. However, we were only able to locate a small number of clear-cut studies that clarified dependability-related problems and assessed the effect of load fluctuation on SDN dependability, as Table 3.5 illustrates.

Table 3.5. *Dependability Issues, Solutions, and Challenges*

Proposal	**Main Purpose/Challenge**
A stochastic model to evaluate reliability and availability (dependability) of SDN architectures and represent SDN controller whose components are organized in a hierarchical topology. This model is based on an algorithm that represents realistic behaviors and changing operating conditions of the network because of workloads.	Presenting and evaluating a dependability model of SDN to pinpoint the key aspects of reliable and available SDN architecture. In particular, the evaluation is mainly based on a parametric controller model, instantiated and populated with different parameters and measures to evaluate the control plane dependability and reliability.

A probabilistic model to analyze dependability of SDN with the PRISM tool. The results of the designed system model are verified and visualized using PRISM. SDN system is modeled using Markov chain model.	Improving the dependability (reliability) of SDN by implementing multicontroller architecture.
Discussing the important aspects of a secure and dependable SDN architecture as well as threats/vulnerabilities. A brief description of the mechanisms required to build a secure and dependable SDN control platform is also introduced.	Dependability is of paramount importance when designing SDN.

3.4.3.2. Service Level Agreement

Even though SLAs frequently include information about the agreed-upon features of the service, like memory and CPU speed, scope, quality, performance, and time delivery, there is no safeguard against one or more of the SLA contract's elements failing. Unpredictable misbehaviors and glitches in systems or networks can actually be caused by malware, phony processes, or bugs that run in the background and use a lot of CPU and memory. As a result, end users may not be able to access services. One more potential problem has nothing to do with the availability of hardware. There have been reported instances of complete blackouts caused by minor misconfigurations or malfunctions in major cloud providers.

Advanced technical HA specifications, including throughput, bandwidth, transfer rates, jitter, latency, and HA metrics, such as mean time between failures (MTBF), mean time to recover (MTTR), mean time to repair (MTTRr), mean time to failure (MTTF), and mean time to detect (MTTD), are usually determined by the service level agreement (SLA). MTBF is a repairable system's "up-time" between inherent failures while it is in use. The mean time to repair (MTTR) is the amount of time a device or network will take to repair itself after a failure. The average time to repair a failed device after determining its underlying cause is known as the Mean Time to Repair (MTTRr). The mean time to failure (MTTF) is measured from the point at which the device recovers. The expected average time to identify a failed network component is known as MTTD.

The availability of SDN can be calculated using the following formula:

$$\text{Availability} = \frac{\text{MTTF}}{\text{MTBF}} = \frac{\text{MTBF} - \text{MTTD} - \text{MTTR}}{\text{MTBF}}$$

$$\text{where} \begin{cases} \text{MTTR} = \text{MTTD} + \text{MTTRr} \\ \text{MTBF} = \text{MTTR} + \text{MTTF} \end{cases}$$

Percentages of availability are sometimes referred to by the class of nines. For example, three nines means nearly 9 h of unavailability per year.

3.4.4. High Availability: Challenges

In an operational cloud, achieving high availability is typically one of the most difficult objectives. Within the traditional network, multiple HA mechanisms (e.g., link aggregation, multipath routing, state synchronization, failure detection and handling, redundancy and backup for systems and networks, and protocols (e.g., includes host standby router protocol, virtual router redundancy protocol, resilient packet ring, link aggregation control protocol, EtherChannel, equal-cost multipath routing, stateful switch-over, nonstop forwarding, nonstop routing, Ethernet automatic protection switching, and fast rerouting.

Similar to all other cloud components, SDN must be operated continuously in order to achieve the HA goals, which include supplying constant physical and virtual resources (e.g., databases, platforms, computational servers, and applications). New difficulties have been brought about by the division of the controllability into a single entity and the separation of the data and control planes. Although the majority of the previously mentioned protocols and mechanisms can be used with cloud infrastructure, they regrettably do not support certain requirements for SDN features, like synchronization amongst SDN controllers, HA interconnection, and correlation of failures between the control plane and the data plane. It goes without saying that managing the SDN's brain is more important than managing a decentralized network where each component's responsibilities are divided and shared. Because they are a single point of failure and hold the authority to make decisions and orders, controllers are essential to HA (Figure 3.6 and Table 3.6).

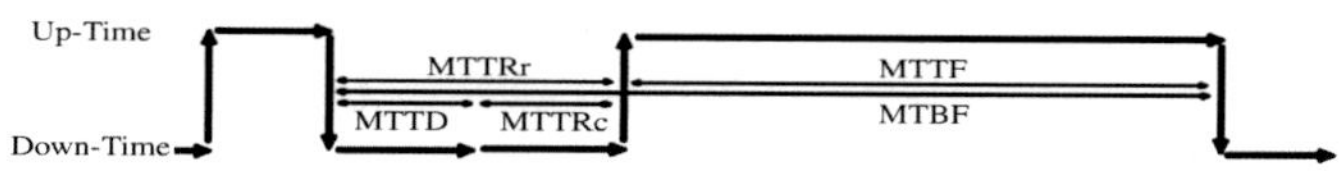

Figure 3.6. *Software-defined networking availability timeline.*

Source: https://web.archive.org/web/20190724155640id_/https://onlinelibrary.wiley.com/doi/pdf/10.1002/sec.1737.

Table 3.6. *Percentage of Availability*

Availability (%)	Downtime per Year	Downtime per Month	Downtime per Week	Downtime per Day
90 ("1 nine")	36.5 d	72 h	16.8 h	2.4 h
99 ("2 nines")	3.65 d	7.20 h	1.68 h	14.4 min
99.9 ("3 nines")	8.76 h	43.8 min	10.1 min	1.44 min

99.99 ("4 nines")	52.56 min	4.38 min	1.01 min	8.66 s
99.999 ("5 nines")	5.26 min	25.9 s	6.05 s	864.3 ms
99.9999 ("6 nines")	31.5 s	2.59 s	604.8 ms	86.4 ms
99.99999 ("7 nines")	3.15 s	262.97 ms	60.48 ms	8.64 ms
99.999999 ("8 nines")	315.569 ms	26.297 ms	6.048 ms	0.864 ms
99.9999999 ("9 nines")	31.5569 ms	2.6297 ms	0.6048 ms	0.0864 ms

Moreover, a key component of the HA idea is controller redundancy. To guarantee HA and reliability, there are a few ways to accomplish this in real time. In a highly available SDN, one of the most difficult tasks is designing a redundant architecture. Latency is yet another significant problem that the network providers are dealing with. HA suffers as a result of latency because it impacts failover times in addition to traffic. Low power RAM/CPU in network components, longer network update/upgrade times, congestion, and insufficient bandwidth are some of the factors that contribute to low latencies.

Basically, latency in SDN can be divided into three categories:

1. **Data Plane Latencies:** Switches and routers or any other network components in the data plane have their specific characteristics that determine their capacity in terms of memory, CPU, and so on. For instance, in an OpenFlow (OF) switch there is an inbound and an outbound latency from the controller perspective:

i. **Inbound Latency:** Represents the time between receiving a packet from the data plane and sending it to the controller. First, the switch relies on the forwarding engine to send packet for a lookup in the rule table. Here, two cases may emerge: In case of (i) reactive OpenFlow operation mode, the OpenFlow agent performs a lookup in the flow tables. If there is no match, the switch automatically creates an OpenFlow "packet-in" packet and sends it to the controller for orders. (ii) In proactive mode, flow tables are already predefined and thus no need to consult the controller for instructions. This could be advantageous in eliminating the latencies resulting in contacting a controller.

ii. **Outbound Latency:** The switch receives the flow from the controller and then parses OpenFlow messages that hold new rules to be applied to the OpenFlow switch's flow table. The whole update process could take a long time.

There is another mode of operation called Hybrid mode when OpenFlow is used. In this mode, the combination of proactive and reactive mode has been made to allow more flexibility and maintain low latencies.

2. **Control Plane Latencies:** In the control plane, the latencies associated with an SDN controller are Input/Output (I/O) performance, processing, and flow setup time. These performance metrics heavily influence when additional SDN controllers are deployed. If the OF switches fire out too many flows, the controller would take longer time to respond, and thus, the latency is increased.
3. **Interconnection Latencies:** These low latencies are measurable and depend mainly on the physical medium capacity (i.e., bandwidth and throughput). Generally, interconnection latencies are negligible.

3.4.5. Reliability

Another crucial component of SDN is reliability, whereby failures should alert the delivery. In the event of a delivery failure, the service providers alert the end user through dependable apps and services. Reliability specifications provide assurances that data delivery via dependable SDN architecture and dependable protocols will only affect the intended recipient.

Because network outages could easily result in disconnections between the control and forwarding plane, increasing reliability is critical. Under increased workload, a dependable SDN should operate continuously without dropping messages from either the control plane or the data plane. Since the control plane is the brains of the production network, its dependability is crucial to SDN.

The SDN networks will systematically lose running processes and packet forwarding if the control plane fails.

Because of the complex interactions between its hardware and software components, SDN reliability is difficult to analyze. Failures of various kinds, including overflow, timeout, unreachable resources, software, hardware, database, and link failures, can affect the dependability of SDN.

While building dependable SDN networks, these kinds of failures should be taken into account as they may be dependent. For instance, invocation between software programs to retrieve the required information may be disabled by network failures. In order to uphold SLAs and please clients, service providers should isolate problematic components in the event of a breakdown and reduce their impact on experience quality.

3.5. PERFORMANCE OF SDN

Better user experience, centralized control, programmable functionalities, and lower network system and equipment costs are all provided by software-defined networking. Nonetheless, the features and capabilities that SDN infrastructure offers affect the overall network performance (e.g., error rate, throughput, jitter, and latency). Actually, because OpenFlow-based SDN systems handle a larger workload of network traffic, SDN may experience performance penalties. Performance is a critical issue, particularly in large-scale network implementations where a heavy request load on an SDN controller may result in longer delays.

The main bottleneck of the SDN architecture is the control plane. In practical terms, addressing SDN performance challenges means adopting novel approaches to traditional problems in line with mainstream practices. SDN performance can still be effectively managed by utilizing a number of current techniques, including data traffic scheduling, load balancing, end-to-end congestion control, and quality of service.

Benchmarking is typically used to analyze network controller performance. In order to decide whether to increase a controller's power processing capabilities, benchmarking is a frequently used technique for evaluating controller performance and locating performance bottlenecks. The benchmarking process has been carried out on current SDN controllers in a number of works. NOX-MT is an enhanced version of NOX that has been developed for enhanced performance. Performance tests have been conducted on a number of controllers, including Floodlight, Beacon, NOX-MT, and Maestro. We came to the conclusion that different architectural features, such as packet batching, switch partitioning, and multicore support, affect how well OpenFlow-based controllers perform.

They have observed that the controllers with high throughput performance are those that use static switch partitioning and static batching. Controllers that use an adaptive batching technique, however, perform reasonably well in terms of latency. Benchmarking on NOX, NOX-MT, Maestro, and Beacon has demonstrated that NOX-MT outperforms the other two in terms of maximum throughput, minimum and maximum response times, and both. Based on the network operating system's (NOX) single thread C++ implementation, the NOX-MT controller takes advantage of multithreading. To enhance baseline performance, the NOX-MT makes use of optimization strategies like I/O batching. On a server with two quad-core 2 GHz processors, NOX-MT outperforms NOX by a factor of 33 thanks to these optimizations. Maestro is an implementation of a controller built on Java. It makes use of throughput optimization techniques as well as parallelism (e.g., core and thread binding, as well as input and output batching). Benchmarking showed that on multicore processors, the Maestro design can ensure good performances and nearly linear performance scalability. We have tested the latency and throughput of both OpenDaylight and Floodlight controllers using the standard Cbench tool. They discovered that OpenDaylight's benchmarking results using Cbench were not very successful and asserted that the controller had multiple memory problems, including memory leakage.

By creating requests for packet forwarding rules and observing the controller's responses, the Cbench tool evaluates the performance of the controller. For every switching device, Cbench provides aggregated controller throughput and response time statistics. It's possible that aggregate statistics won't be adequate to investigate intricate controller behavior. As a result, OFCBenchmark, an additional tool, is thought to facilitate fine-grained statistics. For each switching device, OFCBenchmark offers statistics on response time, response rate, and number of unanswered packets.

Additionally, benchmarks for the data plane components have been carried out. We compared the switching performance of OpenFlow, layer-2 Ethernet, and layer-3 IP routing, and the Linux software SDN switching demonstrated better fairness and higher forwarding performance. They have employed forwarding throughput and packet latency under overload as performance indicators. In order to improve the lookup performance of OpenFlow switching, mechanisms have been proposed to increase the performance of OpenFlow using an architectural model.

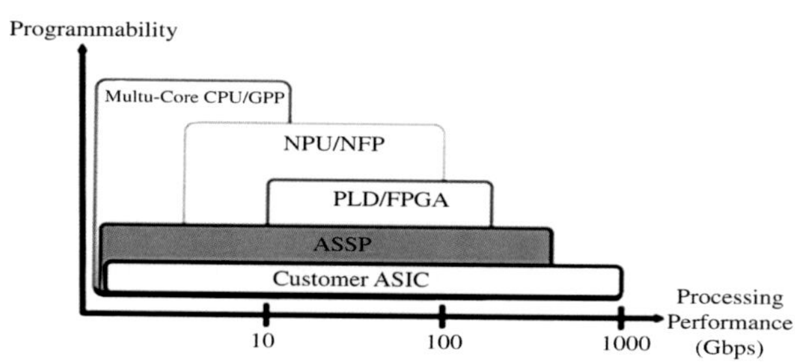

Figure 3.7. *Performance and programmability.*

Source: https://web.archive.org/web/20190724155640id_/https://onlinelibrary.wiley.com/doi/pdf/10.1002/sec.1737.

When comparing the packet switching throughput to regular software-based OpenFlow switching, it increases by 25%. To make performance benchmarking easier, a framework known as OpenFLow Operations Per Second (OFLOPS) has been introduced. Multiple packet generation and capturing mechanisms are supported by OFLOPS. OFLOPS enables detailed performance measurement data plane operations of SDN switching devices in addition to measuring performance metrics for control plane operations like rule insertion delay and traffic statistic query delay (Figure 3.7).

3.5.1. Resilience

Developing robust communication is one of networking's main goals. SDNs are therefore anticipated to provide the same levels of dependability as any new alternative technology or legacy system. When SDN architecture can function in the face of load, failures, and attacks, it is considered resilient. Resilience is typically predicated on concepts of security and reliability. Resilience in SDN refers to the capacity of one or more SDN architecture components, either in the control plane or data plane, to rapidly recover and carry on with operations even in the event of an equipment malfunction, power outage, or other disruption. SLA planning should include SDN resilience in order to guarantee continuous computing services.

Version 1.2 of the OpenFlow protocol includes the ability to use master-slave configuration to handle malfunctioning OpenFlow controllers and boost resilience, as SDN networks are susceptible to failures. This means that in the event of a master controller failure, all switches are under the control of the master controller. In this scenario, a backup controller, or slave, can assume control by quickly detecting a failure and initiating a failover process.

The network topology needs to take into account various challenges in order to create a resilient network. It must, for example, guarantee an identical synchronized network state between the master and slave controllers and contain redundant paths between network nodes. Furthermore, new modules and components added to the network must adhere to the specifications without impairing its functionality or resulting in failures.

Resilience can be modeled as an unforeseeable cycle that starts from an SDN normal state, where every network node behaves as intended and delivers an acceptable service and communicates without any disruption under normal operation S_0, to unacceptable service delivery under severely degraded service Sc. Anomalies are detected early to prevent failures or at least enable a partially degraded network to recover afterwards. However, escaping from severely degraded zone S_c to initial state S_0 requires a successful remediation and then a fast recovery. Figure 3.8 illustrates a multilevel two-dimensional state space that is characterized by two axes representing the operational state N (horizontal) and service parameters P (vertical). This model is commonly used to identify potential network threats and failures so as to anticipate and react in real time to ensure network resilience.

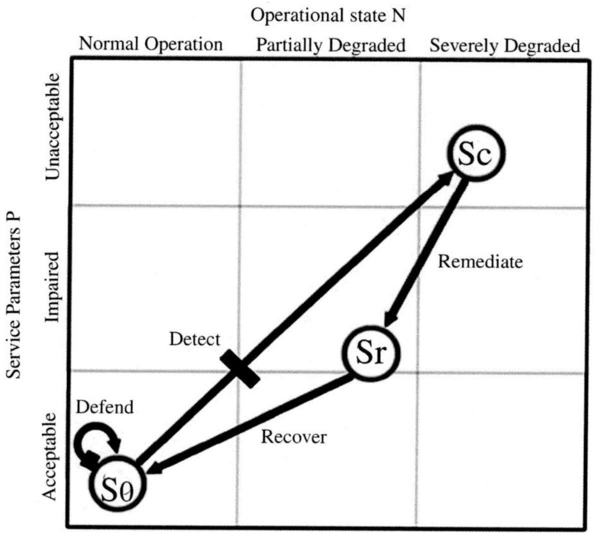

Figure 3.8. *Multilevel two-dimensional state space.*

Source: https://web.archive.org/web/20190724155640id_/https://onlinelibrary.wiley.com/doi/pdf/10.1002/sec.1737.

3.5.2. SDN Security

3.5.2.1. Software-Defined Networking: Vulnerabilities

Since security is not currently a feature of the SDN architecture, security concerns have grown in importance even though SDN offers a new network design that enables a wide range of network applications and services. Based on current technological capabilities (e.g., servers, apps, switches, routers, and so forth), it methodically inherits all of the Open Systems Interconnection model's associated security problems, from the application layer to the physical layer. Still, SDN has introduced new network components (e.g., controllers, components that are virtualized, etc.) and different applications using a new splitting design into the core network.

Although it would remove some minor threats that currently exist in traditional networks, decoupling the data plane from the control plane has introduced new vulnerabilities that are unique to SDN. SDN undoubtedly has significant disadvantages because it primarily depends on different application-layer software to communicate with the underlying infrastructure. This is because security flaws in code can have a major impact. Furthermore, by centralizing management and control on the controller, the entire infrastructure would become vulnerable to a single point of failure. Threats to controllers may come from several sources (i.e., interfaces). The control's entrance doors are located at the northbound and southbound interfaces, respectively, and they could be attractive targets for attackers. Attackers may also choose to target the data plane. An attacker could stop the data flow by flooding the switches or interfering with the communications because of the exchanges that take place between the control and data planes. Certain attacks may also target the OpenFlow protocol, which is in charge of establishing communication between the two planes.

The SDN vulnerabilities can be repartitioned into five major axes:

1. **Application Layer:** These are software-related vulnerabilities that might be exploited through code injection. Some works have been proposed to tackle common issues of the application layer. Such issues include the challenge of detecting and reconciling potentially conflicting flow rules from OF apps and dealing with network applications' failures leading to loss of network control and enabling network resilience to SDN application failures and faults.
2. **Control Layer:** This includes vulnerabilities associated with the controller. Major works have been proposed in the literature to identify and mitigate/reduce vulnerabilities of the controller. Othman and Okamura present a signature algorithm to securely transmit flow installation requests from the controller to the network devices. The system assumes using secure communication with TLS so as to avoid the control channel from being tampered. A hierarchical system of controllers is identified to reduce the impact of a malicious application that can lead to point of failures in the control plane. Other works such as formal methods have been proposed to verify and prove the safety and correctness of the SDN control plane and resolve issues related to security policies.
3. **APIs:** The control plane exposes two types of APIs: vertical (i.e., southbound and northbound) and horizontal (i.e., eastbound, westbound, and management interface). The issue of exposing interfaces is discussed. As a solution, the Security-Enhanced Floodlight is proposed that offers an authenticated northbound API. Another system named Frenetic also focuses on the northbound API to resolve policy conflicts.
4. **Protocols:** In OpenFlow-based SDN architecture, the OpenFlow protocol can be exposed to various threats according to vulnerability assessments, among which is the TLS security layer that has been considered as optional in the specification of the OpenFlow protocol.

5. **Infrastructure Layer:** Vulnerabilities related to data plane components (e.g., switchs, and routers) could engender different attack vectors such as fraudulent rule insertion, rule modifications, and flooding. FlowChecker has been introduced to solve issues of misconfigurations in OpenFlow switches causing variance in flow rules. Anteater is a similar work that introduces a static analysis approach to diagnose network configuration problems. OFHIP is proposed to provide secure mobility with OpenFlow to avoid disrupted flow processing, active TLS session teardown, and mutual authentication issues.

3.5.2.2. Software-Defined Networking: Threats and Attacks

Vulnerabilities in the management, application control, and data planes entail different threats for the SDN model and could be classified into four categories depending on the motivations:

1. **Internal:** These threats come from the inside of SDN, generally from authorized individuals who can have full access to the SDN network (e.g., managing applications, modifying security policies, programming scripts for SDN, etc.). According to improperly high privileges can lead to serious malicious actions into the network either being intentional or accidental. Although intentional malicious activities are rare, they are the most dangerous threats for a productive network. Accidental undesired network manipulations are also non-negligible, which can cause undesired traffic or network loops.
2. **External:** These threats are mainly initiated from the outside of the corporate network and aimed at altering the SDN network by relying on denial of service (DoS) attacks or trying to have unauthorized access by relying on advanced techniques such as malwares, social engineering, man in the middle, and spoofing.
3. **Unstructured:** Generally, this type of threat comes from script kiddies, bugs/misconfigurations, or conflicting rules in the SDN components (e.g., applications, security policies, conflicting rule tables in the switches, etc.).
4. **Structured:** This threat can entail very sophisticated attacks leading to serious damages in the SDN network. In fact, this threat comes from high-level technically skilled attackers who can penetrate into networks by varying their advanced techniques (e.g., spoofing, code exploits, social engineering, malwares, etc.). Skilled hackers can join their forces and lead an organized crime against organizations and network providers.

Depending on their objectives and level of expertise, the attackers may spearhead one or more attacks. In general, there are two categories of attacks against SDN: passive attacks and active attacks. A sophisticated attack typically combines the two attack modalities. Using scanning tools, the attacker's only goals in the first mode are to identify IP addresses, open ports, and running services and communications by monitoring, collecting data, listening in on message contents, and analyzing the traffic. After that, he or she can launch an active attack, also known as a denial-of-service (DoS) attack, to obtain unauthorized access for spying and/or exhaust a resource or service in the SDN infrastructure, based on the network data that has been gathered and the potential vulnerabilities that have been found. The literature has suggested a number of countermeasures to get rid of or lessen SDN threats in the OpenFlow protocol, API, and data/control plane.

REFERENCES

1. Armbrust, M., Fox, A., Griffith, R., et al. (2010). A view of cloud computing. *Communications of the ACM, 53*(4), 50–58.
2. Benson, T., Akella, A., & Maltz, D. (2009). Unraveling the complexity of network management. In *Proceedings of the 6th USENIX Symposium on Networked Systems Design and Implementation* (pp. 335–348). USENIX Association.
3. Benzekki, K., El Fergougui, A., & ElBelrhiti ElAlaoui, A. (2016). A secure cloud computing architecture using homomorphic encryption. *International Journal of Advanced Computer Science & Applications, 1*(7), 293–298.
4. Cai, Z. (2011). *Maestro: Achieving Scalability and Coordination in Centralized Network Control Plane* (Doctoral dissertation). Rice University, Houston, TX, USA.
5. Casado, M., Freedman, M., Pettit, J., Luo, J., McKeown, N., & Shenker, S. (2007). Ethane: Taking control of the enterprise. In *Proceedings of the 2007 Conference on Applications, Technologies, Architectures, and Protocols for Computer Communications* (pp. 1–12). ACM.
6. Doria, A., Salim, J. H., Haas, R., et al. (2010). *Forwarding and Control Element Separation (ForCES) Protocol Specification* (RFC 5810, Proposed Standard).
7. Erickson, D. (2013). The Beacon OpenFlow controller. In *Proceedings of the Second ACM SIGCOMM Workshop on Hot Topics in Software Defined Networking* (pp. 13–18). ACM.
8. Farrel, A., Vasseur, J. P., & Ash, J. (2006). *A Path Computation Element (PCE)-Based Architecture* (RFC 4655).
9. Hassas Yeganeh, S., & Ganjali, Y. (2012). Kandoo: A framework for efficient and scalable offloading of control applications. In *Proceedings of the First Workshop on Hot Topics in Software Defined Networks* (pp. 19–24). ACM.
10. Jarschel, M., Lehrieder, F., Magyari, Z., & Pries, R. (2012). A flexible OpenFlow-controller benchmark. In *Proceedings of the European Workshop on Software Defined Networking (EWSDN)* (pp. 48–53).
11. Jarschel, M., Oechsner, S., Schlosser, D., Pries, R., Goll, S., & TranGia, P. (2011). Modeling and performance evaluation of an OpenFlow architecture. In *23rd International Teletraffic Congress (ITC)* (pp. 1–7). IEEE.
12. McKeown, N., Anderson, T., Balakrishnan, H., et al. (2008). OpenFlow: Enabling innovation in campus networks. *ACM SIGCOMM Computer Communication Review, 38*(2), 69–74.

13. Naudts, B., Kind, M., Westphal, F. J., Verbrugge, S., Colle, D., & Pickavet, M. (2012). Techno-economic analysis of software defined networking as architecture for the virtualization of a mobile network. In *European Workshop on Software Defined Networking (EWSDN)* (pp. 67–72). IEEE.
14. Rimal, B. P., Jukan, A., Katsaros, D., & Goeleven, Y. (2011). Architectural requirements for cloud computing systems: An enterprise cloud approach. *Journal of Grid Computing, 9*(1), 3–26.
15. Scott-Hayward, S., O'Callaghan, G., & Sezer, S. (2013). SDN security: A survey. In *IEEE SDN for Future Networks and Services (SDN4FNS)* (pp. 1–7).
16. Shalimov, A., Zuikov, D., Zimarina, D., Pashkov, V., & Smeliansky, R. (2013). Advanced study of SDN/OpenFlow controllers. In *Proceedings of the 9th Central and Eastern European Software Engineering Conference in Russia* (p. 1). ACM.
17. Tootoonchian, A., & Ganjali, Y. (2010). HyperFlow: A distributed control plane for OpenFlow. In *Proceedings of the 2010 Internet Network Management Conference on Research on Enterprise Networking* (p. 3). USENIX Association.
18. Yang, L., Dantu, R., Anderson, T., & Gopal, R. (2004). *Forwarding and Control Element Separation (ForCES) framework* (RFC 3746, Informational).
19. Yu, M., Rexford, J., Freedman, M. J., & Wang, J. (2010). Scalable flow-based networking with DIFANE. *SIGCOMM Computer Communication Review, 41*(4), 351–362.

CHAPTER 4

NETWORK PROGRAMMABILITY

Contents

INTRODUCTION

One of the fundamental ideas of software-defined networks is the notion of network programmability. Since network management has existed for networked devices since the beginning of time, the idea of programmability can exist in or be a feature of many network devices and software components. What has changed recently is the manner in which those devices—whether physical or virtual—are not only controlled but also used. The objective is to make the target easily programmable and to enable a bidirectional channel of communication between it and the other piece of software that is communicating with it, regardless of the type of target. Between these components, this creates what is known as a tightly coupled feedback loop. In actuality, this idea differs greatly from the conventional paradigm of network management, in which there was often little to no feedback and a significant lag between operations in the manager-agent communication.

Programmatic interfaces that are tightly coupled and bidirectional are required to realize this new paradigm of interaction and communication. To promote their use and widespread deployment, software must also incorporate these interfaces quickly and easily. The term "application friendly" has been used frequently to describe these interfaces. For these interfaces to be reliable, safe, and widely used, developer communities must also create them. De facto standardization and eventually proper standardization will result from this. In order to enable applications to quickly and dynamically discover and comprehend the capabilities of a network element without requiring recompilation, interfaces must have self-describing capabilities. Interfaces that are portable across various controller platforms and that can be safely coded will be the end result.

4.1. THE APPLICATION-NETWORK DIVIDE

Recently, the majority of contemporary network components (e.g., switches, routers, or firewalls) allowed for the communication of those components via a limited number of conventional interfaces. These usually included CORBA, SNMP, a proprietary command-line interface (CLI), and, more recently, a NETCONF variant. These languages share a few essential characteristics. Firstly, they are usually quite static in nature and necessitate the design and declaration of data models in advance. In practical terms, this means that code is frequently generated from these interfaces, which are integrated into both the management software (or applications) and the firmware images that are running on the network elements. This meant that instead of learning on the fly, the interfaces used to communicate with a network element had to be preprogrammed. Second, the grammar of the languages that specify how messages should be structured and the guidelines that elements should follow when handling messages (i.e., read-write, and read-only) are developed specifically for those management interfaces. Third, these protocols frequently employed binary encodings, which made them challenging to program, debug, and otherwise represent even though they were small on the wire. Last but not least, the standard procedures for creating the syntactic modules that describe the schema of any one of these interfaces were frequently nonhierarchical, making it challenging for both applications and people to navigate the schema.

Generally, in order for an application to interact with a network element or its services, it had to follow one of these protocols or, more frequently, use an element management system (EMS) to facilitate communication. Between the network components and the applications, the EMS served as a middleman. Regretfully, the EMS (or NMS) typically did not expose the network elements or the services they offered in a manner that was application friendly. This meant that coding toward these interfaces and paradigms was sometimes difficult and ultimately led to lengthy lags between an application signaling that it wanted to do something and the action actually taking place. As seen in Figure 4.1, this is actually referred to as the application-network divide.

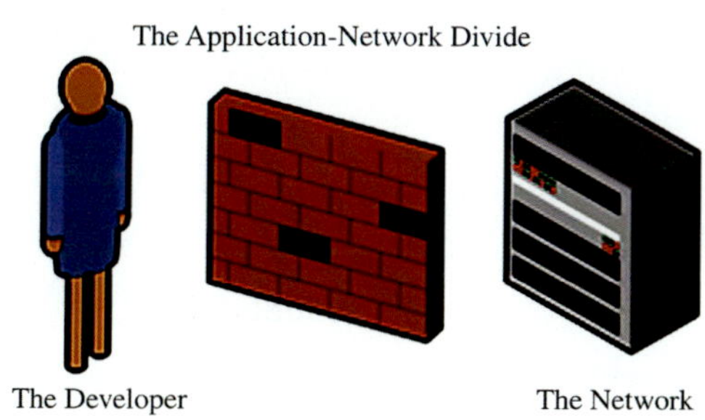

Figure 4.1. *The application-network divide.*

Source: Thomas, D. N., & Ken, G.; SDN: Software Defined Networks; ISBN: 978-1-449-34230-2.

Using application-friendly RESTful (representational state transfer) interfaces is one way to achieve this. It so happens that JSON (JavaScript Object Notation), one of the more contemporary approaches, is typically used to define these interfaces. Because JSON's schema is defined using XML that is readable by humans, it is self-referential, hierarchical, and easily integrated into Java applications—the most popular application programming language of the last 10 years—it addresses many of the drawbacks previously mentioned. The code snippet here demonstrates a JSON example:

```
<!DOCTYPE html>
<html>
<body>
<h2>
JSON Object Creation in JavaScript
</h2>
<p>
Name: <span id="jname"></span><br/>
Age: <span id="jage"></span><br/>
Address: <span id="jstreet"></span><br/>
Phone: <span id="jphone"></span><br/>
</p>
<script>
var JSONObject= {
"name":"John Johnson,"
"street":"Oslo West 555,"
"age":33,
"phone":"5551234567"};
document.getElementById("jname").innerHTML=JSONObject.name
document.getElementById("jage").innerHTML=JSONObject.age
document.getElementById("jstreet").innerHTML=JSONObject.street
document.getElementById("jphone").innerHTML=JSONObject.phone
</script>
</body>
</html>
```

Encouraging a much closer coupled interaction between applications and the network components that support them is one of the fundamental principles of SDN technology. The cycle of provisioning, analysis, and optimization, in particular, stands for three typical and universal actions that were previously frequently regarded as independent. We propose that these be taken into consideration jointly in an SDN approach. As seen in Figure 4.2, this is explained. When an application expresses a wish to perform an action, modify an existing behavior, or generally influence network behavior, it is said to be provisioning. Monitoring or obtaining input from network elements regarding their operational, fault, capacity, or other well-being states constitutes the analysis phase. For instance, collecting statistics or receiving status updates fall under this category. In order for the system to adjust itself in order to function better, optimization is the final step that is completed using the data collected from the analysis phase. It may result in another act of provisioning (possibly through some interaction between external or embedded policy engines). The faster this feedback loop is put into place, the faster the system as a whole may be able to adapt to changes and possibly perform at its best.

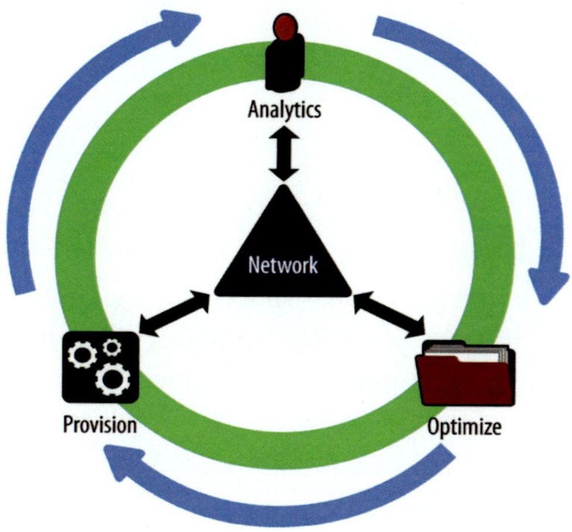

Figure 4.2. *The application-network feedback loop.*

Source: Thomas, D. N., & Ken, G.; SDN: Software Defined Networks; ISBN: 978-1-449-34230-2.

4.1.1. The Command-Line Interface

Since the beginning of time, every vendor has been required to offer a command line interface (CLI) in order for the operator to interact with the device. Usually based on ASCII characters, the CLI is meant to be used as the lowest common denominator (LCD) management interface by default for any given device. In many ways, the CLI is similar to a UNIX shell prompt in that it functions as a syntax parser that, upon depressing the Return key, performs an action based on a string of tokens. The majority of devices allow remote CLI access via a common protocol like Secure Shell (SSH) or Telnet. These protocols are vulnerable to network outages and other issues that could stop a manager from interacting with a device because they function over a network. Because of this, the majority of gadgets, regardless of size, still come with a hardwired attachment and a command set that enables local interaction (e.g., a serial port or USB that is hardwired). Device manufacturers typically divide their command-line syntax into two sections: query, or monitoring, and configuration. When it comes to configuration, a manager can frequently change a device's operating configuration by entering a secure mode of operation. Certain devices enable an operator to store multiple configuration copies, so they have backups in case one configuration doesn't work or they need to configure different scenarios. This is shown in the brief snippet here:

```
RP/0/0/CPU0:ios#config t
RP/0/0/CPU0:ios(config)#interface
MgmtEth 0/0/CPU0/0
RP/0/0/CPU0:ios(config-if)#
RP/0/0/CPU0:ios#
RP/0/0/CPU0:ios#admin
RP/0/0/CPU0:ios(admin)#
```

Additionally, the command-line syntax usually offers a query mode that enables a manager to inquire about the status or condition of specific device functions. For example, in the previous example, one element that a manager could query to make sure they were about to configure the correct device was the name of the system. Another example is shown here, where we query the BGP protocol status of a device:

```
RP/0/0/CPU0:R2#show bgp summary
BGP router identifier 3.3.3.3, local AS number 1 BGP generic
scan interval 60 secs
BGP table state: Active
Table ID: 0xe0000000
BGP main routing table version 561
BGP scan interval 60 secs
BGP is operating in STANDALONE mode.
Process Speaker Neighbor 20.0.101.1
RecvTblVerbRIB/RIB LabelVer ImportVer SendTblVer
StandbyVer 561 561 561 561 561 561
Spk AS MsgRcvdMsgSentTblVerInQOutQ Up/Down
St/PfxRcd 0 1 1068 1036 561 0 0 14:35:30 100
```

Though different CLIs may be used to manage the same conceptual elements, sadly, the CLI syntax specified by any two vendors is usually different and incompatible. For instance, on one system, the name of the system might be permitted to be written in mixed case, but on another, it might be required to be written in all capital letters (or not allow certain reserved characters). As much as it is legal, many net-work equipment vendors have now imitated the Cisco CLI in an attempt to concentrate on a single de facto standard. Even though this has been beneficial, operations like the one we just discussed are still incompatible, which makes these solutions more difficult to implement. Nevertheless, there isn't a standard for CLI syntax. Though none of the attempts to standardize it have been successful.

Using UNIX scripting to communicate with the device's CLI is one of the earliest methods of network programmability within the constraints of the CLI that is still widely used. This can be accomplished with a number of tools, such as Python, UNIX shell commands, Expect scripts, and Perl. In these situations, scripts are configured to establish a connection with a device via a network transport and session protocols, like SSH or Telnet via UDP/IP. The scripts automatically enter commands on the CLI as if a user were typing them after they have connected and possibly authenticated. Because one is not actually interacting with the system but rather behaving as though they are washing windows with a window squeegee, this is commonly referred to as "screen scraping." Regretfully, the most popular method for network programmability is this one. The drawback of utilizing these management robots is that, generally speaking, it takes a while for them to program a device and then gather statistics so that they can modify configuration or take action. This approach's unfortunate lack of application friendliness is just another drawback. Although some contemporary applications are written in Python or Perl, they are typically not designed to comprehend the syntax and semantics of a specific vendor's CLI. Even worse, if a network contains devices from several different vendors, the application needs to know how to communicate with each device in a variety of ways, based on its model, type, make, and firmware version. Most people familiar with this method of operation consider this requirement an inappropriate and undue burden on application programmers, who typically do not understand the details of programming a network device—nor should they!

4.1.2. NETCONF and NETMOD

The IETF standardized the Network Configuration Protocol (NETCONF) as a network management protocol. December 2006 saw the development and publication of it. SNMP was created by the IETF in the late 1980s, and at least for statistical monitoring, it is still widely used as a network management protocol today. Sadly, it was discovered after roughly 10 years of SNMP deployment experience that, contrary to its original purpose, SNMP was primarily being used for network monitoring rather than network equipment configuration. Network operators and members of the IETF's network management community met in 2001 to talk about the state of affairs. The outcomes of this meeting are detailed in RFC 3535, but in short, it was discovered that operators were configuring their boxes mainly through proprietary command-line interfaces (CLI) rather than SNMP. The rationale behind this behavior was the other significant finding from this meeting. Key points included the fact that the operators preferred the CLI's many features, such as its text-based interface compared to the BER-encoded (i.e., binary) SNMP. Furthermore, a lot of equipment manufacturers did not offer the ability to fully configure their products using SNMP. The majority had received the notification from operators earlier and were only permitted to read-only data. Even so, in some ways those that adopted full read-write capability were isolated since, despite the IETF's provision of standards-based MIB modules, each vendor continued to implement its own proprietary MIB modules. Frequently, these extensions were not implemented by other vendors. Last but not least, some standards-based MIBs were de-signed using one implementation's semantics, which eventually did not match another's, making it even harder (or impossible) to use as a configuration vehicle.

Generally speaking, operators preferred writing scripts to control their network elements, but they all felt that the CLI was deficient in several areas. The output's unpredictability stood out the most. The output's content and formatting were prone to erratic changes, even within firmware releases. While some offered documentation and written notice of changes, others did not supply this information, which exacerbated an already challenging situation.

Juniper Networks had been remotely communicating with its devices at this same time via an XML-based network management technique (i.e., as the native language used to specify the model for the CLI and as the protocol for the management interface. As a suggestion for a more standardized and application-friendly management interface, this innovative method was presented to the IETF and disseminated throughout the community. The result of this initial proposal and the meeting detailed in RFC 3535 was the IETF's development of NETCONF, a new network management protocol. Let me summarize by saying that NETCONF offers methods for adding, modifying, and removing network device configurations. A basic remote procedure call (RPC) layer serves as the foundation for its operations. Both protocol messages and data are encoded using XML, or Extensible Markup Language, by the NETCONF protocol. On top of the transport protocol—which may be TCP, HTTP, or HTTPS—this is then implemented. As seen in Figure 4.3, the NETCONF protocol can be divided conceptually into four layers. Now, we will also go over each of these layers.

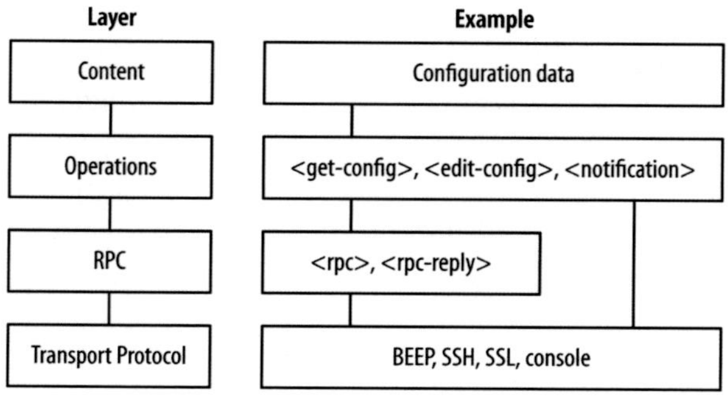

Figure 4.3. *The four layers of NETCONF: Content, operations, RPC, and transport protocol.*

Source: Thomas, D. N., & Ken, G.; SDN: Software Defined Networks; ISBN: 978-1-449-34230-2.

4.1.2.1. Basic NETCONF Operations

The base protocol includes the following protocol operations: get, get-config, edit-config, copy-config, delete-config, lock, unlock, close-session, and kill-session.

4.1.2.2. Capabilities

By defining NETCONF capabilities, the functionality of the base NETCONF can be expanded. During the capability exchange phase of session setup, the server and the client must exchange information about any additional protocol features that the implementation supports. The capability exchange does not include mandatory protocol features because it is assumed that all compliant implementations support them. RFC 4741 defines a few optional capabilities, such as :xpath and :validate.

Support for subscribing to and receiving asynchronous event notifications is another feature provided by NETCONF. Specifically, the function allows an operator to set up replay and real-time subscriptions for alerts. Notifications are sent asynchronously using the construct after they are emitted. The ability for NETCONF to support partial locking of a device's running configuration is one of its most significant features. This is important because it permits nonoverlapping subtrees within the running configuration to be edited by multiple sessions. The only lock that is available in the absence of this feature is for the entire configuration, necessitating an efficient serialization of configuration entities, which could cause the configuration process to lag.

Lastly, the NETCONF protocol itself is capable of being independently managed and watched over. Accessible components that help manage a NETCONF server, like datastores, sessions, locks, and statistics, can be used for critical tasks like server troubleshooting. The most crucial thing is that a NETCONF server specifies how NETCONF clients can find data models that are supported by the server and how to retrieve them. This feature enables a NETCONF-supporting device's capabilities to be dynamically discovered by an application (or SDN controller). This straightforward but effective feature will make it easier to create dynamic, data-driven application code, including that which is contained inside SDN controllers.

4.2. SIMPLE NETWORK MANAGEMENT PROTOCOL

An application layer protocol called Simple Network Management Protocol (SNMP) makes it easier for network devices to share management data. It belongs to the suite of protocols known as Transmission Control Protocol/ Internet Protocol (TCP/IP).

Network administrators can plan for network expansion, monitor network performance, and identify and fix network issues with the help of SNMP. SNMP version 1 (SNMPv1) and SNMP version 2 (SNMPv2) are the two versions of SNMP. While there are many features shared by both versions, SNMPv2 offers improvements like extra protocol operations. SNMP Version 3 (SNMPv3) is a further version of SNMP that has not yet been standardized. The operations of the SNMPv1 and SNMPv2 protocols are described in this chapter. An example of an SNMP-managed basic network is shown in Figure 4.4.

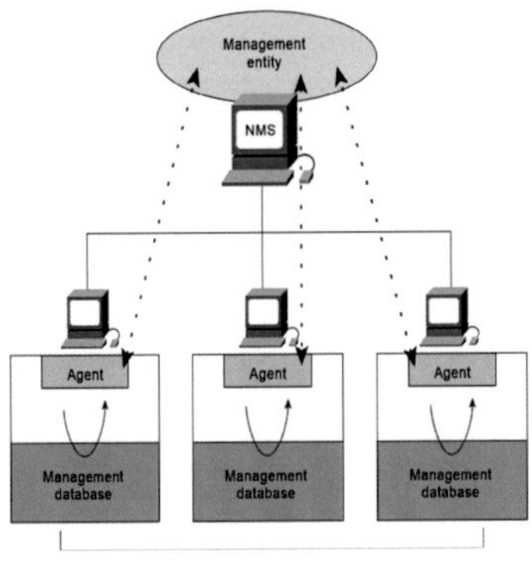

Figure 4.4. *SNMP facilitates the exchange of network information between devices.*

Source: https://faculty.kfupm.edu.sa/ics/salah/082/cse550/slides/snmp/snmp.pdf.

4.2.1. SNMP Basic Components

The three main parts of an SNMP-managed network are network-management systems (NMSs), agents, and managed devices. A network node that is part of a managed network and has an SNMP agent on it is called a managed device. By means of SNMP, managed devices gather, store, and make management data available to NMSs. Hubs, computer hosts, printers, switches, bridges, routers, and access servers are examples of managed devices, also known as network elements. A managed device's resident network management software module is called an agent.

Local knowledge of management data is possessed by an agent, who converts it into SNMP-compatible format. Applications that oversee and manage managed devices are run by an NMS. The majority of the memory and processing power needed for network management is supplied by NMSs. Every managed network needs to have one or more NMSs. The connections between these three elements are shown in Figure 4.5.

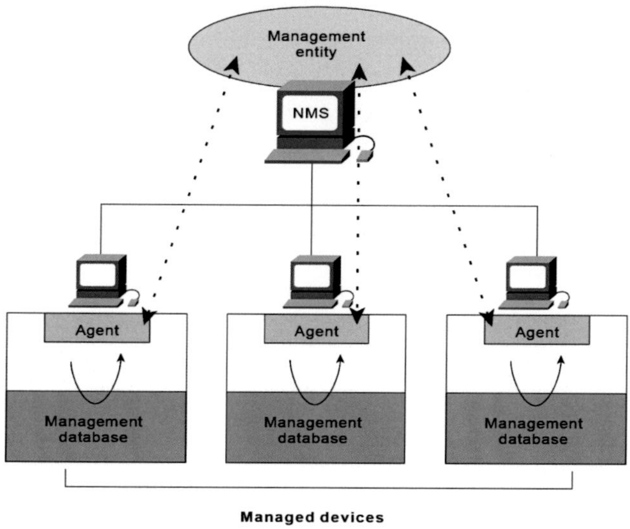

Figure 4.5. *An SNMP-managed network consists of managed devices, agents, and NMSs.*

Source: https://faculty.kfupm.edu.sa/ics/salah/082/cse550/slides/snmp/snmp.pdf.

4.2.2. SNMP Basic Commands

The four fundamental SNMP commands—read, write, trap, and traversal operations—are used to monitor and manage managed devices. An NMS monitors managed devices with the read command. Several variables that are kept up to date by managed devices are examined by the NMS. An NMS uses the write command to take control of managed devices. Variables stored on managed devices have their values altered by the NMS. Managed devices use the trap command to send events to the NMS asynchronously. A managed device notifies the NMS of a trap when specific events take place. To ascertain which variables a managed device supports and to progressively compile data into variable tables, like a routing table, the NMS employs traversal operations.

4.2.3. SNMP Management Information Base

An information collection with a hierarchical organization is called a Management Information Base (MIB). A network-management protocol like SNMP is used to access MIBs. Identified by object identifiers, they consist of managed objects. One of the many distinct features of a managed device is a managed object, also known as an object, an MIB, or a managed object. One or more object instances, which are essentially variables, make up managed objects.

There are two kinds of managed objects: tabular and scalar. A single object instance is defined by scalar objects. Multiple related object instances that are grouped in MIB tables are defined by tabular objects. The integer value that represents the total number of input AppleTalk packets on a router interface is found in the scalar object atInput, an example of a managed object.

There are two kinds of managed objects: tabular and scalar. A single object instance is defined by scalar objects. Multiple related object instances that are grouped in MIB tables are defined by tabular objects. The integer value that represents the total number of input AppleTalk packets on a router interface is found in the scalar object atInput, an example of a managed object. In the MIB hierarchy, a managed object is uniquely identified by its object ID. The MIB hierarchy can be represented as a tree with levels assigned by various organizations and a nameless root.

In Figure 4.6, the MIB tree is shown. While related organizations assign lower-level object IDs, top-level MIB object IDs are owned by various standards organizations. It is possible for vendors to define private branches with managed objects specific to their own products. MIBs in the experimental branch are usually those that have not been standardized.

The managed object atInput can be uniquely identified either by the object name—iso.identified-organization.dod.internet.private.enterprise.cisco.temporary variables.AppleTalk.atInput—or by the equivalent object descriptor, 1.3.6.1.4.1.9.3.3.1.

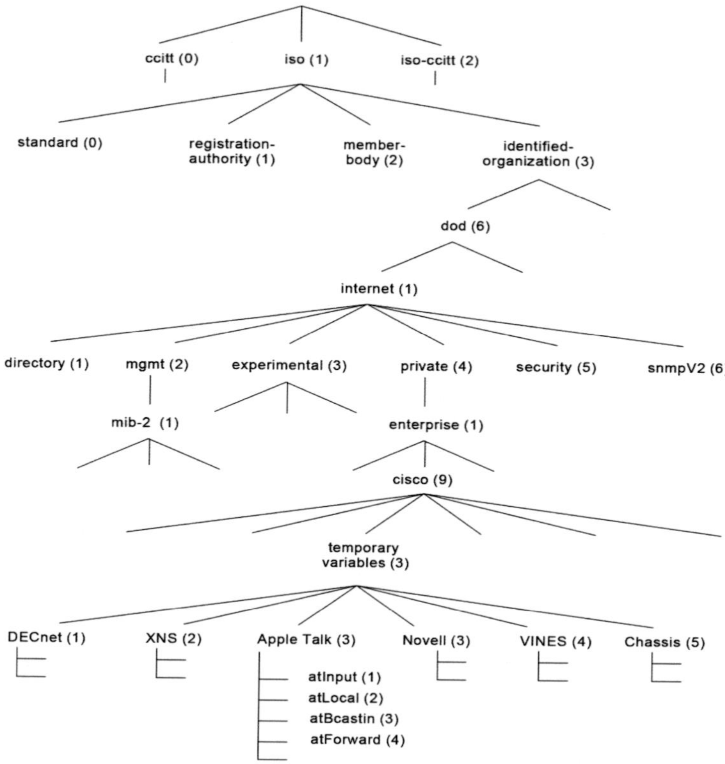

Figure 4.6. *The MIB tree illustrates the various hierarchies assigned by different organizations.*

Source: https://faculty.kfupm.edu.sa/ics/salah/082/cse550/slides/snmp/snmp.pdf.

4.2.4. SNMP and Data Representation

SNMP must account for and adjust to incompatibilities between managed devices. Different computers use different data representation techniques, which can compromise the capability of SNMP to exchange information between managed devices. SNMP uses a subset of Abstract Syntax Notation One (ASN.1) to accommodate communication between diverse systems.

4.2.5. SNMP Version 1

The SNMP protocol was first implemented with SNMP version 1 (SNMPv1). It operates within the parameters of the structure of management information (SMI) and is explained in request for comments (RFC) 1157. User datagram protocol (UDP), internet protocol (IP), AppleTalk datagram-delivery protocol

(DDP), OSI connectionless network service (CLNS), and Novell internet packet exchange (IPX) are among the protocols that SNMPv1 supports. In the Internet community, SNMPv1 is the de facto network-management protocol and is widely used.

4.2.5.1. SNMPv1 and Structure of Management Information

The Structure of Management Information (SMI) defines the rules for describing management information, using Abstract Syntax Notation One (ASN.1). The SNMPv1 SMI is defined in RFC 1155. The SMI makes three key specifications: ASN.1 data types, SMI-specific data types, and SNMP MIB tables.

4.2.5.1.1. SNMPv1 and ASN.1 Data Types

The SNMPv1 SMI specifies that all managed objects have a certain subset of Abstract Syntax Notation One (ASN.1) data types associated with them. Three ASN.1 data types are required: name, syntax, and encoding. The name serves as the object identifier (object ID). The syntax defines the data type of the object (for example, integer or string). The SMI uses a subset of the ASN.1 syntax definitions. The encoding data describes how information associated with a managed object is formatted as a series of data items for transmission over the network.

4.2.5.1.2. SNMPv1 and SMI-Specific Data Types

A variety of SMI-specific data types, which fall into two categories—simple data types and application-wide data types—are prescribed for use in the SNMPv1 SMI. The SNMPv1 SMI defines three unique values for simple data types: integers, octet strings, and object IDs. A signed integer between –2,147,483,648 and 2,147,483,647 is the integer data type. Sequences with a length of 0 to 65,535 octets are called octet strings. The set of all object identifiers assigned in accordance with the ASN.1-specified rules is where object IDs originate.

Seven application-wide data types exist in the SNMPv1 SMI: network addresses, counters, gauges, time ticks, opaques, integers, and unsigned integers. Network addresses represent an address from a particular protocol family. SNMPv1 supports only 32-bit IP addresses. Counters are non-negative integers that increase until they reach a maximum value and then return to zero. In SNMPv1, a 32-bit counter size is specified. Gauges are non-negative integers that can increase or decrease but that retain the maximum value reached. A time tick represents a 100th of a second since some event. An opaque represents an arbitrary encoding that is used to pass arbitrary information strings that do not conform to the strict data typing used by the SMI. An integer represents signed integer-valued information. This data type redefines the integer data type, which has arbitrary precision in ASN.1 but bounded precision in the SMI. An unsigned integer represents unsigned integer-valued information and is useful when values are always non-negative. This data type redefines the integer data type, which has arbitrary precision in ASN.1 but bounded precision in the SMI.

4.2.5.1.3. SNMP MIB Tables

To group the instances of a tabular object (i.e., an object with multiple variables), the SNMPv1 SMI defines highly structured tables. Tables consist of zero or more rows that are indexed so that SNMP can use a single Get, GetNext, or Set command to retrieve or modify the whole row.

4.2.5.2. SNMPv1 Protocol Operations

A straightforward request/response protocol is SNMP. Managed devices respond to requests made by the network-management system. One of the following four protocol operations—Get, GetNext, Set, and Trap—is used to implement this behavior. The NMS uses the Get operation to get an agent's value for one or more object instances. The agent responding to the Get operation does not provide any values if it is unable to provide values for each object instance in a list. The NMS uses the GetNext operation to get the value of the following object instance in a list or table inside an agent. The NMS uses the Set operation to set the values of object instances inside of an agent. Agents use the Trap operation to asynchronously notify the NMS of an important event.

4.2.6. SNMP Version 2

The second version of SNMP, or SNMPv2, is an advancement over the first version, SNMPv1. SNMPv2 is a draft standard that was first published in 1993 as a set of suggested Internet standards. Similar to SNMPv1, SNMPv2 operates in accordance with the Structure of Management Information (SMI) specifications. Theoretically, SNMPv2 provides more protocol operations in addition to several other improvements over SNMPv1.

4.2.6.1. SNMPv2 and Structure of Management Information

The Structure of Management Information (SMI) defines the rules for describing management information, using ASN.1. The SNMPv2 SMI is described in RFC 1902. It makes certain additions and enhancements to the SNMPv1 SMI-specific data types, such as including bit strings, network addresses, and counters. Bit strings are defined only in SNMPv2 and comprise zero or more named bits that specify a value. Network addresses represent an address from a particular protocol family. SNMPv1 supports only 32-bit IP addresses, but SNMPv2 can support other types of addresses as well. Counters are non-negative integers that increase until they reach a maximum value and then return to zero. In SNMPv1, a 32-bit counter size is specified. In SNMPv2, 32-bit and 64-bit counters are defined.

4.2.6.2. SMI Information Modules

A collection of related definitions are specified by information modules, which are also specified by the SNMPv2 SMI. There are three different kinds of SMI information modules: capability statements, compliance statements, and MIB modules. The definitions of related managed objects are contained in MIB modules. A set of managed objects that need to be implemented in order to be in compliance with a standard can be described in a methodical manner using compliance statements. To specify the exact degree of support an agent claims for a MIB group, capability statements are utilized. Based on the capability's statements linked to each agent, an NMS can modify how it behaves with agents.

4.2.6.3. SNMPv2 Protocol Operations

The Get, GetNext, and Set functions utilized in SNMPv1 and SNMPv2 are identical. SNMPv2 improves and adds to a few protocol functions, though. For instance, the SNMPv2 Trap operation replaces the SNMPv1 Trap and performs the same function as the SNMPv1 Trap, but it uses a different message format. GetBulk and Inform are two additional new protocol operations defined by SNMPv2. The NMS uses the GetBulk operation to quickly retrieve big data blocks, like several rows in a table. GetBulk inserts as much of the requested data as it can into a response message. One NMS can communicate trap information to another NMS and receive a response by using the Inform operation. In SNMPv2, partial results are returned by the agent in response to GetBulk operations if it is unable to supply values for all the variables in a list.

4.3. MODERN PROGRAMMATIC INTERFACES

Now that we have described the most common management interfaces, let's move the discussion to modern management interfaces and concepts. These new interfaces and concepts are those that enable and encourage network programmability in the best sense. To that end, these interfaces exhibit most if not all of the key attributes we spelled out in the introduction earlier: bidirectional, application-friendly, and self-describing. They also incorporate robust data models that can translate into data-driven behavior and rapid implementation, and of course are easily developed by communities of developers.

4.3.1. Publish and Subscribe Interfaces

A messaging pattern known as publish-subscribe interfaces, or just pub-sub as it is more widely known, allows message senders, also known as publishers, to send messages to recipients, also known as subscribers. Senders categorize published messages into classes rather than programming the messages to be sent directly to particular recipients. This is carried out without express knowledge of the number of subscribers that may exist at any given time. Subscribing users in this model indicate their interest in one or more classes; as a result, they only receive messages within the messages that interest them. This is carried out without awareness of which publishers, if any, are involved. This creates what is known as a "messaging bus," in which subscribers just pick up messages that are posted on the bus. Because of features like fewer state management requirements, this pattern offers more network scalability and a more dynamic network topology than a point-to-point system would. Similar to virtual networks, message buses can be dependable or unreliable and offer buffer queuing controls. Since the pub-sub paradigm is actually the sibling of the message queuing paradigm, it shares many network principles with it. Most contemporary messaging systems support both the message queue and pub-sub models in their API in order to handle the widest range of use cases. Programmers of Java applications use the Java Message Service (JMS), which is one such example.

Subscribers in the pub-sub model usually receive a portion of all messages published. This is a critical feature because it reduces the overall system load associated with message delivery, accounting, and maintenance while also easing the load on applications related to message processing. Message filtering is the process of choosing which messages to receive and process. Topic-based and content-based filtering are the two most popular types.

Messages are published to topics in a topic-based system, which are similar to logical channels in a broadcast system or that symbolize logical sets. Under a topic-based system, subscribers will only receive messages published to the topics they have subscribed to. The same messages will be sent to all subscribers on a given topic, usually in the same order that they were published. It is not possible to assume that all messaging systems take message ordering and buffering into account because some messaging systems do, and some do not. It is crucial that the publisher first defines the classes of messages to which subscribers can subscribe in order for them to understand the messages. In the event that this isn't done, unsubscribed messages are just ignored (i.e., disregarded) by every member.

On the other hand, a content-based system only sends messages to a subscriber if the content or attributive matches the subscriber-defined constraints. This is comparable to configuring email search filters that match specific message fields. Messages that match are categorized into a unique folder. In this instance, the message is delivered instead of being disregarded, but otherwise it is the same. The subscriber must categorize the messages, just like the publisher in a topic-based approach, or else they will be ignored.

It should be noted that a lot of messaging systems allow subscribers to simultaneously register content-based subscriptions to topics, and publishers can post messages to a topic in a hybrid of the two approaches. Many pub-sub systems allow users to register their subscriptions with a broker, who then handles the filtering on their behalf. Publishers post messages to an event bus or middleman message broker under this model. In order to buffer messages and prevent loss in the event of congestion, the broker typically executes a store and forward function. A message is routed from publishers to subscribers once it reaches the top of its queue. The broker may also give messages in a queue priority before routing. A broker can simply duplicate every message sent over the system so that it can be replayed at a later date because it keeps track of every message that is sent. This is an important feature of such a system because, if one imagines a broker replicating messages to a backup broker that can take over in case this broker somehow stops functioning, it can provide both a high-availability function and a troubleshooting or diagnostic function.

This design pattern's ability to allow subscribers to sign up for particular messages at build, initialization, or runtime is an intriguing feature. This model's adaptability is what makes it so helpful and extensively used. Certain software products and frameworks employ XML configuration files for the purpose of registering subscribers. This approach is known as data-driven, as it can adapt to changes in system configuration, local conditions, or attributes. Publishers do not even need to be aware of subscribers because they are only tangentially linked to them. This is a crucial component of the strategy since it eliminates the need for publishers and subscribers to maintain tabs on each other's financial situation and other details. This is the broker's responsibility; although it creates a single point of failure, it also has the advantage of centralizing these tasks. This implies that once a publisher or subscriber registers with a broker, there is essentially no configuration because publishers and subscribers are also kept in the dark about system topology. This implies that when more people subscribe or unsubscribe to topics, content, or the system as a whole, neither publishers nor subscribers are affected. This implies that any particular element can carry on as usual, independent of the status of all other publishers or subscribers.

Naturally, if a publisher disappears (i.e., crashes, virtual machine paused, CPU busy, etc.), neither the system nor subscribers will receive any more messages from that publisher. It is crucial that each element's state is only tangentially related to the states of the others. Alternatively, a client may not be able to post messages to the server while the server process is not running, and the server may not be able to receive messages unless the client is operating. This is in contrast to the conventional tightly coupled client-server paradigm. The fact that the majority of pub-sub systems can temporally separate subscribers from publishers is an intriguing implementation strategy. To enable subscribers to process a backlog of messages, for instance, a publisher may be disabled. This would limit subscribers' processor usage and messaging bandwidth.

Compared to conventional tightly coupled client-server techniques, the pub-sub model offers the possibility of greater scalability because it allows for parallel operation, message caching, and tree-based or network-based routing. In addition to having superior scalability, the system may be more highly available than the conventional ones. One strategy, for instance, would be to run two publishers simultaneously, as previously mentioned, to give the system some resilience. In this scenario, the generality of the system would not be compromised if one publisher crashed or was taken offline for maintenance while the other continued. Through web syndication protocols like RSS, Atom, and XMPP, the pub-sub paradigm has demonstrated its scalability to volumes far beyond those of a single data center, enabling distributed messaging across the Internet. In order to support large numbers of subscribers, these syndication protocols accept higher latency as well as a decrease in or complete loss of delivery guarantees.

The decoupling of the publisher and subscriber is one of the pub-sub approach's most significant issues. The problem lies in the fact that a broker in a pub-sub system might be programmed to deliver messages for a predetermined amount of time before ceasing to try, regardless of whether it has confirmation from every subscriber that the message was successfully received. A pub-sub system that is designed in this way cannot ensure that messages are delivered to any applications that might need that assurance. Unawareness of this restriction by publishers or subscribers may lead to synchronization problems and other consistency problems. Paradoxically, tightening up the coupling between the publisher and subscriber pair designs is one way to get around this restriction. To achieve assured delivery, this needs to be enforced outside of the pub-sub architecture, which makes this approach undesirable because it places more work on the application programmer.

Using a pub-sub model for inter-controller communication is another example. With this loosely coupled approach, controllers can relay or convey status to one another, allowing them to carry out their necessary tasks without stopping to process, send, or receive messages from other controllers. Lastly, this can also be applied in situations where a controller is desired to be accessed by numerous applications. The pub-sub model can be implemented by installing a broker separately from the controller to mediate, process, and maintain communication between the controller and applications, thereby improving the scalability of the communications between the controller and applications.

4.3.2. XMPP

One example of a pub-sub protocol is the Extensible Messaging and Presence Protocol (XMPP), which has been used to create several publish-sub systems. A communications protocol called XMPP is built on top of XML, or extensible markup language. Near real-time instant messaging, presence data, and pretty much any other type of information that needs to be shared with a subscription group can all be provided via the protocol. As its name implies, it was intended to be extensible, and it has been so on several occasions over the years.

XMPP is an open protocol that has been IETF standardized. The Jabber Software Foundation was renamed as the XMPP Standards Foundation, and it is actively working on developing open XMPP extensions in addition to these core protocols that are standardized at the IETF. Jabber, Google Talk, and Facebook Messenger are just a few of the many implementations that have been created and made available. The architecture of XMPP is quite decentralized and comparable to email in that anyone can operate their own XMPP server; there isn't a single master server that users must connect to or authenticate with. Private groups of publishers and subscribers can, of course, be established. For instance, in the controller and application example we provided in the pub-sub section, this is the case. Like the message broker we discussed in the pub-sub section, the server itself functions. It takes care of all the necessary message passing and registration. In order to register with the server, publishers and subscribers use a topic-based approach, which filters users based on their participation in what amounts to a group discussion. Multiple conversations can be supported by servers. For instance, a lot of instant messaging servers enable several private, multiway chats between user groups at once.

The XMPP network employs a pub-sub client-server architecture, meaning that clients register with a central server that serves as the pub-sub broker function instead of communicating with one another directly. This indicates that clients and servers have a loose coupling and benefit from all of the previously mentioned advantages. Unlike instant messaging services like Facebook Messenger or Google Talk, which have a global authoritative server, the architecture is decentralized by design. This can occasionally cause confusion because many people subscribe to the public XMPP server hosted at jabber.org. But that's limited to that user community. Others can—and currently do—run their own XMPP servers on separate domains or integrated into application frameworks unrelated to these open implementations. Every system user in the XMPP architecture has a distinct Jabber ID. We use the term "user" loosely here because, in the pub-sub paradigm, it really refers to either an application that serves as a publisher, a subscriber, or both. The typical structure of a Jabber ID is similar to that of an email address, consisting of a username, domain name, and IP address, in order to prevent the need for a central server to keep track of IDs. An at symbol (@) can be added after the username to provide additional information about the server that the user is residing on, for example, username@ex ample.com. Although common, this is not necessary, and in fact, it may not work with frameworks that use XMPP. It is very possible to use other localized naming schemes in these situations.

A message priority notation is present in the XMPP system. As we previously discussed, certain pub-sub systems use queuing to deliver messages. An ordered/priority queuing strategy is used in this instance. In order to achieve this, when a resource registers with a server, it may provide a numerical value known as a priority. Messages addressed to that person will be given the proper priority. The largest numerical value designates the highest priority. It should be mentioned that messages sent through the XMPP system are also accepted without a username. These are utilized for controlling the server's unique features and sending out system messages.

The utilization of HTTP and WebSocket transports for XMPP is a significant and captivating deviation from the standard XMPP deployment paradigm. Transmission Control Protocol (TCP) over IP is the original and native transport protocol for XMPP. Long-lasting TCP connections were used for this encoding, and users were free to define and specify the format of the XML streams.

The XMPP community has also developed an HTTP transport for web clients and users behind specific restricted firewalls as an alternative to the TCP transport. XMPP had two options for using HTTP in the original specification: binding models or polling modes. Since the polling method is outdated, we won't be using it.

Through synchronous HTTP, bidirectional streams are used to implement the binding method. With this technique, servers can send messages to clients asynchronously as soon as they're prepared for delivery. This method's popularity stems from the fact that it is far more effective than the outdated polling method. Another benefit of using an HTTP transport is that, in the majority of cases, firewalls don't cause problems for clients trying to fetch and post messages because of port filtering or blocking. By using this method, a server can simply process XMPP-encapsulated traffic as it arrives by listening on standard HTTP or HTTPS ports.

4.3.3. Google's Protocol Buffers

Google's extensible, language-and platform-neutral method for serializing structured data is called a protocol buffer. Google's coders identified shortcomings in both XML and JSON, so they developed protocol buffers as an improvement.

The major refinement of protocol buffers has been to make XML smaller and denser through the use of a binary encoding. One of the downsides to using XML is that while it is presented in a human-readable format, it is quite verbose in terms of the amount of characters that need to be transmitted to convey the same information that one would with a comparative binary format. This in fact was one of the arguments against using NETCONF (versus SNMP) in the early days of NETCONF. Recall that we discussed the relative merits of these earlier, and one of those was the speed at which SNMP could process requests due to its compact, binary format. While it was in a compact format, searching for which information to act on could take considerable time. Approaches such as those in protocol buffers do not necessarily suffer from either limitation. However, in general, the question one has to ask when comparing these approaches is whether or not the compactness outweighs the ability for humans to quickly inspect and understand the text. One way to help decide is whether or not the format will be used for internal or external APIs. In general, the consensus seems to be that it's a good idea to use binary-encoded APIs only for internally consumed APIs and use human-readable ones (i.e., XML, JSON, etc.) for public-facing ones.

A structured data format that is subsequently exchanged and serialized in protocol buffers can only be defined in one way. In a. proto file, this is accomplished by defining a buffer message type. The information in this format is then represented logically by each protocol buffer message. Then, each message uses this syntax to contain a list of name-value pairs. Here is a very basic example of a .proto file that defines a message containing information for an address book entry:

```
message PersonalRecord {
        required string nameFirst = 1;
        required string nameLast = 2;
        required string streetAddress = 3;
        optional string emailAddress = 3;
        enum PhoneType {
                MOBILE = 0;
                HOME = 1;
                WORK = 2;
                HOME_OFFICE = 3;
        }
```

```
        message PhoneNumber {
                required string internationalNumber = 1;
                optional PhoneType type = 2 [default = MOBILE];
                }
        repeated PhoneNumber phone = 4;
}
```

The format of the message is very simple. There is one or more uniquely numbered fields for each type of message, and each field has a name and a value type. Be aware that values can also be numbers (i.e., Booleans, strings, raw bytes, integer or floating-point), or other protocol buffer message types (as in the preceding example). With the help of these other kinds, data can be organized hierarchically in a way that is flexible and customizable to the requirements of the application. We demonstrated that repeated fields, required fields, and optional fields can all be specified in the previous example by indicating that four entries are repeated in the PhoneNumber portion.

Several protocol buffer compiler tools are available that can generate source code from data structure types to write and read them once the types and formats have been defined. These tools are available for many different languages, such as Java, Python, Perl, and C++, and for many different types of data streams. One of the protocol buffer compilers is used for a specific target language after messages have been defined. The .proto file or files are fed into this compiler, which produces data access classes. This procedure includes the generation of access functions for every field (i.e., query(), or set_query()) in addition to functions for serializing or parsing the pre-defined data structures to and from raw bytes. For example, if C++ is your preferred language, the compiler using the previous example will produce a class named PersonalRecord. The Person protocol buffer messages can then be filled, serialized, sent, and retrieved by using this class in your application.

Protocol buffers have the very cool feature of ignoring structures with additional fields not defined in the version of the code compiled when code is generated for message reception. This implies that precise alignment between the opposing viewpoints is not necessary. This is permitted since the designers of the system were worried about the need for server upgrades due to the quick evolution of APIs and wanted to avoid having to upgrade every server at once. While this might not seem like a big deal on a small scale, updating tens of thousands of servers in a short amount of time can definitely be problematic for a large company like Google. Getting back to the example, if you examine the newly generated C++ code, you can imagine populating these classes and using them to transmit a message such as the following:

```
PersonalRecord personalRec;
personalRec.set_name("David Blowfish");
personalRec.set_id(420420420420);
personalRec.set_email("blowfish@lovestogrowgrapes.com");
fstream output("someFile," ios::out | ios::binary);
personalRec.SerializeToOstream(&output);
```

To read the message, you would execute the following:

```
fstream input("someFile," ios::in | ios::binary);
PersonalRecord personalRec;
personalRec.ParseFromIstream(&input);
cout << "Name: " << personalRec.name() << endl;
cout << "E-mail: " << personalRec.email() << endl;
```

Protocol buffers have an interesting feature in that their format is self-describing, which is highly desirable for APIs used in SDN contexts. This is due to the fact that those APIs can be used to dynamically interpret the syntax or semantics in addition to generating code. This is also true if the code is changed because it is generated, which implies that an application has the ability to recognize incompatibility and update itself by inquiring about the updated API. Protocol buffers are used to define self-describing data persistent storage in addition to being used for transient Remote Procedure Call (RPC) requests. Nowadays, protocol buffers are the go-to option for data formatting at major data center providers like Google and many others. They are utilized for persistent data storage as well as in RPC systems.

4.3.4. Thrift

A language for defining interfaces, Thrift is used to define and build services for multiple languages. Similar to protocol buffers, it serves as a framework for remote procedure calls, or RPCs. Similar to protocol buffers, Thrift was created to meet the expanding requirements of Facebook, an application content service provider. Facebook faced difficulties akin to those Google faced several years prior when it first started operating large-scale data centers. Though Thrift's compiler can produce code in several languages, the program is written in C++. Like protocol buffers, Thrift combines a code generation engine to build services with multiprogramming language support, although in the spirit of Facebook's much more flexible development environment, Thrift supports a very wide variety of generated languages including C++, Erlang, Go, Haskell, Perl, Cappuccino, Python, C#, Perl, Ruby, Smalltalk, Node.js, and PHP.

The project was given by Facebook to the Apache Software Foundation in April 2007, and it is currently being developed there. As previously indicated, Thrift comes with a full software library that can be used to build servers and clients, along with an RPC mechanism that makes communication easier. The functional architecture of a Thrift client and server is depicted in Figure 4.7. The Thrift service definition file is used to generate the read()/write() code and service client. The Thrift compiler receives this file and uses it to produce client and processor code, which is then added to the client and server code. Included in the client and server base as a precompiled library, the runtime library includes the protocol and transport layer depicted in Figure 4.7.

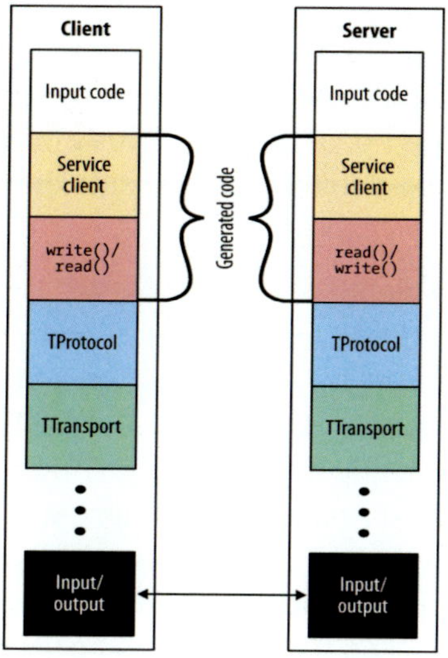

Figure 4.7. *The Apache thrift API client/server architecture.*

Source: Thomas, D. N., & Ken, G.; SDN: Software Defined Networks; ISBN: 978-1-449-34230-2.

The basic Thrift library encompasses server architecture for managing the fundamental I/O requests. Similar to Google's protocol buffers, Thrift allows for the definition of a service and the alteration of the protocol and transport without requiring a code recompile. This is enabled by the generation of code from definition files, along with the capability to disregard unknown fields. Thrift is flexible enough to accommodate a variety of protocols, catering to different application needs. For instance, Thrift supports TBinaryProtocol, a basic binary format that can be utilized when raw textual format is not suitable due to performance concerns. Another example is TJSON Protocol, which incorporates JSON encoding of data. Thrift supports numerous protocols overall.

This is an example of a Thrift service description file:

```
enum PhoneType {
        HOME,
        WORK,
        MOBILE
}
struct Phone {
        1: i32 id,
        2: string phoneNum,
        3: PhoneType type
}
```

As you can see, this code is quite similar to how structures would be defined in C++, which (for those familiar with that language) should be straightforward. Thrift will generate the code out of this descriptive information. For instance, in Java, the PhoneType will be a simple enum inside the C++ class Phone.

4.3.5. JSON

JSON, also referred to as JavaScript Object Notation, is a simple format for exchanging data. The fact that JSON is based on XML and is therefore simple for people to read and write is one of its key selling points. Additionally, machines can parse and generate it fairly easily. Although JSON is a completely language-independent text format, programmers working in the C-family of languages—C, C++, C, Java, JavaScript, Perl, and Python—are likely familiar with its conventions. These characteristics make JSON a very attractive language for data exchange, and it has shown to be very effective when building APIs for SDN controllers and applications.

The basic idea behind JSON is the interplay between two structures: an ordered list of values and a collection of name/value pairs. This is realized as an object, record, or struct, among other things, in different languages. An ordered list of values is referred to as an array, or list, in most programming languages. Though the exact form varies from language to language, these constructs are supported by the majority of modern programming languages. It makes sense that these structures would also serve as the foundation for a data format that is compatible with programming languages. The data format in JSON can take these forms.

An object is an unordered set of name/value pairs. An object begins with a { (left brace) and ends with a } (right brace). Each name is followed by a colon (:) and the name/value pairs are separated by a comma (,). The following is an example of a JSON definition:

{"menu": {
"header": "SVG Viewer,"
"items": [
{"id": "Open"},
{"id": "OpenNew," "label": "Open New"},
null,
{"id": "ZoomIn," "label": "Zoom In"},
{"id": "ZoomOut," "label": "Zoom Out"},
{"id": "OriginalView," "label": "Original View"},
null,
{"id": "Quality"},
{"id": "Pause"},
{"id": "Mute"},
null,
{"id": "Find," "label": "Find…"},
{"id": "FindAgain," "label": "Find Again"},
{"id": "Copy"},
{"id": "CopyAgain," "label": "Copy Again"},
{"id": "CopySVG," "label": "Copy SVG"},
{"id": "ViewSVG," "label": "View SVG"},
{"id": "ViewSource," "label": "View Source"},
{"id": "SaveAs," "label": "Save As"},
null,
{"id": "Help"},
{"id": "About," "label": "About Adobe CVG Viewer…"}
]
}}

4.4. I2RS

Tom Nadeau, Ping Pan, Alia Atlas, and David Ward were among the group that started considering standardizing programmability ideas, such as network topology, (rapid) device programming, and a controller's northbound interface. These were all central to the SDN debate, although there were numerous interpretations, explanations, and applications of these ideas. In certain instances, there were incomplete standards in place or being developed, and in others, the components' future was up to a closed forum. These reasons gave rise to the idea of doing this work at the IETF, a body renowned for producing open and high-quality standards. We were able to get the organization off the ground after a lot of organizing and writing work. It is currently known as the Interface to the Routing System (or I2RS, as the IETF abbreviation for it) at the IETF.

There are three key aspects at the head of the I2RSL:

- First, the interface is a modern programmatic interface much in the sense that we have been discussing in this chapter (meaning that it is asynchronous and offers fast, interactive access). It should be self-describing and easily consumed and/or manipulated by modern applications and programming methods.
- Second, the I2RS gives access to information and state that is not normally modeled or manipulated by existing implementations or configuration protocols. For example, this might be the active forwarding table of a device.
- Third, the I2RS gives applications the ability to learn additional, structured information, such as topology and events, from a device. This information will be offered in a manner that is filterable in order to support flexibility, scalability and ease of consumption by applications.

In order to assess the viability and applicability of I2RS for various use cases, an initial survey and analysis of the mechanisms in place were conducted. SNMP and NETCONF were the last competitors since they both supported writing and reading of state to and from devices, but they ultimately fell short of meeting all the essential requirements specified for I2RS. For instance, modern applications find the overhead of programming within the SNMP infrastructure to be relatively costly. Furthermore, many MIBs are not suitable for configuring a device's state because they are not (by definition or in practice) implemented in a read-only manner.

It was found that adding new application-specific state to be distributed via the routing system is extremely limited in the case of NETCONF. While NETCONF has many helpful features, including configuration replay, rewind, and verification, these can be time-consuming and are not recommended for quickly configuring devices that may already have these functions handled by an external SDN controller. The interface might also need to create ephemeral state in the target due to the nature of RIB data and the possibility of high transaction rates in SDN programmatic interfaces. This is a flaw in a lot of the current interfaces, like NETCONF. In light of this, the I2RS effort has produced recommendations that increase its capacity to generate and control ephemeral state.

A few interesting use cases around I2RS are:

1. **Route Control via Indirection:** Enabling an application to install routes in the RIB may result in an application-installed route being used, for instance, when BGP uses the RIB to resolve its IGP next-hop. Generally speaking, the RIB is used to redistribute a route from one protocol to another. The I2RS interface could have been used to install such a route.
2. **Policy-based Routing of Unknown Traffic:** Installing a static route within the RIB could guide traffic that would not otherwise be recognized toward an application for additional handling, via whatever tunnel that may be necessary. An indirection program could be used to program a static route like this, such that its outgoing path is whatever is used by another specific route (e.g., to a specific server).
3. **Services with Fixed Hours:** An application could install a specific route in the RIB of the local router and use the IGP to advertise the associated prefix as being attached to the local router if it were limited to providing services during certain times. The installed state could be temporary and automatically removed at roughly the appropriate time if the application was aware of the set hours.

Today, there are many management interfaces available that let the routing system be indirectly programmed. These consist of SNMP, NETCONF, and the proprietary CLI. All of these methods do not, however, enable the direct, quick, and application-friendly programming of a device's routing system. Applications that are time-based and dynamic require such asynchronous interfaces to function.

Instead of forcing applications to use outdated mechanisms that are more difficult to comprehend, implement, and use, these interfaces should take into account how applications normally interact with one another and with network services. Applications should be able to access the network with restricted, filtered, or abstracted knowledge thanks to the interfaces. In order for a network application that is granted some access to I2RS but is not entirely under the network operator's control to use it, authorization and authentication are also essential. The standard data models and their corresponding semantics are being developed by the I2RS working group.

Although many routing protocols have been standardized, the corresponding data models have not yet been made available. Instead, every router has its own set of data, protocols, and CLI, which makes creating and maintaining a standard interface for use by applications very difficult.

There are well-known data modeling languages like YANG, which have some data models in progress and could be used to define the required data models for I2RS; however, further research into alternatives is needed. It is acknowledged that future extensions and proprietary extensions must be supported by the data models; ideally, only a small portion of the data will remain as proprietary extensions.

In order to facilitate communication between the application and the routing system, a protocol-defined transfer syntax must be provided by at least one standard mechanism that has been identified and defined.

This is necessary because the I2RS must facilitate remote access between applications running on hosts or servers and routers in the network. Request-reserve-commit, notifications, and acknowledgements are common features that I2RS must support.

The I2RS Working Group is currently in the process of defining suitable candidate protocols. The chosen protocols should ideally not require applications to comprehend and use current routing protocols in order to communicate with I2RS. Instead, these interfaces ought to be built using lightweight, quickly deployable techniques; technological approaches need to be assessed, but possible examples include JSON, XMPP, XML, and ReSTful web services. Self-describing features (e.g., a web services interface) so that programs can rapidly inquire about and discover a device's active capabilities. It might be advantageous to specify the local syntax as well (e.g., programming language APIs) that can be utilized by local applications on a router.

I2RS is expected to evolve over time, so it's critical that versioning and backward compatibility be fundamentally supported features. Similar to this, common, uniform error-handling and acknowledgement procedures that don't significantly impair these interfaces' scalability and responsiveness are needed. We will only speculate that, given the I2RS effort's relative youth, it has been somewhat successful in mobilizing the community to start defining the interfaces and other components needed to meet its ambitious objectives. Time will tell whether they are attainable or not.

4.5. MODERN ORCHESTRATION

In the last few years, it has become necessary to coordinate several essential components of data centers as well as networks. To achieve the fastest, least expensive, and most optimized deployments, it is especially necessary to motivate and monitor storage, compute, and storage within these deployment scenarios. These tasks were previously either completed manually or with antiquated, cumbersome management systems. To accomplish these goals, a few rather concurrent efforts have persisted to define standards as well as, more crucially, de facto standards based on open-source code that has been deployed and utilized in production data center environments, including those of Yahoo, Bloomberg, Rackspace, and other companies.

From an SDN perspective, the network-activation APIs from these efforts represents a subset of the capabilities of the API of an SDN controller (largely because of their focus on a specific application).

4.5.1. OpenStack

The goal of the international partnership OpenStack is to create the open standard cloud operating system for public and private clouds. Massively scalable cloud environments can be constructed using OpenStack, a software system licensed under the Apache license and available for free. In addition to the Common Project that unites them, OpenStack presently consists of numerous software projects (*see* Figure 4.8): OpenStack Image Service (code-named Glance), OpenStack Networking (code-named Quantum), OpenStack Compute (code-named Nova), OpenStack Object Storage (code-named Swift and Cinder), OpenStack Dashboard (code-named Horizon).

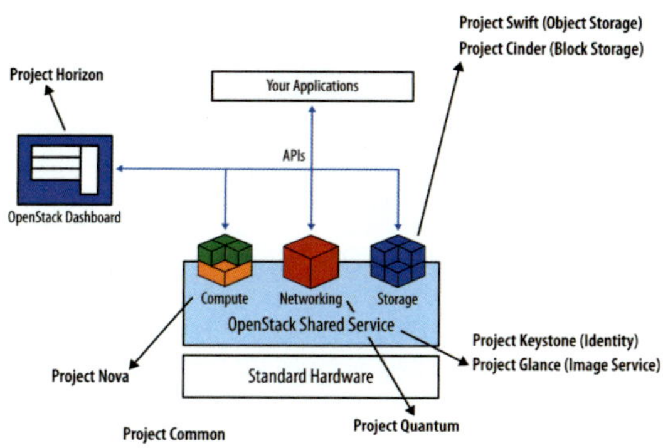

Figure 4.8. *Components of the OpenStack architecture.*

Source: Thomas, D. N., & Ken, G.; SDN: Software Defined Networks; ISBN: 978-1-449-34230-2.

The framework created by these projects can be expanded and plugged in to create an open-source operating system for both public and private clouds. Due to its tight integration with the most widely used hypervisors in the market, the OpenStack system has become more and more popular over the past year. Support for Xen, XenServer, KVM, LXC, QEMU, ESX, and Hyper-V are a few examples.

Open-source software called Swift and Cinder can be used to build scalable, redundant data storage by storing multiple blocks of accessible data in clusters of standard servers. It is a system for long-term, retrievable, and updateable storage of massive amounts of static data, not a filesystem or real-time data system. Using a distributed architecture, object storage avoids having a single point of failure. Along with the obvious benefits of scalability, redundancy, and performance, this also gives the user more deployment options.

For virtual disk images, Glance offers delivery, registration, and discovery services. A clear RESTful web services interface is offered by the Image Service API server for information queries regarding virtual disk images. OpenStack Object Storage is one of the backend stores where these disk images could be kept. Customers can utilize the Image Service's client library to stream virtual disk images, register new virtual disk images, and query for details on disk images that are made available to the general public. Subsequently, these pictures can be referred to in a manner similar to how a restaurant's menu can be presented to a customer. Figures 4.9 and 4.10 show how each of OpenStack's three components must first exist in order for an image to be launched (i.e., called upon through a hypervisor) and linked to virtual storage, and afterwards after an image is called.

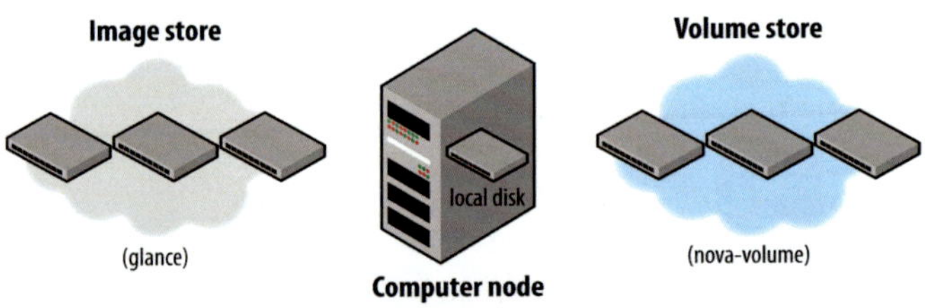

Figure 4.9. *Each of the three major components of OpenStack representing storage, compute, and image management.*

Source: Thomas, D. N., & Ken, G.; SDN: Software Defined Networks; ISBN: 978-1-449-34230-2.

Nova will not configure physical network interfaces but will automatically create all virtual network bridges (e.g., br100) and VM virtual interfaces (through the Nova network subset of functions). Nova assigns a private IP address to each VM instance it deploys. This address is then attached to the Linux Bridge via the nova-network API and then (potentially) to a NAT function that allows the virtual interfaces to connect to the outside network through the physical interface. The network controller with nova-network provides virtual networks to enable computer servers to interact with one another and with the public network.

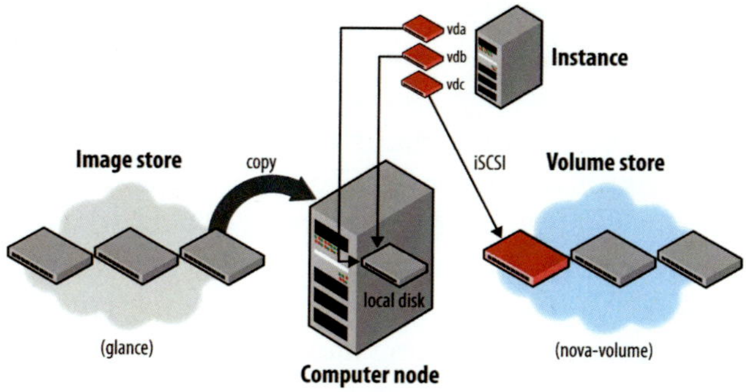

Figure 4.10. *Each of the three components after an instance creation has been implemented using one of the cataloged images.*

Source: Thomas, D. N., & Ken, G.; SDN: Software Defined Networks; ISBN: 978-1-449-34230-2.

Currently, Nova (nova-network) supports three kinds of networks, implemented in three Network Manager types: Flat Network Manager, Flat DHCP Network Manager, and the VLAN Network Manager. The three kinds of networks can coexist in a cloud system. Nova will automatically create all network bridges (i.e., br100) and VM virtual interfaces. All physical machines must have a public and internal network interface. Quantum provides the API that builds required network connectivity between OpenStack physical nodes (i.e., between the vNICs managed by OpenStack Nova—providing them network as a service functionality).

Because it focuses on delivering primitives needed for a single application—orchestration—the Quantum API is most relevant to discussions about SDN and network programmability. However, it should be noted that the Quantum API only exposes a subset of the capabilities that could be made available through the northbound API of the majority of SDN controllers, frameworks, and systems. The goal of quantum is to create sophisticated virtual topologies and services, such as the widely used layer 2-in-layer 3 overlay, which gets around the limitations of conventional VLAN-based deployments in larger deployments. In other words, Quantum uses an underlying topology made up of both virtual and physical systems with a wealth of capabilities to try and separate the what (service specification APIs) from the how (service implementation). Plug-ins, which can be distributed privately or as part of the public Quantum release, are used to deploy Open-Stack functionality. Vendors can support the standard API in network service configuration by hiding the details of their own backend implementations thanks to the plug-in architecture.

Simple L2 connectivity is offered by the API's current release (version 2.0) through seven to 10 plug-ins. Because of the plug-ins' single-service/single-device architecture, it is difficult to support a multivendor vSwitch environment. For instance, there are distinct plug-ins for Linux Bridge, OVS, and Cisco Nexxus. In a similar vein, the Ryu and NEC OpenFlow controllers each have their own plug-ins. Furthermore, physical devices are usually managed out of band and by hand (although an increasing number of network element providers are offering their own plug-ins). Version 2.0 introduces two implicit semantics to the term "network": a grouping of ports and services (layer 2 connectivity) and services provided to ports (working under the premise that the grouping of ports was necessary only to provide them with network layer 2 connectivity).

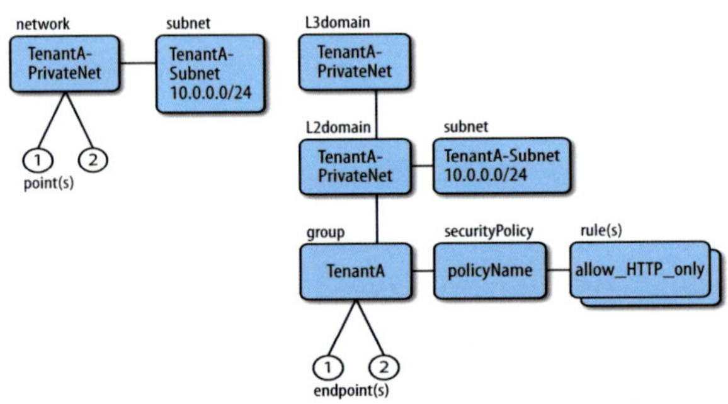

Figure 4.11. *The elements and relationships of quantum version 2.0 (left) and the proposed elements and relationships of quantum version 3.0 (right).*

Source: Thomas, D. N., & Ken, G.; SDN: Software Defined Networks; ISBN: 978-1-449-34230-2.

The network (connectivity service), subnet (policy), and port (tenant endpoint) are the components of version 2.0. The Quantum API, also known as Grizzly, is currently in the proposal stage with version 3.0. Among the suggestions are layer 3 network APIs (e.g., VPN), the inclusion of APIs for network services (e.g., load balancing, security, and possibly a shift in the direction of a multiservice/multivendor plug-in architecture. A sketch of the variations between the elements and relationships in Quantum versions 2.0 and 3.0 can be found in Figure 4.11.

4.5.2. CloudStack

Building public, private, and hybrid Infrastructure as a Service (IaaS) clouds is possible with the help of CloudStack, a platform for cloud orchestration. A cloud infrastructure's network, storage, and compute nodes are managed by CloudStack. Because of its hierarchical structure, a CloudStack cloud can scale to oversee tens of thousands of physical servers from a single management interface.

4.5.2.1. Availability Zones

The largest organizational unit in a CloudStack deployment is called an Availability Zone. Although a data center (DC) implementation will typically have one Zone, there are no hard and fast rules, and a DC may have more than one Zone. Virtual instances and data storage can be placed in particular locations to adhere to an organization's data storage policies, etc., by organizing CloudStack into geographical Zones. A minimum of one Pod and shared Secondary Storage are the components of an Availability Zone. End users can choose which Zone to create their virtual instances in after seeing the zones. All users can see a public zone, but you can also create private zones that are only accessible to members of a specific domain and any subdomains that are associated with it (Figure 4.12).

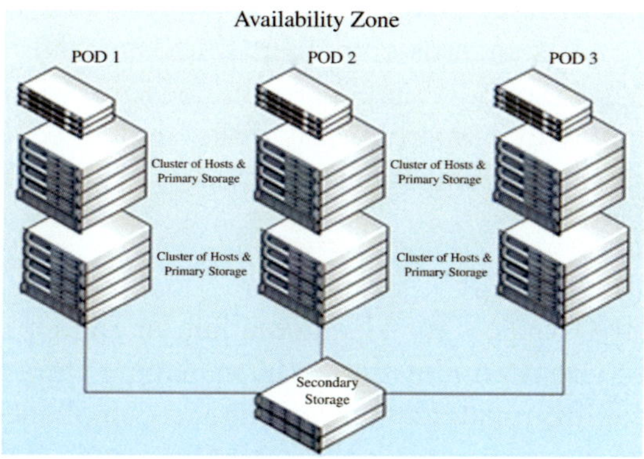

Figure 4.12. *A CloudStack availability zone.*

Source: Thomas, D. N., & Ken, G.; SDN: Software Defined Networks; ISBN: 978-1-449-34230-2; https://www.shapeblue.com/wp-content/uploads/2023/11/Availability-Zone.gif.

4.5.2.2. Pods

A group of hardware components arranged to create clusters is called a pod. A pod is typically a rack with one or more clusters and a shared Layer 2 switch architecture among all the clusters in the pod. End users are not conscious of or able to see Pods.

4.5.2.3. Clusters

A cluster is a collection of homogeneous hosts that share a hypervisor. A pre-configured VMware cluster in vCenter, a set KVM server, or a pool of XenServers could all be examples of clusters. The virtual machine instances are housed on a specific Primary Storage device for each Cluster. High Availability and Load Balancing are standard features of a CloudStack deployment with multiple Hosts within a Cluster.

4.5.2.4. Secondary Storage

Snapshots, ISO images, and virtual machine templates are kept on secondary storage. All PODs in a Zone can access the storage, and it can also be automatically replicated between Availability Zones, giving the entire Cloud a common storage platform. The Network File System (NFS) is used by secondary storage to guarantee that any host in the zone can access it.

4.5.2.5. Primary Storage

Every cluster has a distinct primary storage system that houses the virtual machine instances. All standards-compliant iSCSI and NFS servers that the underlying hypervisor supports are compatible with CloudStack. A high-performance system with numerous fast disks should be used for primary storage, as it is an essential component.

4.5.3. Puppet

One of a set of software tools for IT automation, or DevOps tools, is Puppet. These tools assist system administrators in managing infrastructure at every stage of its lifecycle, from patch management and compliance to provisioning and configuration. A diagram of the Puppet DevOps management cycle is shown in Figure 4.13. IT managers can swiftly deploy vital apps, automate tedious operations, and proactively manage change servers with Puppet. In addition to being open source, Puppet comes in a number of commercial enterprise editions.

Puppet automates IT using a declarative, model-based methodology. An IT administrator can effortlessly specify the intended configuration state of the infrastructure by utilizing Puppet's declarative configuration language, thanks to this language. Before implementing configuration changes, it enables an administrator to simulate them. It makes it possible for the deployed infrastructure to automatically enforce the desired state. Administrators can also use this to undo any changes they may have made to the configuration. In the end, Puppet gives an administrator reports that they can use to identify discrepancies between the desired and actual states of the infrastructure, as well as any modifications made to enforce the desired state.

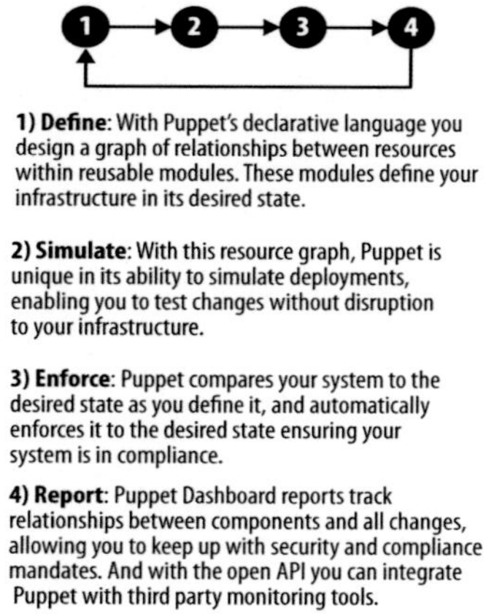

Figure 4.13. *Puppet DevOps high-level management cycle.*

Source: Thomas, D. N., & Ken, G.; SDN: Software Defined Networks; ISBN: 978-1-449-34230-2.

Initially, one must choose from pre-built, freely down-loadable configuration modules or create custom modules using Puppet's configuration language in order to define the desired state of an infrastructure. Once defined, these configurations can be used to manage and orchestrate infrastructure components across operating systems and in physical, virtual, and cloud environments. To build entire application configuration stacks, configuration modules can also be added, removed, or mixed and matched.

For instance, these stacks can be helpful when incorporated with SDN controllers or infrastructure management software. Once set up, every infrastructure node's Puppet agent automatically updates the Puppet master server about its current state by periodically communicating with it. The puppet master can then decide whether to monitor and report any deviations from the expected configurations, or it can instruct the nodes to maintain the desired states. The node's Puppet agent communicates with the Puppet master server by sending back what the Puppet architecture refers to as facts or data regarding the node's status. This is carried out on a recurring basis or in response to an occurrence. With the help of these details, the Puppet master server creates a catalog—a comprehensive collection of data regarding the optimal configuration for the node. The Puppet agent receives this data back on a regular basis. A diagram of the Puppet configuration/provisioning cycle can be found in Figure 4.14.

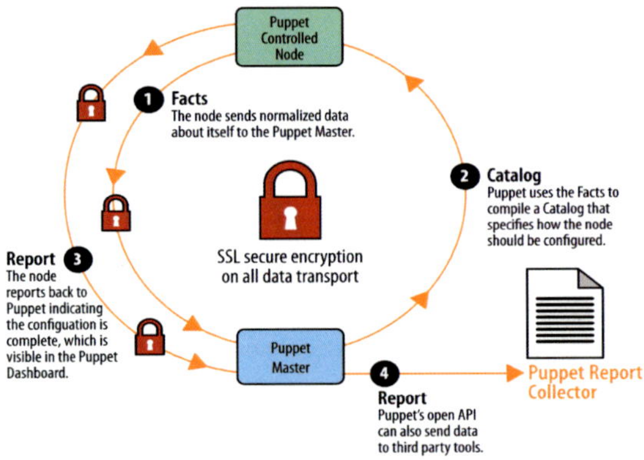

Figure 4.14. *Puppet configuration/provisioning cycle (specific).*

Source: Thomas, D. N., & Ken, G.; SDN: Software Defined Networks; ISBN: 978-1-449-34230-2.

The Puppet agent sends the Puppet master a comprehensive report after making the necessary adjustments to get back to the desired state. The reports can be integrated with other IT systems completely via open APIs. The possibility of running these reports in "no-op mode," which enables an administrator to simulate changes without actually altering the network elements, should be noted. For this reason, Puppet is a valuable planning and "what if?" scenario testing tool.

REFERENCES

1. Alexander, D. S., Arbaugh, W. A., Hicks, M. A., Kakkar, P., Keromytis, A., Moore, J. T., Nettles, S. M., & Smith, J. M. (1998). The SwitchWare active network architecture. *IEEE Network, 12*(3), 27–33.
2. Angin, O., Campbell, A. T., Kounavis, M. E., & Liao, R. R. F. (1998). The Mobiware toolkit: Programmable support for adaptive mobile networking. *IEEE Personal Communications, 5*(4), 31–37.
3. Brakmo, L., & Peterson, L. (1995). TCP Vegas: End to end congestion avoidance on a global Internet. *IEEE Journal on Selected Areas in Communications, 13*(8), 1465–1480.
4. Caini, C., & Firrincieli, R. (2004). TCP Hybla: A TCP enhancement for heterogeneous networks. *International Journal of Satellite Communications and Networking, 22*(6), 547–566.
5. Cataltepe, Z., & Moghe, P. (2003). Characterizing nature and location of congestion on the public Internet. In *Proceedings of the Eighth IEEE International Symposium on Computers and Communication* (pp. 324–329).
6. Chan, M. C., Huard, J. F., Lazar, A. A., & Lim, K. S. (1996). On realizing a broadband kernel for multimedia networks. In *Proceedings of the 3rd COST 237 Workshop on Multimedia Telecommunications and Applications* (pp. 1–6). Barcelona, Spain.
7. Chiu, D. M., & Jain, R. (1989). Analysis of the increase/decrease algorithms for congestion avoidance in computer networks. *Journal of Computer Networks, 17*(1), 1–14.
8. Jacobs, S. (2015). *Engineering Information Security: The Application of Systems Engineering Concepts to Achieve Information Assurance* (p. 367). John Wiley & Sons.
9. Mauro, D., & Schmidt, K. (2005). *Information Security Management Handbook* (6th ed., pp. 21–22). O'Reilly Media, Inc.
10. Schwartz, B., Jackson, W. A., Strayer, W. T., Zhou, W., Rockwell, R. D., & Partridge, C. (1999). Smart packets for active networks. In *Proceedings of the Second International Conference on Open Architectures and Network Programming (OPENARCH)* (pp. 99–110). New York.
11. Wetherall, D., Guttag, J., & Tennenhouse, D. (1998). ANTS: A toolkit for building and dynamically deploying network protocols. In *Proceedings of the IEEE OPENARCH'98* (pp. 1–12). San Francisco, CA.

CHAPTER 5

DATA CENTER CONCEPTS AND CONSTRUCTS

Contents

INTRODUCTION

In today's rapidly evolving technological landscape, data centers play a crucial role in the functioning of enterprises, cloud services, and the broader internet infrastructure. Traditional data centers, with their rigid hardware-centric models, are increasingly being challenged by the need for greater flexibility, scalability, and efficiency. This is where Software-Defined Networking (SDN) emerges as a transformative paradigm.

Software-Defined Networking (SDN) is an innovative approach that decouples the control plane from the data plane, enabling centralized and programmable network management. By abstracting the underlying network infrastructure, SDN allows for dynamic, automated, and efficient network configuration, which is essential for modern data center operations. This decoupling enables network administrators to manage network services through abstraction of lower-level functionality, simplifying the overall network design and operation.

The integration of SDN into data centers revolutionizes how networks are designed, deployed, and managed. Traditional data centers often face challenges related to scalability, resource utilization, and operational overhead. SDN addresses these challenges by providing a framework that supports automation, agility, and enhanced control over the network. With SDN, data centers can dynamically adjust to varying workloads, optimize resource allocation, and implement robust security measures with greater ease.

"Data Center Concepts and Constructs in Software-Defined Networking (SDN)," delves into the foundational elements and advanced topics related to data centers and SDN. Students will explore the architecture and components of modern data centers, understand the principles and mechanisms of SDN, and examine real-world applications and case studies. By the end of the course, participants will gain comprehensive knowledge of how SDN can be leveraged to build efficient, scalable, and resilient data center infrastructures, positioning them at the forefront of network innovation and management.

5.1. THE MULTITENANT DATA CENTER

One important observation about the Amazon AWS model is that, in addition to virtualizing its services, it now requires a different paradigm for resource management and access controls because, by allowing external users to access its network, it has effectively created a multitenant data center environment. Naturally, this led to the creation of a new challenge: how to divide up to thousands of tenants, each with resources that must be dispersed randomly among virtual machines in various physical data centers, while still providing them with ubiquitous, private Internet access to their own portion of the AWS cloud?

Noting that execution environments were typically managed by a single company or organization during the shift to hyper virtualized environments is another way to observe this conundrum. That is, they functioned as if they were a single, flat local area network (LAN) connecting a huge number of virtual or physical machines and network attached storage, owning and operating all of the computing and storage (though some rented co-location space). Financial institutions were an exception, as mandated by regulatory requirements requiring separation. On the other hand, in these instances, there were comparatively few departments (or tenants)—less than 100. The same private network IP address space was also used to address these departments. Using the readily available tools at the time, such as MPLS layer 2 or layer 3 VPNs, this was easily resolved. However, in both situations, the network components that had previously connected all of the computing and storage resources were fairly basic—typically, a flat Ethernet LAN linked all of the virtual and physical machines. Since a single enterprise owned the machines and required access to them, the majority of these environments assigned IP addresses to all of the devices—virtual or physical—in the network from a single network, possibly with IP subnets. Because all of the virtual machines in that enterprise were part of the same routed domain and could communicate with one another regardless of physical location, moving them between different data centers was also typically not a problem (Figure 5.1).

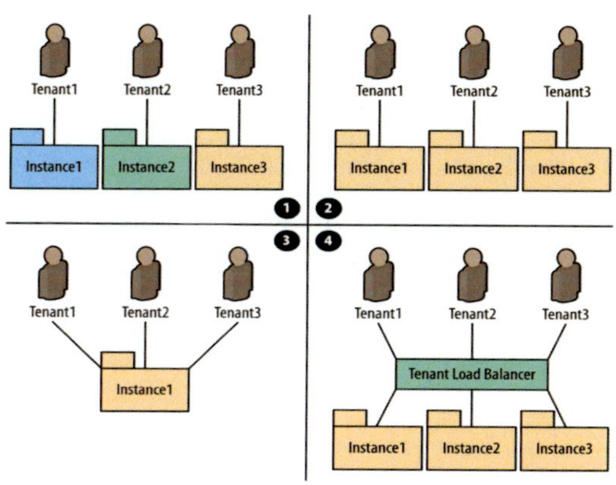

Figure 5.1. *Multitenant data center concept; in multitenant data centers, users must have access to virtual slices of compute, storage, and network resources that are kept private from other tenants.*

Source: Thomas, D. N., et al., (2013). SDN: Software Defined Networks, See http://oreilly.com/catalog/errata.csp?isbn=9781449342302.

Depending on the situation, the definition of a tenant can change. It entails being a client in a data center run by a service provider that offers public cloud services. It can refer to a department (which can be thought of as an internal customer) in an enterprise data center that is implementing a private cloud solution. While not synonymous with multiuser or multienterprise, multitenancy is distinct from these concepts. Above the user or enterprise boundary is where tenancy occurs. Multitenancy is not exclusive to Infrastructure as a Service (IaaS) data center offerings; it is also prevalent in private and public clouds. When cloud computing was starting to gain popularity in 2008, Phil Wainewright 1 attempted to define the term "multitenancy" as an architectural consideration that was set up at the application layer in a blog post. Tenants utilize a shared application environment or, depending on the blog, a specific portion of it. The degree of multitenancy was used to define the differences in the definition of multitenancy in the original posting. This idea centered on how much of the application is shared, all the way down to the database, where the structure of the database is defined by the schema. The example used was Salesforce.com, which at the time of the article was achieving an amazing 1:5000 database instance-to-customer ratio and had deployed a single schema (shared by all customers) that scaled on a distributed system using database replication technology.

By 2012, this idea was revisited, and several notable cloud architects were mapping the degree to common data center application/service archetypes:

1. **Infrastructure as a Service (IaaS):** Infrastructure (compute, storage, and network) are shared. Exemplified by Amazon.
2. **Platform as a Service (PaaS):** An application development environment is shared. Exemplified by Google Apps.
3. **Software as a Service (SaaS):** An application is shared. Exemplified by Salesforce.com.

The architects introduced a second axis of multitenancy (other than the degree to which schema are shared across customers). In this model:

- The highest degree of multitenancy occurs in the IaaS and PaaS aspects of the data center service–offering hierarchy.
- The overall highest degree of multitenancy occurs when all three aspects of the service offering, including SaaS, are fully multitenant.
- A middle-degree of multitenancy may be seen when IaaS and PaaS are multitenant, but SaaS is multitenant in physical clusters or for various subcomponents of SaaS.
- The lowest degree of multitenancy occurs when SaaS is single tenant.

The degree to which application components are tightly coupled to the network and security architectures needed to support them is described by these degrees. These dependencies are crucial for the mobility of a single virtual machine (VM) or the distributed but dependent collection of application/service components, or VM mobility—the poster child of SDN applications (Figure 5.2).

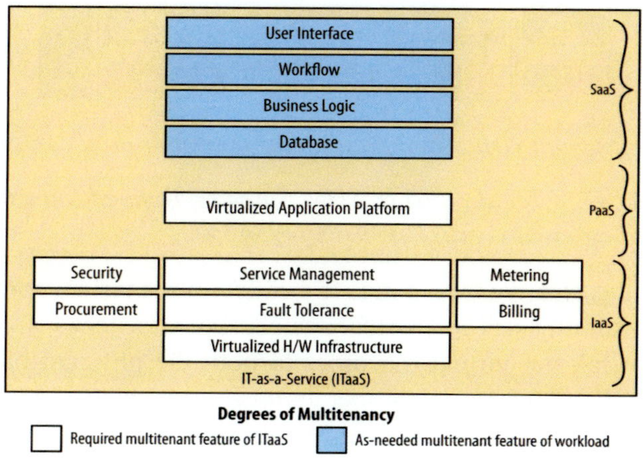

Figure 5.2. *Degrees of multitenancy.*

Source: Thomas, D. N., et al., (2013). SDN: Software Defined Networks, See http://oreilly.com/catalog/errata.csp?isbn=9781449342302.

We will examine the fundamental ideas of the multitenant data center, the architecture that goes along with it, and the various control plane options that are vying to be accepted as industry standards for SDN in data centers.

5.2. THE VIRTUALIZED MULTITENANT DATA CENTER

Multiple tenants can be hosted in a data center with private access to virtual slices of resources thanks to the virtualized multitenant data center. There's a chance the data center network has multiple tiers. A third tier, known as the aggregation tier, has emerged as a result of further growth, despite the original designs being a two-layer, spine-and-leaf structure. Another option for the data center is a single-tier network (e.g., Q-Fabric by Juniper (Figure 5.3).

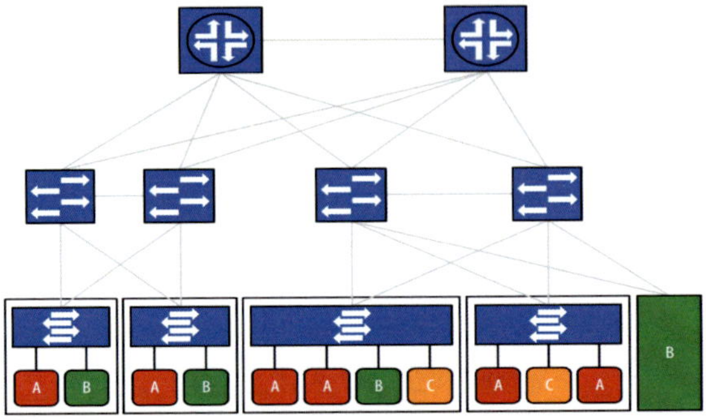

Figure 5.3. *Multitenant virtualized data center (multitier data center network).*

Source: Thomas, D. N., et al., (2013). SDN: Software Defined Networks, See http://oreilly.com/catalog/errata.csp?isbn=9781449342302.

Each tenant typically corresponds to a collection of virtual machines housed on hypervisor-running servers. Virtual switches, or vSwitches, are built into the hypervisors to link the virtual machines to both the physical network and to each other. Applications can also operate on a server that is bare metal. That is, as demonstrated by the B server in Figure 5.4's lower right corner, they are executed on a whole machine devoted to that application rather than running in a virtual machine. A physical network, usually a high-speed Ethernet network, is used to connect servers, though there are some variants that use optical rings instead. The network is shown as a two-tier layer 2 network (access, core). It might also be a layer 2 network with three tiers (access, aggregation, and core) or one tier (e.g., QFabric) network layer. The data center network may also be a layer 3 network (IP, GRE, or MPLS) for overlay solutions.

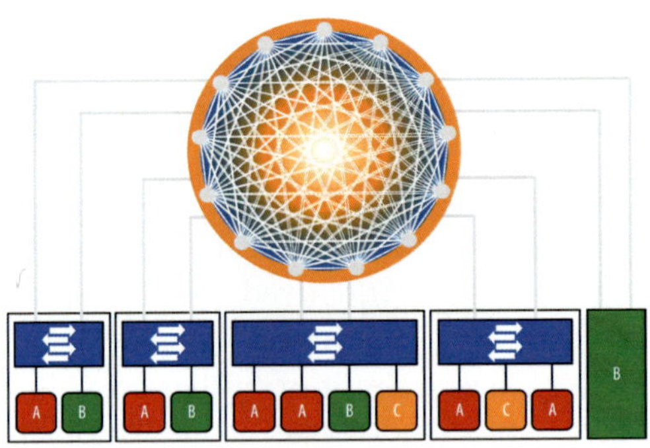

Figure 5.4. *Multitenant virtualized data center as a single-tier data center network (Ju - Niper's Q-Fabric).*

Source: Thomas, D. N., et al., (2013). SDN: Software Defined Networks, See http://oreilly.com/catalog/errata.csp?isbn=9781449342302.

A private network is allotted to every tenant. Subject to policy limitations, every service instance within a tenant's network can communicate with every other instance within that tenant.

In practice, this means that every physical or virtual machine hosting the service needs to be connected to the other machines in its logical tenant grouping via either layer 3 or layer 2 of the network. Tenant networks are segregated from one another; unless permitted by policy, a tenant's virtual machine cannot communicate with another tenant's virtual machine (Figure 5.5).

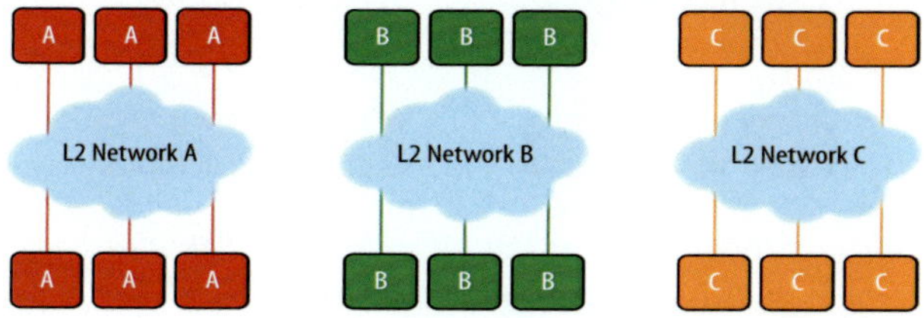

Figure 5.5. *Logical network abstraction as presented to tenants.*

Source: Thomas, D. N., et al., (2013). SDN: Software Defined Networks, See http://oreilly.com/catalog/errata.csp?isbn=9781449342302.

Virtual machines on a tenant network are configured within the same layer 3 IP subnet, and tenant private networks are typically layer 2 networks. The cloud provider may assign the IP addresses to the virtual machines (VMs), or the tenant may be able to choose his own.

In any case, it's possible that tenants' IP addresses aren't all the same (i.e., two virtual machines belonging to two distinct tenants may use the same IP address). If tenants are permitted to communicate with one another or with people outside the network (for example, by using the services via the public Internet), then a network address scheme (NAT) needs to be implemented.

For the purpose of establishing security zones, merging departments, as in the case of Infrastructure as a Service (IaaS), or using multiple cloud providers to host services, a single tenant may have multiple networks. An enterprise's local data center can be extended by connecting multiple cloud providers, as shown in Figure 5.6, to offer elastic cloud services.

The benefits of this configuration include geographic coverage for services that are deployed over a large geographic area, redundancy, and the utilization of the least expensive cloud provider resources (much like when electricity is consumed from multiple providers).

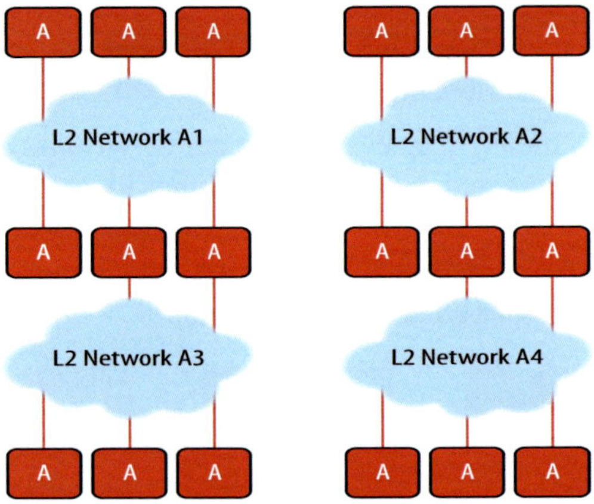

Figure 5.6. *Multiple networks for a tenant enterprise; tenant cloud networks A1, A2, A3, and A4 span multiple geographic and logical service providers to weave together a consistent yet virtual service offering for customer A.*

Source: Thomas, D. N., et al., (2013). SDN: Software Defined Networks, See http://oreilly.com/catalog/errata.csp?isbn=9781449342302.

5.2.1. Orchestration

Orchestration is a key component of a virtualized multitenant data center solution. A service provider needs to use logically centralized orchestration in order to deploy and administer a multitenant data center solution. In a data center, orchestration serves as a central point of control for other network controllers and gives network operators a logically centralized point of interaction and control. At a high level, the orchestration layer provides the capability of:

- Adding and removing tenants;
- Billing system interface after provisioning operations are executed;
- Workflow automation;
- Adding and removing virtual machines to and from tenants;
- Specifying the bandwidth, quality of service, and security attributes of a tenant network.

All aspects of the data center, such as interacting with the network, storage, compute, and storage systems or controllers, must be covered by this orchestration layer. And in order to facilitate true elastic compute services, it needs to do so at a high rate of change (Figure 5.7).

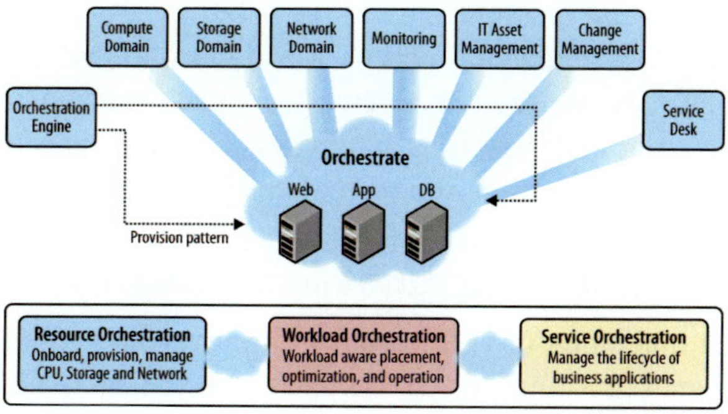

Figure 5.7. *Data center orchestration engine example; orchestration in a data center provides the logically centralized control and interaction point for network operators and is a central point of control of other network controllers.*

Source: Thomas, D. N., et al., (2013). SDN: Software Defined Networks, See http://oreilly.com/catalog/errata.csp?isbn=9781449342302.

5.2.2. Connecting a Tenant to the Internet/VPN

Tenants of data centers usually use a VPN to access their corporate network or the Internet. The VPN may be of the following types: L3 MPLS, L2 MPLS, SSL, IPsec, or another kind. The specific VPN type has a variety of benefits and drawbacks, and it also relies on the underlay network (such as Ethernet, VLANs, stacked VLANs, VxLAN, and MPLS) that is used in the data center (Figure 5.8).

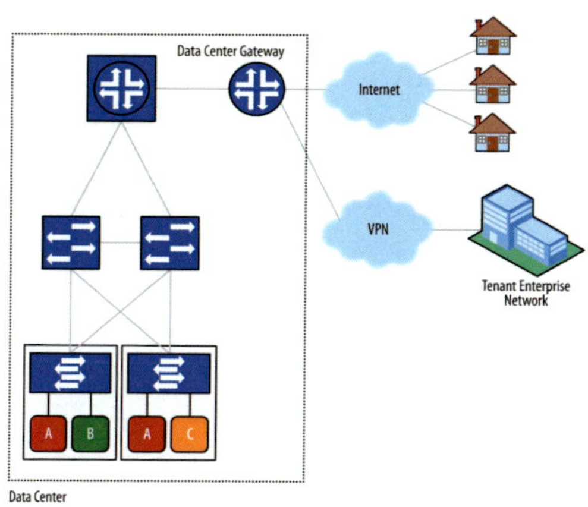

Figure 5.8. *Connect tenant to internet/VPN.*

Source: Thomas, D. N., et al., (2013). SDN: Software Defined Networks, See http://oreilly.com/catalog/errata.csp?isbn=9781449342302.

Tenant networks can be connected to the Internet, other VPN sites, or both through the data center gateway function. Keep in mind that, depending on the network architecture used, several gateways may be used. Although physical devices are still commonly used as gateways, software can also be used to implement the gateway function as a virtualized service.

5.2.3. Virtual Machine Migration and Elasticity

Moving a virtual machine (VM) from one compute server to another is known as virtual machine migration. This covers both instances in which it is operating and instances in which a virtual machine is dormant, paused, or shut down. The process typically entails a file copy between servers or storage arrays near the new computing resource (although this need not always be the case).

The motivations for VM migration include:

- Data center maintenance;
- Workload balance/rebalance/capacity expansion (including power management);
- Data center migration, consolidation or expansion;
- Disaster avoidance/recovery;
- Geographic locality (i.e., moving access to a service closer to users to improve their experience).

The simplest example to demonstrate is the notion that migration is restricted to a single server instance, given the previous definition of tenancy and the notion of the degree of tenancy. Sometimes the application is multitier, consisting of a closely coupled ensemble of virtual machines and network components. In this case, moving a single virtual machine could cause bandwidth and performance issues. The ensemble's dependencies must be known to the operator and/or orchestration system. But in other situations, where the different layers of an application are loosely coupled (i.e., VM migration, or more commonly, destruction and creation, usually only has positive effects on the service., compute, frontend load-balancer/web-services, and a backend distributed database), much as applications written to take advantage of Hadoop or other granular process distribution architectures. Live virtual machine migration is usually not used in these situations. In Figure 5.9, the three-tiered architecture is displayed. Each of the three layers of the system in the three-tiered architecture must be implemented by a single virtual machine (VM), but additional component VMs can be spun up at any time to run locally on the same compute server or remotely to adjust the amount of computing power available. This granular and elastic computing paradigm is made possible by technologies like Hadoop, which manage the seamless distribution of job processes, while

Cassandra, a technology, manages the seamless, easily scalable, and extremely resilient backend database functionality.

The frequency of live migration between data centers as a DCI use case is still up for debate. The justification is that a file copy of the running virtual machine (VM) to a new compute server is necessary for any migration to occur, and a VM cannot be running during the copy operation lest the file change. As a result, the practice of this operation is becoming less and less common. It is much easier (and safer) to switch to a three-tiered application architecture where creating and destroying machines is the standard.

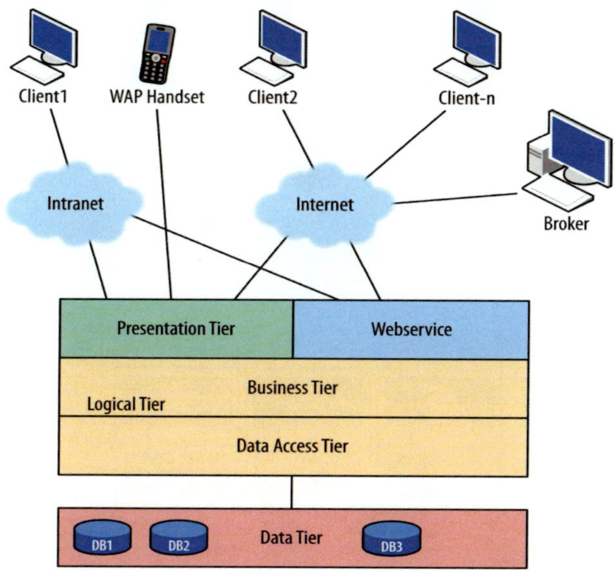

Figure 5.9. *Three-tiered application architecture employed by modern applications.*

Source: Thomas, D. N., et al., (2013). SDN: Software Defined Networks, See http://oreilly.com/catalog/errata.csp?isbn=9781449342302.

A virtual machine is moved between two compute servers in Figure 5.10. If both servers are located in the same data center, the VM migration is intra-data center and only needs to be completed by copying the VM file from one location to another after the VM has been paused. A file copy between two IP end points is still necessary if the two servers are located in different data centers; however, the file transfer may need to travel over a longer and more complicated network path. This type of migration is known as an inter-data center virtual machine migration. On the basis of this and keeping in mind the talk about live virtual machine moves, the network needs to stay operational during the migration, and all sessions (e.g., TCP connection) needs to be active. The hypervisor system, which controls virtual machines and their movements, is in charge of this little bit of magic.

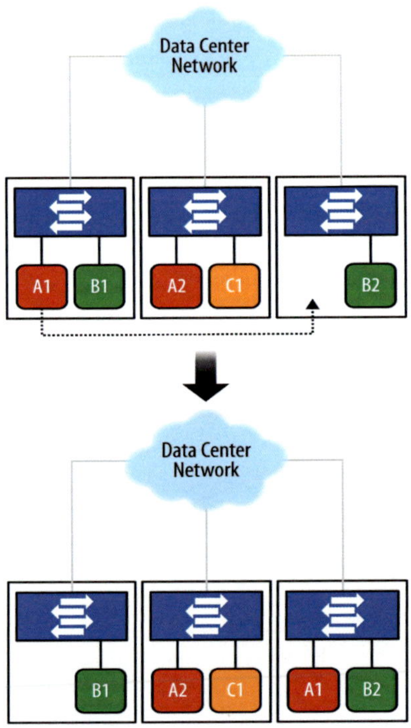

Figure 5.10. *VM migration.*

Source: Thomas, D. N., et al., (2013). SDN: Software Defined Networks, See http://oreilly.com/catalog/errata.csp?isbn=9781449342302.

The fact that, in many situations, the MAC address, IP address, and any associated configuration state of the virtual machine (VM) must stay the same to enable a smooth transition only serves to further complicate matters. This covers additional network-related components like firewall rules, security policies, ACLs, and QoS configuration. These items all need to be moved to the new access switch or server. This encompasses all runtime states both in the vSwitch and within the virtual machine. Furthermore, the physical network's switches need to be quickly adjusted to reflect the virtual machine's new location. ARP tables, MAC tables, and multicast group membership tables are examples of this. Because of these complexities, using the three-tiered application design pattern and creating and destroying component virtual machines (VMs) is far simpler.

The VM migration can be implemented in one of three ways:

1. **Network Data-Plane Driven Approach:** The supporting network devices can identify virtual machine migration by keeping an eye on network traffic going to and coming from the virtual machine (for instance, by looking for extraneous ARP messages).
2. **Hypervisor Driven Approach:** The vSwitch or vGW, which are components of the hypervisor, use introspection to identify the VM migration. One method to accomplish this is to have the new hypervisor detect the VM's appearance while the old hypervisor detects the VM's disappearance.
3. **Orchestrator Driven Approach:** The orchestrator specifically initiates the change of runtime state prior to carrying out the VM migration, rather than detecting it at runtime automatically.

The runtime state can be updated in one of two ways:

i. **Data-Plane Driven Approach:** To compel an update to the runtime state, the virtual machine sends some traffic. To force all MAC tables in the tenant network to be updated with the new location of the VM's MAC address, for instance, the VM can broadcast a gratuitous ARP.

ii. **Orchestrator or Control-Plane Driven Approach:** The orchestrator updates the runtime state explicitly everywhere it is required by using a control-plane signaling protocol.

To execute VM migration, the entire state—including the disk, memory, registers, etc.—must be copied.) between different servers. Usually, this is done by copying the VM's file, which combines all of these components into one file. The copying process happens in the background while the virtual machine (VM) is still operating on the original server during the first phase, which can take several minutes. When the copying is almost finished, the virtual machine is suspended, its final state is copied, and it is reanimated on the new server in the final fraction of a second. Because the time required to replicate this final state equals time spent with the VM's service being unresponsive, this process requires high bandwidth and low latency between the two servers.

An alternate method is to take a virtual machine snapshot, pause it, and then move the snapshot to a different server, whereupon the virtual machine will be unpaused by the hypervisor. Though not a live migration, this is one, nonetheless. Live migration involves a storage component, especially if the two virtual machines (VMs) utilize the shared storage model, which allows I/O to continue while the two VMs share a common physical disk (array) and logical volume. The disk access protocol (iSCSI, NFS, Fiber Channel) determines the maximum distance and latency that can be used for this process. The application can also be divided into multiple tiers, with state and other data being stored in a common backend database. That state is locked right before the virtual machine pauses to make its move. It just reconnects to this store and carries on when it comes to life again somewhere else.

The type of service offering (IaaS, PaaS, or SaaS) and the level of tenancy will determine the scale and performance of virtual machine moves. An entry-level Intel/ARM processor from the current generation offered as part of a standard service provider's IaaS offering, c. 2012 could show the approximate scale numbers as follows:

1. **Number of Data Centers:** Multiples of tens (depends entirely on the geography of the offering; the example given would be for a country the size of Japan).
2. **Number of Servers per Center:** Tens of thousands.
3. **Number of Servers per Cluster/Pod:** 1,000.
4. **Number of Tenants per Server:** Approximately 20 (current generation of processor, expected to double with next generation).
5. **Number of VMs per Tenant:** Approximately five.
6. **VM Change Rate:** Highly variable.
7. **VM Change Latency:** This is a target that varies by provider and application.

5.2.4. Data Center Interconnect (DCI)

After going over the fundamentals of what a data center is and how one can be constructed, let's talk about connecting one or more data centers. Data centers are connected via some type of Wide Area Network (WAN) in configurations where multiple data centers are needed for disaster recovery, geographic diversity, service, or cloud bursting. This is true even in situations where data centers are located next to each other; in these situations, a metro access network is usually utilized to link them. There are numerous technological options available to accomplish these connections. These include pseudowires, EVPN, VPLS, MPLS L3 or L2 VPNs, and even regular old IP.

When there are two or more data centers, you need to think about how to connect them. An arbitrary number of virtual machines could be owned by a tenant in each of these various data centers, but they still need to be at least logically connected. All of a tenant's virtual machines (VMs) are placed on the same L2 or L3 underlying network across all data centers via the Data Center Interconnect (DCI) tenant network (below). It turns out that you can use one of the concepts derived from the previously discussed multitenant data center concept to treat data centers almost like Lego blocks that snap together in order to interconnect them (Figure 5.11).

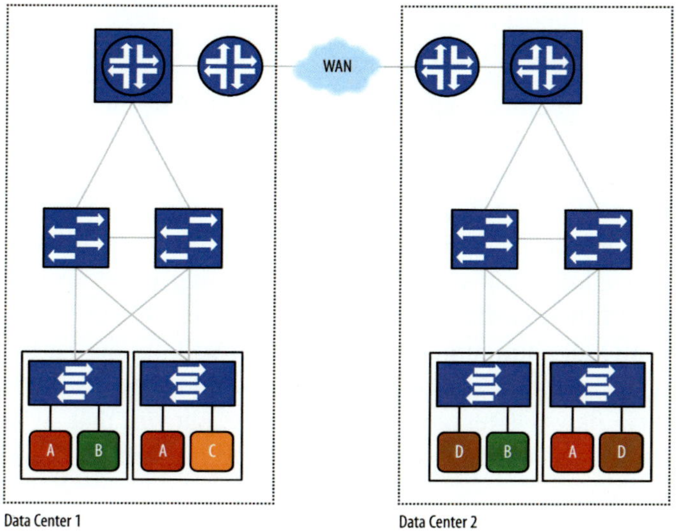

Figure 5.11. *Data center interconnect (DCI).*

Source: Thomas, D. N., et al., (2013). SDN: Software Defined Networks, See http://oreilly.com/catalog/errata.csp?isbn=9781449342302.

It turns out that there are a number of considerations to make when connecting data centers, so the process is not always straightforward. Nevertheless, let's first go over some of the prerequisites for any decent DCI solution and, more importantly, some of its myths, before diving headfirst into all the different ways that DCI can be implemented.

5.2.5. Fallacies of Data Center Distributed Computing

It is inevitable that one must include a list of the interconnection's requirements when building a data center and an architecture, or strategy, for connecting two or more data centers. These frequently begin with a range of assumptions, and we have discovered that many of these actually fit into a category of things that, while they may seem reasonable in theory, are actually hard to guarantee or assume. These assumptions include the following:

- The network is reliable;
- Latency is zero;
- Bandwidth is infinite;

- The network is secure;
- Topology doesn't change;
- There is one administrator;
- Transport cost is zero;
- The network is homogeneous.

While these ideas might appear reasonable at first, they are actually very difficult, if not impossible, to implement in real life. For instance, the first four points assume certain things about the technology in use and the tools that make it work. It is usually a safer bet to assume the opposite of these first points because no equipment is flawless or perfect. Points four through six relate to personnel or administrative matters. If everything is set up correctly, your network should function that way until it is altered. Herein lies the problem: errors in operational configuration (i.e., errors involving the fat finger) can be disastrous for the network's regular functioning and may also unintentionally create security flaws. (Research has actually shown that when network operations staff is on holidays or vacations, the number of network failures actually decreases.).

5.2.6. Data Center Distributed Computing Pitfalls to Consider

It turns out that the DCI needs to take into consideration the possibility of tenant address spaces overlapping. To prevent this, the DCI can use tunneling techniques like L2 MPLS VPNs, L3 MPLS VPNs, GRE tunnels, SSL VPNs, or other methods. These might be covered by the DCI fallacies that were just covered, depending on the address management strategy that is selected. Specifically, if a new tenant is operationally misconfigured and unintentionally able to view another tenant's virtual machines (VMs), the assumption that addresses overlap but are isolated from one another can quickly unravel. Therefore, bear in mind that selecting an addressing scheme involves more than just making the obvious choice; operations and management verification and checking schemes should also be taken into account.

Additionally, there are performance requirements for the interconnection. Many of the limitations stem from the idea of live migration between data centers (including disk I/O, as was previously mentioned), and given the obstacles that live migration must overcome to be functional, there is much discussion about whether live migration is actually a use case that should be taken into account in Data Center Interconnect design. For instance, discussions about DCI in the Broadband Forum state that the VMware VMotion solution suggests a Round-Trip Time (RTT) of less than 5 ms between source and destination servers and necessitates a minimum bandwidth of 622 Mbps between data centers. In effect, this places physical restrictions on the separation between servers. Actually, it is possible to determine how much bandwidth you require using data that is already known. Although this data is generally applicable, it is primarily influenced by target constraints and tenant service behavior. DCI bandwidth is especially important since it has a direct impact on the length of the change window and the volume of data that needs to be replicated. Another restriction is the RTT and, consequently, the separation between data centers. The example that was just given was for a three-hour change window for a specific data product with the link's bandwidth set to a fixed value, but a calculation could optimize for all constraints. Naturally, the results of these computations will vary depending on whether they are done for a single operational action or the total of all operational actions (Figure 5.12).

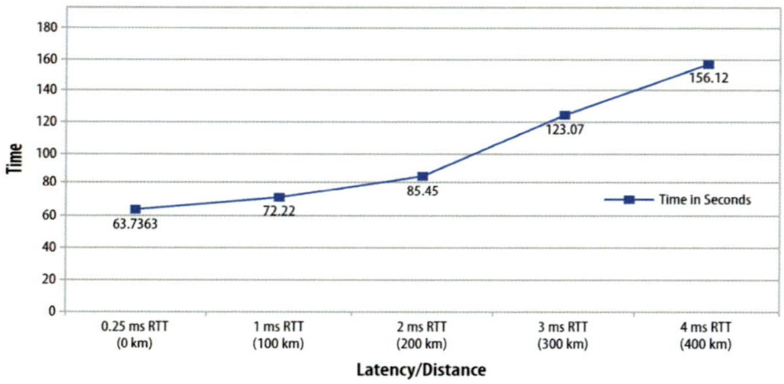

Figure 5.12. *Distance limitations for recommended vMotion latency (at interconnect rate of 622 Mbps).*

Source: Thomas, D. N., et al., (2013). SDN: Software Defined Networks, See http://oreilly.com/catalog/errata.csp?isbn=9781449342302.

To review, the general scale concerns when designing the DCI include:

- MAC address scalability is an issue on the DC WAN edge for solutions that use L2 extension (e.g., 250k client MAC addresses in a single Service Provider data center multiplied across interconnected SP data centers and Enterprise data centers).
- Pseudowire scale (i.e., the number of directed LDP sessions, MAC learning).
- Control plane scale (i.e., whether or not an L2 control plane domain is extended between data centers).
- Broadcast, unknown unicast, and multicast traffic handling (BUM).

Ultimately, it might be necessary to combine IP interconnection with layer 2 extensions. The latter could be L3VPN or just plain IP forwarding. The unanswered concerns center on whether or not the control planes of the various centers are divided or disjoint.

5.2.6.1. DCI Approaches

The commonly used DCI approaches that have been discussed can be categorized into the following groups to better illustrate their benefits and drawbacks, ranging from the most straightforward to the most complex.

- VLAN Extension uses 802.1q trunking on the links between the data centers and is fraught with the same concerns of VLANs in the data center; MAC scalability, potential spanning tree loops, unpredictable amounts of BUM traffic and little control that allows effective load balancing over multiple links (traffic engineering).
- There are some proprietary solutions to the VLAN extension problem. For example, Cisco vPC (virtual port channel) suggests bonding inter-DC links and filtering STP BPDUs to avoid STP looping.
- VPLS uses MPLS to create a pseudowire overlay on the physical connection between the data centers. The MPLS requirement comes with an LDP and/or multiprotocol BGP requirement (for the control plane of the overlay) that may (to some operators) mean additional complexity, though this can be mitigated with technique like AutoDiscovery.
- MPLS brings additional potentially desirable functionality: traffic engineering, fast reroute, multicast/broadcast replication, a degree of isolation between data centers allowing overlapping VLAN assignments and hiding topology, and fairly broad support and interoperability.

5.2.6.2. VLANs for DCI

The most straightforward way to handle DCI is to use VLANs. Use of VLANs as a segregation mechanism is perfectly acceptable (and scalable) in any given data center where the tenant count is less than approximately 4,000. The majority of hardware, including commodity switches and expensive routing and switching equipment, supports this technique.

The benefits of employing this mechanism are that it is relatively easy to design and initially cheap to run. The drawbacks include the possibility of complexity in managing modifications in the future. In other words, if changes are needed in the future, a sizable number of points may require VLAN/tag mapping modifications.

To implement VLAN for DCs, one needs only map the tagged traffic between data center gateways to intra-DC IP or Ethernet paths, which subsequently forward the traffic to the local data center.

5.2.6.3. VPLS for DCI

If you need to accommodate more than 4,000 tenants, you will need to find alternative solutions. Virtual Private LAN Service (VPLS) is one such choice. The fundamental workings of the VPLS solution are comparable to those of the VLAN service, with the exception that data centers are connected via MPLS (L2TPv3) and pseudowires, and VLANs (or stacked VLANs) are mapped to the pseudowires at the gateways, connecting the VLAN-to-VM mappings between the data centers. Depending on how far down the network the architecture requires the VPLS to extend, the CE in Figure 5.13 represents either the gateway router/switch or the top of rack switch (ToR). In the first scenario, the mapping of the VLAN-to-VPLS tunnel takes place at the gateway; in the second scenario, it occurs on the ToR. Both cases have pros and cons in terms of scale, operations and management, and resilience to change, but in general the VPLS solution has the following characteristics:

- Flooding (broadcast, multicast, unknown unicast);
- Dynamic learning of Mac addresses;
- Split-Horizon and full-mesh of PWs for loop-avoidance in core (no STP runs in the core, so the data center SPT domains are isolated);
- Sub-optimal multicast (though the emergence of Label Switched Multicast may provide relief);
- The VLAN to pseudowire mapping may place an artificial limit on the number of tenants supported per physical interface (4K);
- VLAN-based dual homing may require the use of virtual chassis techniques between the PE/DCI gateways and pseudowire redundancy (for active/active redundancy);
- Load balancing across equal cost paths can be only VLAN based (but not flow-based unless we introduce further enhancements like Entropy Labels or Flow Aware Transport (FAT) pseudowires).

Even though VPLS is a step up from a straightforward VLAN or stacked VLAN approach, there are still problems with it. For example, the approach is still encumbered by MAC scaling problems due to data plane learning, similar to the VLAN or stacked VLAN approaches. The CE points depicted in Figure 5.14 may experience problems as a result of these problems. Furthermore, because the network configuration calls for the implementation and deployment of pseudowire tunnels between the PEs, i.e., depending on the architecture, either the gateway or the ToR) and raises the possibility of pseudowire scale and maintenance problems.

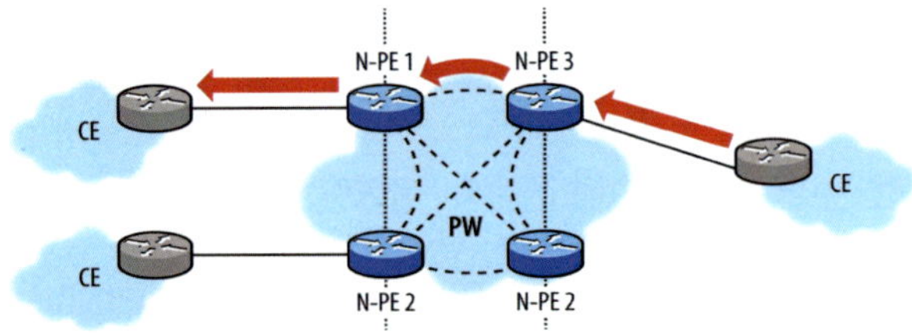

Figure 5.13. *VPLS for DCI (split horizon has eliminated the paths to the target CE via N-PE2, NPE-4, and alternate LSPs on N-PE3).*

Source: Thomas, D. N., et al., (2013). SDN: Software Defined Networks, See http://oreilly.com/catalog/errata.csp?isbn=9781449342302.

5.2.6.4. EVPN for DCI

To address some of the drawbacks of VPLS solutions, Ethernet VPN (EVPN), another MPLS-based solution, was created. A control plane solution for automated MAC learning between data centers is added by EVPN to the data plane MAC learning paradigm. By transforming MAC addresses into routable addresses, EVPN generates a new address family for BGP and uses this to share MAC learning information amongst network PEs. Additional improvements have also been made to EVPN to improve MAC learning and increase its scalability.

EVPN can use a number of different transport LSP types (P2P/P2MP/MP2MP) and can provide some distribution advantages over VPLS:

- Flow-based load balancing and multipathing (Layers 2, 3, and) in support of multihoming devices.
- The same flow-based or VLAN-based load balancing for multihomed networks (this can be based on auto-detection).
- Multicast optimization using MP2MP multicast distribution trees.
- Geo-redundancy for PE/gateway nodes.

EVPN introduces some new conceptual devices:

- The MES-MPLS edge switch;
- The MFI-EVPN forwarding instance;
- The ESI-ethernet segment identifier (which is important in link aggregation scenarios).

In the EVPN model, local MAC addresses are still learned through standard data plane learning within the data center, as shown in Figure 5.15. Although MESs can also acquire local MACs through other means, such as management plane protocols or extensions to discovery protocols like LLDP, they can still use split horizon and other MAC bridging optimization techniques to distribute these addresses to other PEs. In order to distribute MAC routes, the fundamental function of EVPN also involves populating the table for the new address family in the MES and notifying neighboring MES(s) about it through BGP updates. Additionally, a MES adds the associated adjacency information and the BGP learned MAC addresses to their layer 2 forwarding table. This can now be done in a far more scalable way than the typical VLAN approach previously described. WAN border routers, for instance, might only forward on the label, and other MES points might only include active MACs in the forwarding plane. This is not the same as requiring every endpoint to acquire every MAC address from every VLAN. Similar to how BGP aggregates network addresses behind a network and only distributes reachability to those networks rather than the actual end point addresses, MAC addresses are effectively aggregated behind each MES.

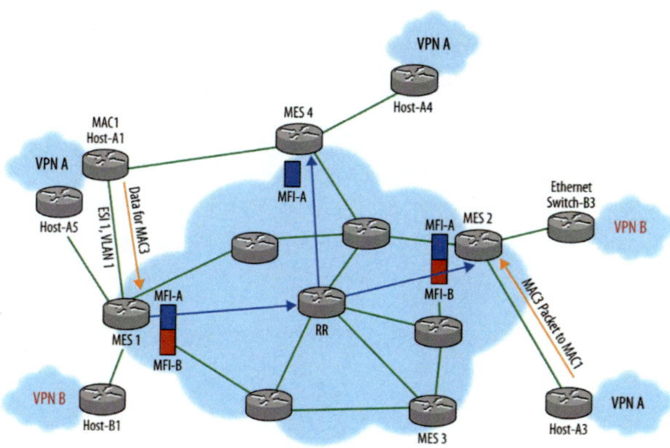

Figure 5.14. *EVPN MAC-learning model.*

Source: Thomas, D. N., et al., (2013). SDN: Software Defined Networks, See http://oreilly.com/catalog/errata.csp?isbn=9781449342302.

Apart from these benefits, EVPN significantly lessens ARP flooding, which may also cause scalability problems. Switch forwarding bandwidth can be rapidly depleted by ARP storms. In order to achieve this, the MES executes proxy ARP, answers ARP queries for IP addresses it represents, and doesn't forward ARP messages unless the requested IP address is carried by a binding on the BGP MAC routes.

Similar to how BGP policies are used to improve regular IP reachability, EVPN also uses BGP policies to improve MAC learning and selective VLAN distribution. An EVPN's membership is defined by its Route Targets (RTs), which include the MES(s) and Ethernet interfaces/VLANs that link CEs (e.g., switches, routers, and hosts). In particular, if an EVPN and a VLAN are mapped one to one, RTs can be automatically generated from a VLAN ID. In the VPNs it engages in, every MES discovers the ESI membership of every other MES. For BUM traffic, this procedure permits split horizon and designated forwarder election (for multihomed CEs).

The ability of EVPN MES(s) to distribute various MFI to other MES that have members of the same VPNs is demonstrated by the example in Figure 5.14. In order to increase the solution's scalability, a route reflector is typically used in its implementation. Additionally, BGP features like inter-AS, Route Reflectors, and constrained distribution are reused.

Also on Figure 5.14, both MES1 and MES4 advertise Ethernet Tag auto-discovery routes for < ESI1, VLAN1>along with MPLS label and VPNA RT. For example, MES1 advertises MAC Route in BGP:

< RD-1, MAC1, A1-VLAN, A1-ESI ID, MAC lbl L1, VPN A RT>

In the example, MES2 learns via BGP that MAC1 is dual homed to MES1 and MES4. This still works despite the fact that MES4 might not yet have advertised MAC1 because MES2 knows via the Ethernet Tag auto-discovery routes that MES4 is connected to ESI1 and VLAN1. If MES2 decides to send the packet to MES1, it will use inner label < EVPN label advertised by MES1 for MAC1> and outer encapsulation as < MPLS Label for LSP to MES1> or < IP/GRE header for IP/GRE tunnel to MES1>.

MES2 can now safely load-balance the traffic to MAC1 between MES1 and MES4.

5.2.6.5. Comparison of VPLS and EVPN for DCI

Given their similarity, we believe that contrasting and comparing the last two DCI solutions is instructive. It is evident from Table 5.1 that EVPN seems to be the best option for DCI.

Table 5.1. *Comparison of VPLS and EVPN for DCI*

Desirable 1.2 extension attributes	**VPLS**	**E-VPN**
VM Mobility without renumbering L2 and L3 addresses	√	√
Ability to span VLANs across racks in different locations	√	√
Scale to few 100K hosts within and across multiple DCs	√	√
Policy-based flexible L2 topologies similar to L3 VPNs		√

Multiple points of attachment with ability to load-balance VLANs across them	√	√
Active-Active points of attachment with ability to load-balance flows within a single VLAN		√
Multi-tenant support (secure isolation, overlapping MAC, IP addresses)	√	√
Control-Plane Based Learning		√
Minimize or eliminate flooding of unknown unicast		√

Source: Thomas, D. N., et al., (2013). SDN: Software Defined Networks, See http://oreilly.com/catalog/errata.csp?isbn=9781449342302.

5.3. SDN SOLUTIONS FOR THE DATA CENTER NETWORK

We discuss SDN solutions for the contemporary data center in this section. We will specifically talk about how SDN concepts are being used in the recently described modern data centers to increase and improve their efficiency, scalability, and flexibility in providing hosting services. It is important to remember that SDN solutions don't always equate to standard solutions, and some of the solutions mentioned may in some way be vendor proprietary.

Conventional data centers, as previously mentioned, comprise storage, compute (i.e., servers), as well as some network technology that connects the two. Similar to how virtualization has affected servers and apps, it has also affected networks. VLANs were the most virtualized network configuration possible in the traditional network deployment. The network paths between VMs were being virtualized by the VLANs in this way. This marked the beginning of the network's virtualization process. The network fabric of the data center can be formed using a variety of protocols, as we previously discussed in the DCI section. As you will see, these protocols can also be used to virtualize the fabric. We will specifically present the idea of network overlays as a concept that makes it possible to virtualize the network underlay, or underlying network fabric.

5.3.1. The Network Underlay

The technologies that make up the network underlay are numerous. These can generally be categorized as Layers 1, 2, or 3 solutions, but they are all made to essentially do the same thing: transfer data between servers in the data center. An overlay network builds a logical network on top of the physical underlay network, as shown in Figure 5.15. Usually, virtual network components like switches, routers, and logical tunnels are used to build the overlay network. A standard network, like an Ethernet, MPLS, or IP network, makes up the underlay network.

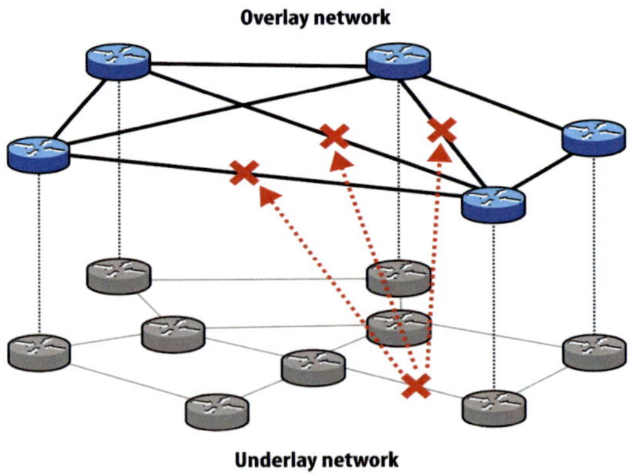

Figure 5.15. *Data center overlay and underlay network relationships.*

Source: Thomas, D. N., et al., (2013). SDN: Software Defined Networks, See http://oreilly.com/catalog/errata.csp?isbn=9781449342302.

To be honest, all of the existing methods will be able to provide an overlay-carrying underlay network.

The question is how well each solution hosts a specific overlay technology and how optimal it is at what it does. For instance, a certain approach may be more scalable for layer 2 MAC address learning, but it may not be as effective when handling VM moves or external cloud bursting. While one example may require more time for semi-automated (or even manual) operator intervention, another may scale well in terms of how quickly it adapts to changes in the network. In the section that follows, we will examine each of these perspectives.

5.4. VLANS

Although the new SDN technologies are the main topic of this chapter, remember that simplicity is key when managing a network. In light of this, VLANS continue to be the most straightforward and efficient option when internal tenant tenancy is required, and the number of tenants does not exceed roughly 1,000.

The most basic type of network overlay is obviously a flat IP network that runs over a VLAN substrate or underlay since it's a well-known method that's very simple to use and supported on the broadest range of hardware. In actuality, this is the way that data centers were initially built.

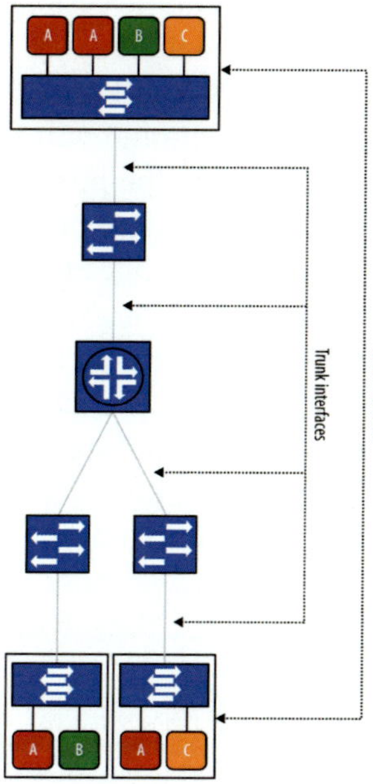

Figure 5.16. *End-to-end tenant VLANs in the data center.*

Source: Thomas, D. N., et al., (2013). SDN: Software Defined Networks, See http:// oreilly.com/catalog/errata.csp?isbn=9781449342302.

The overlay was still largely a flatly addressed IP network at the time, and there was no real need to support multiple tenants. VLANs were invented to help separate resources based on departmental access. This method even briefly succeeded in granting external users access to data centers (recall the Amazon AWS example). However, the number of tenants eventually exceeded the available address spaces, and the frequent turnover of these virtualized network components necessitated the rapid (re)programming of these resources. In these cases, a single tenant could be supported by a basic IP over Ethernet network, which could be easily and covertly expanded with VLANs to accommodate up to approximately 4,000 tenants. Figure 5.16 shows how an IP overlay and a comparatively simple DC interconnection can be implemented together with a localized data center overlay using a basic VLAN approach. For each application (app, db, and management) in the example, three 801.1Q VLANs are created, and traffic is divided throughout the network using these VLANs. This method gives the VMs hosting those services layer 3 access by using the same flat IP addressing space inside the DCs. An access interface is the interface that connects the virtual machine to the hypervisor. This interface is allocated to the tenant's VLAN by the hypervisor. All switch-to-switch interfaces and the interface connecting the server to the access switch are trunk interfaces. Even though implementing VLAN solutions is relatively simple, unless routing is added between VLANs, it is well known that using just bridging or the Spanning Tree Protocol (or its variations) will not scale to more than 300 hosts on a single VLAN. The issue with the protocol arises from the fact that changes, moves, or failures resulting in a large number of host MAC addresses cause massive processing inside the net-work elements. Network components may overlook additional malfunctions during these extremely busy times or may simply become so overwhelmed that they are unable to respond rapidly enough. Black holes or network loops may arise from this. Equal cost waste was another problem with early iterations of Spanning Tree, i.e., parallel) links, as the protocol served as a pre-venting loop by effectively blocking all other parallel links to the same bridge. The ability to provide multipath capabilities is limited, even in the most recent versions of these protocols. Ultimately, when bridges reconnect to other bridge links, they typically experience a loss of several seconds in forwarding.

5.5. EVPN

The PE function might end at the DC gateway or the ToR, as we mentioned when we first presented EVPN as a DCI solution. We demonstrated how VLANs—stacked, tagged, or flat—would be used as the underlay in the former scenario. We also mentioned that EVPN and VPLS could be used to increase the number of tenants in a network above the maximum of 4,000 VLAN tags.

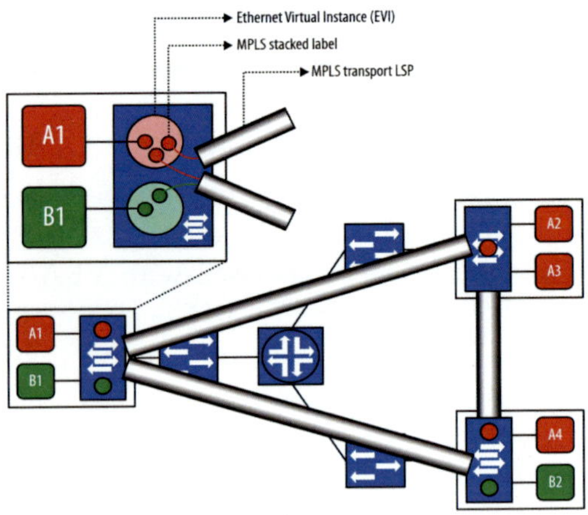

Figure 5.17. *EVPN (data plane).*

Source: Thomas, D. N., et al., (2013). SDN: Software Defined Networks, See http://oreilly.com/catalog/errata.csp?isbn=9781449342302.

Figure 5.17 provides an example of how EVPN can be used in a data center to transfer traffic from one tenant to another. Traffic is transmitted as an MPLS encapsulated frame containing an Ethernet frame, making the overall operation straightforward. Depending on the implementation, MPLS tunnels end at the physical or virtual switch, which decapsulates the traffic and sends it as a layer 2 frame to the virtual or physical host. In a similar manner, layer 2 frame transmission from the end stations is sent to additional end hosts after being encapsulated in an MPLS tunnel. This behavior is the same as what was previously described.

Additionally, Figure 5.18 shows how the control plane uses RSVP or LDP to create a full mesh of transport MPLS LSPs between the access and core switches. The access switches use the same procedure as previously outlined in the DCI section to run MP-IBGP in order to signal MAC learning reachability information.

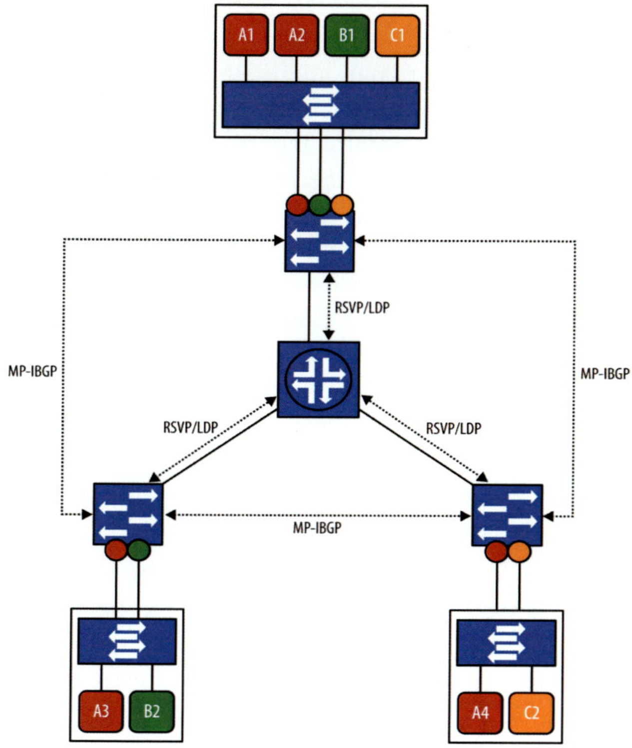

Figure 5.18. *EVPN (control plane).*

Source: Thomas, D. N., et al., (2013). SDN: Software Defined Networks, See http://oreilly.com/catalog/errata.csp?isbn=9781449342302.

It is crucial to take into account how this strategy scales in comparison to the other previously mentioned methods. Specifically, the physical network will scale and function in the same well-known ways as MPLS networks because it is a layer 3 (MPLS) network. Similar to this, all layer 2 traffic is tunneled via MPLS across the network, which helps with scaling as it eliminates the need for big layer 2 domains and the scaling issues that come with them. One must also take into account the quantity of actual tunnels that need to be set up and maintained when comparing this method to VxLAN or NVGRE. Because stacked labels can be used, there usually shouldn't be as many as in the VxLAN and NVGRE scenarios. The use of BGP route reflectors in this scheme further expands the scope of this approach in terms of processing load on the switches. These can significantly improve the solution. Finally, the protocol configuration load on the end hosts may be reduced by using XMPP between the local switches (or vSwitches) and the MP-IBGP points in the architecture.

5.5.1. Locator ID Split (LISP)

The Internet's current routing and addressing architecture uses a single namespace to express two aspects of a network element: its network identity and its network attachment. Essentially, the issue lies in our desire to maintain the device's identity irrespective of the network or networks it is linked to. When the current addressing scheme was developed, network elements were thought to be comparatively static, and it was assumed that the ID binding between the network and the element would also be relatively static. We now need to take into account the dynamic user behavior of today, where mobile components frequently switch between base stations and radio access networks. Because of this, when a network element switches networks, its whole address may change, making it challenging to manage network connections, resources, and other items that should be pinned to it based on its identifier. Moreover, traffic engineering (TE) or address allocations that prohibit aggregation are required when network elements are multihomed.

Two circumstances have made this issue worse. The first is the depletion of IPv4 address space, which has caused the space to be allocated more and more finely, reducing the amount of aggregation potential. The prevalence of dualstack routers that support both IPv4 and IPv6 protocols is the second. Since IPv6 did not alter how IP addresses are used, it continues to have the same problems as IPv4.

These problems were identified by several IETF members, who worked to address them by developing a new address and network element address split known as Locator ID Split, or LISP, as it is currently known. They developed a new semantic for IP addressing through the creation of a network architecture and set of protocols. For every network device, LISP essentially uses two IP addresses and two namespaces. The first is an Endpoint Identifier (EID), which is linked to an end host and stays with it no matter what network it is connected to. A Routing Locator (RLOC) is the second, and it is linked to a network device (i.e., among the components of the global routing system, a router). The components that make up the LISP system and enable it to operate are these routers, the unique device identifier, and the protocols that are used to manage them over the Internet.

The separation of device identifier from its network identifier offers several advantages:

- Improved routing system scalability by using topologically aggregated RLOCs.
- Improved traffic engineering for cases where multihoming of end-sites are employed.
- Provider independence for devices that are assigned an EID rom a common EID space. This facilitates IP portability, which is an important feature, too.
- LISP is a simple, incremental, network-based implementation that is deployed primarily in network edge devices, therefore requiring no changes to host stacks, Domain Name Services, or the local network infrastructure used to support those hosts.
- IP mobility (EIDs can move without changing—only the RLOC changes!).

The IETF and other academic institutions and researchers have been studying the idea of a location/ID separation for more than 15 years. Greater aggregation of RLOCs can be attained by partitioning the device identity, its Endpoint Identifier, and Routing Locator into two distinct namespaces, thereby improving the scalability of the routing system.

Data centers can benefit from LISP's ability to segment traffic on a large, worldwide scale with little impact on the infrastructure. In fact, this is a method of achieving virtualization/multitenancy support, similar to how we have explained VPNs or VLANs inside of DCs. This is achieved by mapping VRFs to LISP instance IDs in order to segment control and data plane traffic, which gives this overlay solution exceptional flexibility and scalability. Because the DC network switches perform the mapping automatically, there is also a chance that this will have intrinsically low operating costs.

Another advantage of this strategy is that data center VM-Mobility can give IP endpoints location flexibility not just within the data center network but also over the Internet because it uses the IP protocol. In actuality, because the server identifiers—which are essentially EIDs—are isolated from their location (RLOC) in the same manner as any other LISP implementation, virtual machine hosts that utilize this scheme are free to migrate between data centers. As a result, this solution can deploy virtual machines anywhere, independent of their IP addresses, and bind IP endpoints to them. Moreover, support for virtual machine mobility within and between data center rows, racks, and PDs is feasible. This technique can also be applied across organizations, enabling data centers' cloud-bursting capabilities.

5.6. VXLAN

Using current VLAN technology, Virtual Extensible LAN (VxLAN) is a network virtualization technology that aims to address scalability issues with large-scale cloud computing deployments. VxLAN was initially developed by VMware and Cisco to address issues that arose in these environments. At the moment, Juniper Networks, Arista Networks, Broadcom, Citrix, and Red Hat are among the other supporters of the technology.

VxLAN encapsulates MAC-based layer 2 Ethernet frames within layer 3 UDP packets using a VLAN-like encapsulation technique. For similar reasons as to why LISP was created, VxLAN uses a MAC-in-UDP encapsulation to give virtual machines (VMs) a layer 2 abstraction regardless of where they are located. Figure 5.19 shows the packet format that VxLAN uses. Take note of the inner and outer MAC/IP sections of this approach that enable virtual tunneling.

Outer MAC	Outer IP	Outer UDP	VXLAN	Inner MAC	Inner Payload	Outer CRC

Figure 5.19. *VXLAN packet format.*

Source: Thomas, D. N., et al., (2013). SDN: Software Defined Networks, See http://oreilly.com/catalog/errata.csp?isbn=9781449342302.

The 802.1Q VLAN Identifier space is restricted to just 12 bits, or roughly 4,000 entries, as was previously mentioned. With 24 bits available for the identifier, the VxLAN Id space can grow by more than 400,000% to accommodate more than 16 million unique identifiers. This ought to leave ample space for growth in the years to come. Additionally, Figure 5.20 demonstrates how the Internet Protocol is used by VxLAN as the transport protocol between VxLAN hosts. This is accomplished for both multicast and unicast operations. The use of IP as the transport is crucial because it enables a VxLAN segment's reach to be significantly expanded beyond what is normally possible with VLANs using 802.1Q.

In essence, VxLAN separates virtual machines (VMs) from their physical networks by enabling inter-VM communication via a transparent overlay hosted over physical overlay networks. To support intra-DC scenarios, these overlay networks can also cross layer 3 boundaries. Because the endpoint virtual machines (VMs) only see the virtual layer 2 adjacencies, they are completely unaware of the physical network constraints, which is a significant benefit of VxLAN. More significantly, this technology allows virtualization to be extended across conventional network boundaries, supporting the portability and mobility of virtual machine hosts. Similar to the VLAN technique, VxLAN enables the division of logical networks from one another, making true multitenancy implementation easier. However, it goes one step further by surpassing the 4,000 VLAN limit with a significantly larger virtualization space.

Virtual Tunnel Endpoints (VTEPs), which are equipped with all the features required to offer Ethernet layer 2 services to linked end systems, are essential to the regular functioning of VxLAN. The network's edges are home to VTEPs. An IP transport network and an access switch are normally connected by VTEPs. Keep in mind that these switches might be real or virtual.

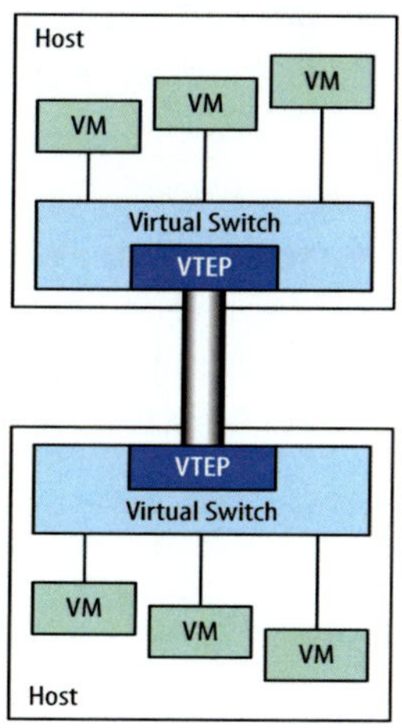

Figure 5.20. *VTEP as part of a virtual (or physical) switch connecting VMs together across a data center infrastructure.*

Source: Thomas, D. N., et al., (2013). SDN: Software Defined Networks, See http://oreilly.com/catalog/errata.csp?isbn=9781449342302.

To get its packets to other hosts, every end system linked to the same access switch communicates with one another via the access switch. The behavior of the access switch is similar to that of a conventional learning bridge. In particular, when it doesn't know the destination MAC of an incoming packet, it will flood packets out of all ports save the one it arrived on. It only transmits out of a specific port when it knows the direction of a forwarding destination. As usual, broadcast traffic is sent out all ports, and multicast is managed in a similar manner. Several bridge domains, which are commonly recognized as VLANs with corresponding VLAN IDs carried in the 802.1Q header on trunk ports, can be supported by the access switch. On the other hand, if the switch were VxLAN enabled, the bridge domain would be linked to a VxLAN ID.

In typical operation, the VTEP looks up the IP address of the VTEP for a destination by examining the destination MAC address of the frames it handles. The standard L2 bridge learning process populates the MAC-to-OuterIP mapping table. A VM typically sends a broadcast ARP to another VM it wants to talk to, and its VTEP forwards this ARP to the multicast group for its VNI. This packet contains information that all other VTEPs will need to know, including the sending VM's Inner MAC address and its Outer IP address. The original VTEP can also learn the destination mapping since the destination VM will reply to the ARP by sending a unicast message back to the sender.

A MAC address shifts to a new virtual or physical switch port (i.e., a VM is moved), the other VTEPs use the previously described learning process to determine its new location. The learning action is triggered by the first packet the other VTEPs see from its new VTEP.

By offering a single interface for authoritatively programming a layer 2 logical network overlay, VxLAN excels in terms of programmability. To program and manage virtual machines (VMs) and the bandwidth and security features that go along with them, VxLAN has been incorporated into VMware's vSphere DVS, vSwitch, and network IO controls within a virtualized environment.

5.7. NVGRE

A network virtualization technology known as Network Virtualization using Generic Routing Encapsulation (NVGRE) was developed to address the scalability issues that arise in large data center environments that experience the problems previously mentioned in relation to the VLAN underlay option. It uses a packet tunneling scheme that encapsulates layer 2 data inside of a layer 3 packet, much like VxLAN. In particular, layer 2 packets are tunneled over layer 3 networks by NVGRE using the generic routing encapsulation (GRE). Fundamentally, NVGRE is just an IP packet carrying an Ethernet layer 2 Frame encapsulated. As a consequence, virtualized L2 subnets that can span actual L3 IP networks can be created. Draft-sridharan-virtualizationnvgre-00, the protocol's initial specification, was defined by the Internet Engineering Task Force. The main sponsor of it is Microsoft.

By enabling the connection between two or more L3 networks, NVGRE gives end hosts the impression that they are connected to the same L2 subnet. This enables inter-VM communications across L3 networks to seem to the end stations as though they were connected to the same L2 subnet, much like VxLAN. An L2 overlay scheme over an L3 network is called NVGRE (Figure 5.21).

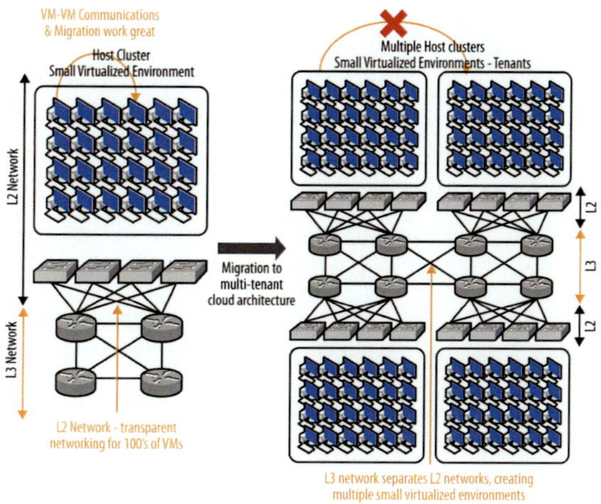

Figure 5.21. *NVGRE overlay networks: Enabling network scalability for a cloud infrastructure.*

Source: Thomas, D. N., et al., (2013). SDN: Software Defined Networks, See http://oreilly.com/catalog/errata.csp?isbn=9781449342302.

Tenant Network Identifiers (TNIs), which are distinct 24-bit IDs used by NVGRE, are appended to L2 Ethernet frames. The top 24 bits of the GRE Key field are mapped with the TNI. More than 16 million L2 (logical) networks can now function within the same administrative domain thanks to the new 24-bit TNI, which is a scalability improvement of many orders of magnitude over the 4,094 VLAN segment limit previously discussed. After the GRE encapsulation of the L2 frame, an outer IP header and an outer MAC address are added to the encapsulation (Figure 5.22).

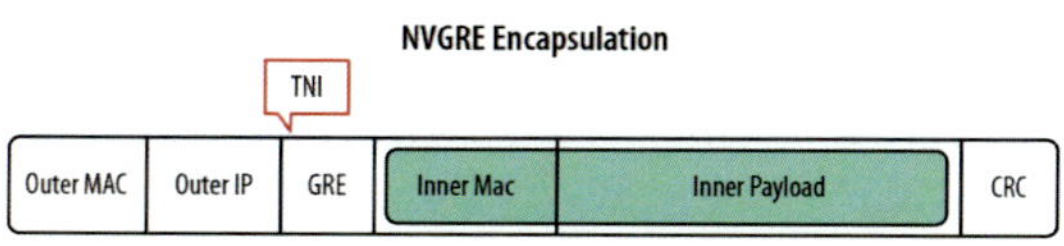

Figure 5.22. *NVGRE packet format.*

Source: Thomas, D. N., et al., (2013). SDN: Software Defined Networks, See http://oreilly.com/catalog/errata.csp?isbn=9781449342302.

Based on the GRE routing protocol as defined by RFC 2784, NVGRE is a tunneling scheme that extends it according to RFC 2890. As its name implies, a TNI uniquely identifies a cloud tenant's unique virtual subnet and is linked to a single GRE tunnel. Because NVGRE makes use of the pre-existing GRE protocol between hypervisors, it isn't a new standard per se; rather, it is a modification of an existing protocol. This offers benefits for managing and operating the system as well as comprehending the other features of the protocol.

When VM traffic is encapsulated using the NVGRE protocol, a server, switch, or physical NIC that does so behaves in a predictable way. The 24-Bit TNI is appended to each frame of traffic coming from a virtual machine (VM), and it is subsequently routed via the relevant GRE tunnel. The incoming packet is de-encapsulated at the destination and forwarded as the original Ethernet L2 packet to the destination virtual machine.

The Customer Address (CA) is the internal IP address. The Provider Address (PA) is the term for the external IP address. An NVGRE endpoint must be aware of the PA of the destination NVGRE endpoint in order to send a packet to the destination virtual machine.

5.7.1. OpenFlow

Several underlay techniques that roughly correspond to variations of current layer 2 network protocols have been described by us. The only exception to this is if the underlay network—over which, say, an IP network can be overlaid—is established and maintained using the OpenFlow protocol. We won't reiterate the protocol's general operation here because we already covered it. It is helpful to illustrate the construction process of such an underlay, which is fortunately fairly straightforward.

The standard configuration of an OpenFlow controller to manage a switch zone in a network is shown in Figure 5.23. Although the BigSwitch FloodTM light controller is depicted in the figure, any OpenFlow controller can be substituted for it and function essentially in the same way. The switches in the figure are typically configured so that the controller has total control over them; however, a clear (and feasible) option is the hybrid mode of operation. Every switch has a designated control channel that connects it to the controller and facilitates communication via the Open-Flow protocol. Take note that both virtual (vSwitch) and real (switch) representations of the controlled switches are displayed. It is crucial to realize that, in most cases, it makes no difference in this situation whether the switch is real or virtual.

In order to create layer 2 switching paths between the switches, the controller typically builds and configures the switches. Layer 3 is then added at the network's entry and exit points to handle ARP and other layer 3 operations. It should be noted that while a true combined layer 2 and 3 underlay can be built with this configuration, most people agree that doing so would be too challenging in terms of scale, failure resistance, and overall operational complexity.

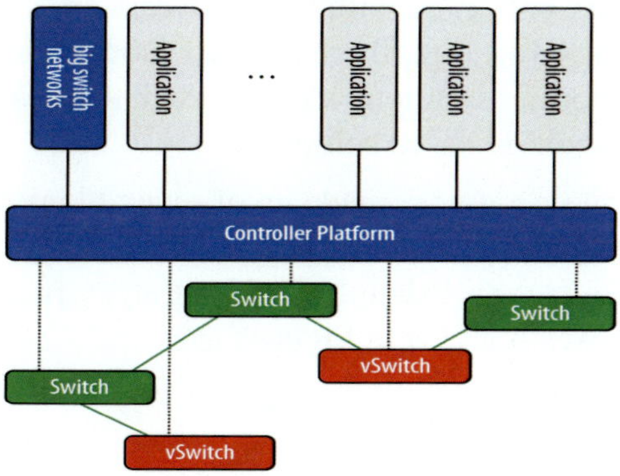

Figure 5.23. *Creating a layer 2 network underlay using OpenFlow-controlled switches.*

Source: Thomas, D. N., et al., (2013). SDN: Software Defined Networks, See http://oreilly.com/catalog/errata.csp?isbn=9781449342302.

5.7.2. Network Overlays

Logical network overlays are not a concept that SDN created, but it is undeniably one of the things that inspires and propels SDN in the modern day, particularly in data center networks. We presented the notation of a network underlay earlier in this chapter. The technologies used by data centers and other network operators today for their network infrastructure make up the majority of the underlay. These fundamental technologies have been enhanced or modified to support more virtualization, user contexts, or entire virtual slices of the network itself, with a few notable exceptions being VxLAN and NGVRE. Similar to the range of network underlays, there are numerous types of network overlays. We'll go over each of these, beginning with the broad ideas of where virtual machine tunnel termination points can be found.

5.7.2.1. Tunnels Terminated at the vSwitch

Today, there are many of these in both the open source and commercial domains. One could argue that the Open Virtual Switch, or OVS, is the most well-known.

In this type of solution, tenant traffic is carried between vSwitches via tunnels that are established between them. The vSwitch serves as a local termination and translation point for virtual machines (VMs) because it typically resides within the hypervisor space. The fact that it isn't altered in any way to take part in the overlay—or un-derlay, for that matter—is another benefit.

Rather, since virtual machines (VMs) happily live in non-overlay environments, they are presented with an IP address and MAC address. When terminating tunnels at vSwitches, there are two subclasses of solutions: single and multitiered. The former solution, which we will discuss in more detail later, is typical of many standards-based solutions.

In general, it shows a network made up of several logical and physical tiers that, when connected, form the underlying infrastructure that the overlay rides over. Figure 5.24 provides an example of this strategy in action. The VMs are represented by the boxes A and B in Figure 5.24.

The group membership of a specific overlay, or VPN, is indicated by the letters. The larger boxes that house them are symbolic of the actual host computer, or server. The vSwitch is represented by the rectangle inside this box. Take note of how logical network tunnels end and originate from this location. This holds true irrespective of the underlay or underlying network.

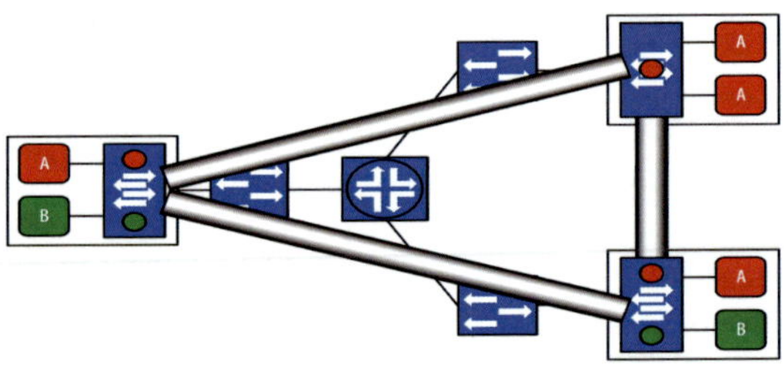

Figure 5.24. *Overlays—tunnels terminated at the vSwitch for a multitier network.*

Source: Thomas, D. N., et al., (2013). SDN: Software Defined Networks, See http://oreilly.com/catalog/errata.csp?isbn=9781449342302.

A single-tiered approach is the alternative strategy for overlays. These are commonly known as "data center fabrics," and they are typically vertically integrated, primarily proprietary, vendor-specific solutions.

As in the multitiered solution, each overlay tunnel in these solutions starts and ends in a vSwitch. It is different from the multitiered solution, though, in that these solutions typically create a complete network of tunnels connecting the vSwitches to form a logical switching fabric.

The network operator (or their OSS) need not be involved in any special tunnel signaling, movement, or maintenance because the fabric management system handles all of this and merely presents tunnels to the virtual machines

(VMs) as if they were plugged into a real network. This could potentially simplify signaling and network operations (Figure 5.25).

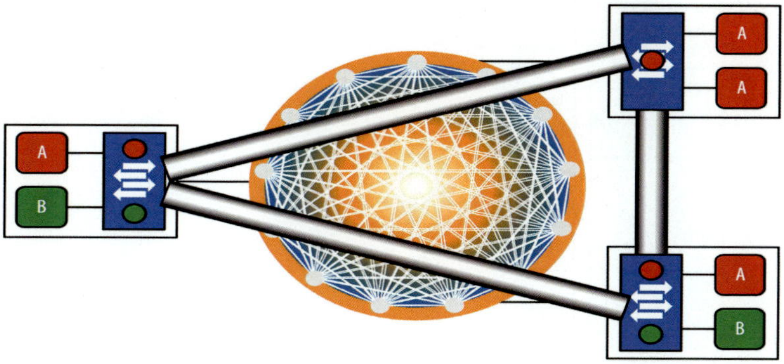

Figure 5.25. *Overlays—tunnels terminated at the vSwitch using a single-tier network (a.k.a. a fabric).*

Source: Thomas, D. N., et al., (2013). SDN: Software Defined Networks, See http://oreilly.com/catalog/errata.csp?isbn=9781449342302.

5.7.3. Network Overlay Types

There are network overlays that simulate various network logical layers. These consist of layers 2 and 3, as well as a more recent strategy that closely combines layers 1 and 2.

5.7.3.1. Layer 2 Overlays

In this case, OpenFlow is the obvious variant, where the usual approach is to build a network out of entire layer 2 segments, as previously described. It can be argued that most overlay tunneling protocols available encapsulate layer 2 tenant network traffic over some layer 3 networks.

Although, as we've seen, it can also be OpenFlow, GRE, or even MPLS—which is actually layer 2.5 but is included here—the layer 3 network is commonly IP. The tunneling encapsulation determines the exact format of the tunnel header, but the general concept is the same for all encapsulations.

In the past, server clustering technologies, storage synchronization, and the requirement for greater flexibility for the network operator of an OSS to assign IP addresses to virtual machines (VMs) have been the main drivers of layer 2 networking. But more and more of these applications are moving to layer 3, so they are no longer just layer 2 (Figure 5.26).

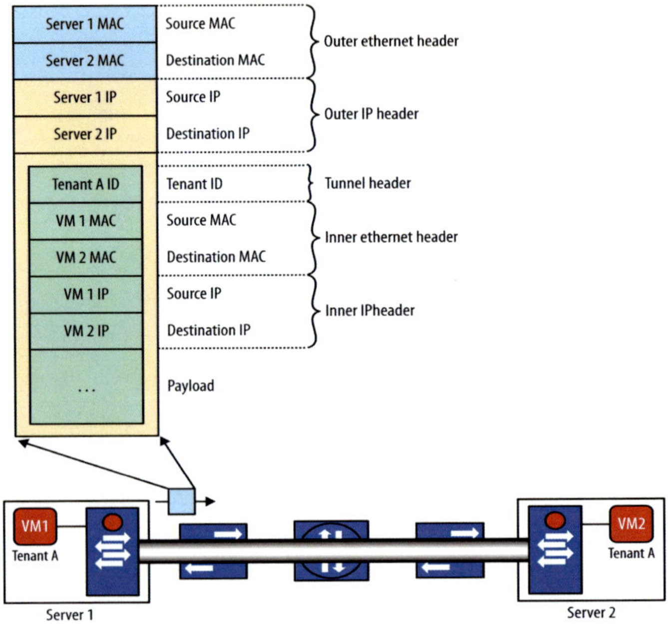

Figure 5.26. *Layer 2 encapsulation for overlay tunnels.*

Source: Thomas, D. N., et al., (2013). SDN: Software Defined Networks, See http://oreilly.com/catalog/errata.csp?isbn=9781449342302.

All of the tunnel encapsulation used in these solutions uses some sort of tenant identifier field in the tunnel header to de-multiplex the packets received from the tunnel into the context of the right vSwitch bridge:

- GRE uses the 32-bit GRE key [GRE-KEY-RFC] (32 bits).
- VxLAN uses the 24-bit VxLAN segment ID, also known as the VxLAN Network Identifier (VNI).
- NVGRE uses the 24-bit Virtual Subnet ID (VSID), which is part of the GRE key.
- VmWare/Nicera's STT uses the 64-bit Context ID.
- MPLS uses the 20-bit inner label.

Global reach throughout the data center is possessed by the VNI in VxLAN, the VSID in NVGRE, and the context ID in STT. In MPLS, the inner label also has local scope inside the vSwitch (Figure 5.27).

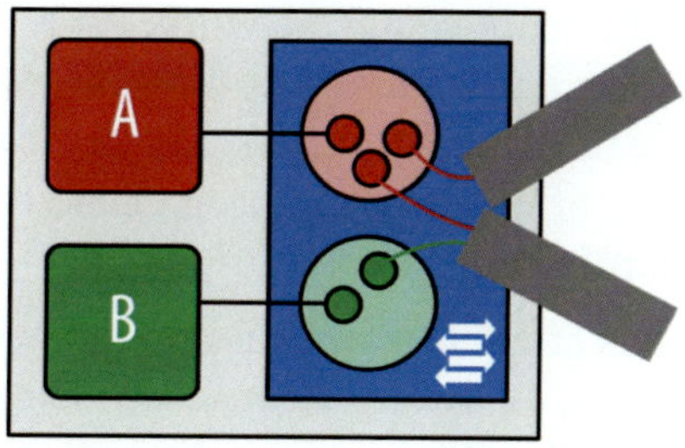

Figure 5.27. *Using the tenant ID in the tunnel header to de-multiplex to the correct tenant.*

Source: Thomas, D. N., et al., (2013). SDN: Software Defined Networks, See http://oreilly.com/catalog/errata.csp?isbn=9781449342302.

5.7.3.2. Layer 3 Overlays

Layer 3 (i.e., network overlays) are an additional type (i.e., IP) overlays. Instead of layer 2 overlays, these overlays display IP-based overlays. These overlays differ from layer 2 overlays in that they display a layer 3 network between virtual machines (VMs) as opposed to a layer 2 logical topology. These methods have benefits that are similar to those of layer 3 VPNs currently in use. Specifically, it is simple to combine private and public addressing, making tasks like cloud-bursting and external cloud attachment feasible. Arguably, moves are also simpler. In this method, a layer 3 tunnel is terminated at a vRouter as opposed to a layer 2 tunnel at the vSwitch. The duties of a vRouter are comparable to those of a vSwitch, with the exception that it serves as a layer 3 VPN's Provider Edge (PE) element. In actuality, a modified layer 3 MPLS approach that integrates with a vRouter inside the hypervisor space is the most common of these approaches that are currently being proposed.

5.7.3.3. Hybrid Overlay-Underlay Approach

One method from a recent startup named Plexxi is different from the strictly layer 2 or strictly layer 3 approaches previously discussed. This solution offers a tightly integrated overlay while functioning as an underlay. This is what we call a hybrid overlay-underlay. Operators still need to be aware of network capacity in the context of overlays because it is a limited resource. Overlays have no idea about the network at all, and as far as the overlay administrator is aware, they are supported by an endless amount of bandwidth. The capacity of conventional network designs, such as leaf/spine designs, is statically structured. A large portion of the capacity in such a network is idle, according to studies. Plexxi's method involves optically connecting switches within a single tier that is created by collapsing the data center network. As a result, the system may require far less transceivers and cabling, as well as fewer boxes. This means that applications can have the capacity they need when they need it without pre-structuring a large amount of otherwise unused capacity when combined with dynamically maintained affinities.

Even though endpoints are hidden within the overlay, this method converts overlays into affinities, enabling dynamic capacity management in the network. This is made possible by the fact that a connector pulls the necessary data from the overlay management system and sends it to the Plexxi controller via its API.

REFERENCES

1. Arora, D., Benson, T., & Rexford, J. (2014). Proactive routing in scalable data centers with PARIS. In *Proceedings of the ACM SIGCOMM 2014 Workshop on Distributed Cloud Computing (DCC)* (pp. 5–10). ACM. https://doi.org/10.1145/2627566.2627571.
2. Ba, J., Wang, Y., Zhong, X., Feng, S., Qiu, X., & Guo, S. (2018). An SDN energy saving method based on topology switch and rerouting. In *Proceedings of the 2018 IEEE/IFIP Network Operations and Management Symposium (NOMS)* (pp. 1–5). IEEE. https://doi.org/10.1109/NOMS.2018.8406202.
3. Bari, M. F., Ahmed, R., et al. (2013). Data center network virtualization: A survey. *IEEE Communications Surveys and Tutorials, 15*(2), 909–928. https://doi.org/10.1109/SURV.2012.091312.00082.
4. Baucke, S., Ben Ali, R., Kempf, J., Mishra, R., Ferioli, F., & Carossino, A. (2013). Cloud Atlas: A software defined networking abstraction for cloud to WAN virtual networking. In *Proceedings of the IEEE Sixth International Conference on Cloud Computing (CLOUD)* (pp. 895–902). IEEE. https://doi.org/10.1109/CLOUD.2013.44.
5. Cohen, R., Gokhale, P., et al. (2013). An intent-based approach for network virtualization. In *Proceedings of the 2013 IFIP/IEEE International Symposium on Integrated Network Management (IM)* (pp. 42–50). IEEE. Retrieved from: http://www.scopus.com/inward/record.url?eid=2-s2.0-84883484060&partnerID=40&md5=33835fe721726b09a32273e97e948440 (accessed on 2 August 2024).
6. Ferguson, D., Guha, A., Liang, C., Fonseca, R., & Krishnamurthi, S. (2013). Participatory networking: An API for application control of SDNs. In *Proceedings of the ACM SIGCOMM 2013 Conference on Applications, Technologies, Architectures, and Protocols for Computer Communication* (pp. 327–338). ACM. https://doi.org/10.1145/2486001.2486003.
7. Foster, N., McKeown, N., Rexford, J., Parulkar, G., Peterson, L., & Sunay, O. (2020). Using deep programmability to put network owners in control. *SIGCOMM Computer Communication Review, 50*(4), 82–88. https://doi.org/10.1145/3431832.3431842.
8. Gandhi, R., Ganjali, Y., et al. (2014). Duet: Cloud scale load balancing with hardware and software. In *Proceedings of the 2014 ACM Conference on Special Interest Group on Data Communication (SIGCOMM)* (pp. 27–38). ACM. https://doi.org/10.1145/2619239.2626317.
9. Hu, S., Liu, L., Zhang, X., Xu, S., & Jiang, C. (2015). Explicit path control in commodity data centers: Design and applications. In *Proceedings*

of the 12th USENIX Conference on Networked Systems Design and Implementation (pp. 1–14). USENIX Association.

10. Hyojoon, K., & Feamster, N. (2013). Improving network management with software defined networking. *IEEE Communications Magazine, 51*(2), 114–119. https://doi.org/10.1109/MCOM.2013.6461195.
11. Kang, N., Liu, Z., Rexford, J., & Walker, D. (2013). Optimizing the "one big switch" abstraction in software-defined networks. In *Proceedings of the 2013 ACM International Conference on Emerging Networking Experiments and Technologies (CoNEXT)* (pp. 13–24). ACM. Retrieved from: http://www.scopus.com/inward/record.url?eid=2-s2.0-84893398564&partnerID=40&md5=198adea3b54a99cfcb044ee2f143cc52 (accessed on 2 August 2024).
12. Kreutz, D., Ramos, F. M. V., Verissimo, P. E., Rothenberg, C. E., Azodolmolky, S., & Uhlig, S. (2014). Software defined networking: A comprehensive survey. *Proceedings of the IEEE, 103*(1), 14–76. https://doi.org/10.1109/JPROC.2014.2371999.
13. Lee, S., Kim, J., Shin, S., Porras, P., & Yegneswaran, V. (2017). Athena: A framework for scalable anomaly detection in software-defined networks. In *Proceedings of the 47th Annual IEEE/IFIP International Conference on Dependable Systems and Networks (DSN)* (pp. 249–260). IEEE. https://doi.org/10.1109/DSN.2017.42.
14. Liu, J., Li, Y., & Jin, D. (2014). SDN-based live VM migration across datacenters. In *Proceedings of the 2014 ACM Conference on SIGCOMM* (pp. 1–2). ACM.
15. Mekky, H., Hao, F., Mukherjee, S., Zhang, Z. L., & Lakshman, T. V. (2014). Application-aware data plane processing in SDN. In *Proceedings of the ACM SIGCOMM 2014 Workshop on Hot Topics in Software Defined Networking (HotSDN)* (pp. 13–18). ACM. https://doi.org/10.1145/2620728.2620735.
16. Moshref, M., Yu, M., Govindan, R., & Vahdat, A. (2014). DREAM: Dynamic resource allocation for software-defined measurement. In *Proceedings of the 2014 ACM Conference on Special Interest Group on Data Communication (SIGCOMM)* (pp. 419–430). ACM. https://doi.org/10.1145/2619239.2626291.
17. Rasley, J., Koponen, T., et al. (2014). Planck: Millisecond-scale monitoring and control for commodity networks. In *Proceedings of the 2014 ACM Conference on Special Interest Group on Data Communication (SIGCOMM)* (pp. 407–418). ACM. https://doi.org/10.1145/2619239.2626310.

18. Shen, G., Li, Q., Ai, S., Jiang, Y., Xu, M., & Jia, X. (2019). How powerful switches should be deployed: A precise estimation based on queuing theory. In *Proceedings of the IEEE Conference on Computer Communications (INFOCOM)* (pp. 811–819). IEEE. https://doi.org/10.1109/INFOCOM.2019.8737629.
19. Sherwin, J., & Sreenan, C. J. (2018). Reducing the latency of OpenFlow rule changes in data centre networks. In *Proceedings of the 21st Conference on Innovation in Clouds, Internet and Networks and Workshops (ICIN)* (pp. 1–5). IEEE. https://doi.org/10.1109/ICIN.2018.8401629.
20. Tran Manh, N., Nguyen Huu, T., Ngo Quynh, T., Hoang Trung, H., & Covaci, S. (2015). Energy-aware routing based on power profile of devices in data center networks using SDN. In *Proceedings of the 12th International Conference on Electrical Engineering/Electronics, Computer, Telecommunications and Information Technology (ECTI-CON)* (pp. 1–6). IEEE. https://doi.org/10.1109/ECTICon.2015.7207042.
21. Zheng, J., Xu, H., Chen, G., & Dai, H. (2016). Minimizing transient congestion during network update in data centers. In *Proceedings of the International Conference on Network Protocols (ICNP)* (pp. 1–10). IEEE. https://doi.org/10.1109/ICNP.2015.33.

CHAPTER 6

NETWORK FUNCTION VIRTUALIZATION

Contents

INTRODUCTION

Using IT virtualization technologies, network functions virtualization (NFV) is a concept in network architecture that allows entire classes of network node functions to be virtualized into building blocks that can be connected, or chained together, to create and deliver communication services.

NFV (Network Function Virtualization) expands upon some of the fundamental SDN subjects covered in earlier chapters, such as virtualization, control/data plane separation, SDN controllers, and data center concepts (especially orchestration applications). The intersection of these topics is depicted in Figure 6.1.

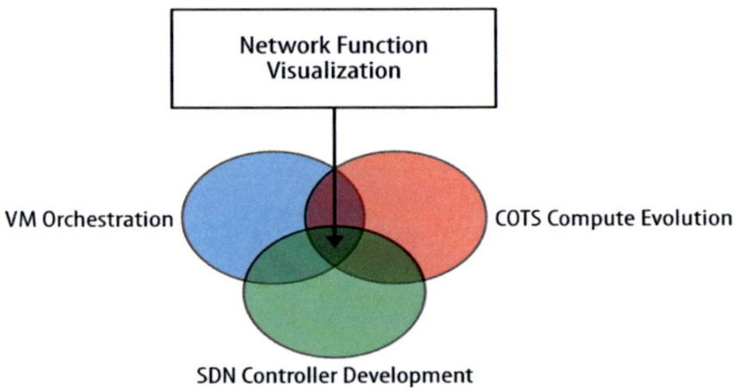

Figure 6.1. *The intersection that makes network function virtualization possible.*

Source: Thomas, D. N., & Ken, G. SDN: Software Defined Networks. O'Reilly Media, Inc. ISBN: 9781449342302.

Network function virtualization stems from a number of previously discussed issues related to network operations, specifically the consequences of network equipment manufacturers bundling services within their platform operating system. Appliance vendors are also affected by NFV in a way that misses out on the processing innovation and scale that many customers observe in their data centers.

Since many big service providers offered cloud services of their own, virtual machine orchestration was assumed to be part of how they operated. Additionally, they were monitoring Intel's I/O innovations in this field, such as SR-IOV support, VT-d, DDIO, and DPDK. In an autumn 2012 paper presented at the Layer123 SDN Conference (Darmstaad, Germany), these providers formally announced their support for the development of standards surrounding service virtualization and their desire for it. In the end, this work was sponsored by ETSI. Apart from this chapter, suppliers have shown a consistent preference for commodity-priced, off-the-shelf software-powered, ODM-built top-of-rack switches by voting with their wallets. Vendors were also monitoring the developing I/O capabilities of COTS platforms in the background and planning their approaches for the upcoming service appliances and dedicated network platforms with a significant services component. These include other platforms for service-oriented access and aggregation, the Broadband Network Gateway (BNG), its cable-space counterpart, the CMTS, the node-B in the mobile space, and others.

The discourse surrounding network services and functions has progressed to encompass three overarching classifications: basic virtualized services, service chaining, and services or platform virtualization. An SDN controller is mentioned in all of these talks; for basic virtualized services, it's at least somewhat involved, and in other cases, it may even be necessary.

6.1. CONCEPT OF NETWORK FUNCTION VIRTUALIZATION (NFV)

The need for telecom service providers all over the world to support their revenue and expansion goals, as well as to expedite the deployment of new network services, gave rise to the concept of Network Function Virtualization, or NFV. These days, proprietary hardware appliances are overly prevalent in today's overcrowded telecom networks. Consequently, in order to introduce a new network service, it is frequently necessary to introduce yet another type of proprietary hardware, which means finding the room and resources to support these configurations—a task that is getting harder and harder. This is made worse by factors like rising energy prices, capital requirements, the need for a large workforce with specialized skills, etc.

The range of abilities required to create, incorporate, and manage progressively intricate hardware-oriented appliances presents a significant obstacle for network operators and developers alike. Furthermore, hardware-based appliances quickly approach their end of life, and other cost-related problems have little to no positive impact on revenue. Due to the limitations of hardware-based appliances (such as firewalls and routers), they were forced to consider alternatives to the conventional network system. As a result, they developed a variety of IT virtualization technologies, established standards for them, and integrated them into their networks. Service providers from all over the world got together to negotiate with various standardization organizations, like the European Telecommunications Standards Institute (ETSI), in order to expedite the progress towards this shared objective. The lead group in charge of developing specifications, architecture, and other pertinent issues for the virtualization of various functions within telecommunication networks is the ETSI Industry Specification Group for Network Functions Virtualization (ETSI ISG NFV).

With Network Function Virtualization (NFV), hardware-centric, dedicated network devices are replaced with software running on general-purpose CPUs or virtual machines that run on standard servers. This new approach to designing, deploying, and managing networking services decouples the physical network equipment from the functions that run on it. NFV has the ability to significantly lower operating and capital expenses by severing the Network Functions (NFs) from the physical devices they operate on. This will enable the deployment of new services with greater agility and a quicker time-to-value. The idea of network function virtualization (NFV) is relatively new, but it is built on technologies that have shown to be effective in the IT sector. It is the outcome of rigorous testing and assessment conducted in the last few years by both industry and academic players.

By developing standard IT virtualization technology to consolidate a variety of network equipment types onto high-volume, industry-standard servers, switches, and storage that may be found in data centers, network nodes, or end user premises, Network Function Virtualization seeks to revolutionize the way network operators architect networks. There is no need to install additional hardware because these virtual appliances can be instantiated on demand. For instance, network administrators may use a Virtual Machine (VM) to run an open-source firewall program. It entails implementing network functions in software that can operate on a variety of industry-standard servers and that can be instantiated or moved to different parts of the network as needed, all without requiring the installation of additional hardware. Put differently, network function virtualization encourages the use of software that can implement network functions and be managed (e.g., moved, replicated) without requiring changes to the physical infrastructure. This software can run on a variety of common IT hardware in data centers.

6.1.1. History of NFV

A white paper on software-defined networking (SDN) and OpenFlow was released by a consortium of telecom operators during a conference held in Darmstadt, Germany, in October 2012. The Network Functions Virtualization (NFV) Industry Specification Group (ISG) was established within the European Telecommunications Standards Institute (ETSI) as a result of the Call for Action that concluded the White Paper. Representatives from the telecom sector in Europe and beyond made up the ISG (Le Maistre & Ray, 2012). Numerous topics are covered by ETSI ISG NFV, such as functional architecture, protocols, APIs, data models, information models, testing, security, and future developments.

In an effort to create new specifications and expand the ones that have already been published based on new features and improvements, the ETSI ISG

NFV has announced the release of Version 5 of its specifications, which will go into effect in May 2021. The team has published more than 100 publications since the white paper's release, many of which are being used in well-known open-source projects like OpenStack, ONAP, and Open-Source MANO (OSM), to mention a few. These publications have been more widely accepted in the industry. Owing to ongoing collaboration, other SDOs such as 3GPP, IETF, ETSI MEC, and others are referencing the ETSI NFV specifications.

6.1.2. NFV Framework

The NFV framework consists of three main components:

1. Virtualized network functions (VNFs) are software implementations of network functions that can be deployed on a network functions virtualization infrastructure (NFVI).
2. Network functions virtualization infrastructure (NFVI) is the totality of all hardware and software components that build the environment where NFVs are deployed. The NFV infrastructure can span several locations. The network providing connectivity between these locations is considered as part of the NFV infrastructure.
3. Network functions virtualization management and orchestration architectural framework (NFV-MANO Architectural Framework) is the collection of all functional blocks, data repositories used by these blocks, and reference points and interfaces through which these functional blocks exchange information for the purpose of managing and orchestrating NFVI and VNFs.

The NFV platform is the fundamental component of both the NFVI and the NFV-MANO. Virtualization software, in addition to physical and virtual processing and storage resources, play a part in the NFVI function. It is composed of virtualization software running on a hardware controller, as well as VNF and NFVI managers, in its NFV-MANO role. In order to manage and monitor the platform's components, recover from failures, and offer effective security—all necessary for the public carrier network—the NFV platform implements carrier-grade features.

6.1.3. Practical Aspects of NFV

One or more virtualized network functions, or VNFs, are implemented by a service provider that adheres to the NFV design. Customers of the provider are not automatically provided with a useable good or service by a VNF on its own. The idea of service chaining, in which several VNFs are used sequentially to deliver a service, is used to create more complex services. An additional facet of NFV implementation involves the orchestration procedure. NFV requires the network to be able to instantiate VNF instances, monitor, repair, and—most importantly for a service provider business—bill for the services rendered in order to build highly reliable and scalable services. These characteristics—also known as carrier-grade features—are assigned to an orchestration layer with the goal of offering low operation and maintenance costs, high availability, and security (Ashton & Charlie, 2014). Crucially, VNFs need to be managed by the orchestration layer regardless of the underlying technology within the VNF. For instance, an orchestration layer needs to be capable of managing both an IMS VNF from vendor Y running on KVM and an SBC VNF from vendor X running on VMware vSphere.

6.1.4. Distributed NFV

Initially, the idea behind Network Function Virtualization (NFV) was that data centers should use virtualized capabilities. This strategy is effective in many situations, but not always. The greatest degree of flexibility with regard to the physical location of the virtualized functions is assumed and emphasized by NFV.

Therefore, the best place for virtualized functions to be located is wherever they are most cost-effective and efficient. This implies that a service provider ought to have the liberty to deploy NFV anywhere it can be deployed, be it the data center, a network node, or the customer's premises. When NFV was being developed and standardized, this strategy—known as distributed NFV—was highlighted from the start. It is also highlighted in the most recent NFV ISG documents (Tom Nolle, 2013). In certain instances, a service provider may find it advantageous to have this virtualized functionality located at the client's premises. These benefits include those related to performance, economy, and the viability of the virtualized functions (Carol Wilson, 2013).

In June 2014, the initial multi-vendor proof of concept (PoC) approved by ETSI NFV ISG for D-NFV, led by Cyan, Inc., RAD, Fortinet, and Certes Networks, was carried out in Chicago. CenturyLink sponsored this event. The demonstration utilized RAD's dedicated customer-edge D-NFV equipment, which ran Fortinet's Next Generation Firewall (NGFW) and Certes Networks' virtual encryption/decryption engine as Virtual Network Functions (VNFs). Cyan's Blue Planet system managed the entire ecosystem. By the end of the same month, RAD's D-NFV solution, a Layer 2/Layer 3 network termination unit (NTU) with a D-NFV X86 server module acting as a virtualization engine at the customer edge, became commercially available. Additionally, throughout 2014, RAD established a D-NFV Alliance, a collaborative network of vendors and international systems integrators specializing in innovative NFV applications.

6.1.5. Relationship Between NFV and SDN

NFV and SDN are sometimes confused when talking about software-based networking, which results in the terms being mispronounced. Actually, NFV and SDN are two closely related, separate, but complimentary, and helpful technologies that work well together. Figure 6.2 illustrates how Network Functions Virtualization complements Software Defined Networking (SDN) rather than being dependent on it. SDN technologies are not necessary for the virtualization and deployment of network functions, and they can be used to manage nonvirtualized functions. The main distinction between the two is the domain to which they apply: SDN deals with replacing standardized networking protocols with centralized control, whereas NFV replaces proprietary hardware network elements (NEs) with software running on standard servers. A network's programmability, centralization of control, and separation of data are all part of SDN function, whereas network function transfers from specialized appliances to generic servers are the focus of NFV. SDN can be supported by Network Functions Virtualization since it offers the infrastructure needed to run SDN software. Moreover, the SDN goals of using commodity servers and switches are closely aligned with Network Functions Virtualization (Liyanage & Madhusanka, 2015).

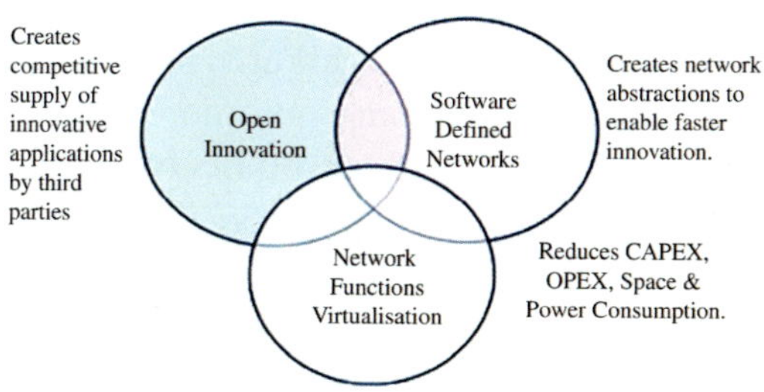

Figure 6.2. *Network functions virtualization relationship with SDN.*

Source: https://tec.gov.in/pdf/Studypaper/Network_Function_Virtualization%20.pdf.

6.1.6. Benefits of Network Function Virtualization

In the last few years, network functions virtualization (NFV), an emerging theme in the telecom sector, has acted as a catalyst for significant network transformations. Use of Network Functions Virtualization has greatly benefited network operators and changed the telecommunications sector in important ways.

Benefits include:

- Reduced equipment costs and reduced power consumption through consolidating equipment. Cost efficiency is a main driver of NFV.
- NFV allows to abstract underlying hardware, and enables elasticity, scalability and automation. Improves the flexibility of network service provisioning and reduce the time to deploy new services.
- Increased speed of deployment by minimizing the typical network operator cycle of innovation. Economies of scale required to cover investments in hardware-based functionalities are no longer applicable for software-based development, making feasible other modes of feature evolution. Network Functions Virtualization will enable network operators to significantly reduce the maturation cycle.
- The possibility of running production, test and reference facilities on the same infrastructure provides much more efficient test and integration, reducing development costs and time to market.
- Services can be rapidly scaled up/down as required. In addition, speed of service deployment is improved by provisioning remotely in software without any site visits required to install new hardware.
- Enabling a wide variety of eco-systems and encouraging openness. It opens the virtual appliance market to pure software entrants, small players and academia, encouraging more innovation to bring new services and new revenue streams quickly at much lower risk.
- Reduced energy consumption by exploiting power management features in standard servers and storage, as well as workload consolidation and location optimization. For example, relying on virtualization techniques, it would be possible to concentrate the workload on a smaller number of servers during off-peak hours (e.g., overnight) so that all the other servers can be switched off or put into an energy saving mode.
- Improved operational efficiency by taking advantage of the higher uniformity of the physical network platform and its homogeneity to other support platforms.

6.2. VIRTUALIZATION AND DATA PLANE I/O

Virtualization of network services doesn't necessarily mean separate hypervisor partitioned VMs that contain each service instance; instead, it could also mean:

- Services implemented in a machine with multiple/compartmentalized OS(s);

- Services implemented within the hypervisor;
- Services implemented as distributed or clustered as composites;
- Services on bare metal machines;
- Services implemented in Linux virtual containers.

By utilizing Network Attached Storage (NAS) or other shared storage/memory architectures, these techniques may share state. Figure 6.3 shows a sketch that demonstrates these techniques. Virtual machines are the main vehicle for Network Function Virtualization (NFV) because they offer significant management benefits. Linux containers outperform virtual machines in terms of performance and density (more instances per host), but they lack the virtual machines' management ecosystem and OS flexibility. Of course, in terms of performance, bare metal machines are superior to both alternatives, but in terms of flexibility and management, they are frequently regarded as being behind the times.

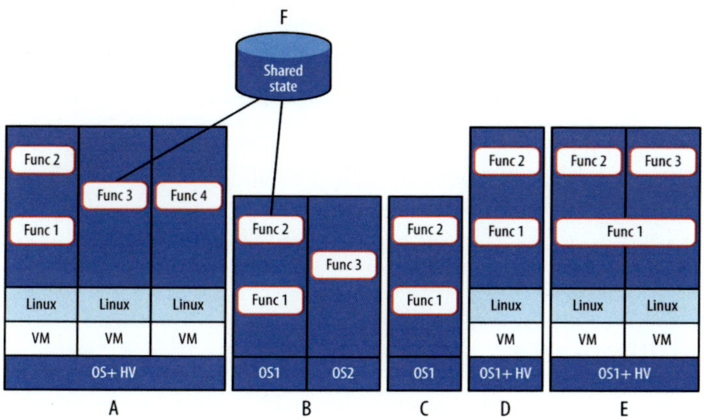

Figure 6.3. *Methods of virtualization survey: hypervisor partitioned (A); compartmentalized OS (B); bare metal (C); hypervisor embedded (D); and distributed/clustered composite functions (E); and two of these methods ((A) and (B)) also are depicted sharing state through shared storage (F).*

Source: Thomas, D. N., & Ken, G. SDN: Software Defined Networks. O'Reilly Media, Inc. ISBN: 9781449342302.

In a switch/router context, technologies such as the Virtual Ethernet Port Extension (VEPA) port extension may also offer a chance to deliver per-VM services through integrated or auxiliary services.

Virtualization of network services will introduce reliability concerns that NFV practices and recommendations need to address:

- The introduction of the hypervisor and the potential of multiple virtualized services on the same physical hardware can lead to contention for physical resources, resulting in a potential degradation experienced by individual services/functions or a whole chain via that single component. Not only will the NFV orchestration system need to monitor for such degradation, but it will also need visibility into the hypervisor and host resources to troubleshoot and potentially isolate/mitigate the contention.
- The hypervisor itself introduces a potential single point of failure (SPOF) that can impact many concurrent VMs on a host and potentially many different service chains.
- The hypervisor virtual switch can congest while serving the multiple vNICs of the various VMs and needs to be able to identify and prioritize control traffic to avoid application and management failure.
- Additionally, the hypervisor can isolate the applications from awareness of changes in physical machine state like failure of a NIC port. This management awareness needs to be bridged by SDN controller and Orchestration cooperation.
- Finally, virtual machines can also be migrated while operating as part of a high availability (HA) strategy. This behavior can impact a service chain in different ways, and so this behavior is sometimes intentional or unintentional as part of this strategy insofar as being used for HA capabilities.

6.2.1. Data Plane I/O

In general, the ability to run services on COTS hardware has been greatly facilitated by developments in data-plane I/O. There have been developing hardware and software strategies for penalty mitigation because the hypervisor vSwitch used in NFV/service virtualization methods adds an additional performance overhead for I/O due to the fact that virtualization/abstraction is not free. Software-based I/O acceleration methods like Virtio and SR-IOV are based on operating systems or hypervisors.

- The primary platform used by Linux, FreeBSD, and other operating systems for virtualizing disk and network I/O is called Virtio. In contrast to full virtualization, Virtio offers an abstraction layer over devices in a para-virtualized hypervisor/VMM and offers advantages for input/output.
- The PCI-SIG Single Root I/O Virtualization, or SR-IOV, is compatible with the PCIe-based class of I/O hardware. The I/O

MMU can distinguish between different traffic streams, apply memory/interrupt translations, and carry out delivery directly to a virtual machine (VM) thanks to the PCIe specification, which divides a device into multiple PCI Express Requester IDs (it splits physical functions into lighter-weight virtual functions). Each PCI Express virtual function, mapped to an ID, can be assigned to a VM. This lessens the effect of software emulation on I/O by avoiding the software switch layer. 1:256 is the mapping ratio between physical and virtual devices.

To the virtual machine (VM), the PCIE virtual functions look like hardware. Between the particular guest OS and the virtual function, all data packets travel directly via interrupts, DMA stream, and independent memory space. There is an improvement in latency, CPU utilization, and I/O throughput.

The BIOS, operating system instance, and hypervisor must all meet the hardware (NIC) and software support requirements for SR-IOV.

Additional I/O acceleration may be limited to vendor-specific hardware I/O enhancements (NIC and CPU). For developers who have been advancing with the capabilities of their CPUs and NICs (those based on Intel architecture), Intel has been refining a number of I/O performance boosts, such as:

- Pure hardware design improvement—pipeline depth, direct cache access, integration of the memory controller, and integration of high bandwidth PCIe Gen3.
- Intel Virtualization Technology (Intel VT)—VTx, c, and d.
- VT-x provides CPU-level hardware assist for VM migration and 32-bit guests (supported by VMware, Microsoft, Xen, KVM, Citrix, Red Hat, Novell, and Parallels).
- VT-d accelerates I/O virtualization by enabling direct assignment of an I/O device to a VM (requires BIOS support on OEM platforms, and a wide variety of hypervisor/VMM support).
- VT-c hardware assists in Intel Ethernet for network and storage connectivity, including VMDq and SR-IOV. Virtual Machine Device Queues (VMDq) refers to the sorting/grouping of network packets with multiple queues using LAN silicon instead of the VMM.
- Intel QuickAssist technology that enables Middleware for accelerated packet handling workloads (e.g., DPI, cryptography). Applications can integrate at different levels: program to the Intel QuickAssist technology API or program to open-source framework (e.g., OpenSSL libcrypto, Linux kernel crypto API—scatterlist, and zlib) through patches/shims.

- Commercial integration partners (e.g., 6Wind and Wind River) offer scheduling and other enhancements that dedicate cores to packet I/O integrated via special packaging (e.g., Wind River Linux, and Wind River Hypervisor).
- Intel Data Direct I/O Technology (Intel DDIO)—leverages integrated PCIe lanes on the CPU, reducing memory accesses and speeding up CPU data transfer, which is sometimes referred to as NIC core pinning.
- Intel DPDK—Intel's most recent innovation in I/O virtualization improvements, Dataplane Development Kit (Figure 6.4), provides data plane libraries and optimized (poll-mode) NIC drivers (for Intel NICs) in Linux user space that provide advanced queue and buffer management, and flow classification through a simple API interface (supported via a standard tool chain—gcc/icc, gdb, and profiling tools).
- RoCE (RDMA over Converged Ethernet) is potentially useful application of APIs for cluster computing between/among the virtualized network functions (an I/O virtualization technique). Mellanox is a primary proponent of RoCE technology and its potential use in NFV. Their NICs accelerate RoCE support and provide dynamically linked, user-space libraries that offload network packet processing from the CPU by allowing applications to directly access the NIC.

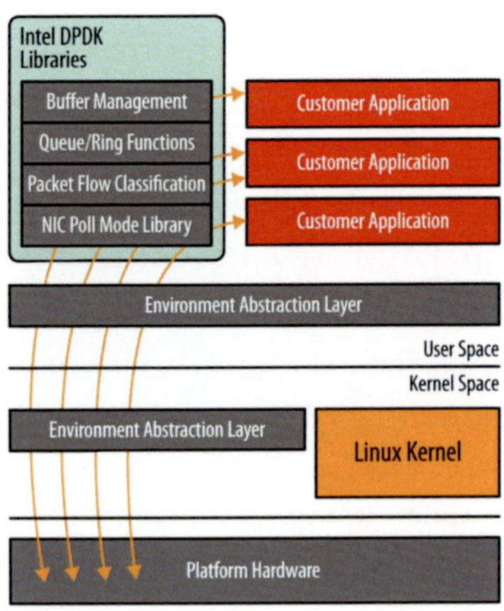

Figure 6.4. *Intel DPDK.*

Source: Thomas, D. N., & Ken, G. SDN: Software Defined Networks. O'Reilly Media, Inc. ISBN: 9781449342302.

- Similarly, other specific, specialized virtual application acceleration (e.g., PCoIP— Teradici offers NICs optimized for PCoIP) could potentially find applicability in the NFV virtual services space.

Data-plane processing, such as batch processing, differs from (raw) data-plane input/output (e.g., implementing access control lists or changing packets at the vSwitch or bridge) that could affect how well some virtualized services or functions work. There are many instances of throughput fall-off in the presence of such operations throughout the history of routing and switching development (that were successfully optimized over time).

6.2.2. I/O Summary

Although a lot of information has been provided here, the main takeaway is that interrupt density reduction, context switching, and buffer memory copies (i.e., zero-copy strategies) are being closely examined and worked upon. The explosion in virtualized service development is the main driving force behind this effort, which makes sense given their intrinsic I/O component and the need to increase overall performance and scale.

The primary objective for NFV going forward will be to identify optimization techniques that the community finds to be reasonably open (i.e., not dependent on the hardware technology of a single vendor), unless a clear de facto hardware standard develops, possibly similar to the ones previously mentioned.

6.3. SERVICES ENGINEERED PATH

Jim Guichard, a principal architect in the CTO Office at Juniper Networks at the time, proposed in 2010 to separate the Service and Network infrastructure (plane). Although it was a Juniper-specific solution, the Service Engineered Path (SEP) concept (Figure 6.5) was presented as a potentially novel method of service delivery for the Service Provider community. The issue was resolved before the concept was standardized.

The issue that needed to be addressed in SEP was that the requirement to deploy the service appliances, or dedicated services blades, which would make up the service offering, limited the ability of service providers to create new services. Within the edge routers that would service their anticipated markets, service offerings included firewalls, load balancers, intrusion prevention systems (IPS), and intrusion detection systems (IDS).

Due to these limitations, introducing new services was time-consuming and disruptive to network operations. It also made it crucial to forecast the markets for a service because there is a chance that there will be too few subscribers, leaving resources stranded, or too many subscribers, necessitating the installation of additional appliances or blades.

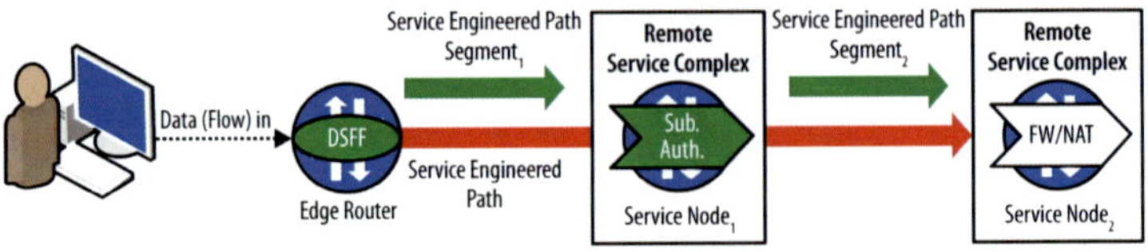

Figure 6.5. *Basic SEP concept.*

Source: Thomas, D. N., & Ken, G. SDN: Software Defined Networks. O'Reilly Media, Inc. ISBN: 9781449342302.

The motivation for the idea was manifold:

- Network devices that provide Service Enabling Technologies (SETs) would be transparent to the general network infrastructure.
- Changes/additions/upgrades to one or more service instances wouldn't affect routing in the network, providing a more stable service introduction environment.
- Provide flexible service SET and instance placement, and streamlined capacity planning of services.
- Faster time to market for services from a design, upgrade, testing, and deployment perspective.
- Edge routers need not be upgraded every time a new service is added or upgraded with new functionality.
- Providing the ability to link together services of differing types, thereby enabling new and innovative bundled services.

In essence, if these SETs could be pooled locally or remotely, these providers could benefit from lower costs and more efficient operations (the same basic appeal of host virtualization in data centers).

By determining qualifying flows at the edge and guiding them through these SETs via a SEP (Service Engineered Path), which could be built utilizing the overlay technologies that were available at the time—VLANs, MPLS, or IP tunnels—new services could be created.

The construction of service was a hierarchy of the following components:

1. **Service:** A service function, application, or content used singularly or in collaboration with other SETs to enable a service.
2. **SET Sequence:** Predetermined sequence of SETs that form the service.

3. **Set Sequence Path:** As an instance of a SET may be available at multiple points in the network, there are potentially several combinations of Service Nodes that could form part of the SET sequence. The SET sequence path is a list of (service node, SET) combinations available that could be used to satisfy the service.

To make provisioning and continuing management easier, a service orchestration and registration service was envisaged.

Initially, MPLS encapsulation controlled the paths, while Dynamic Service Flow Filters identified and guided traffic onto the paths.

SDN technologies were eventually introduced, most notably PCE and OpenFlow (Figure 6.6). The concept was honed, though there was some experimentation with the idea of generating the overlay abstraction/encapsulation through LDP label distribution.

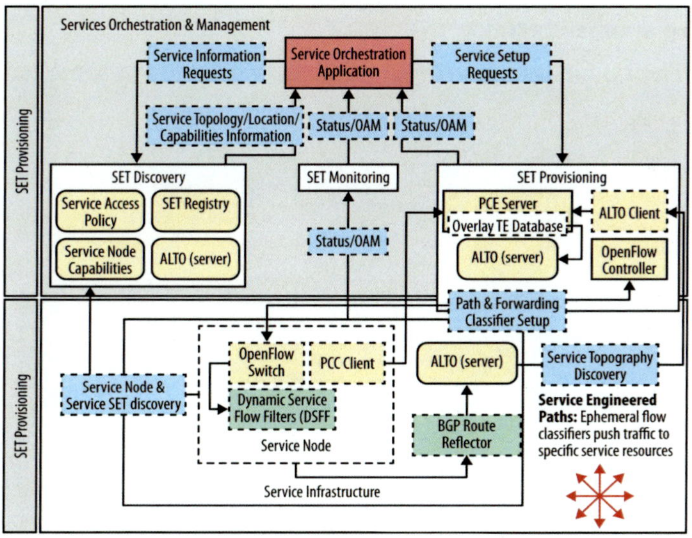

Figure 6.6. *Evolved SEP concept with OpenFlow, ALTO (topology), and PCE.*

Source: Thomas, D. N., & Ken, G. SDN: Software Defined Networks. O'Reilly Media, Inc. ISBN: 9781449342302.

The proposal did not include the wholesale virtualization of the service plane on COTS, unlike ETSI NFV, because virtualization techniques and virtual I/O improvements were still in their infancy when the SEP concept was introduced. However, this concept is the origin of the concepts of service chaining, network function virtualization, and separation of the service plane (as do some commercial products).In the end (and regrettably), network function virtualization became the ETSI work group's name and the superset nomenclature for previous ideas like those presented with SEP.

6.4. SERVICE LOCATIONS AND CHAINING

Although this may be a long-term objective of service providers for their edge/ access deployments, the concept of service chaining shouldn't assume that all of the service elements are virtualized or that they are all located in data centers.

Network boundaries can naturally be associated with services, for instance, by placing a load balancer or affixing a security policy to a boundary. As shown in Figure 6.7, this network boundary may be:

- The boundary between a tenant network and an external network (the Internet or the VPN to the enterprise network);
- The boundary between the network of one tenant and the network of another tenant;
- The boundary between multiple networks of the same tenant.

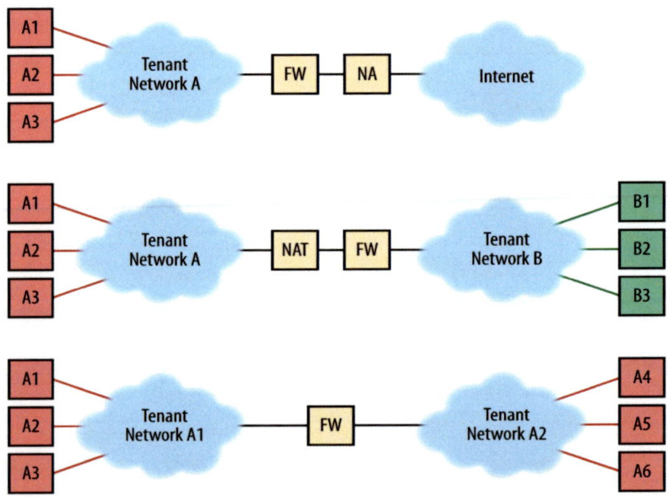

Figure 6.7. *Services at network boundaries.*

Source: Thomas, D. N., & Ken, G. SDN: Software Defined Networks. O'Reilly Media, Inc. ISBN: 9781449342302.

Ultimately, services can be implemented with greater precision and linked to specific flows or clusters of flows (i.e., aggregate flows), as depicted in Figure 6.8. For cloud service providers and per-subscriber services in the Edge/Access network domain, this is the main model of interest.

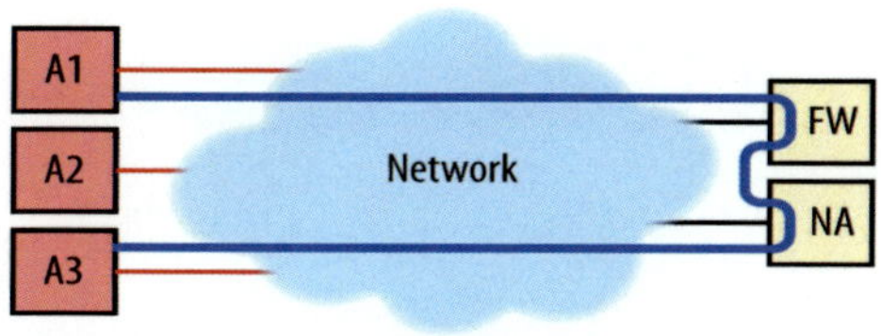

Figure 6.8. *Services for flows.*

Source: Thomas, D. N., & Ken, G. SDN: Software Defined Networks. O'Reilly Media, Inc. ISBN: 9781449342302.

Applying services to flows of traffic involves several steps:

1. Defining the elements and the ordering and configurations required to implement a service. This definition includes the constraints on the placement of service elements.
2. Identifying and steering the flow of traffic to visit the service node or the sequence of service nodes.
3. Vendors have begun to label their current methodologies for doing service chaining. In the case of Cisco Systems, this is called vPath, and in the case of Juniper Networks, The Service Engineered Path (SEP).
4. Control plane signaling to the service nodes to inform them which services to apply to which flows, including the service parameters.
5. There are also optimizations possible around original placement of the service node and/or the ongoing placement of additional service instances to alleviate performance bottlenecks.

An SDN controller is a good fit for each of these responsibilities. SDN controllers are equipped with hooks to orchestration systems (API), domain/network-wide topology views, and the capability to manage/provision a network overlay (or the abstraction that may be used to match and direct traffic). In the context of service chaining in the data center, the use of an SDN controller might seem obvious, but less so in the Edge/Access domains (where the potential interaction delay between the agent and controller could be problematic but the additional cost of a co-located controller might be prohibitive). This brings us full circle to the concept of an embedded controller, as illustrated in Figure 6.9. This concept was first introduced in research studies pertaining to the identification of "mice and elephant" flows and the management of forwarding table size in OpenFlow controlled networks as an optimization to the control feedback loop. As a slave subcontroller to a master controller, the data plane element that closes the circuit at the edge in this instance functions as an interface with orchestration applications, merely updating state, rules, and configuration.

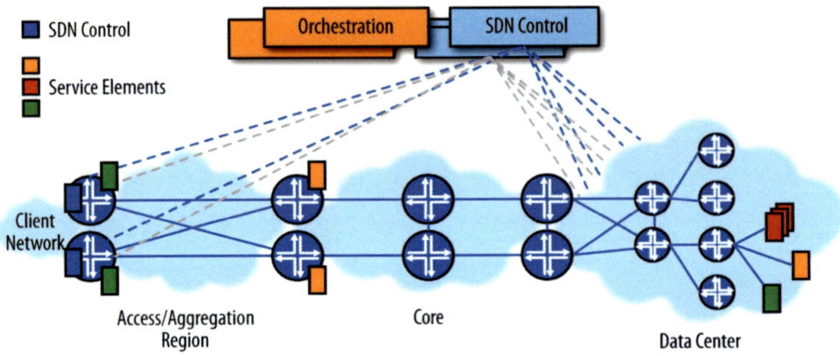

Figure 6.9. *For non-data center regions of the network, embedded SDN control processes in network elements may be appropriate.*

Source: Thomas, D. N., & Ken, G. SDN: Software Defined Networks. O'Reilly Media, Inc. ISBN: 9781449342302.

In a combination setting (i.e., virtualized and legacy service elements) or a fully legacy environment, the components might not be able to support native agents that work well with the SDN controller or some of the tunnel encapsulations used in SDN overlays. In order to establish service chains, it may be necessary to combine VLANs and tunnel encapsulations with configuration/control protocols between controllers and network elements.

6.4.1. Metadata

There are still unanswered questions about the traffic matching protocol (or protocols) used to create service chains and paths, as well as the standardization of the overlay encapsulation.

The idea of whether metadata needs to be inserted into the flow further complicates these questions. This latter consideration stems from the understanding of how service applications are currently designed in integrated systems, which use metadata to transfer hints between different processing blocks within the integrated system, as well as the possibility of partial decomposition and virtualization of service functions, as envisaged in the ETSI NFV workgroups.

The controller's role and its service chaining application may determine whether or not metadata is necessary. Specifically, it may determine whether or not the controller will be tasked with establishing a chain that forbids any inter-block knowledge.

The answer might also depend on whether the virtualization vision divides the external chain/overlay from the internal chain, which uses some

IPC mechanism to allow internal embedded metadata, by restricting function decomposition to the same virtual device or composite.

The most popular examples that are used to illustrate the requirements for metadata involving contexts that aren't available through flow packet header analysis—e.g., the treatment of a video flow with subscriber-specific ad insertion (where some additional clue is embedded that reflects geography, interests, or other triggers for the ad insertion).

A Metadata Access Point (MAP) might have a place in the overall architecture if passing metadata between NFV functional blocks was necessary and if the metadata was flow-associated rather than per-packet associated. For the creation and distribution of metadata, existing specifications such as IF-MAP may offer server/protocol solutions; however, these solutions must be integrated during the flow setup or SDN control stages of developing service chains.

Metadata can be implicit (e.g., associated with an MPLS label) or explicit. In order to pass metadata from one chain member to another, the explicit alternative—embedding the metadata—may result in packet extensions or overhead. Standardization will almost certainly be necessary to maintain an open environment, and this could raise unintended concerns about the transparency of such augmented flows to the current network infrastructure.

6.4.2. An Application-Level Approach

The network construct view requires tunneling because data flows have intrinsic routing that needs to be obscured (i.e., don't forward on destination address). But what if we're approaching the service chaining aspect of NFV incorrectly? Should we investigate a solution using application-based protocols instead of network-based constructs?

This perspective makes the assumption that, with the help of a controller, network protocols can be changed to control metadata and flow direction.

Data flows are treated as application inputs and outputs in the application construct view (Figure 6.10). Discrete sockets are used by applications to run on servers, which have DNS (resolvable names).

The load balancer (or an anycast address for a bank of ADC/load balance capacity—the assumption of a load balancer is quite common) for a set of components that run the service is identified by that service instance name to IP address binding, along with potentially multiple input and output ports that represent different application personalities (i.e., arrangements or actions). Two personalities are used in bidirectional flows.

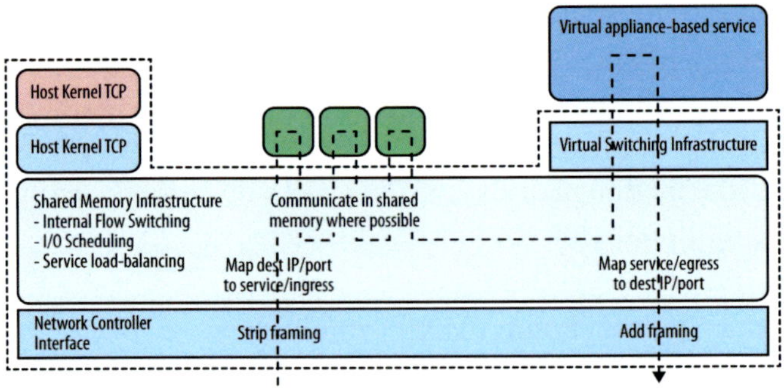

Figure 6.10. *The application-level proposal for service chaining leverages an optimized stack to communicate with virtual appliances and allows a runtime environment for some virtualized network services that use shared memory to communicate (an optimization).*

Source: Thomas, D. N., & Ken, G. SDN: Software Defined Networks. O'Reilly Media, Inc. ISBN: 9781449342302.

Each service's mapping from internal service ports to external transport ports as well as the connectivity between the transport ports are specified in the service path. These service paths are propagated or applied from a management system to the service instances (via an as-yet-undetermined API) and are created from a data model that expresses the relationships between a service component, services, and service paths. In more detail, the model describes the relationships between internal port/socket mappings to external ports, load balancing, scaling/constraints, and other more general features, as well as how the functions work together to form a service.

Although still in the concept/exploratory stage, this method of chaining using a number of well-known application-keyed technologies (e.g., ADC/LB, DNS, and others) along with a few novel application management technologies (e.g., controllers and their API) might be intriguing in the event that there are an excessive number of chains and tunnels. One of the benefits of the various ideas discussed here is that functional elements on the same device may employ shared memory IPC mechanisms to enhance performance in scenarios where the application interaction is a combination of internal IPC and external protocol.

6.4.3. Scale

Since that SDN is currently a working entity that we can experiment and develop with, even if the network construct is palatable in its current state, scale and complexity issues cannot be disregarded. Furthermore, the application-level approach discussion cannot be steered by scale or complexity.

Major components of the complexity discussion revolve around placement of the service nodes and constraints that may restrict the service path (Figure 6.11):

- How many chains will there be, and what are the constraints on the path selection of service chains (e.g., overall latency of the delivered service, administrative boundaries, and tariffs)?
- How do those constraints affect the HA policy for a service (e.g., should individual SETs be added to or from the chain if their placement causes trombone flows in the network, or should the flow fail over to an entirely new chain)?
- How often will the chain topology change, and how dynamic/elastic is the loading of the elements in the chain?
- Is there a benefit to service placement algorithms that minimize the potential for network bottlenecks and contribution to overall delay in a serviced flow?
- What role does policy play in the service chain embedded within the chain as a decision/branch point or when expressed as multiple different chain topologies? When would packets be sent to a remote in-line service (i.e., not a proxy)?

Raw scale is also a factor in the complexity discussion:

- Number of subscribers/sessions;
- Length/duration of sessions/flows and profile of packet lengths;
- Packet throughput expectations, and both the capabilities of the overall chain and each individual element (e.g., load balancer).

Virtual service function placement and the ensuing service chains are probably going to be highly localized given the possible scale implications and overall service constraints. The connectivity between an edge/access domain device and a centralized COTS resource bank (a data center), with a failover to another such resource bank, may have the highest path diversity in the chain.

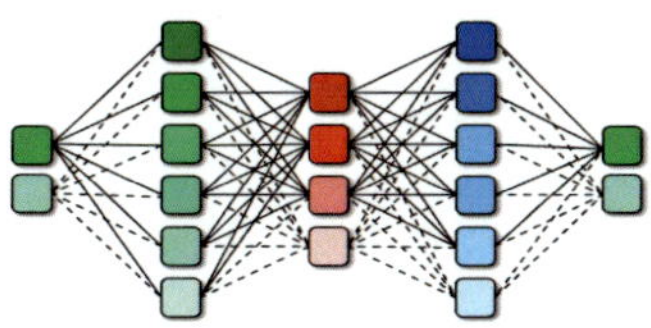

Figure 6.11. *How complex will service chaining be? Load balancing and HA introduce a requirement for many tunnels to be set up between service nodes. Elasticity and dynamic paths require potentially large-scale tunnel creation/deletion.*

Source: Thomas, D. N., & Ken, G. SDN: Software Defined Networks. O'Reilly Media, Inc. ISBN: 9781449342302.

6.5. NFV AT ETSI

These and other service virtualization-related questions are intended to be addressed by NFV activity within ETSI. An Industry Specification Group (ISG) is what NFV in ETSI is called. There will be no standards defined by the NFV workgroups (Figure 6.12). Rather, they aim to specify needs, detect optimal methodologies, pinpoint deficiencies in existing guidelines, and offer suggestions on how to close those gaps. NFV is composed of a technical steering committee (TSC), a main organizational body, and numerous subgroups with specialized interests. Though they are welcome to participate in the conversations, vendors are overwhelmingly represented on the list of NFV officials due to organizational structure.

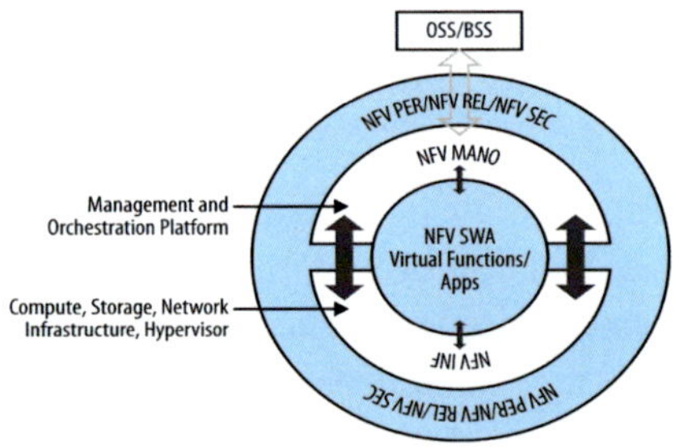

Figure 6.12. *ETSI NFV work group organization/structure. Both MAN and INF have interfaces with NFV SWA as well as with each other. Cross-functional work-groups (PER, REL, and SEC) don't have defined interfaces with MANO, INF, and SWA, but work in conjunction with them. NFV SWA anticipates an interface to legacy OSS/BSS systems (not shown).*

Source: Thomas, D. N., & Ken, G. SDN: Software Defined Networks. O'Reilly Media, Inc. ISBN: 9781449342302.

Virtualized network functions (VNFs) can be provisioned, configured, and operated using the framework defined by Management and Orchestration (MANO), which is essentially an orchestrator that manages all of the VNFs. Both an element (southbound) and an application (northbound) interface are available in the MANO Orchestrator. The northbound interface offers VNF lifecycle services (instantiation, operation, and monitoring), policing (usage controls), infrastructure monitoring (which would essentially be a pass-through function), and registration/topology, while the southbound interface is defined in a different group (infrastructure).

The idea that additional management tools might be required to handle virtualized network services in the traditional OAM&P model is reinforced by MANO. This is suggested as the NFV Orchestrator (NFVO) in the MANO case, and it will communicate with the legacy OSS/BSS.

It remains to be seen if this means that this application interface, other application interfaces, or some intrinsic interface at the SDN controller level to the legacy OSS/BSS represent a significant portion of the management data that may have been gathered by the SDN controller/agent mechanism. The MANO Orchestration platform in the DC Orchestration example can cooperate with a Cloud Management System, which is logically displayed in some NFV documents below the MANO Orchestration. Determining data models (Yang, TMN) for these different tasks/interfaces and offering an open API will be a part of the MANO work. In collaboration with NFV INF, this work includes network and cloud models that could make it possible to develop a macro-management tool for virtual infrastructure—a Manager of Managers, perhaps. The ability to match functional capacity to demand and possibly offer a service topology with an API and visualization component should be present somewhere in the orchestration function. The topology and endpoint mappings will need to be managed by the SDN controller.

Infrastructure— (NFV INF) defines common infrastructure for NFV. The intention is to incorporate both hardware and software, as seen in Figure 6.13. With their prolific writing, this group has already cataloged about 14 interdomain interfaces in the NFV architecture. They are in charge of endorsing the data model that was discussed in the MANO section as well as the hypervisor-level architectures that minimize context switching and streamline I/O.

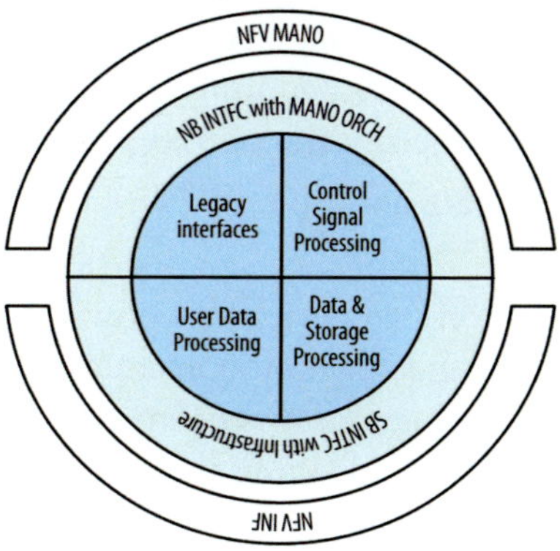

Figure 6.13. *Interaction of ETSI MANO, INF, and SWA work groups (SWA view with proposed inner functional groups).*

Source: Thomas, D. N., & Ken, G. SDN: Software Defined Networks. O'Reilly Media, Inc. ISBN: 9781449342302.

The question of which of the popular I/O optimization techniques in the field is most appropriate for NFV has been well-discussed (e.g., DPDK in comparison to SR-IOV) performance. This subject depends on the suggested

Reliability and Availability architecture since it may incorporate the idea of VM-motion, which could conflict with an SR-IOV optimization plan. It has been argued in the discussion that SR-IOV is less accommodating to VM-motion.

Software Architecture— (NFV SWA) defines use cases and how solutions should be structured and possibly decomposed into functional blocks. What services can be virtualized and how is an intriguing question for NFV in general. Potential solutions range from fully virtualized services operating in a single virtual machine (VM) to multipart services, which are fully virtualized services made up of functional sub-blocks, to services that need to run on bare metal. Keep in mind that, from an operations standpoint, the latter could still profit from orchestration.

The virtualized functions should be able to communicate with INF directly or indirectly through MANO, according to NFV SWA, in order to express operational requirements (e.g., memory resources, compute, storage, security, QOS) and support requirements (e.g., keeping an eye on, charging, and measuring).

- Their proposed Control Signal Processing Function Group will focus on authentication/authorization, policy, state management, mobility, and mobility-related support functions, including call record collection and lawful intercept.
- Their proposed User Data Processing FG will focus on packet forwarding, duplication, counting, processing, load balancing, and application layer steering (i.e., proxy).
- Their proposed Data and Storage FG will focus on data storage and management.

A SET or service function can be broken down into component pieces or functional blocks (assuming the set may consist of more than one functional block—e.g., signal processing, transaction management, and content processing). This is how NFV builds upon the SEP concept of a SET (in NFV, now called a VNF) in SWA.

If broken down into multiple functional blocks, those blocks can operate in a variety of configurations. Therefore, it is also necessary to describe the operational behavior, constraints, and relationships and communication among the parts (e.g., topology). These function descriptors bear resemblance to the policies that are affixed to SDN applications and that are to be communicated to or enforced upon SDN controllers. These policies outline the availability/disaster-recovery, consistency, routing, security, performance, QoS, geofencing, access control, and other operational expectations and parameters for each application.

Determining how to define the descriptors so that flow-through provisioning is possible is a critical task for the SWA. In other words, even though the SDN controller and orchestration system can work together to arrange, route, and instantiate network functions, their separate and combined configurations can be fairly complicated and are presently vendor-specific. Open Virtual Format (OVF), which is currently the de facto standard for packaging virtual machines, needs to be expanded or enhanced because it can only express a limited amount of configuration metadata at this time and cannot handle the potential complexity of some of the envisioned services. The intention is to avoid retouching the group of machines that make up the individual or composite service by requiring the operator to exit to separate configuration entities post-instantiation.

Among the instances given is the Evolved Packet Core (EPC) application (in general), which comprises the following sub-functions: layer 3 packet processing, layer 7 traffic steering function, user/session state management, policy/rule-set processing, and so forth. Figure 6.14 provides an illustration of this functional decomposition.

1. **Security (NFV SEC):** Defining how to secure both infrastructure and the virtualized service functions (including the API). This would also include authentication, identity management, monitoring, detection, and mitigation of threats.
2. **Performance and Scale (NFC PER):** This is self-evident. The group will try and define practices that provide optimal performance, describe performance/scale/portability tradeoffs, and present performance test data (several carriers have proposed tests including the impact on performance of the use of various vendor's NICs and different types of I/O mechanisms).
3. **Reliability and Availability (NFV REL):** Defines deployment and management practices that assure reliability and availability. At this point, they've defined some useful terminology for the expression of application requirements and constraints: delay/traffic/disruption/fault tolerances, performance (e.g., QOS requirements), security (non-repudiation, confidentiality, authorization, etc.), and dependability/reliability.

Additionally, this group has discussed some intriguing issues regarding potential application involvement, in-chain failure (one component or function fails in the chain), the removal of single points of failure (e.g., hypervisor), the requirement for heartbeat mechanisms between subcomponents, and the impersonation of watchdogs (hardware/software) that could have existed in solutions that weren't virtualized.

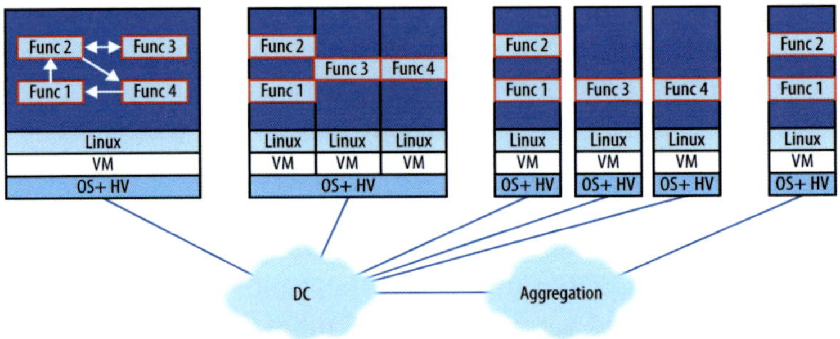

Figure 6.14. *Functional decomposition. If a service (e.g., EPC) is virtualized, will all its subcomponents run in the same VM, in separate VMs on the same host, as separate VMs on different hosts in the same logical domain (e.g., data center), or as separate VMs on different hosts in multiple logical domains (e.g., data center and aggregation)?*

Source: Thomas, D. N., & Ken, G. SDN: Software Defined Networks. O'Reilly Media, Inc. ISBN: 9781449342302.

Additionally, some potential issues in a virtualized environment that must be resolved for a carrier-grade deployment will be addressed by NFV REL.

Use case documents appear to originate from multiple sources, not just the SWA. Use cases are defined by the Network Operations Council (NOC), and the INF group has also supplied examples of use cases. Your creativity is the only restriction on these, which contain details (e.g., WAN Optimization, Firewall, Router, IPTV Head-end, DPI, Residential Gateway/CPE, Mobile Base Station, and Mobile Packet Core) in addition to more general service descriptions (e.g., using purpose-built hardware, sharing compute between VNFs, and partial decomposition of a function).

6.6. NON-ETSI NFV WORK

The fact that the ETSI workgroup exists doesn't mean that other organizations aren't doing research on service virtualization and developing standards for it, nor does it mean that commercial service virtualization products aren't already available. This is far from the case; for example:

- The academic community is beginning to study some of the questions around NFV as part of the burgeoning SDN research they are performing.
- Many existing controller/framework vendors are targeting service chaining as one of their applications and a few startups (e.g.,

LineRate, Embrane) are positioning controllers for layer 2 through layer 7 that work with their own virtualized services.

- Existing vendors of highly integrated network elements are investigating intermediate or total virtualization of their platform/ solutions.
- Though it is too early for a complete section in this revision, the IETF has begun soliciting interest in the area of service chaining. A proposed work group (network service chaining (NSC)) is currently collecting drafts in its BoF (birds of a feather) stage. This includes drafts proposing formalized packet headers for expressing service context and metadata as well as the need for a standardized generic service control plane.

6.6.1. Middlebox Studies

Recent research in the academic community has concentrated on Middlebox appliance optimization. Middlebox appliances are essentially the virtual service appliances (or a subset of them) that are the subject of NFV studies. The studies, in particular, concentrate on the capacity to scale, integrate, and manage an entire Middlebox deployment—keeping in mind that these may consist of multiple devices, or a service chain. Based on an application-reported performance metric, the University of Wisconsin has developed a series of studies (called Stratos, which seems to progress as CloudMB) that suggest optimizing the performance of such chains by monitoring serviced streams and (using a greedy heuristic) spinning up or down instances of specific middleboxes to relieve bottlenecks (caused by a significant change in performance over some time threshold) while maintaining a predetermined level of application performance. In order to prevent inter-rack traffic (network-aware placement and flow distribution), another source of bottlenecks, the study also looks at optimizing the initial middlebox placement, the heuristic (scale), and in-flow assignment to the middleboxes.

There was also emphasis on not moving existing flows (no service interruption or make-before-break behavior) in the scale up/down phases (the scale down phase is an interesting inclusion because there could be cost savings during idle network periods). There are interesting concepts in the research around the heuristic and some of the simplifying operations assumptions/ assertions (in respect to service chaining):

- The operator would prefer not to manually intervene at all (fully automated solution) and that the nature or function of the middlebox was somewhat irrelevant to the process (or could be made so by the process).

- The preferred solution to congestion in the service chain can be solved in place (relatively), without diverting or "trombone(ing)" traffic to an instance or chain segment in another location (i.e., minimizing branching).
- The assertion that monitoring can't be derived from traditional traffic counters in the infrastructure because of the nature of operation of some of the devices. Nor can the simple monitoring of resource consumption in the VMs be assumed to reflect end-to-end application performance. Thus, application involvement in monitoring is preferred.
- The iterative heuristic was chosen over other strategies: scaling all middleboxes in the path, reliance on function-specific monitoring, reliance on packet processing time estimates, and monitoring CPU load on the service elements.

The solution defines service chains using a high-level topology abstraction, and it uses a central controller to program forwarding (e.g., using an OpenFlow controller). According to the abstracted topology chains, the controller was enhanced with a topology file populated with middlebox and application instances, from which it can generate service-chain forwarding rules for the switching infrastructure. More broadly, this augmentation modifies the controller's conventional (simple) topology and path computation to make it service aware.

In order to initially position the service virtual machines (VMs) and to add or remove instances as the heuristic spins up or down scale, the system/process collaborates with a virtual machine orchestration system.

Slick adopts a distinct strategy. Although the potential to transform a (v) switch into a network service appliance has been hinted at by the semantics of SDN protocols, current implementations and protocol limitations have hindered this possibility from being realized. Slick stays within two main domains: circumventing the constraints of the current static semantics of flow matching in SDN and potentially unintentionally utilizing dynamic service chaining.

In this project, an agent on a programmable device (e.g., a server, possibly with a programmable network element—FPGA, NPU, or GPU) communicates with a specialized controller (a Slick controller and agent) in order to dynamically load application functions and send back triggers to the controller from those functions.

Applications work in conjunction with the controller to install features and a corresponding set of flow specifications in the network. The controller is in charge of deciding where the functions are placed (a task shared by CloudMB) and creating the pathways via which flows lead to the functions. By eliminating the a priori assignment of functionality (i.e., the device is no longer a firewall per se, but could perform some of the functions of a firewall), the concept appears to break the vertical integration of middleboxes. Thus, Slick discusses virtualized service definitions in addition to service chaining in general (Figure 6.15).

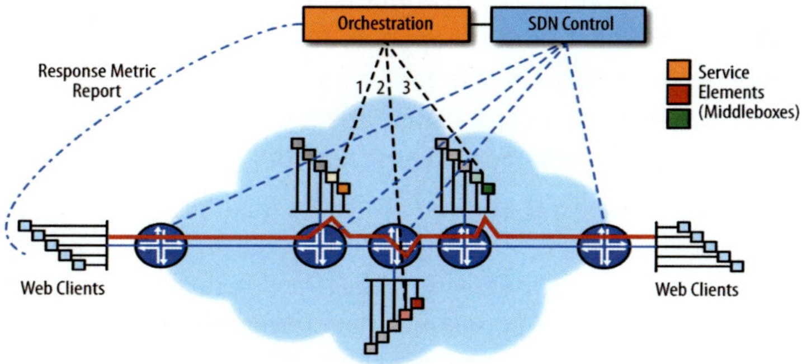

Figure 6.15. *An iterative middlebox optimization technique; when web clients report out of specification response times, the orchestrator (in conjunction with the SDN controller) iteratively tries to add (localized) capacity to the different middleboxes in the service path to remove the bottleneck.*

Source: Thomas, D. N., & Ken, G. SDN: Software Defined Networks. O'Reilly Media, Inc. ISBN: 9781449342302.

6.6.2. Embrane/LineRate

Heleos is a platform that allows virtual network services to be provisioned; it is marketed by Embrane. It becomes a little confusing to distinguish between controller, orchestration, and management system because it doesn't rely on any standard SDN protocols and integrates the service management application directly into their application. The Elastic Services Manager (ESM) control processes of Embrane exclusively function with their devices, the Distributed Virtual Appliances (DVAs), similar to certain other SDN controller/agent architectures. For COTS compute, a DVA is essentially a virtual service element. At the moment, Embrane provides firewall and load balancing services.

A major concern with Embrane, and to be fair, all SDN-like solutions that are being introduced to the market, is whether or not they will create an open ecosystem for the creation and administration of third-party applications, or if they will stick to their proprietary course. It is ultimately reasonable to question this solution's viability in light of whether or not customers will adopt it in sufficient numbers to create a de facto standard, should it opt for the latter course.

F5 Networks acquired LineRate Systems. At the time, LineRate was a spin-off from the University of Colorado and only offered one (public) product: a virtual load balancer known as LineRate Proxy. The virtual service was a complete application layer proxy with traffic-steering capabilities that was powered by an external policy. This product is directly related to the virtualized services/NFV discussion. LineRate appears not to have a separate controller/agent architecture or controller offering, which sets it apart from Embrane. It offers an external policy server as an alternative. LineRate did offer an intriguing viewpoint on how SDN is defined and how network functions are broken down:

- LineRate has what appears to be a DPI-like approach to SDN but claims to be different because it doesn't steer traffic based on packet-based matching/forwarding behaviors. Instead, it uses its ability to cache and replay application-level requests in combination with policies applied to the responses to do the steering. This allows the solution to potentially re-issue the request to a different source or an intermediary service, e.g., video optimization.
- LineRate points out in its marketing literature that perhaps as integrated network services (e.g., EPC) decompose, the LineRate solution is positioned to be even more effective as a control point.

Contributions from the NFV work in ETSI also imply that different points in the flow may require a combination of high-touch control, like full proxies, and low-touch control, like flow matching, as found in OpenFlow. High-touch control is used to divide or aggregate traffic, while low-touch control is helpful for setting up flows and performing some location steering.

Both Linerate and Embrane have promoted flexible licensing models, such as usage-based, subscription, and keyless models (each company refers to these models differently, but the concepts are the same). Pricing and licensing can be quite flexible, so things can turn historic very quickly. However, licensing is still another crucial factor to take into account when talking about NFV, or service virtualization. For instance, a usage-based pricing model with automation and optimizations similar to those offered by Stratos/CloudMB would be preferable.

6.6.3. Platform Virtualization

The networks used by service providers today are made up of a variety of integrated, purpose-built components or platforms. A core routing platform's basic architecture, for instance, is to forward packets at a very high speed and low latency while using packaging that is sensitive to factors like physical footprint, power consumption, and associated heat. It might be challenging to deploy this platform at the network/provider edge without a completely separate set of forwarding and service blades, as tradeoffs between forwarding rate, session state management, protocol session scale, and other services might be necessary.

Some vendors developed into experts in packaging particular kinds of platforms over time. The Evolved Packet Core and Broadband Network Gateway components are the most popular examples.

Competitors of the established "big three or four" providers of these platforms started looking into new packaging models that lowered costs and made use of some of the service virtualization concepts as network operators started investigating SDN.

The suggested general designs called for the use of an SDN Controller (e.g., an OpenFlow controller) to develop application-specific state (protocol or user session state) on a related server-based application and program forwarding state into a (much simpler and lower cost) switching element. Aside from the aforementioned initiatives, there are also newer efforts like IP Infusion (ZebOS BGPD) and RouteFlow (BGP and IGP on OpenFlow), which use less expensive components to replace or centralize the functions of the current generation of routers.

Low-hanging fruit in conventional network operations, such as the BGP Route Reflector (vRR); Figure 6.16, are being virtualized by traditional vendors in response. These devices can be converted to operate in a virtual machine (VM) the easiest because they are not intended to be in the data plane.

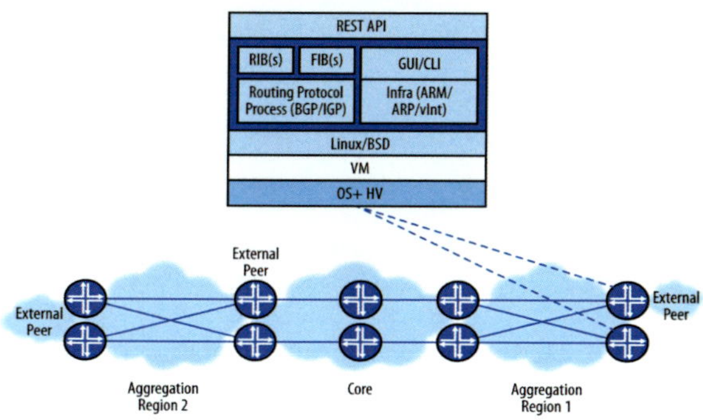

Figure 6.16. *Conceptual virtual route reflector (vRR) as programmable control point for service provider network (e.g., injecting routes into aggregation network).*

Source: Thomas, D. N., & Ken, G. SDN: Software Defined Networks. O'Reilly Media, Inc. ISBN: 9781449342302.

The vRR becomes a potential centralization point for SDN control if it has a standardized controller/agent control session and standardized programming interface. Subsequently, current Provider Edge implementations begin to resemble SDN implementations (despite mostly still utilizing the current distributed control plane), serving as a link between current operations and a future that will be increasingly virtualized. This model is being presented by other traditional network element vendors and was investigated in the Juniper Networks/Contrail and ALU/Nuage SDN controllers. In the context of a data center, this is especially simple to visualize: tenant virtual machines (VMs) appear as virtual Customer Edge (vCE) entities, a virtual Provider Edge (vPE) manifests as a vRR, and a companion host-based agent (which programs a hypervisor-based routing entity for the data/forwarding plane) as a control plane. To centralize and optimize processing for WaaS, IPSec, and other services, the vCE could also be implemented as part of a managed service offering for the enterprise VPN market (presumably through flow tunneling). A conceptual drawing of a vCE proposal can be found in Figure 6.17.

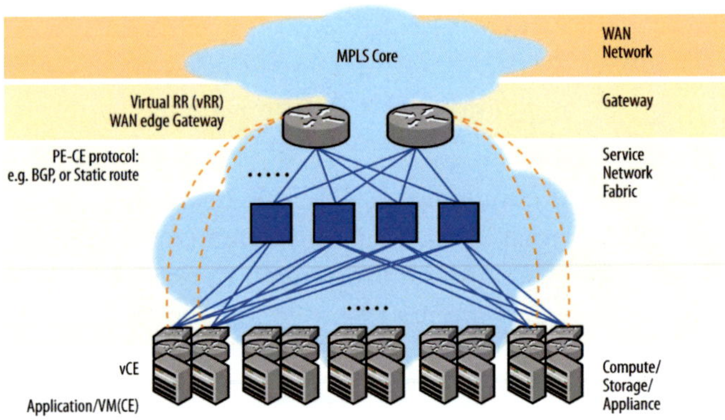

Figure 6.17. *Fang/Bitar vCE proposal from MPLS and Ethernet World Congress (2013).*

Source: Thomas, D. N., & Ken, G. SDN: Software Defined Networks. O'Reilly Media, Inc. ISBN: 9781449342302.

Traditional network element providers can also employ certain strategies to gradually divide their services offering from their hardware offerings. Some vendors, for instance, have programs that let their services run on tethered servers initially, then virtualize them later (by means of extensions to their SDK/APIs that chain services in the integrated platform). As the chaining orchestration and protocols are developed, this permits some temporary scaling of the service on shared compute (Figure 6.18).

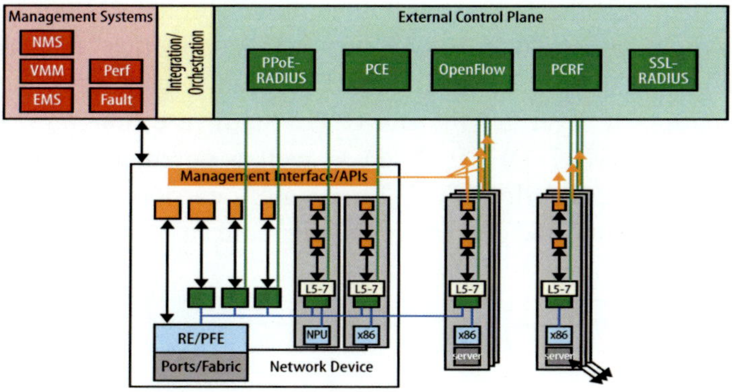

Figure 6.18. *Transitional/integrated service virtualization strategies.*

Source: Thomas, D. N., & Ken, G. SDN: Software Defined Networks. O'Reilly Media, Inc. ISBN: 9781449342302.

Internal NPU or CPU blades, tethered COTS with API extensions enabling internal management, forwarding/chaining techniques on the tethered compute, and finally an autonomous entity under external control are all possible operating environments for services. Although proprietary, this degree of virtualization and chaining allows for some scale out on COTS compute and can be used in conjunction with localized static routing and application-level load balancing to create new services (e.g., the mobile space's Service Delivery Gateway). However, in this model—especially in the tethered-appliance model—the router/switch may act as the manager of the virtualized service. The early market service chains could be established using GRE encapsulation and route-leaking techniques because there was no immediate standardization in service chaining protocols and encapsulation (Figure 6.19).

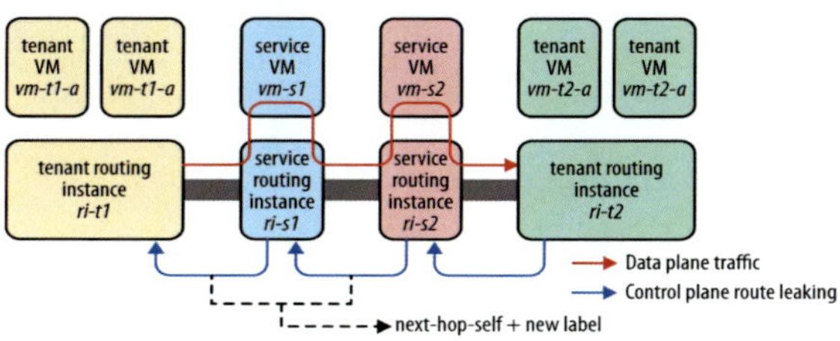

Figure 6.19. *Service chaining using routing instances.*

Source: Thomas, D. N., & Ken, G. SDN: Software Defined Networks. O'Reilly Media, Inc. ISBN: 9781449342302.

A lot of broadband aggregators, or public service providers, are also considering switching to virtualized CPE devices (vCPE). These investigations have led to the hypothesis that the conventional broadband aggregation PE (Provider Edge) device (BNG/BRAS) could also function well as a virtual entity (vPE). By shifting the functions of (arguably exhausted) layer 3 CPE to a combination of layer 2 CPE and COTS hardware running layer 3 CPE basic services (e.g., NAT, DHCP, DNS), as well as potentially more advanced/ future services (e.g., security, HTTP Proxy, etc.), carriers were able to create new services, cut costs, and decrease customer care calls (*refer to* Figure 6.20).

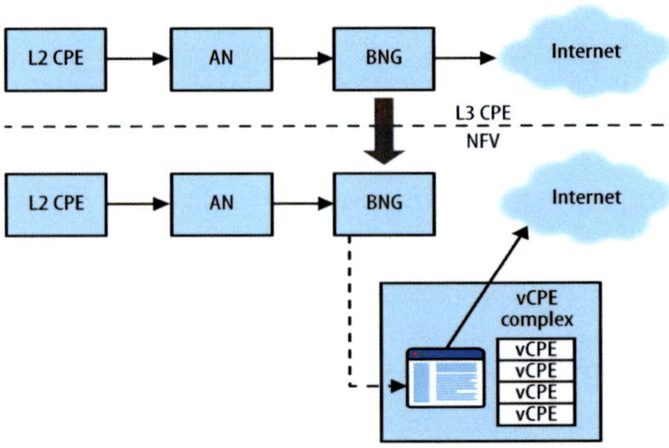

Figure 6.20. *Network function virtualization applied to layer 3 CPE in service provider networks (proof of concept).*

Source: Thomas, D. N., & Ken, G. SDN: Software Defined Networks. O'Reilly Media, Inc. ISBN: 9781449342302.

The ultimate goal of this work is to determine whether it is possible to integrate the vCPE functionality with the BNG functionality (Figure 6.21).

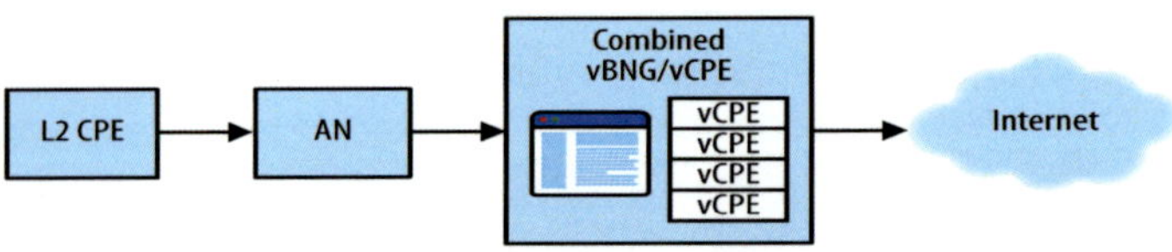

Figure 6.21. *A broadband aggregation platform constructed by integrating and virtualizing the functions of both the BNG and the CPE.*

Source: Thomas, D. N., & Ken, G. SDN: Software Defined Networks. O'Reilly Media, Inc. ISBN: 9781449342302.

Research in this field (beyond proof of concept) involves examining how the placement of the virtualized functions may affect performance (e.g., south or north of the BNG, colocated with the AN, etc.) and how the integrated functionality can be broken down to produce a solution that is horizontally scalable. This includes I/O optimization techniques and container strategies, which are also being researched and discussed in ETSI NFV forums. The new virtualized services will need to meet the extremely low-price points per subscriber of the currently integrated solutions (for the vCPE/vBNG example). If these new designs for virtual platforms are technically possible, the cost per subscriber may only fit the business case when the COTS price/performance curve crosses the right thresholds at a later date.

6.7. ENABLERS FOR NETWORK FUNCTION VIRTUALIZATION

The Network Functions Virtualization (NFV) became achievable with several recent technology developments, such as given in susbections.

6.7.1. Cloud Computing

Cloud computing and other contemporary technologies are leveraged by Network Functions Virtualization. Virtualization mechanisms, such as using virtual Ethernet switches (e.g., vSwitch) to connect traffic between virtual machines and physical interfaces and hardware virtualization through the use of hypervisors, are the foundation of these cloud technologies. High-speed multi-core CPUs with large I/O bandwidth, smart Ethernet NICs for load sharing and TCP offloading, poll-mode Ethernet drivers (instead of interrupt driven ones, like Linux NAPI and Intel's DPDK), and packet routing directly to virtual machine memory are all ways to achieve high-performance packet processing for communication-oriented functions.

By using orchestration and management mechanisms, cloud infrastructures can improve resource availability and utilization. These mechanisms can be applied to the automatic creation of virtual appliances within a network, resource management through the assignment of virtual appliances to the appropriate CPU core, memory, and interfaces, re-initialization of failed virtual machines, snapshotting of virtual machine states, and VM migration. Finally, an additional level of integration between Network Functions Virtualization and cloud computing is made possible by the availability of open APIs for management and data plane control, such as OpenFlow, OpenStack, OpenNaaS, or OGF's NSI.

6.7.2. Industry Standard High-Volume Servers

The utilization of high-volume, industry-standard servers is a crucial component of the Network Functions Virtualization business case. A server manufactured with standardized IT components (such as the x86 architecture) and sold in millions is referred to as an industry standard high-volume server. A prevalent characteristic of high-volume servers that are industry standard is the competitive supply of interchangeable subcomponents within the server.

Network appliances that rely on custom Application Specific Integrated Circuits (ASICs) will lose ground to general-purpose processors in the long run because creating ASICs gets more expensive the smaller the features you want. For commodity functions implemented at scale, merchant silicon will continue to be useful, while ASICs will still be useful for some kinds of very high throughput applications.

6.7.3. Software Defined Networking (SDN)

Although NFV and software defined networking (SDN) can be used separately, SDN greatly simplifies the implementation and management of NFV. Through a network-wide software platform that allows for centralized network coordination, control, and programmability, SDN manages network complexity. At various levels of abstraction, SDN offers a programmable and adaptable interface that manages and synchronizes the operation of a group of devices. With it, users can use only software mechanisms to dynamically reconfigure the network to plug in a function that is running on a server at the proper location in the network. Without it, configuring the network to properly plug in software-instantiated functions would require a lot more manual intervention from NFV users.

6.8. TECHNICAL REQUIREMENT/CHALLENGES FOR NETWORK FUNCTION VIRTUALIZATION

Network function virtualization (NFV) is a relatively new technology in the network industry. It presents a number of challenges to network operators, including ensuring network performance for virtual appliances, managing their dynamic installation and migration, and strategically placing them. Prior to implementing the Network Functions Virtualization, these implementation challenges must be resolved.

6.8.1. Interoperability and Compatibility

The primary need for network function virtualization (NFV) is to create standard interfaces between a variety of virtual appliances and between the virtualized implementations and legacy equipment. The promotion of openness is one of NFV's objectives, so in a multi-tenant NFV environment, network carriers may need to integrate and manage servers, hypervisors, and virtual appliances from various vendors. A single interface is necessary for their smooth integration in order to promote interoperability. The NFV solutions that are developed must function in a hybrid environment that combines virtual and physical network functions, and they must be compatible with the current Element and Network Management Systems (EMS/NMS) and Operation and Business Support Systems (OSS/BSS). Eventually, network operators will need to be able to transition seamlessly from proprietary physical network appliances to open standard-based virtual ones, as they might not be able to maintain all of their current services and hardware in proprietary physical network appliances.

6.8.2. Performance Trade-Off

Since the Network Functions Virtualization approach is based on using industry standard hardware (i.e., avoiding any proprietary hardware such as acceleration engines) along with a virtualized networks & appliances, a probable decrease in performance may arise.

Using the right hypervisors and contemporary software technologies to minimize performance degradation and its negative effects on latency and throughput is the challenge. In order for virtual appliances to know what they can get out of the hardware; the available performance of the underlying platform needs to be precisely identified and understood. Selecting the appropriate technology will enable virtualization of data/user plane functions in addition to network control functions.

6.8.3. Migration From and Co-Existence of Legacy While Ensuring Compatibility with Existing Platforms

If Network Functions Virtualization (NFV) and IT orchestration are to converge, NFV implementations must coexist with network operators' legacy network equipment and be compatible with their current Element Management Systems, Network Management Systems, OSS, and BSS, as well as possibly with their existing IT orchestration systems.

A migration path from the current proprietary physical network appliance-based solutions to more open standards-based virtual network appliance solutions must be supported by the Network Functions Virtualization architecture. Stated differently, Network Functions Virtualization needs to function in a hybrid network made up of both virtual and traditional physical network appliances. Therefore, in order to work with physical appliances that carry out the same functions, virtual appliances must utilize and support the North Bound Interfaces that are currently in place (for management and control).

6.8.4. Management and Orchestration

Network Functions Virtualization offers a chance to quickly align management and orchestration with North Bound Interfaces to well-defined standards and abstract specifications thanks to the flexibility provided by software network appliances operating in an open and standardized infrastructure. As a result, integrating new virtual appliances into a network operator's operating environment will be much less expensive and time-consuming. This is further extended by Software Defined Networking (SDN), which streamlines the incorporation of packet and optical switches into the system, e.g., SDN can be used by a virtual appliance or Network Functions Virtualization orchestration system to regulate how physical switches forward traffic.

6.8.5. Security and Resilience

Operators must make sure that the security features of their network won't be negatively impacted when deploying virtualized network functions. Notwithstanding its advantages, NFV might also introduce fresh security risks. The initial hypothesis is that by enabling the on-demand replication of network functions following a failure, network functions virtualization will increase network availability and resilience. Provided that the infrastructure is secure, particularly the hypervisor and its configuration, a virtual appliance ought to be just as safe as a physical appliance. Tools for managing and confirming hypervisor configurations will be sought after by network operators. Virtual appliances and hypervisors with security certifications will also be necessary.

6.8.6. Reliability and Stability

When providing particular services (e.g., network operators must ensure reliability, e.g., voice calls, and on-demand videos), whether they are made using real or virtual network appliances. Carriers must ensure that the transition to NFV does not negatively impact service level agreements or reliability. When switching to hardware platforms that are prone to errors, NFV must incorporate resilience into its software in order to meet the reliability requirement. Each of these processes adds a new potential point of failure that ought to be managed automatically.

Another issue with NFV is maintaining service stability, particularly when moving or reconfiguring a big number of software-based virtual appliances that are powered by various hypervisors and software providers. It should be possible for network operators to transfer virtual network functions (VNFs) from one hardware platform to another while meeting the requirements for service continuity. To achieve service stability and continuity, they must also specify the values of a number of key performance indicators, such as the maximum rate of call/session drops and non-intentional packet losses, the maximum per-flow delay and latency variation, and the maximum amount of time it takes to identify and recover from failures.

6.8.7. Simplicity

It is imperative to guarantee that virtualized network platforms will be easier to use than current ones. Hence, while preserving continuity to support crucial revenue-generating services, network operators must prioritize the simplification of the numerous complex network platforms and support systems that have developed over decades of network technology evolution. It is crucial to refrain from exchanging one set of operational difficulties for another, equally difficult set.

REFERENCES

1. Ashton, C. (2014). Don't confuse "high availability" with "carrier grade". *Embedded Community.*
2. Chatras, B. (2018). On the standardization of NFV management and orchestration APIs. *IEEE Communications Standards Magazine, 2*(4), 66–71. https://doi.org/10.1109/MCOMSTD.2018.1800032.
3. Le Maistre, R. (2012). Tier 1 carriers tackle telco SDN. *Light Reading.*
4. Lemke, A. (2014). 5 must-have attributes of an NFV platform. *Techzine, Alcatel-Lucent.*
5. Liyanage, M. (2015). *Software Defined Mobile Networks (SDMN): Beyond LTE Network Architecture.* John Wiley. ISBN 978-1-118-90028-4.
6. Nolle, T. (2013). Is "distributed NFV" teaching us something? *CIMI Corporation's Public Blog.*
7. Stephenson, R. (2013). How low-cost telecom killed five 9s in cloud computing. *Wired.*
8. Wilson, C. (2013). RAD rolls out distributed NFV strategy. *Light Reading.*

CHAPTER 7

NETWORK TOPOLOGY AND TOPOLOGICAL INFORMATION ABSTRACTION

Contents

INTRODUCTION

A small number of applications have long had access to topological information and its availability to them when they want to make use of what is practically undiscovered gold in the networking world. A few crucial requirements had to be met by these submissions. They must have mastered one of the many routing protocols first. Second, their access to routing had to be granted in the strictest sense possible; they needed to connect to a routing network directly; this required more than simply setting up a server and connecting it to the internet. Like any other networking device in that network, the application frequently had to pass security and other quality assurance tests. In many cases, this required testing for years to finish. The application's understanding of network topology was also restricted to active topology—that is, topology that is currently in use to route or steer traffic—when the time came for it to be approved for use on the network.

Generally speaking, dormant or inactive topological data is not needed for routing computations and is therefore not exchanged in routing protocols. Some applications still require this information, so in order to obtain it, the application had to search for it manually using out-of-band methods like the command-line interface or other management protocols. The way in which topology information was formatted was one last drawback of conventional topology methods.

The information was, predictably, formatted so that a router could obtain and process the topology for the quickest routing computations in a timely manner. If the information were obtained outside of band, it was also formatted in a different way that would be appropriate for a command-line interface, but not for performing other calculations. Unfortunately, these formats were frequently not the best for other purposes these applications had, necessitating additional processing to make it workable—more work, money, and kludges. Thankfully, fresh perspectives on the identification, retrieval, and processing of topological data have recently been pursued. The way in which applications are able to access this new topology through SDN controllers and frameworks is what's really new and innovative.

7.1. NETWORK TOPOLOGY

Network topology is the arrangement of the elements (links, nodes, etc.) of a communication network (Groth & Toby, 2005). Network topology can be used to define or describe the arrangement of various types of telecommunication networks, including command and control radio networks (Grant, 2014), industrial field busses and computer networks.

A network's topological structure, or network topology, can be represented physically or logically. This is a graph theory application in which the links or lines connecting the nodes represent the connections between the communicating devices, which are modeled as nodes. Physical topology refers to how a network's various components are arranged (e.g., cable installation, and device placement), whereas logical topology shows how data moves through a network. Despite having the same logical topology, two networks may differ in terms of node distances, physical connections, transmission rates, or signal kinds. The physical layer of the OSI model is specifically concerned with the physical topology of a network. Local area networks (LANs), which are widely used computer networks, are a common source of examples of network topologies. Every LAN node has one or more physical links connecting it to other network nodes; these links can be graphically mapped to create a geometric shape that represents the physical topology of the network. Numerous physical topologies, such as ring, bus, mesh, and star, have been employed in local area networks (LANs). On the other hand, the network's logical topology is established by mapping the data flow among the constituent parts. Comparatively, Controller Area Networks—which are frequently found in automobiles—are essentially distributed control system networks made up of one or more controllers connected to actuators and sensors via a physical bus topology.

7.1.1. Types of Network Topology

Network topology is the configuration of a network consisting of sender and receiver pairs and connecting lines between nodes. Various network topologies that include are discussed in subsections.

7.1.1.1. Mesh Topology

Every node in a mesh topology has a specific point-to-point link with every other node. Because there is a unique link between any two devices and non-redundant links cannot be added to the main network, this type of network is referred to as complete.

- In a mesh topology, where N devices are connected to each other, the total number of ports needed by all the devices is N–1. Since there are five devices linked to one another, each device needs a total of four ports. N * (N–1) is the total number of ports needed.
- Assuming a mesh topology with N devices connected to one another, the total number of dedicated links needed to link them is NC2, i.e., N(N–1)/2. Since there are five connected devices in Figure 7.1, five times four is two, or ten, links are needed in total.

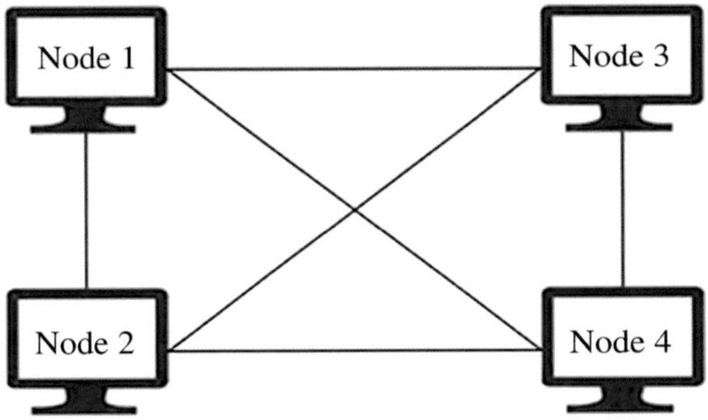

Figure 7.1. *Mesh topology.*

Source: https://www.geeksforgeeks.org/network-topology/.

There are two types of Mesh topologies:

i. **Full Mesh Topology:** All the nodes within the network are connected with every other If there are n number of nodes during a network, each node will have an n–1 number of connections.

ii. **Partial Mesh Topology:** The partial mesh is more practical as compared to the full mesh. In a partially connected mesh, all the nodes aren't necessary to be connected with one another during a network.

- **Advantages of Mesh Topology:**
  - Easy fault identification and isolation.
  - Failure during a single device won't break the network.
  - There is no traffic problem as there is a dedicated point to point links for every computer.
  - It provides high privacy and security.
  - Data transmission is more consistent because failure doesn't disrupt its processes.
  - Adding new devices won't disrupt data transmissions.
  - This topology has robust features to beat any situation.
  - A mesh doesn't have a centralized authority.
- **Disadvantages of Mesh Topology:**
  - Each node must have an interface for every other node.
- There is only a limited number of I/O ports in a computer.
  - The cost to implement mesh topology is high.

- There is a high risk of redundant connections.
- Maintenance needs are challenging with a mesh topology.

7.1.1.2. Star Topology

Every node (PCs, printers, and peripherals) in a star topology is connected to the main server. It has a hub or switch—a central point of connection. Every device in a star topology is linked to a central hub (Figure 7.2).

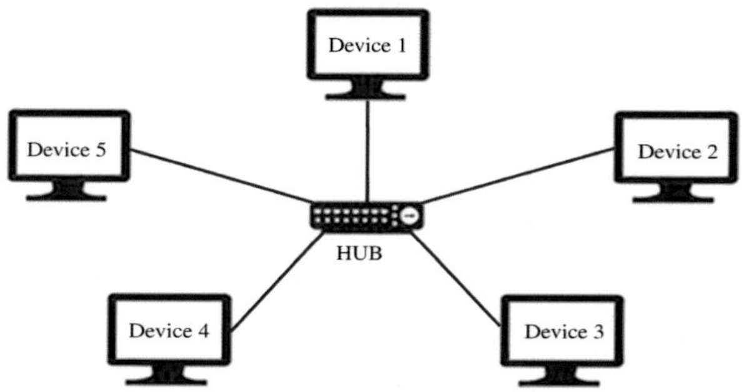

Figure 7.2. *Star topology.*

Source: https://www.geeksforgeeks.org/network-topology/.

- Advantages of Star Topology:
  - If N devices are connected to each other in a star topology, then the number of cables required to connect them is N. So, it is easy to set up.
  - Each device requires only 1 port, i.e., to connect to the hub, therefore the total number of ports required is N.
  - It is Robust. If one link fails only that link will affect and no other than that.
  - Easy to fault identification and fault isolation.
  - Star topology is cost-effective as it uses inexpensive coaxial cable.
- Disadvantages of Star Topology:
  - Star networks can require more cable length than a linear topology.
  - More expensive cabling.
  - Performance is based on the single concentrator, i.e., hub.

7.1.1.3. Bus Topology

Every station in a bus topology is connected to a single cable. Messages are sent from one point to both directions in the bus network. Signals are broadcast to all stations in the bus topology. Every computer on the bus verifies the address on the signal, or data frame, as it travels by. The computer processes the signal if the address on it matches its address. The computer proceeds down the bus without doing anything if the address doesn't match (Figure 7.3).

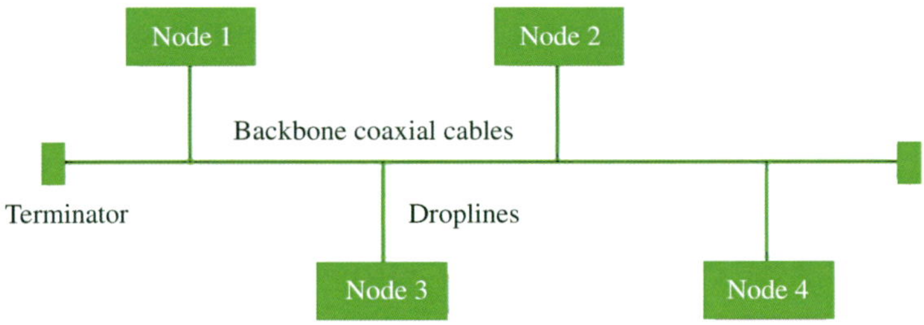

Figure 7.3. *Bus topology.*

Source: https://www.geeksforgeeks.org/network-topology/.

7.1.1.4. Ring Topology

In a ring topology, every node is wired into a closed circle. Transmitted messages circle the ring unit to which they are addressed, with each node refreshing the signal. Every device in a ring network has two neighbors that it can communicate with (Figure 7.4).

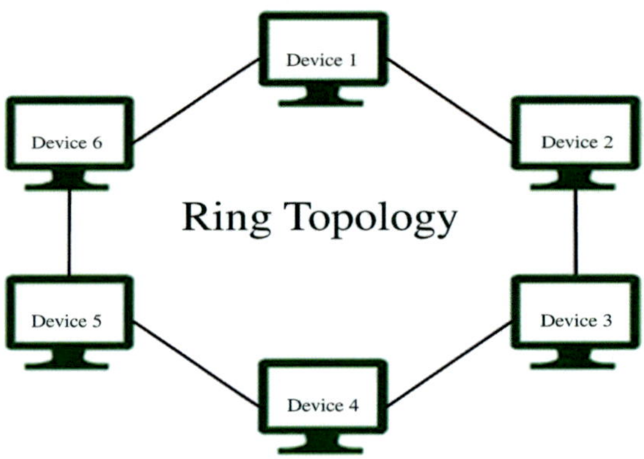

Figure 7.4. *Ring topology.*

Source: https://www.geeksforgeeks.org/network-topology/.

The most common access method of ring topology is token passing:

i. **Token Passing:** It is a network access method in which a token is passed from one node to another node.

ii. **Token:** It is a frame that circulates around the network.

- Advantages of Ring Topology:
  - The data transmission is high-speed.
  - The possibility of collision is minimum in this type of topology.
  - Cheap to install and expand.
  - It is less costly than a star topology.
- Disadvantages of Ring Topology:
  - The failure of a single node in the network can cause the entire network to fail.
  - Troubleshooting is difficult in this topology.
  - The addition of stations in between or the removal of stations can disturb the whole topology.
  - Less secure.

7.1.1.5. Tree Topology

Nodes are connected in a hierarchical structure to form a tree in a tree topology. In a nutshell, tree topology is a mix of bus and star topology, with a root node and the remaining nodes being child nodes. A level in the tree is represented by each star-configured network, and the central bus serves as a communication channel. The branching cable in a tree topology creates a hierarchy by connecting the root node to every other node via a communication loop that is devoid of loops (Figure 7.5).

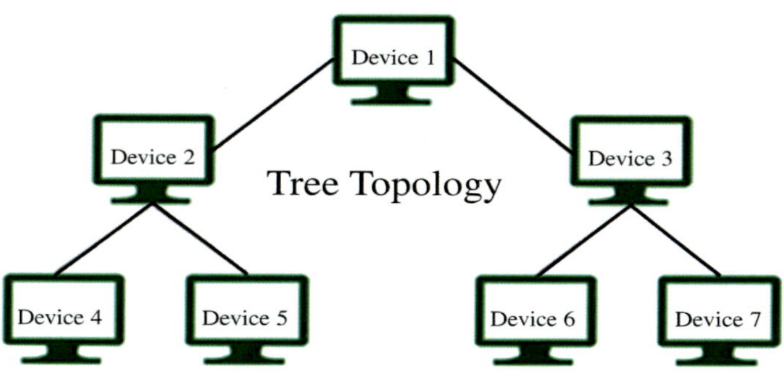

Figure 7.5. *Tree topology.*

Source: https://www.geeksforgeeks.org/network-topology/.

- Advantages of Tree Topology:
  - Security is high in tree topology.
  - Tree topology is more reliable.
  - Tree topology is more scalable.
  - It allows more devices to be attached to a single central hub thus it decreases the distance that is traveled by the signal to come to the devices.
  - We can add new devices to the existing network.
  - Error detection and error correction are very easy in a tree topology.
- Disadvantages of Tree Topology:
  - If the central hub gets fails the entire system fails.
  - The cost is high because of the cabling.
  - If new devices are added, it becomes difficult to reconfigure.

7.1.1.6. Hybrid Topology

The term "hybrid network topology" refers to a configuration that combines two or more different topologies. It is created when various network topologies are integrated (Figure 7.6).

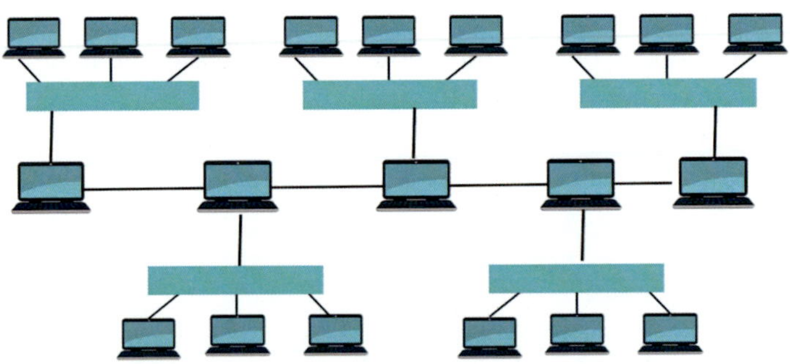

Figure 7.6. *Hybrid topology.*

Source: https://www.geeksforgeeks.org/network-topology/.

- **Advantages of Hybrid Topology:**
  - Hybrid Topology provides more flexibility than other topologies.
  - Hybrid topology is more robust than the other.
  - Hybrid Topology provides optimized performance.

- **Disadvantage of Hybrid Topology:**
  - It is challenging to design the architecture of the hybrid network.
  - Hubs used in this topology are very expensive.
  - The infrastructure cost is very high as a hybrid network requires a lot of cabling and network devices.

7.1.1.7. Point to Point Topology

The functionality of the sender and recipient is the focus of point-to-point topology. It is the most basic kind of communication between two nodes—one acting as the sender and the other as the recipient. Broadband is abundant with point-to-point (Figure 7.7).

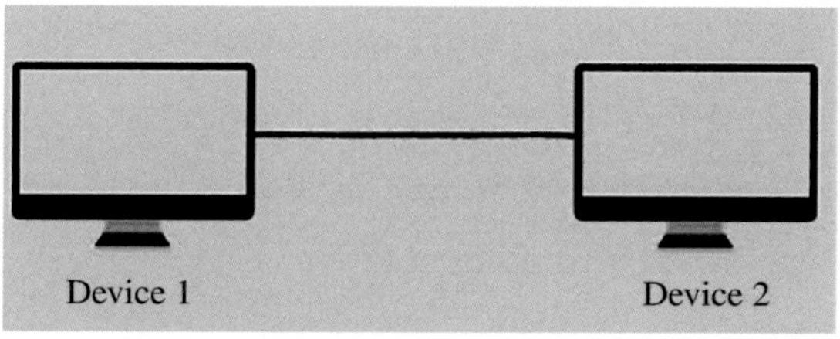

Figure 7.7. *Point to point topology.*

Source: https://images.shiksha.com/mediadata/images/articles/1709110764phpgvtttB.jpeg.

- **Advantages of Point-to-Point Topology:**
  - P2P networks are highly efficient as they allow for direct communication between two devices without any intermediate devices or network components.
  - P2P networks are relatively more secure than other topologies as they do not rely on intermediate devices that can be compromised or attacked.
  - P2P networks are easy to configure and require minimal management or administration.
- **Disadvantages of Point-to-Point Topology:**
  - P2P networks are not scalable as adding new devices requires establishing a separate link between each new device and the existing network, which can be time-consuming and expensive.
  - P2P networks can be difficult to maintain as each device has to be managed separately.

– P2P networks do not provide redundancy, which can be a problem if a link fails, or a device goes offline with a dedicated communication connection between two systems.

7.1.1.8. Daisy Chain Topology

Nodes are connected by a chain of connections using the daisy chain topology. Up until it arrives at its destination, data is moved from one node to the next. Daisy chain network topologies come in two varieties: ring daisy chains and linear daisy chains (Figure 7.8).

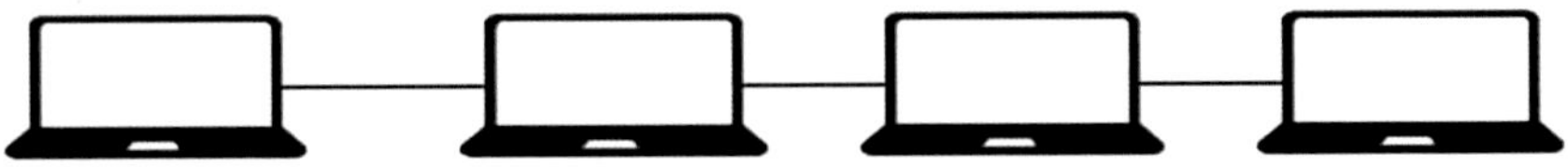

Figure 7.8. *Daisy chain.*

Source: https://www.geeksforgeeks.org/network-topology/.

- **Advantages of Daisy Chain Topology:**
  - Easy to create and maintain.
  - Less cable usage.
  - Cost-effective.
- **Disadvantages of Daisy Chain Topology:**
  - It provide slow data transmission.
  - Easy failure, particularly in linear daisy chain topologies.
  - Every node needs two transmitters and two receivers for successful data transmission.

7.1.2. Importance of Network Topology

To ensure the best possible network management and functionality, it is essential to understand network topology. Moreover, it offers understanding of the intricate structure of a network and helps with the effective resolution of network nodes.

1. **Impacts how a Network Functions:** When a suitable network topology is used, it ensures that the network will function at maximum efficiency with improved data transfer rates.
2. **Helps IT Administrators Understand How the Entire Network Infrastructure is Organized:** Network topology tool enables the IT operations team to visualize the network better and understand the dependencies of each device.

3. **Enables Geographic Visualization of a Distributed Network:** This ensures that an IT admin can effectively chart the organization's network spanning across multiple countries.
4. **Explains How Devices and Applications Impact Others in the Network:** Knowing the device dependency through network topology helps identify what device or application might be affecting other devices and causing network bottleneck.
5. **Helps Find and Resolve System-Wide Issues:** With the right network topology map in place, diagnosis of problems, troubleshooting, and network resource allocation becomes easier.

7.2. NETWORK LAYERS

Every networking book discusses the OSI model, which is a common seven-layer model. Higher-layer protocols are supposed to be layered on top of lower-layer protocols. However, this model understates how straightforward and complex reality actually is. In real networks, a Layer 3 network (or occasionally a Layer 2 network) is layered on top of another Layer 3 network with a distinct logical topology using mechanisms like virtual private networks (VPN tunnels). Thus, while it's critical to comprehend the layers, it's equally critical to avoid becoming overly technical about them.

When talking about network topology, we're mostly interested in the bottom few layers.

1. **Layer 1 is the Physical Layer:** This refers to the tangible components of a network, such as the cables and hardware, for design purposes. However, in a technical sense, it also refers to the optical and electrical signaling characteristics. The characteristics of the cables required to transport the signals are specified in Layer 1. In cases where wireless signaling is employed, Layer 1 is also concerned. As network designers, it is our responsibility to ensure that the appropriate cables are used and to be aware of any distance restrictions. Naturally, we also need to confirm that the appropriate devices are physically linked to one another.
2. **Layer 2 is the Logical Link Layer:** Ethernet is the foundation of the majority of contemporary networks. We have Ethernet available in speeds ranging from 10 Mbps to 100 Gbps. Ethernets have LAN and WAN ports. Additionally, the majority of WAN providers will prefer to deliver it to you via an Ethernet handoff, despite the fact that there are numerous other WAN protocols, such as DSL and T1. Therefore, you typically have no issues with those other Layer

2 protocols. Wi-Fi is another crucial Layer 2 protocol to take into account. Given that Wi-Fi and Ethernet use very similar signaling, I view Wi-Fi as just an Ethernet variant. While there are undoubtedly significant concerns about radio frequency (RF) propagation and isolation when using Wi-Fi, those are Layer 1 rather than Layer 2 problems.

3. **Layer 3 is the Network Layer:** That will refer to either IPv4 or IPv6 throughout this book. Though I highly advise keeping IPv6 in mind as a potential future option, you'll most likely be building your network to support IPv4 in 2014 or 2015. Thankfully, an IPv4 network topology that is sound will usually support an IPv6 network flawlessly, though this may not always be the case.
4. **Layer 4 is Called the Transport Layer:** It is the place where protocols like the well-known User Datagram Protocol (UDP) and Transmission Control Protocol (TCP) are defined. Common protocols such as HTTP and HTTPS are discussed as running on TCP ports 80 and 443, respectively. DNS uses port 53 on UDP. Specific IP protocol numbers for protocols such as TCP, UDP, and ICMP are defined in the Layer 3 portion of the IP packet header. The port numbers of these higher layer protocols, such as DNS and HTTP, are then used to identify them in the Layer 4 portion of the header.
5. **Layer 5 Session Layer:** This layer guarantees security and is in charge of connection establishment, session maintenance, and authentication.

Functions of the session layer:

1. **Session Establishment, Maintenance, and Termination:** The layer allows the two processes to establish, use, and terminate a connection.
2. **Synchronization:** This layer allows a process to add checkpoints that are considered synchronization points in the data. These synchronization points help to identify the error so that the data is re-synchronized properly, and ends of the messages are not cut prematurely, and data loss is avoided.
3. **Dialog Controller:** The session layer allows two systems to start communication with each other in half-duplex or full duplex.

6. **Layer 6 Presentation Layer:** The Translation layer is another name for the Presentation layer. Here, the data from the application layer is taken out and formatted for transmission across the network.

7. **Layer 7 Application Layer:** The Application layer, implemented by network applications, is the highest layer in the OSI Reference Model stack of layers. These programs generate the data that needs to be sent across the network. This layer also acts as a window through which application services can access the network and show the user the data they have received.

7.2.1. Ethernet, Bus, and Switched

Since Ethernet has a bus architecture, every device is connected to it on a peer-to-peer basis. A bus allows only one device to communicate at a time, and all communications between the connected devices are visible to one another. This is still how Wi-Fi functions and how Ethernet was originally intended to function. It isn't very effective, though. When there are fewer devices on the bus, the system works well. However, as the number of devices increases, they eventually have to wait longer and longer to speak with one another. For example, in order for A to speak with B, it must first wait for C to finish speaking with D dot. To get the same architecture without all the waiting, use an Ethernet switch. Every device in a switched Ethernet architecture communicates with the switch, which is the only other device. The devices are arranged in a star-or hub-and-spoke-connected configuration. A sends its packet to the switch first before attempting to communicate with B. The switch locates the interface that contains the destination Ethernet MAC address by reading it from the frame it received from A and looking it up in its internal MAC address table. Subsequently, the switch transfers the frame to the destination interface by means of its own backplane. Apart from removing waiting, a switch's other significant benefit is that each interface can run in full duplex. When a switch is configured for full duplex, it allows connected devices to send and receive Ethernet frames simultaneously. Therefore, the network does not even need to wait for the switch to stop talking before sending a frame; it can send a frame before waiting for every other device to stop talking. Although a switch uses bandwidth far more effectively than a basic bus, it is also undoubtedly much more complicated. The switch can forward Ethernet frames simultaneously and in all directions between all connected devices without waiting if the backplane is fast enough.

Two significant internal switch architectures exist. The switch has two modes of operation: cut through and store-and-forward. When a switch is configured to store and forward, it reads an entire Ethernet frame and stores the data in a memory buffer before sending it to the destination interface. In contrast, a cut-through switch reads just enough of the Ethernet frame header to determine its destination. After that, it starts sending that frame out to the destination interface right away. Lower latency is a feature of cut-through switches (the time it takes to forward a packet from one port to another). The other significant distinction is that a cut-through switch has already begun transmitting, but a store-and-forward switch has the ability to drop a frame containing errors. Luckily, Layer 2 mistakes don't happen very often.

7.3. TRADITIONAL METHODS

Several fundamental operations are part of traditional topological approaches. These include figuring out a network's topology from the beginning and staying abreast of any changes made to it (i.e., rediscovery), and after it has been gathered and judged stable, the topology's management and exposure. There are two main categories of methods for gathering and interacting with the network topology: joining routing, SNMP MIBs or NETCONF access, or a haphazard combination of screen scraping using a CLI. In the first scenario, an application would typically rely on a network management station to collect its diverse topological data, which it would then combine, filter, and abstract into a format that was exclusive and made available to other applications or managed services. Once assembled, an application could look through the frequently enormous amount of data to find the bits and pieces it required, at which point it could proceed. In other situations, any modifications to the current topology would need to be communicated to interested applications by the management station. For example, it was crucial to promptly inform applications of any changes if a new node was found.

Diverse strategies were employed when interacting with devices. This included IP ICMP ping discovery, SNMP, NETCONF, and even ARP probing. This patchwork of methods would yield a variety of data, such as reachability on layers two or three, attached neighbors, logical tunnels/paths, and the fundamental status of each of these components. After being gathered, this data is processed into a format that allows it to be analyzed, abstracted, and eventually used by other applications. Applications that carried out the aforementioned operations gave rise to numerous prosperous businesses. Certain products, like the original Cabletron Spectrum (now known as CA Infra-structure Manager), advanced the field of topology discovery to unprecedented heights. These applications could find non-routed (i.e., unrouted) networks in addition to active layer 3 topology layer 2) topology of switches and hubs, among other devices. Lastly, they could find paths, links, or devices that were not yet advertised in routing protocols, failed, or were in a dormant state. Figure 7.9 displays a screenshot of the CA Spectrum/IM product. Figure 7.9 illustrates how an operator can create a more comprehensive view of the network by superimposing logical and physical data on a display. As with the previous approaches, other companies have adopted the strategy of joining routing to obtain the majority of their topological information; however, they must supplement this information with data obtained from other management interfaces, like the CLI.

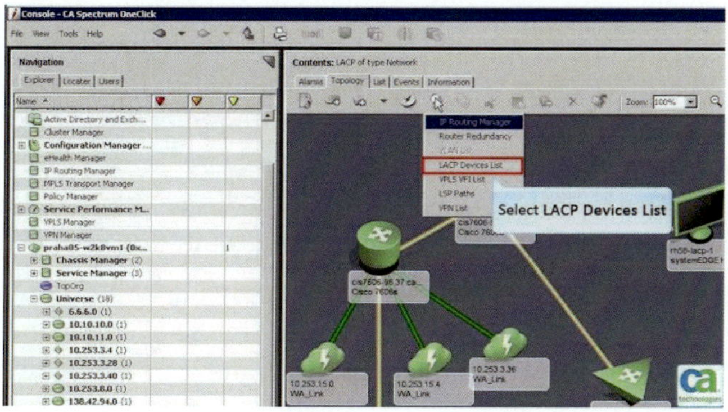

Figure 7.9. *CA spectrum/IM topology.*

Source: https://i.ytimg.com/vi/f9teO8oGa3s/hq720.jpg?sqp=-oaymwEhCK4FEI-IDSFryq4qpAxMIARUAAAAAGAElAADIQj0AgKJD&rs=AOn4CLB0RlOQ0q1GJCoeJ0D3X5FxCpfwGg

The Route Explorer product from Packet Design is one such example of a product in this market. Route Explorer essentially joins routing as an OSPF, BGP, or ISIS speaker and just listens to routing exchanges. By doing this, it discovers the topologies of the entire network that are advertised by the network's routers. This is demonstrated in Figure 7.10. Route Explorer requires at least one interface on the server it runs on (i.e., it obtains knowledge of both IGP and BGP adjacencies from the Ethernet port.

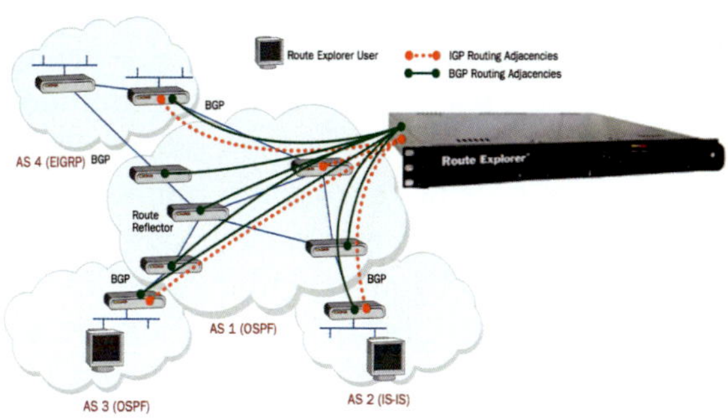

Figure 7.10. *Packet design's route explorer product joins active routing and masquerades as if it were a real router in order to listen to routing protocol updates in order to gather network topological information.*

Source: https://dataedge.ie/wp-content/uploads/2013/11/Packet-Design-Route-Explorer.png.

The topology management system's responsibility is to normalize the topology into a format that the rest of the system can use, regardless of how the topology is obtained. The operational support system (OSS) or other components of the management application used to make up the remainder of the system in the past. Due to the vendor's tight coupling of these components, the topology format may be proprietary, or at the very least, defined by the vendor and exposed as needed to allow for interaction with external applications. One of the main features of the SDN controller architecture of today is a standardized northbound API, though. Just having this API is crucial since it enables applications to be programmed to communicate with that controller; but this is only the start.

Having a common API to program SDN applications to is crucial not only conceptually but also practically and financially in the ever-expanding world of SDN controllers. It implies that a network operator can purchase or develop a single application to carry out a specific function, and then have it communicate with every controller that is set up in the network. Network Change Modeling, also referred to as "what if" scenario planning, is an intriguing application of network topology.

Once a network topology has been assembled and determined to be a stable topology, this is one feature that can be put to use. Once one is aware of a network topology and comprehends how it was created (i.e., routing topology algorithms, restrictions, network policies, interface status, link band-width utilization, etc.) the topology can be seen as a highly realistic representation of the real network.

Furthermore, it is now known how that state came to be. At this point, modifications could be made to observe the impact on the model. Network operators find it fascinating to see how traffic patterns and behaviors are impacted by various failure scenarios, such as a link, node, or entire network failure, changes to link metrics, bandwidth utilization, link addition or removal, and back-up path addition. Furthermore, as we demonstrated, once a layered topology is established, it is possible to observe running applications as well as the servers that house them. One can also envision operations like capacity future planning as a possibility. Network function virtualization and the service chaining of those virtualized functions to other real or virtual ones is a major SDN application that is currently applicable. The topological perspective of the services and how they are linked together is, in fact, one of the secrets to the effectiveness of these methods.

7.3.1. LLDP

This data was not available because, in general, the switches were waiting to be programmed by the controller in their initial state and did not have any paths set up until they were set up. This information was necessary for the controller to plan, provision, and monitor the network paths between the switches. This exemplified a paradox of opposites. In order to address this, the LLDP protocol was turned on by default on the switch ports.

However, rather than exchanging information with the remote switches directly through the discovery frames, the information was sent to the SDN controller, which gathered it into a centralized view of the network topology before forwarding it to the nearby switches. At the time, this functioned well within the OpenFlow deployment architecture.

An industry standard protocol called Link Layer Discovery Protocol (LLDP) enables networked devices to find and advertise identity information and capabilities on a layer 2 LAN.

The Cisco Discovery Protocol (CDP) and other proprietary protocols put in place by different equipment vendors are replaced by the layer 2 protocol that the IEEE standardized. Network equipment functioning at the lower echelons of a protocol stack (e.g., layer 2 bridges and switches) to discover some of the features and powers of LAN devices that are accessible to protocols at higher layers (e.g., IP addresses). The data acquired by the LLDP operation is kept in a network device and is queryable via the CLI, NETCONF, or SNMP protocol. This database can also be used to obtain information about a device's neighbor topology and related details. Some of the information that can be gathered by LLDP includes the following:

- System name and description;
- Port name and description;
- VLAN name and identifier;
- IP network management address;
- Capabilities of the device (e.g., switch, router, or server);
- MAC address and physical layer information;
- Power information.

When a device is set up for LLDP operation, PDUs are sent on all of its interfaces that have the protocol enabled. The PDUs are transmitted in the form of an Ethernet Frame or PDU at a predetermined interval.

One of the previously mentioned attributes is encoded in a series of type-length value (TLV) structures found in each LLD PDU. These frames are delivered to a unique, non-forwarding multicast address. In situations where forwarding loops occur, broadcast storms are avoided in this way (Figure 7.11).

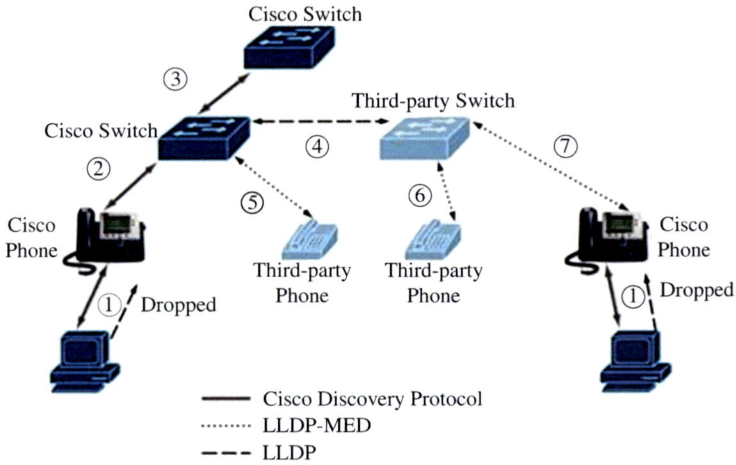

Figure 7.11. *LLDP-MED and cisco discovery protocol.*

Source: https://www.cisco.com/en/US/technologies/tk652/tk701/images/0900aecd804cd46d_null_null_null_06_28_06-2.jpg.

LLDP can be used as a switch discovery protocol in an SDN environment. The network topology can then be built using the information that is gathered. Packet_in and packet_out messages are used to accomplish OpenFlow network discovery. As previously mentioned, when network ports broadcast their discovery information, the switch processes and sends the information to the SDN controller through the "packet in" rule. After that, it is sent to the nearby switches so they can discover the MAC address. However, the creation of the network topology database is the key point (Figure 7.12).

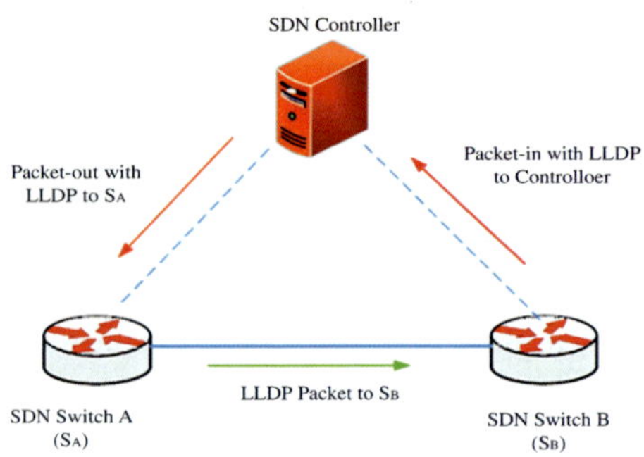

Figure 7.12. *The use of LLDP as a switch port discovery protocol by an SDN controller.*

Source: https://www.researchgate.net/profile/Zhaogang-Shu-2/publication/304365495/figure/fig2/AS:571254618374144@1513209122466/Detection-process-using-LLDP-for-SDN-topology.png.

Although the neighbor switch topology discovery problem is resolved by the just described method for exchanging LLDP neighbors, there are drawbacks to this strategy. First off, only switches that support LLDP can use this method. While this is generally not a major issue, applications find these approaches to be highly unappealing, much like the other methods that call for speaking a particular routing (or, more recently, switching) protocol. Second, only the switch's immediate layer 2 neighbors are included in the LLDP topology information.

If some ports are misconfigured (i.e., their initial configurations are off), then those ports are not open for discovery. Lastly, there may be a problem piecing this information together for topologies that span the zones of purely OpenFlow-controlled switches to those that are not, or hybrid zones. The reason for this is that there is currently no standard for extension over these zones, as we previously discussed with the northbound APIs of a controller; as a result, applications or other controllers that comprehend a specific proprietary definition are the only ones that can exchange this information. In keeping with that, both the topology format and its contents are proprietary.

7.3.2. BGP-TE/LS

Network topology information can be obtained primarily through two methods: routing protocols and management protocols. BGP Link State, also referred to as BGP-LS, is a recent addition to the latter group. The routing protocols contain information appropriate for routing computations, which may not be optimal for other computations requiring topological information. This is something we mentioned but did not go into detail about in the previous discussion of routing protocol-based approaches.

BGP-LS aimed to address this shortcoming. An addition to BGP that enables it to carry link-state data is called BGP-LS. As is customary with other state data, this link state data was obtained from the IGP, but in this instance, it came from the local traffic engineering database (TED). By combining data from several sources and independent systems, intriguing network state analyses can be carried out.

The topological data acquired via BGP-LS and the IGP's TED ought to yield identical information. Nonetheless, BGP-LS was created expressly to take advantage of certain BGP features that improve its scaling capabilities.

These include the intelligent application of route reflector(s) and TCP-based flow control. Because of this, BGP-LS is also a more scalable option than traditional methods of gathering multi-area topology information from individual ASs through more labor-intensive means. An engineer for traffic engineering (e.g., BGP-LS will be used by an application of the PCE Server to obtain the routing topology. This is, of course, just another application/controller pairing within the context of SDN. Additionally, BGP-LS offers a policy mechanism that allows users to restrict access to specific nodes, links, or user-partitioned topologies. The necessary knobs to enable this feature will be supplied by a TE controller.

The topology information can reach the TE controller much more quickly thanks to the IGP flooding mechanism than it could with BGP-LS in the event of a topology change event, such as a link or node going down. This is because before BGP-LS notifies its peers of this change event, it must wait for the local IGP on the network's routers to update the TED. This latency shouldn't have a negative impact on the BGP-LS collection's real-time properties. As we just discussed, there were already manual ways to obtain the network topology and join routing to obtain routed link state information. So why was BGP-LS invented? What problem is it solving that wasn't previously solved? For topological purposes, there are a number of issues with the data in routing protocols.

7.3.3. BGP-LS with PCE

To compute MPLS-TE paths, one can use a path computational element (PCE). The computation of those paths took place inside a domain, like an autonomous system (i.e., an IGP area), or calculated over several area domains or ASs. In these scenarios, we explained how PCE could provide routers with potentially outdated or underpowered hardware with increased computational power by utilizing COGS hardware to run the CSPF algorithm offline. Alternative CSPF algorithms may also be used for customized calculations that some specific commercial hardware may not support. The issue is that in these situations, the computations' accuracy may be hampered by the absence of global topology (multi-domain).

For instance, selecting the incorrect transit node or exit router for a given path are examples of incorrect choices. Other times, decisions may be made that are merely not the best ones. The PCE needs access to the overall, or global, TED in order to solve this issue. The PCE was treated as a passive listener to the IGP, similar to what we just discussed in the solutions that combined routing to extract topology. However, as we have discussed, this approach does not always yield the most useful format for this data. Figure 7.13 illustrates how a PCE can use BGP (BGP-LS) and join routing to obtain its TED information. In the future, BGPLS peering over several domains will enable the PCE server to obtain a global topology.

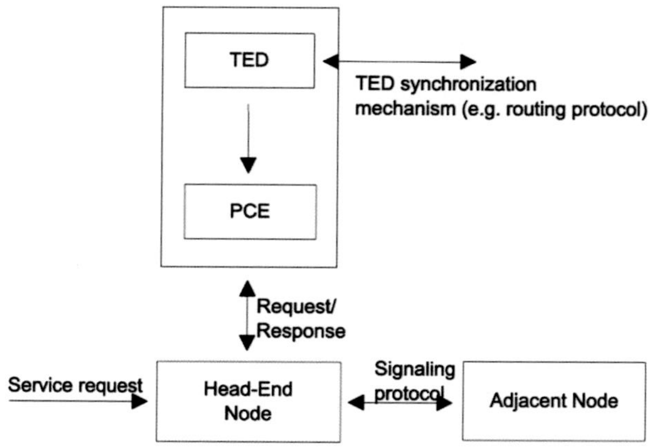

Figure 7.13. *External PCE node using a TED synchronization mechanism.*

Source: https://www.researchgate.net/profile/Rahamatullah-Khondoker/publication/293174387/figure/fig1/AS:645698508840969@1530957929742/PCE-architecture-with-external-PCE-node-3-p12.png.

7.3.4. ALTO

The Application-Layer Traffic Optimization (ALTO) Net-work Service was one of the first attempts to standardize not only the topology information format but also to make that standard format available to applications that do not directly interact with routing protocols. This is a significant modification because most contemporary apps aren't made to do this. Applications can access network information from ALTO, including the network's location, configuration, and preferred paths to different services. At the moment, ALTO is being used with the intention of giving content delivery networks (CDNs) these paths. The purpose of making this data available is to help applications that are looking for the nearest CDN server. Applications like this one can enhance application performance by providing this information. The potential for this service to further optimize patterns of network resource consumption is an intriguing side effect that network operators would find very desirable. An ALTO service's foundational data is derived from logical or abstract network topology maps. The topology that the ALTO server consumes can be either logical or physical and used to build the maps. Network topologies can be either logical or physical; in this instance, they are both logical and at the network service level. An abstracted view of CDN nodes and the relative weights of paths connecting those nodes in the network is offered by the abstract topology maps. As a result, the topology scope is reduced to a set of topics that are relevant to applications pertaining to CDNs. They can then consult other topological resources, like the previously mentioned routing-based resources or management interfaces, if they are interested in more information.

Through a web services API, network-aware applications can access the ALTO server, which is a network service. The ALTO protocol encodes its requests and responses in JSON and has a RESTful architecture. This method is preferred by modern application programmers due to its adaptability and scalability. We also see ALTO as a forerunner of the current paradigm shift and SDN movement. Seen from this perspective, the ALTO server and protocol can be regarded as a pioneer in the SDN controller implementation field.

7.3.5. BGP-LS and PCE Interaction with ALTO

Due to the quicker, more reliable, and more scalable acquisition of link state topology information, BGP-LS and PCE can be combined to create a more optimal solution for cross-AS path computation. Additionally, we defined an ALTO server as an entity that creates an abstracted network topology and makes it available via a web service-based API to network-aware applications. P2P clients, trackers, and CDNs are a few examples of applications. Two maps represent the abstracted network topology: a network map that details the prefix distribution to PIDs and a cost map that details the cost between PIDs on the network map.

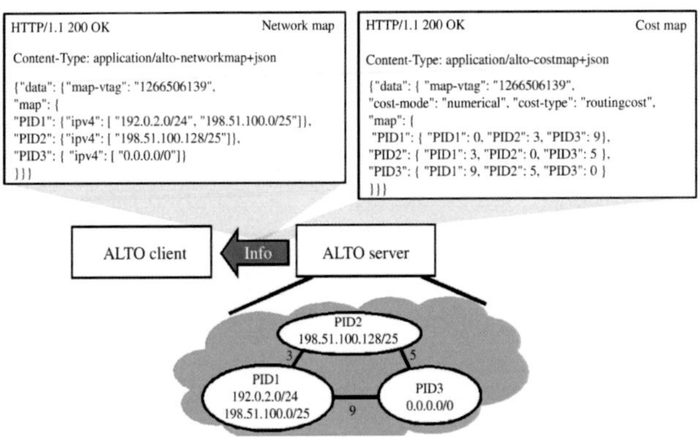

Figure 7.14. *ALTO server using network topology information.*

Source: https://www.researchgate.net/profile/Nishat-Mowla/publication/282750705/figure/fig1/AS:391738159058945@1470409063139/Application-Layer-Traffic-Optimization-ALTO-server-14.png.

The underlying network's physical topology can be used to automatically generate ALTO abstract network topologies. Usually, the generation would follow the guidelines and policies established by the operator. In order to create

ALTO network maps, prefix data is needed, and in order to create ALTO cost maps, TE (topology) data is needed. While TE data originates and is carried in an IGP, prefix data is carried and originated in a BGP. Even though ALTO offers a single interface via which an ALTO server can obtain from the underlying network all required prefix and network topology data, the server can also obtain network data through alternative means (e.g., peering with multiple IGP and BGP speakers). Although ALTO is still being used and deployed, its application is still restricted to CDNs. There isn't much support for those who venture outside of this region. We speculate that this is because, despite the fact that the architecture and protocol are sufficiently versatile to be used for other purposes, there appears to be a belief that CDN is the primary application for ALTO (Figure 7.14).

7.3.6. I2RS Topology

A number of people started an early project called SDNP to standardize some important parts of what was considered to be the canonical SDN architecture at the time. A logically centralized controller that interfaced with and/or managed the data and control planes of several network devices made up this architecture. Using a RESTful web services API, the controller displayed the services it had implemented. This endeavor petered out and was premature. An initiative at the IETF known as the Interface to the Routing System (IRS) emerged from those ashes. The name was somewhat changed to the Interface to the Routing System, or I2RS, after an excessive number of people objected to it, claiming it gave them excessive heartburn by making them think of Uncle Sam. Even though it is still in its early stages, this initiative currently enjoys strong industry support and, as of the writing of this chapter, is proceeding successfully. The standardization of the northbound API (I2RS can read and write network state), and, more pertinent to this chapter, the standardization of a generalized network topology service, are two of the more difficult problems surrounding SDN that we hope this effort will continue to tackle. The IETF's initial attempt to create a standardized topology collection and representation service that applications could use with an application-friendly API was called ALTO. Regretfully, it appears that this endeavor is stalled on CDN. In order to achieve this, generalized topology was included as one of the main work items in the I2RS working group's charter. To help you better understand the significance of this endeavor, let us explain what this means and the current status of these matters.

The gathering of topology (and topology related/co-incident) data from various sources, such as network elements, routing protocols, inventory collection, and statistics collection, is a crucial component of the I2RS topology manager. From the descriptions of the above topology efforts and approaches, it should be evident why gathering information from a wide range of sources, including routing protocols, is essential to forming an accurate and comprehensive picture of the network topology. In order to achieve this, sources of topology data may be found in several IGP areas, several ASes, and/or various network layers (including administrative domains/systems found in a single organization, such as routing and transport). The topology map can be enhanced by adding additional data sources, such as explicit node functions (of network service appliances), statistics, or physical inventory, in addition to the standard links and nodes (both virtual and physical) that are provided by these sources.

The topology manager may use this information (e.g., in offering a map/view interface for operations), but it's probably even more intriguing for uses like network analytics, service location, and provisioning. Global topology view creation is the topology manager's ultimate objective. In actuality, this will be implemented and made available to applications using a shared data model, which will be used to standardize gathered data and make it portable and easily readable by various applications. Ultimately, the topology view can encompass several network layers, autonomous systems, or entire networks, contingent upon the degree to which distinct administrative domains will collaborate and share formation.

Whether or not they are being used, all network components and infrastructure resources must be included in the global view. Rebuilding the network's global view, which includes available but unused router or switch ports, is one example. Creating a global view of the network, which includes the router/switch ports and the underlying transport network elements that are both used and unused, might be another. These are necessary to calculate "what if" scenarios. The information is simply not present in any active routing updates, which makes this kind of operation extremely difficult to accomplish using routing protocol-based approaches, for example (though the need has been demonstrated through modifications to routing like the recent introduction of the SRLG concept in the MPLS-TE). It is only possible to accomplish it with extra tools, like a proprietary CLI. After topology data has been acquired, it is crucial to present it in a way that is suitable for contemporary applications. The information will be assimilated by the topology manager, who will then use a standardized object model to normalize it. The REST API that applications will use to obtain this data will also be generated using this object model. All of this sounds great on the surface, but then you start to realize how much data a topology server could contain. Therefore, it is crucial that the topology manager can use its shared global topology database to generate numerous (possibly application-specific) views. This lets an application set a filter criterion for information viewing, in a sense. For instance, an ALTO server was just discussed. A topology server could be asked to provide it with the CDN topology layer by returning only CDN-tagged nodes and paths from the database. Figure 7.15 illustrates how topology information from network elements is sent into the topology manager function via its southbound API. Network components at various tiers of the network, such as routers, appliances, Level 2 switches, optical transponders, and optical switches, as well as tools for provisioning, monitoring, and network analytics (like inventory subsystems or statistics collection subsystems), can be sources of topology information.

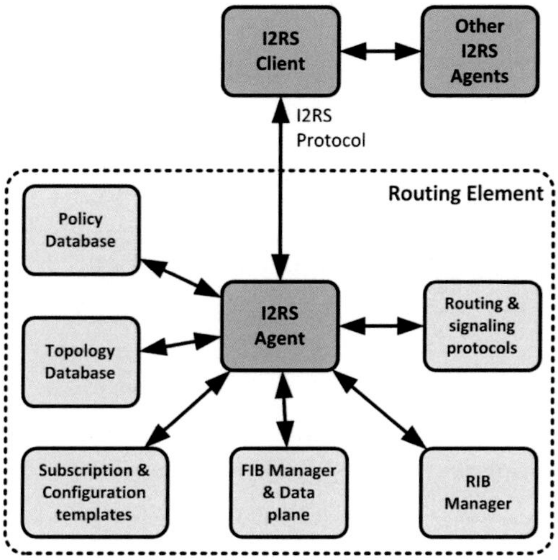

Figure 7.15. *I2RS topology manager operational model.*

Source: https://www.researchgate.net/profile/Eduardo-Jacob/publication/311338103/figure/fig11/AS:668461449637901@1536385037698/Main-components-of-the-I2RS-architecture-highlighted-the-I2RS-Agent-that-communicates.ppm.

The topology manager function can be implemented in a variety of ways, including as an embedded component of a routing element, a standalone server, or a comprehensive orchestration, data collection, and presentation framework. Applications and functions in upper layer frameworks, like policy functions, can be considered clients.

An entire network may not be visible to a topology manager, depending on the information it gathers. The topology manager may use a peer topology manager API to obtain complementary partial topology views from other topology managers in order to build a global topology.

7.4. METRICS FOR TOPOLOGY ANALYSIS

The different metrics that were taken into account when ranking potential topology candidates:

1. **Average Path Length:** The average distance between two nodes in the network over all pairs of distinct nodes. The distance between any two distinct nodes is the shortest path between those two nodes. This can be mathematically represented as:

$$L_{ave} = \frac{\sum_{x=1}^{n-1}\left[\sum_{y=x+1}^{n} d(x,y)\right]}{\sum_{z=1}^{n-1} z}$$

where; d(x, y) is the distance (number of hops) between nodes 'x' and 'y.'

One of the key elements in network speed and efficiency optimization is average path length. Short average path lengths guarantee that messages don't have to travel far to reach their destination, which prevents them from spending a lot of time in the network. Short average path lengths lower message latency and overall network utilization. It is frequently possible to increase average path length when working with numerous "organized" or structured topologies (particularly those that adhere to some geometric pattern) by rewiring a small number of links in the topology at random. As a result, the topology starts to resemble small-world networks, which are a class of random graphs with longer average paths than structured topologies and where most nodes are not next to each other but are reachable with a limited number of hops.

2. **Diameter:** The network path that is the longest between two nodes. A network's diameter can be determined by taking the maximum of all the shortest paths between any two distinct nodes.

$$DIAMETER = \{\max[d(x,y)] \mid x = \{1,2,3,\dots,n\}, y = \{1,2,3,\dots,n\}, x \neq y\}.$$

Although diameter should be reduced whenever feasible, average path length is typically a more crucial factor to take into account because diameter only accounts for the separation between the two farthest nodes. Though a topology with a large diameter will typically have a larger average path length, and a topology with a small diameter will typically imply a smaller average path length, the two factors will typically be related.

3. **Node Degree:** The number of links that a node is connected to determines its degree, or dG(x). Small degrees and fixed, matching

degrees for all nodes are preferred in order to minimize node, network, and routing complexity. Reliability and node degree are trade-offs; more redundant networks will need more links to be used as redundant paths within the network, which will increase node degree. Note that the opposite is not always true: redundancy or reliability are not always indicated by a high node degree. When the network is represented pictorially, degree can be ascertained visually by counting the number of links connected to a specific node (*see* Figure 7.16). The degree of a network can be mathematically obtained by summing values within a row or column of the adjacency matrix, which represents the network. This will yield the degree for a specific node. Alternatively, the adjacency matrix can be multiplied by itself to determine the node degree using standard matrix multiplication in linear algebra. Next, each node's degree would be represented along the matrix's diagonal.

0	1	0	0	← 0+1+0+0 = 1, Node 1 has degree 1
1	0	0	1	← 1+0+0+1 = 2, Node 2 has degree 2
0	0	0	0	← 0+0+0+0 = 0, Node 3 has degree 0
0	1	0	0	← 0+1+0+0 = 1, Node 4 has degree 1

$$\begin{bmatrix} 0 & 1 & 0 & 0 \\ 1 & 0 & 0 & 1 \\ 0 & 0 & 0 & 0 \\ 0 & 1 & 0 & 0 \end{bmatrix} \begin{bmatrix} 0 & 1 & 0 & 0 \\ 1 & 0 & 0 & 1 \\ 0 & 0 & 0 & 0 \\ 0 & 1 & 0 & 0 \end{bmatrix} = \begin{bmatrix} 1 & 0 & 0 & 1 \\ 0 & 2 & 0 & 0 \\ 0 & 0 & 0 & 0 \\ 1 & 0 & 0 & 1 \end{bmatrix}$$

Figure 7.16. *Two methods for obtaining degree from the adjacency matrix.*

Source: https://digital.library.unt.edu/ark:/67531/metadc845229/m2/1/high_res_d/1028919.pdf.

The average degree, minimum degree, and maximum degree are additional significant factors that can be obtained from the node degree. The average degree is calculated by dividing the total number of nodes in the network by the sum of the degrees of all the nodes. Out of all the nodes, the maximum degree, $\Delta(x)$, is the largest, and the minimum degree, $\delta(x)$, is the smallest.

4. **Number of Links:** While more links may result in lower latency, longer average paths, less network congestion, and better overall performance, their increased node degree can also raise the cost and complexity of network wiring and routing. In order to maximize the number of links, one must weigh the trade-off between redundancy and high performance less inter-node links, less power, and cheaper costs.

5. **Worst-Case Connectivity:** To cause an additional type of failure in the system, this is the minimum number of nodes (node connectivity $\kappa(x)$) or links (edge connectivity $\lambda(x)$) that must fail. If all of a live node's neighbors were to experience node failures, for instance, then a failure in this scenario would be the inability of any live node to communicate with any other currently operational node. The inequality $\kappa(x) \leq \lambda(x) \leq \delta(x)$ limits the network's connectivity. In other words, the network's worst-case connectivity will be less than or equal to the lowest node degree that is present. This is because the node with the lowest degree is most vulnerable to isolation from both the failure of the nodes it is connected to and the failure of the links surrounding it. Furthermore, less than or equal to the number of node failures required, the number of link failures required to disconnect the network will occur. The network's algebraic connectivity is the lower bound for worst-case connectivity. Improving the network's algebraic connectivity is a good place to start when trying to improve overall connectivity.

6. **Algebraic Connectivity:** A metric called algebraic connectivity comes from mathematical graph theory. Graphs that are "well-connected" will have a high algebraic connectivity. In order to guarantee high reliability and general connectivity, being "well connected" means having a lot of loops in addition to good average path lengths. Therefore, depending on the routing algorithm being used, graphs with high algebraic connectivity typically show effective link placement with lots of redundant paths between nodes as well as good traffic distribution. On the other hand, graphs with low algebraic connectivity have relatively clean bisections, making it simpler to split them in half. The graph's algebraic connectivity also suggests a lower bound for the expansion and connectivity of nodes and edges. As a result, it is preferable to maximize this value at all times.

   The algebraic connectivity of a network is determined by finding the eigenvalues of the Laplacian matrix L. The Laplacian matrix L is determined by $L = D - A$, where D is the degree matrix of the network (a diagonal matrix where the term $d_{i,i}$ is the degree of node I) and A is the adjacency matrix representation of the network. Once the matrix L is found, the algebraic connectivity will be equal to the second smallest eigenvalue (λ_2) of this matrix. Algebraic connectivity $\lambda_2(x)$ relates to node connectivity $\kappa(x)$ and edge connectivity $\lambda(x)$ as shown by Fiedler's inequality: $\lambda_2(x) \leq \kappa(x) \leq \lambda(x)$.

7. **Scalability:** The simplicity with which a network's node count can be altered. The goal is a high scalability. Certain topologies can only function with a certain number of nodes in a particular structure, while other topologies might support any number of nodes. This is solely reliant on the network's topology selection.
8. **Routing Complexity:** It is important to take into account the complexity of routing algorithms, particularly in situations where node or link failure requires the routing table to be dynamically generated. Certain topologies lend themselves to simple routing algorithms based on mathematics (e.g., hypercube or toroidal layouts), but some might make use of broader routing methods and algorithms.
9. **Bottlenecks or Points-of-Failure:** Numerous other issues can arise from the presence of bottlenecks, such as the possibility of network overload (resulting in packet drops or delays), higher latency, and the emergence of specific nodes or links as critical points-of-failure. The benefit of short transmission distances for networks with short average path lengths could be compromised if bottlenecks prevent traffic from moving freely between nodes. Keep in mind that bottlenecks can be nodes or links. Bottleneck failures will have a serious, even disastrous, effect on the system. Bottlenecks should be avoided from a reliability perspective because a single link or node failure can have a moderate to severe impact. Performance-wise, bottlenecks significantly reduce network performance. Avoiding bottleneck nodes and links is advised whenever feasible.

REFERENCES

1. Ahuja, R. K., Magnanti, T. L., & Orlin, J. B. (1993). *Network Flows: Theory, Algorithms, and Applications*. Prentice Hall.
2. Appenzeller, G., Keslassy, I., & McKeown, N. (2004). Sizing router buffers. In *Proceedings of ACM SIGCOMM.*
3. Bhandarkar, S., Jain, S., & Reddy, A. (2005). Improving TCP performance in high bandwidth high RTT links using layered congestion control. In *Proceedings of the 3rd International Workshop on Protocols for Fast Long-Distance Networks*.
4. Bradley, R. (2001). *Understanding Computer Science (for Advanced Level): The Study Guide*. Cheltenham: Nelson Thornes. p. 244
5. Cavraro, G., & Kekatos, V. (2019). Inverter probing for power distribution network topology processing. *IEEE Transactions on Control of Network Systems, 6*(3), 980–992. https://doi.org/10.1109/TCNS.2018.2873299.
6. Chen, S., Wang, S., & Zhou, M. (2010). A new physical network topology discovery algorithm. *Journal of Electronics Information & Technology, 32*(1), 172–177.
7. Donetti, L., Neri, F., & Munoz, M. (2006). Optimal network topologies: Expanders, cages, Ramanujan graphs, entangled networks and all that. *Journal of Statistical Mechanics: Theory and Experiment, 08*, P08007.
8. Ge, J. X., & Xiao, W. Y. (2013). Network layer network topology discovery algorithm research. *Applied Mechanics and Materials, 380–384*, 1327–1332. https://doi.org/10.4028/www.scientific.net/AMM.380-384.1327.
9. Grant, T. J. (2014). *Network Topology in Command and Control*. Advances in Information Security, Privacy, and Ethics. IGI Global. pp. xvii, 228, 250
10. Groth, D., & Skandier, T. (2005). *Network+ Study Guide* (4th ed.). Sybex, Inc. ISBN 0-7821-4406-3.
11. Jian, F., & Li, Z. (2013). WebNMS-based topology discovery in EPON network. *International Journal of Future Generation Communication and Networking, 6*(6), 161–168.
12. Katseff, H. P. (1988). Incomplete hypercubes. *IEEE Transactions on Computers, 37*(5), Correspondence.
13. Wazirali, R., Ahmad, R., & Alhiyari, S. (2021). SDN-OpenFlow topology discovery: An overview of performance issues. *Applied Sciences, 11*(15), 6999. https://doi.org/10.3390/app11156999.
14. Wenxing, L., Xiaofei, S., & Xinying, C. (2020). The impacts of weak links on topology discovery process in large-scale wireless multi-hop

networks. *International Journal of Distributed Sensor Networks, 16*(11), 155014772097452. https://doi.org/10.1177/1550147720974521.

15. Zhao, R., Liu, Y., Dobre, O. A., Wang, H., & Shen, X. (2020). An efficient topology discovery protocol with node ID assignment based on layered model for underwater acoustic networks. *Sensors, 20*(22), 6601. https://doi.org/10.3390/s20226601.

CHAPTER 8

BUILDING AN SDN FRAMEWORK

Contents

INTRODUCTION

The concept of software-defined networks (SDN) can be traced back to its inception in 2007–2008, when initiatives from universities such as Nicira/VMware, NOX, and others emerged. Since then, SDN has developed and advanced technologically, but regrettably, it has continued to oscillate between various proposals for proprietary controllers without a concrete plan in place for these controllers to communicate with one another. Even worse, the inability of controllers to communicate with one another makes it impossible for third-party software houses, network operators, or controller vendors to create applications that work flawlessly with a variety of controllers. In 2013, there are a variety of controllers and controller strategies available, but none of them are still compatible, at least not readily. This is undoubtedly a problem in need of a solution, one that we believe can be achieved by defining an SDN framework based on an open-source code foundation to guarantee both syntactic and semantic correctness. Then, at a standards body like the IETF, that framework and its auxiliary parts—like protocols or protocol extensions—can be standardized.

8.1. BUILDING SDN FRAMEWORK USING OPENDAYLIGHT CONTROLLER

The standard platform for open SDN is OpenDaylight (ODL), which allows network services across a variety of hardware in a network, regardless of network size or scope. Numerous networks are built with the ability to meet demands and specifications at any given moment.

The kind of networking that can easily adapt to changes in user requirements and improve the current network is known as software-defined networking. This is because OpenDaylight can build the universal platform so that it can set up in multiple ways, which enables it to deal with network challenges. The SDN platform is handed over by Standard OpenDaylight using open source and open APIs, preparing the network for highly adoptable, programmable, and intelligent devices.

The OpenDaylight controller uses a model-driven approach to represent the network and accomplish certain tasks. OpenDaylight helps with complex problem solving by providing data structures in a recognizable massaging framework and data store, as well as by enabling the creation and fusion of elegant services (McKeown et al., 2008).

ODL improves the programmability of existing networks and supports a large collection of protocols for both traditional and emerging networks on the SDN platform. SDN platforms, for instance, support protocols such as BGP/

PCEP, CAPWAP, and NETCONF in addition to OpenFlow and Table Type patterns, which are extensions of OpenFlow. Furthermore, it unifies with Open Vswitch and OpenStack via the OVSDB Integration plan. Here are a few more multiprotocol services that the ODL offers:

- Easily set up into current or greenfield network.
- There are huge number of protocol support from NETCONF o OpenFlow protocol.
- The ODL allows for endless innovations since it is open-source model.
- Ability to install required functions and protocols that user needs.
- To overcome complicated issues, ODL allows incorporating different protocols and many services.
- Computable model of ODL environment allows to influence the new designs.

Software Defined Networking programmability can be managed and abstractions of north or south over the controller can be built by developers by broadcasting similar API structures.

The OpenDaylight controller is software of java virtual machine, and it can be installed in any operating system and any platform which supports java. To implement SDN, OpenDaylight controller uses following tools:

1. **MAVEN:** ODL uses Maven to create automation. Model of Project Objects (pom.xml) to start and load bundles, as well as to write dependencies within them.
2. **OSGI:** This structure allows bundles to be bound for information transactions and allows OpenDaylight to load bundles and JAR files as an active back-end system.
3. **JAVA Interface:** This interface serves as a primary route for different bundles to exhibit their understanding of a particular state. The Java interface is utilized for requirements, event acceptance, and pattern formation.
4. **REST APIs:** Rest APIs such as host tracker, topology controller, flow programmer, and passive routing are examples of northbound APIs.

Northbound APIs are used by applications and are made available by the controller. The OSGi framework and duplex REST support the northbound APIs. Applications that use the same address spaces are supported by OSGi, while those that use different address spaces are supported by the controller's REST APIs (Figure 8.1).

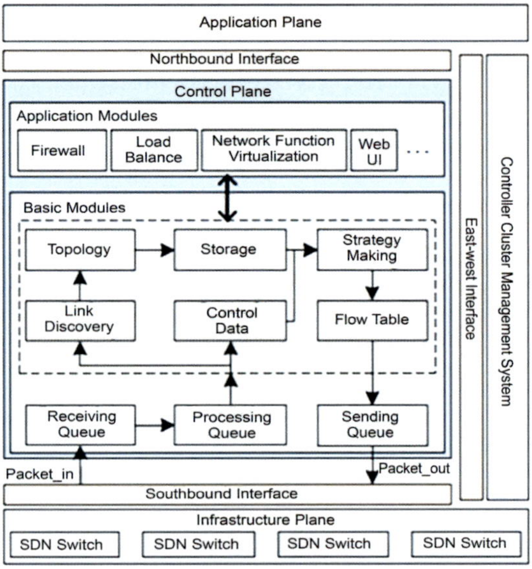

Figure 8.1. *Framework of the SDN controller.*

Source: Prakruthi & Usha, K. P. Building SDN framework using OpenDaylight controller, national level PG project symposium on electronics and communication, computer science.

Business logic persists in network algorithms and applications, which gather network agility; logical analysis is performed by running an algorithm and coordinating the new rules across the network. Numerous protocols and southbound APIs, such as BGP-LS, OpenFlow, and others, support a wide range of plugins. This module's Service Abstraction Layer (SAL) is actively linked to it, and it shows the purpose for which northbound APIs are written.

Protocols make up controllers and network devices; SAL responds to protocol requests. When protocols like OpenFlow and others are developed, this further improves application security. The data that the controller needs to control the devices based on their reachability and capability is managed and stored by the topology manager. The switch manager, APR handler, device manager, and host tracker are among the components that the topology manager uses to create the topology database (Al-Somaidai & Yahya, 2014).

8.2. IMPLEMENTATION OF SDN USING OPENDAYLIGHT CONTROLLER

The internet has been used for information sharing and network device interconnection for 45 years. Although Ethernet devices and protocol are the most widely used, the number of end devices connected to the internet has increased to more than one per person due to changing circumstances. Once more, new technologies like the Internet of Things (IoT) enable nearly all devices to be remotely managed and connected via the internet, which leads to a sharp rise in traffic. Under such circumstances, managing the data center to store user data on one side and controlling congestion on the other become crucial research topics. Researchers are motivated to work on the topic because it involves configuring large and varied network equipment, like switches and routers, using low-level commands and pre-defending protocols to build up network topology, and it lacks innovation.

A novel approach to networking called Software Defined Networking (SDN) seems to alter the architecture of network devices like switches by streamlining the complex node structure. In place of multiple, disorganized devices, it offers a single, software-based centralized controller with programmability and straightforward forwarding capabilities. Various network societies develop a variety of controllers with varying features and functions. However, we chose Open Daylight over the many other controllers with verity that were available (Mendonca, Nunes, Nguyen, Obraczka, & Turletti, 2014).

8.2.1. Architecture and Problem of Traditional Networking

In modern networks, endpoints like switches and routers that are in charge of forwarding and routing packets across the network must carry out three distinct tasks. The first is the data plan, which processes transit traffic in accordance with decisions made by the control plan; the second is the control plan, which determines and manages what is happening based on its type and configuration; and the third is the management plan, which consults with the administrator.

The foundation for traffic transiting over an IP network is comprised of both distributed and transport protocols. When a packet enters the data plan through port, the data plan uses the header information and forwarding table to determine which port to send it to. If there is insufficient information, the data plan may decide to drop the packet or send it to the control plan. Interface, IP subnet, and routing protocol are configured by the control plan, or brain, of the device. Additionally, it gathers and stores the data in a queue, creates route tables, computes the Spanning-Tree Protocol, and forwards a copy of the table to the data plan so that it can handle packet arrivals going forward without requiring the control plan. Administrators use a variety of CLI commands to configure the Control plan via the management plan.

The intricate design of conventional devices, which has the data plane and control plan vertically and strongly coupled to one another, leads to a number of problems, including increased complexity, management challenges, a lack of network visibility, discomfort with dynamic change, fault persistence, decreased flexibility, and a hindrance to innovation.

8.2.2. Architecture of Software Defined Networking

In actuality, traditional networks are incapable of meeting the needs of today's enterprise networks and picky end users. SDN, or software-defined networking, is a networking advancement that addresses issues with conventional networks. Network architecture is being revolutionized by SDN, which offers previously unheard-of features like automation, programmability, flexibility, and stability through programmable controllers.

By separating the control plan from the data plan, SDN aims to simplify complex network devices, turning endpoints into straightforward forwarding devices. By separating the logically centralized controllers and network intelligence (control plan), this is made possible.

Between the application and data plans is the brain, or control plan. It makes use of Application Interfaces (APIs) to manipulate and control the data and management plan; Open Flow, created by ONF (Open Network Foundation), is the most well-known example of this southbound API. Specific network components can communicate with low-level components like end nodes through the southbound interface. It gives the controller the ability to communicate with switches and other nodes in order to ascertain network flows, identify topology, and carry out requests that are sent to it through northbound interfaces.

In contrast to the previous scenario, the higher-level Components can communicate with each other through the northbound interface. Through the controller, the network's services and apps establish communication via the northbound interface. Business applications can function on a platform made possible by APIs connecting controllers and applications, freeing them from the constraints of their implementation.

SDN offers an abstraction for the top layer, eliminating the need for researchers and developers to tamper with the network element's underlying infrastructures. Dynamic network architecture fortifies the network for the future while safeguarding current investments. Additionally, SDN enables network management via intelligent orchestration and provisioning systems.

In recent years, a growing number of controllers using various platforms have experienced success. For instance, different platforms and architectures, both open source and commercial, different vendors, and different language bases are used by NOX, POX, Floodlight, ONOS, Ryu, and so forth.

8.2.3. OpenDayLight Controller Architecture

Developed by the Linux Foundation, OpenDayLight is an open source, Java-based SDN controller that is supported by over 40 businesses, including Cisco, IBM, Juniper, VMware, and several other significant networking vendors. It is regarded as the most extensively documented controller available. It is compatible with all hardware and operating systems that support Java. The Open Services Gateway Initiative (OSGI) architecture serves as the foundation for ODL. The Dynamic Module System for Java, or OSGI, establishes a framework for creating modular applications.

ODL is comprised of three layers as well as numerous projects and components. Applications that use the controller to collect network intelligence and run algorithms to control and monitor network behavior are found in top layer business and network logic applications. The framework layer, or core, is where the controller is located. It unlimbers the application requirement services from the network devices and stabilizes both north- and south-bound APIs. By offering an abstraction, controllers' free developers from having to write device-specific drivers and enable them to concentrate on creating application functionality. Additionally, physical and forwarded devices make up the bottom layer. Three layers make up the majority of architecture, as shown in Figure 8.2. The middle platform includes basic network service functions, as shown in Figure 8.2. Topology Manager is a service that helps applications searching for network view by learning the layout of the network. Storage of nodes found on the physical layer is the responsibility of both switch manager and topology management. Network flow state registration and preservation are services offered by forwarding along Topology manager and switch manager.

Several protocols, including OpenFlow 1.0, OpenFlow 1.3, BGP-LS, LISP, SNMP, and others, are supported by ODL in the southbound interface. Since ODL was developed to lessen vendor locking, it supports protocols in addition to Open Flow. Multiple protocols, including OpenFlow and BGP-LS, can be supported by the southbound interface as separate plug-ins.

Regardless of the underlying protocol that is used between the controller and the network devices, the SAL decides how to provide the requested service.

8.2.4. Implementation of Scenario via ODL

OpenDaylight is a feature-rich platform that is quite large. This could lead to initial confusion and the impression that it is complicated for those who are unfamiliar with it. So let's keep things easy and go over the implementation process step by step.

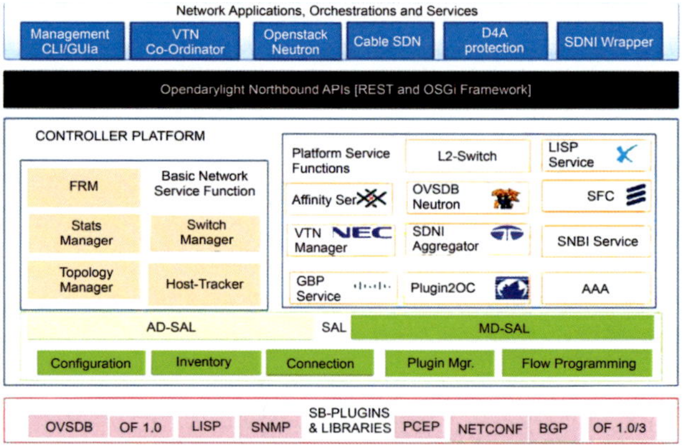

Figure 8.2. *ODL detailed architecture.*

Source: Saleh, A., Bhargavi, G., & Atul, M. G. Implementation of SDN using Open-DayLight Controller, https://www.researchgate.net/publication/320347086.

1. **Step 1:** Using its Karaf distribution, ODL-Beryllium is the simplest to download and install. The Karaf pre-built package is available for download from OpenDaylight's downloads page in both a .zip and a .tar file (same content).

   We already have our new Ubuntu server running, with a NAT access to the Internet. In my case I'm running test@ubuntu, with eth0 as network interface, and an IP address of 192.168.42.137 via DHCP. Let's manually configure this interface to have a static IP:

   Assing IP to both interface public and private for Ubuntu

   Interface.

   eth0 → Nat, public

   eht1 → Private

   This command can be used to assign the IP to specific interface through DHCP service.

   test@ubuntu:~$ sudo dhclient interface

2. **Step 2:** The Java SE Platform is implemented open-source by the OpenJDK project. This is the standard Java version that comes from an Ubuntu repository that is supported. OpenJDK-6 and OpenJDK-7 are the two versions that are currently available.

   The next step is to install the Java Runtime Environment (JRE). ODL-Be runs on Java 7 or higher JVM versions.

   test@ubuntu:~$ sudo apt-get install openjdk-7-jre

3. **Step 3:** At last, we need to define the JAVA_HOME environment variable —Karaf will need it. By default Java is located in "/usr/lib/jvm/java-" directory. To persist the JAVA_HOME variable we must edit our ".profile" file and append a JAVA_HOME definition:

   test@ubuntu:~$ nano.profile

   add blow command to end of this file.

   export JAVA_HOME=/usr/lib/jvm/java-1.7.0-openjdk-amd64 → for 64bit OS

   export JAVA_HOME=/usr/lib/jvm/java-1.7.0-openjdk-i386 → for 32bit OS

4. **Step 4:** Download the OpenDaylight Beryllium

   test@USERVER:~$ wget \

5. **Step 5:** Unpack the tarball on same <HOME> directory —or wherever we want ODL-Be to stay:

   test@ubuntu:~$ tar-xvzf distribution-karaf-0.4.0-Beryllium.tar.gz

6. **Step 6:** Run ODL controller.

   First run OpenDaylight and start the Karaf container in regular mode, by doing

   test@ubuntu:~$./distribution-karaf-0.4.0-Beryllium/bin/karaf

   As can be seen in Figure 8.3, OpenDayLight is up and running and prepared to implement every feature we require for our scenario. Now let's configure ODL-Be with these features. Figure 8.3 confirms that OpenDayLight has been implemented successfully, and we are now prepared to implement the scenario of our choosing instead of ODL. We should investigate a number of ODL's features because it offers a large range of options.

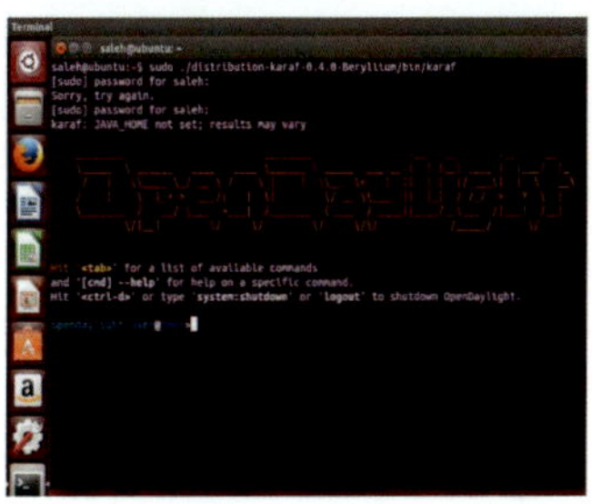

Figure 8.3. *Running ODL controller.*

Source: Saleh, A., Bhargavi, G., & Atul, M. G., Implementation of SDN using Open-DayLight Controller, https://www.researchgate.net/publication/320347086.

The features we're going to use in our simple example:

- The OpenFlow southbound plugin to talk OpenFlow protocol — version 1.3.x— to our OpenFlow-enabled switches —we'll take care of these switches later. Other southbound plugins are available too, but we won't use them in this example.
- The Service Abstraction Layer (SAL), which is the core layer, will act to us as an abstraction layer for all the southbound plugins — only OpenFlow in our case.
- The basic-network-functions bundle, which covers things such as handling packets and flows, being able to discover switches and managing them, tracking hosts, discover addresses and so on, what's been named the L2switch bundle.
- And finally we'll install the DLUX bundle, which is a web-based GUI application, in order to graphically see the topology of our network, its switches, hosts, flow. This application has dependencies on the REST northbound API, among others.

  opendaylight-user@root>feature:install odl-l2switch-switch

  opendaylight-user@root>feature:install odl-dlux-all

7. **Step 7:** Open ODL through Firefox

   ODL provide web GUI facility. You may to insert following address to run it.

   http://192.168.42.137:8181/index.html#/topology

   192.168.42.137 (eht0) is the IP of Linux public interface which ODL could run on it.

To log in as indicated in Figure 8.4, enter Admin as the username and password. And with Mininet's assistance, we will now put our scenario into practice.

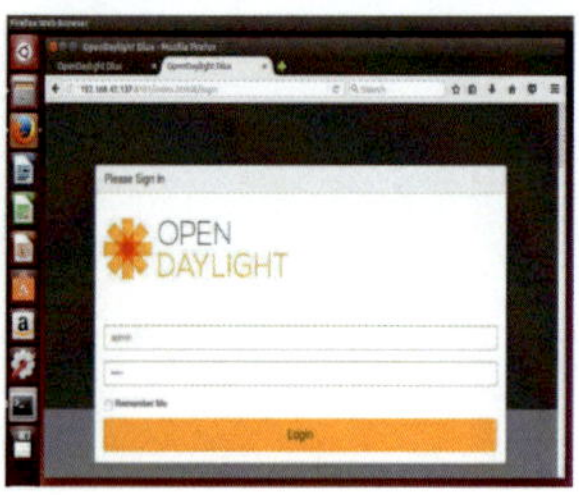

Figure 8.4. *Using ODL web GUI option.*

Source: Saleh, A., Bhargavi, G., & Atul, M. G., Implementation of SDN using Open-DayLight Controller, https://www.researchgate.net/publication/320347086.

8. **Step 8:** The next step is to connect our brand-new ODL-Be controller to a basic OpenFlow-enabled network. Using OpenvSwitch, a free and open-source virtual switch that is compatible with OpenFlow and is simple to install on our computers, is one way to accomplish this. However, there's an even simpler method called Mininet. Mininet is an amazing tool that lets you install an entire virtual network of connected OpenvSwitch switches and virtual hosts on a single machine.

   Consequently, after downloading the Mininet VM image from its website, you turned on NAT on your network adapter and powered it on. Mininet is the default password and login. To configure a network topology inside Mininet VM consisting of four interconnected OpenFlow1.3-capable switches, each with a single host, and connect it to our ODL-Be SDN controller.

8.3. SDN FRAMEWORK FOR CAMPUS NETWORK MANAGEMENT

A university's internal network, or campus network, is a bustling place where a lot of activities take place. It is an assembly of Local Area Networks (LANs) in a condensed geographic area made up of numerous network devices, including switches and routers, where the communications links and networking hardware are owned and operated by the university. Since most administrative, academic, and research processes are now carried out through networks, every campus requires a network that is safe, quick, efficient, accessible from a distance, and has centralized management capabilities. The process of creating a network that can accommodate these features will become more complex, resulting in a highly heterogeneous network, particularly when services, applications, and equipment are offered by various suppliers and manufacturers.

In order to enable data flow and communication within the network, routers, switches, and other physical hardware are connected in a manner consistent with traditional architectural approaches when designing networks on university campuses today. Each of these devices must be manually configured for traffic and security events, and operators, administrators, and system managers are solely responsible for keeping each device up to date with the most recent configuration settings (Rana et al., 2019).

As the network develops, intricate network administration becomes more difficult since crucial management choices are still made by these physical devices. Network operators must constantly be present during the laborious, complex, time-consuming, and error-prone manual configuration of these devices using the low-level device-specific syntax that these devices support (Sahay et al., 2019).

The management interfaces and the management plane provide a suitable platform for a university's (campus) network to be coordinated. The management interfaces offer a conduit for the appropriate information flow between the management plane and other planes (forwarding, control, and application), while the management plane allows for the organization of all operations and management functions within the network. All reports to the network administrator are sent through the management interfaces, and all changes made to the forwarding plane's network device settings are enforced at the management plane. These generic interfaces are designed to support newly added software to the network.

In order to allow the network administrator to assign management functions to the right controllers and planes using software, the management plane and interfaces will be integrated into the administrator's platform and connected to a specific controller in the control layer.

The core management functions of the management plane, domiciled in the administrator's end, include:

- Configuration of network devices and hosts considering the heterogeneity of the network devices and Bring Your Own Device (BYOD) phenomenon.
- Coordinating device deployment so as to dictate the behavior of the network.
- Grouping the different network users into appropriate groups based on status (teaching staff, non-teaching staff and students).
- Assigning different level of access (access control) and privileges to different groups of users of the network with appropriate log-in duration.
- Carrying out proper authentication and authorization of users through web-portal registration and validation of users' devices MAC addresses and users' login details.
- Monitoring and reporting on unexpected conditions within the SDN campus network due to software changes, device reconfiguration, unauthorized access and threats.

All of the data plane's switching devices are compatible with the OpenFlow protocol, and they get rules from the control plane's SDN controller. These rules outline the policies that inspect and govern the network, support packet forwarding on switching devices, and collect and report network status information for every packet handled. The rules are updated as a result of configuration modifications and dynamic control, and they are installed in the proper switching devices for operations. In order to create a comprehensive picture of the entire network and give the application layer the data it needs, the controller also uses traffic statistics and network status, which are gathered and stored by the switching devices. In order to enhance rapid network convergence and facilitate the processing of network administrator policies, the controllers share traffic statistics and network status among themselves (Kutay & Ercan, 2016).

Packet forwarding rules are created by the controller (in the control plane) based on application requirements. The programming language (protocol) that connects the application and control planes is necessary for this function to work. The programming language's programmability makes it possible to automate the controller using application policies that are accessible through the northbound interface. Since the network devices are compliant with SDN, the southbound interface uses the OpenFlow protocol.

The web-based GUI of the northbound interface governs a collection of APIs that control the OpenFlow switch parameters. The Java-based OpenFlow controller floodlight, which is backed by an open-source development community, serves as the work's northbound interface. The industry and developer community have actively tested and improved this commercial SDN product, which is made by Big Switch company. When administrators are familiar with Java programming, require production-level performance, and would like industry support, Floodlight is advised.

8.4. AGILITY WITHOUT COMPROMISE WITH JUNIPER SDN

The next generation of cloud, mobile, M2M, and big data applications are being widely adopted, and this is significantly affecting network and IT infrastructures. These applications have far shorter life cycles than traditional ones. They need to be able to grow, shrink, and spin up and down on demand. Moreover, these application workloads need to be able to be moved between data centers or within one; this will increase the complexity of management.

It's likely that you have been using more and more SDN-style techniques to virtualize your networks and enable your cloud-building endeavors by utilizing SDN technologies. However, in order to fully utilize SDN, you must have a plan that guarantees choice, allowing your network to change over time without being constrained by outdated technology. With its extensive product portfolio, Juniper offers a cutting-edge SDN solution that divides the intelligence and muscle of your network, giving you a centralized network view for more effective orchestration and automation. You can reduce total cost of ownership, shorten time to market, and scale up and down to satisfy shifting market demands by freeing the network from its restrictive history.

8.4.1. The Challenge

Businesses such as yours aim to design their networks to satisfy the service and connectivity needs of numerous ever-changing applications. The network must be automated, scalable, programmable, and policy-driven in order to achieve that. However, networks built using the conventional method of networking and service implementation in hardware are manual, inflexible, static, and unable to adapt quickly to changes in application requirements. According to Juniper, there are three main categories of businesses that stand to gain from SDN. They all tackle SDN from somewhat different angles in the beginning. They all, however, aim to achieve the same commercial objectives, which are enhancing application performance, increasing business agility, and cutting costs.

8.4.1.1. Service Providers

Improving the functionality of the network functions that underpin the services you offer to clients is your goal if you're a service provider, like a telecom company. Your carrier network is your most valuable asset, which you should utilize. You intend to create the most elastic cloud possible by utilizing service orchestration and network services virtualization. To do this, you need to be able to program network resources and paths in real-time response to traffic patterns and loads to be more efficient, enable business agility, contain CapEx and OpEx, and meet elastic service turn-up requirements.

8.4.1.2. Enterprises

If your company is an enterprise, you have to invest in IT because you need to be able to deliver applications to users on a flexible basis while keeping costs as low as possible. The next step up in enterprise cloud architecture is hybrid clouds, which offer scale-out federated architecture performance, maximum agility, and the highest level of resource elasticity.

However, getting there is not easy. You virtualized your data center before adding orchestration software to give it a "cloud-like architecture" as part of your transition from legacy IT data centers to the cloud. But complete network, compute, and storage automation is required to provide true IT as a Service (ITaaS) supported by private cloud infrastructure. Additionally, location-independent connectivity must be achieved, and the network must be seamlessly integrated into the cloud orchestration. Next, you want to incorporate public cloud into the mix so that workloads can be run in tandem with your own data center by enabling on-demand resource consumption from a cloud service provider's data center.

Only location-independent scale-out connectivity, federated workload orchestration across hybrid clouds, and public-private cloud integration can accomplish this.

8.4.1.3. Emerging Cloud Companies

You're what Juniper refers to as an "emerging cloud company" if you're pursuing your business goals by utilizing open cloud infrastructure principles to offer cloud services to your clients. You aim to establish a distinct market position in the broader everything-as-a-service (XaaS) arena by utilizing agile, highly advanced, and open standards that do not impose vendor lock-in. As the de facto orchestration solution for the server, storage, and network integrated cloud infrastructure stack, you are aware of OpenStack.

But you're also having trouble keeping up with the various community release versions, intricacies, and flaws in the networking and storage components in terms of setup, scaling, dependability, and monitoring. You try to strike a balance between open source, commercial solutions, and community-sourced open-source software stacks integrated into commercial alternatives in order to reduce the inherent risks that come with depending solely on open source.

8.4.2. The Juniper Networks SDN Solution

Juniper cloud service orchestration and management solutions are all-in-one SDN solutions that simplify operations, boost business agility, and expedite service delivery for a wide range of organizations, including enterprises, emerging cloud companies, and service providers. They do this by combining virtual and physical switches, routers, security, and software.

1. **Juniper Networks MetaFabric Architecture:** A key element of the Juniper SDN solution, enabling simple, open and smart networks that accelerate the deployment and delivery of applications within and across multiple data centers and clouds. A verified and tested implementation of Juniper's robust switching, routing, and security platforms—which make use of feature-rich silicon, programmable systems, network orchestration, SDN, and open APIs to facilitate integration with the technology ecosystem—delivers the MetaFabric architecture.

2. **Juniper Networks® Contrail Networking:** A simple, open, and agile SDN solution that automates and orchestrates the creation of highly scalable virtual networks, these virtual networks let you harness the power of the cloud—for new services, increased business agility, and revenue growth.
3. **Juniper Networks NorthStar Network Controller:** A software platform providing online and offline WAN analysis and optimization, NorthStar combines Juniper Networks Junos® operating system carrier-grade peering capabilities with WANDL IP/MPLSView's proven multilayer optimization expertise in a unified, highly integrated controller package.
4. **Junos® Space Network Director:** A smart, comprehensive, and automated network management tool that simplifies network operations by unifying wired and wireless management for the complete life cycle of campus and data center networks from a single pane of glass.
5. **Juniper Networks SRX Series Services Gateways:** High-performance network security solutions for enterprises and service providers that pack high port density, advanced security, and flexible connectivity into easily managed platforms.
6. **Juniper Networks Firefly:** This delivers purpose-built security for virtualized and cloud environments and provides flexible and comprehensive protection for enterprises and service providers by delivering a multilayered solution that secures traffic from all directions.
7. **Service Control Gateways (SCGs) and Service Delivery Gateways (SDGs):** This provide consolidated network service delivery and automation based on Juniper Networks MX Series 3D Universal Edge Routers for either Juniper or third-party services. Subscriber aware service chaining and service auto scaling in the Juniper SDN solution deliver significant efficiencies as well.
8. **Juniper Networks EX Series Ethernet Switches, QFX Series Switches, MX Series Routers, and PTX Series Packet Transport Routers:** This provide highly optimized routing and switching forwarding planes, enabling Juniper's SDN solution to interconnect multiple data centers and clouds seamlessly.

8.4.3. Features and Benefits

The Juniper SDN solution gives you freedom of choice, intelligent automation, and always-on reliability (Table 8.1):

1. **Freedom of Choice:** Juniper provides a multi-use case, multi-network-domain SDN solution that is ready for production. You can easily take advantage of all the benefits of SDN while safeguarding your current networking investments because there is no need to completely replace your current infrastructure. With an open architecture that works with a variety of networking and service options—physical or virtual, implemented in hardware or software, Juniper or third party—you can avoid costly vendor lock-in. With the help of open, well-established standards and an open ecosystem, you can select the best-in-class building blocks for your SDN solution and integrate multivendor solutions seamlessly, whether they are in physical or virtual format. You can virtualize and automate in multiple domains within your network, allowing it to expand and change over time. You can also choose from a variety of domains, including data centers, WANs, core, edge, access, and campuses.
2. **Intelligent Automation:** Because of its policy-driven architecture and exceptional responsiveness to network and service demands, Juniper makes it possible to reduce OpEx and streamline operations. Using a feedback loop that is fueled by detailed, rich analytics, you can make decisions based on facts. Network telemetry, capacity planning and optimization, troubleshooting, and precision measurement are all enhanced by the correlation of physical and virtual network data points. The capacity to automatically scale and tune networks and services enhances resource provisioning and opens up new revenue streams for networks.
3. **Always-on Reliability:** Scale-out distributed software that is highly available, always on, elastic, and Network Equipment Building System (NEBS) compliant is the foundation of the Juniper SDN solution and can be deployed by service providers in a variety of scenarios. Strong security with perimeter- and hypervisor-level security that leverages open source for transparency is ensured by enhanced security integrated with cloud platforms. Additionally, the Juniper SDN solution guarantees that you can scale your network infrastructure beyond data center and cloud boundaries, elastically scale services up and down, and scale software out to satisfy any control and management requirements.

Table 8.1. *Juniper SDN Overview*

	Open	Intelligent	Reliable	Automated
Orchestration: OpenStack, CloudStack, Third-Party Orchestration Systems	REST APIs to third-party orchestration systems; OpenStack	Open to support third-party analyst engines; policy rendering	OpenStack deployed in HA mode	Common platform for physical, virtual NF orchestration and management.
Control: Contrail Networking, NorthStar	OpenContrail; MP-BGP and VPN to the host	Contrail networking analytics, overlay underlay analytics correlation; contrail networking policy engine.	Scale-out distributed software and ISSU; multi-DC and inter-cloud federation; virtual security.	Respond to dynamic network changes in automated fashion.
Services: SCG, SDG, SRX Series, Firefly, DDoS Secure	Support for third-party VNFs	Range of interfaces to policy engines (PCRF, AAA) Works with existing policy servers.	High-availability security; data center security.	Subscriber-aware service chaining; service auto-scaling.
Forwarding MX series, vMX, switch fabric	Physical or virtual, multivendor interoperability.	Physical status; Network Director 2.0	NEBScompliant hardware; HA and ISSU.	Chef, Puppet, and Mirantis fuel integration; network director.

Source: https://www.copperriverit.com/wp-content/uploads/2015/09/juniper_sdn.pdf.

8.4.4. Solution Components

8.4.4.1. Orchestration

Juniper SDN integrates seamlessly with orchestration software to automate compute, storage, and network infrastructure, enabling applications and services to be scaled up or down as needed.

Decisions about the allocation and modification of resources can be made holistically through orchestration, taking into account the states of the infrastructure and business processes. Juniper SDN is combined with OpenStack as a core orchestration technology via Junos Space Network Director for network management orchestration and Contrail Networking for overlay network control.

Via REST APIs, Juniper's SDN solution can also be integrated with other orchestration platforms like VMware vCloud and IBM Smart Cloud Orchestration. All of this results in a common orchestration management platform, both virtual and physical.

8.4.4.2. Control

You can create virtual networks with Contrail Networking that work with a variety of hypervisors and orchestration systems that smoothly connect with already-existing physical networks. Wide-area network (WAN) analysis and optimization are other features offered by the NorthStar network controller, both online and offline. Scale-out distributed control software with multiple data center and inter-cloud federation capabilities is made possible by the entire Juniper SDN solution. To provide you with the most controller options, Juniper is also working with VMware to integrate NSX controller capabilities on some of its routing and switching products. Juniper SDN's extensive feature set enables you to manage your dynamic network changes in a highly automated manner.

8.4.4.3. Services

Juniper SDN offers a range of network services, including content caching, WAN optimization, load balancing, deep packet inspection (DPI), and firewall security. They can operate as virtual machines on computer platforms, standalone appliances, or routers, and they can be physical or virtual. Virtual network functions (VNFs) from third parties as well as internally developed products (Firefly and the SRX Series) are part of the Juniper SDN solution.

8.4.4.4. Forwarding

Depending on where it is located in the network or on performance/scaling requirements, the Juniper SDN forwarding plane can be virtual (Contrail Networking vRouter, vMX) or physical (MX Series, EX Series, QFX Series, or PTX Series platforms). It can be implemented in hardware or software. When compared to software implementations on generic hardware, forwarding implemented in ASICs typically offers the same level of performance for high-performance and high-scaled systems with a much smaller footprint, power consumption, and cooling requirements. With the use of standards-based protocols in the forwarding layer, Juniper's SDN solution facilitates multivendor interoperability. It also offers intelligent analysis of network statistics through the use of Junos Space Network Director's analytics features.

8.5. ABNO: A FEASIBLE SDN APPROACH FOR MULTI-VENDOR IP AND OPTICAL NETWORKS

Transport networks are responsible for moving aggregated traffic pipes between various cities, regions, or continents, originating from multiple users and services.

The networks operated by traditional carriers are extremely complex and are not easily programmable or adaptable to changes in traffic. The core and metro network nodes require numerous manual configuration steps. Furthermore, vendor-specific Network Management System (NMS) implementations are commonly used in network solutions from various vendors.

IP/MPLS and optical networks can be used to forward application service requests thanks to Software Defined Networking (SDN) and network programmability. Due to resource optimization and a decrease in network operation complexity, the SDN approach can assist operators in lowering CAPEX and OPEX in their networks. The SDN controllers that are currently being proposed for the market, however, are not tailored to the current heterogeneous network environments because they are based on monolithic software.

Such SDN solutions are like a "black-box" and its deployment leads to different problems for the operator:

- Vendor lock-in (solutions in the market are mono-vendor);
- Lack of support with non-Open Flow (OF) networks; and
- Problems to support E2E multi-domain path establishment in current networks.

Application-based Network Operations (ABNO) is a term used by the Internet Engineering Task Force (IETF) to describe a solution built on common components and protocols. The Path Computation Element (PCE) is the central element of the ABNO architecture. Based on currently defined IETF standard blocks (PCE, ALTO, and VNTM), the IETF ABNO architecture can be implemented in a distributed or centralized manner depending on the needs of network operators. Because ABNO architecture is modular, different vendors, third parties, or even a single provider can deploy different building blocks. The operators' issue with vendor lock-in is resolved by the modules' standard interfaces and modular design. Conversely, ABNO is specifically designed for multidomain and multivendor networks, allowing control plane based and OF based domains to work together. In this chapter, we experimentally validate the ABNO architecture for a multilayer use case in two scenarios: one with OF in the optical layer and the other with control plane.

8.5.1. Application-Based Network Operations Architecture

Numerous technological components, mechanisms, and procedures are combined in the ABNO architecture. By coordinating the parts that run and administer the network, the ABNO architecture and its ensuing components offer a range of services. The central element of the architecture, the ABNO

Controller, is in charge of coordinating the workflows and calling the appropriate parts in the proper sequence. A repository of workflows involving network operations (MPLS provisioning, L3VPNs, etc.) is kept by ABNO. The component that manages path computation throughout the network graph is called the Path Computation Element (PCE). The PCE can directly operate in the nodes to generate LSPs if it is active. Path computation in multi-domain (inter-AS, for example) or multi-layer networks also requires coordination between multiple PCEs operating on different TEDs. Virtual Network Topology Manager (VNTM) is an essential component for multi-layer scenarios. By using connections in the lower layer, VNTM is responsible for preserving the topology of the upper layer. This entity hides the optical connections that the LSP has established, making decisions about traffic engineering and upper-layer routing easier.

The Topology Module (TM) contains three databases: an inventory database containing the resource configuration parameters, an inter-layer relation, and a view of each layer. Obtaining and keeping up with the topology from the available sources (such as routing protocols) takes up one section of the module. Information requests from parties like the Provisioning Manager, PCE, or VTNM are handled by the other portion of the module (Figure 8.5).

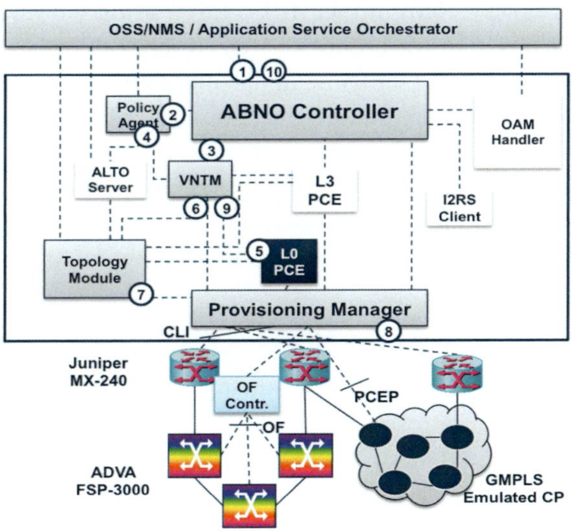

Figure 8.5. *ABNO architecture and its interactions for IP Link provisioning use case.*

Source: http://www.vlopezalvarez.com/Profesional/Publications/Conferences/2014_OFC_1.pdf.

Lastly, the department in charge of configuring the network components is the Provisioning Manager (PM). It can accomplish this by setting up the resources in each node (CLI, OF, or NetConf) or by using PCEP to send a series of commands to the control plane (Figure 8.6).

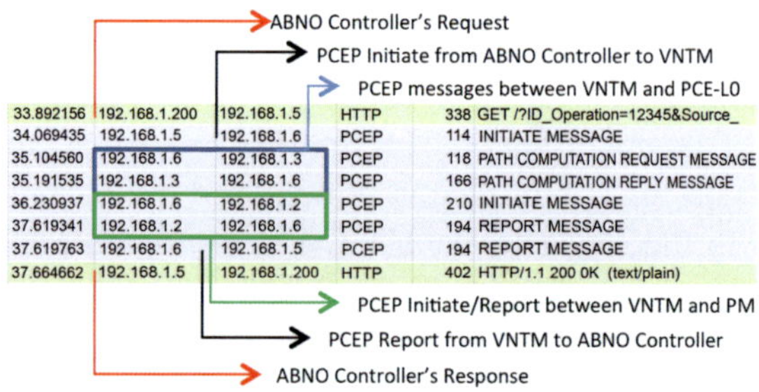

Figure 8.6. *Message flow in IP Link provisioning use case.*

Source: http://www.vlopezalvarez.com/Profesional/Publications/Conferences/2014_OFC_1.pdf.

8.5.2. PCEP to Remotely Initiate GMPLS LSPs

It is possible to remotely configure GMPLS LSPs using the PCE protocol. The goal is to make it possible for an active PCE to configure GMPLS LSPs. On the other hand, any network element can use these extensions to request a path setup. This ABNO framework feature makes it easier for different architecture modules to communicate with one another. It is evident that this interface can be used by any module communicating with PCE to request a new path. Other modules, however, are able to communicate with each other through this interface. For example, the VNTM can be asked to create a new path via this interface by the ABNO controller.

Another module that can benefit from PCEP is PM. The PM requests information about each node from the TM when it receives a PCInitiate message. The TM provides the node's layer, the configuration protocol (CLI, NetConf, OF, or PCEP), and the precise parameters needed to configure the node for each IP in the ERO. Currently, the primary benefit of PCEP is that the PM only needs to forward the PCInitiate message to the network element, negating the need for any other actions on its part. PM must be familiar with the CLI commands or, in the case of NetConf, the XML network configuration for equipment that does not support PCEP.

OF is an additional node configuration option. Despite being a very promising technology for L2, OF has not yet been implemented in actual core networks. Although there are vendor-specific extensions to the OF protocol, some vendors have completed implementations for transport networks. For this reason, our PM uses an external OF controller to get configuration information about a single node via OF. Concerning the particular implementation for optical networks, this OF controller is responsible. Future support for OF in the PM for packet and optical technologies is possible.

8.5.3. Experimental Validation of the ABNO Architecture for IP Link Provisioning

In order to support an IP link provisioning workflow, we implement the ABNO architecture. We wish to show off the architecture's ability to function in OF and GMPLS enabled networks in addition to supporting multi-layer scenarios. In order to accomplish this, we used a CP emulator created in TID, three Juniper MX-240 routers, four ADVA FSP 3000 optical nodes, and five GMPLS nodes. Virtual machines called ABNO architecture modules are installed on a server that has two Intel Xeon E5-2630 2.30 GHz processors with six cores apiece and 192 GB of RAM. Likewise, every GMPLS node uses a virtual machine (VM) to simulate the control plane.

Figure 8.5 illustrates how the modules interact to provide an IP link, and Figure 8.6 depicts the exchange of HTTP and PCEP messages. To make messages easier to read, some are left out, such as the KeepAlive and Open messages. Each step is following explained:

1. The NMS sends a request to the ABNO controller using a HTTP Message with the operation type or workflow (IP Provisioning), its ID and the parameters for this operation (source and destination).
2. ABNO asks the policy agent to check whether it has sufficient rights to make the request.
3. The VNTM is instructed to establish a link between the two routers by the ABNO Controller after it has verified the permission. The module that possesses the inter-layer data, enabling it to determine which optical nodes every router is connected to, is the VNTM. The source and destination IP addresses are included in the End-Points object by the PCInitiate.
4. The VTNM also needs to verify with the Policy Agent if it can provide the service.
5. For a path between two optical nodes, the VNTM module sends a PCRequest message to the L0-PCE. The L0-PCE then responds with the computation in a PCResponse. The L0-PCE in this experiment lacks instantiation capabilities and is stateless. The L0-PCE is only used by the VNTM to obtain the path through the optical layer.

6. The L0 path, endpoints, and interlayer data are all contained in the VNTM. The PM uses a PCInitiate message to configure the nodes after receiving this information. This request contains the same data as the PCInitiate message sent from the ABNO controller to the VNTM, but it also includes the ERO that was acquired from the L0 PCE.
7. The PM asks the TM for each node's description. Because there are hops between the IP and the optical layer, the response enables the PM to determine the layer and technology for each node. As a result, a new link is formed in the optical layer.
8. PM chooses a different protocol to fulfill the request based on the technology and configuration mode. Initially, the IP nodes are configured, followed by the optical layer. PCEP, CLI, and NetConf are the available options for configuring the IP layer. In this experiment, we have used CLI since PCEP is not yet supported. Using PCEP, OF, or even UNI from the router, the optical layer can be configured.

   We have tested two operations mode here:

   i. To configure the ADVA nodes, an OF controller is used with extensions for wavelength switching. A web service interface is used to trigger ADVA's controller.
   ii. For GMPLS CP, we have implemented the extensions to support PCInitiate forwarding to RSVP in TID control plane nodes. The RSVP message contains the information of the PCInitiate.
9. Once the network elements are configured, PM notifies the VTNM using a PCRpt message.
10. Similarly, the VNTM advertises to ABNO controller, which sends a HTTP Reply to the NMS. This response has the ID of the operation, an error code, the source, the destination and the result of the operation. To support any correlation in the NMS.

8.6. SCOPE OF SDN FRAMEWORK AND ARCHITECTURE

The scope of the SDN Framework and Architecture is summarized below:

1. **Controller Plane – Data Plane Decoupling (Logical Separation):**
   i. Distributed, hierarchical and federated deployment of SDN Controller instances, with Intra-Domain and Inter-Domain connectivity between SDN Controller instances;

ii. Northbound Interfaces (NBIs), enabling the development of SDN Clients (within applications) that interact with the SDN Controller plane;

iii. Permitting abstract views of the network to be created, interrogated and manipulated. These abstract views can exist at various levels, and they can be combined with virtualization to create sliced or partitioned views. Furthermore, a comprehensive view may encompass all aspects of a network, whereas a more limited view may focus on specific aspects, e.g., security, reliability, quality of service, et cetera.

2. Network Elements:

i. Modeling of forwarding and processing behavior, where processing includes computation, storage and/or physical or virtual network functions (NFs), whether these are directly related to traffic flows or whether they are associated with networking in general (e.g., processing of aggregated statistics or monitoring of events);

ii. Support for a variety of media and connectivity types (e.g., packet and circuit switching technologies);

iii. Support for diverse hardware and software platforms, with varying port counts, throughput, capacity, and flexibility, e.g., platforms supporting a fixed set of protocols (i.e., pre-defined protocol parsing and fixed matching/action pipelines), platforms supporting protocol independent forwarding (configurable parsing, matching and actions), as well as platforms supporting stateful classification and processing.

iv. Here a Network Element is defined as a collection of resources managed as a unit, i.e., a network node, at any level of abstraction, not necessarily a single "box" in the network.

3. Network Virtualization Related Technologies:

i. Support for static and dynamic network provisioning technologies;

ii. Support for tunnels – used to create overlay networks.

4. Support for Network Functions Virtualization (NFV), L4–L7 Services, and Data Plane Services:

i. Identifying relevant traffic and diverting it to/through individual services, service chains or Virtual Network Function forwarding graphs;

ii. Service specific forwarding, e.g., application aware QoS, or service specific processing, such as encryption and content replication.

iii. Managing services and VNFs.

5. Enabling Traditional and SDN Controlled Networks to Coexist ("Hybrid" Scenario):

i. Partitioning elements with some ports being traditionally controlled, others SDN controlled;

ii. SDN control of an overlay network, with traditional control of the underlying network, and vice versa; c. Partitioning of responsibilities, for example, traditional management/monitoring and SDN forwarding configuration or vice versa;

iii. Enabling traditionally controlled and SDN controlled networks to be interconnected (for both intra-domain and inter-domain scenarios).

Requirements and criteria to evaluate the SDN Architecture are defined. These can be grouped in the following categories:

- Simplicity and expressiveness;
- Applicability;
- Interworking;
- Interoperability;
- Scalability;
- Security;
- Resilience and fault tolerance;
- Management and monitoring.

The high-level reference points and interfaces utilized in a Software Defined Network, such as those connected to the SDN Controller and the SDN-controlled Network Element, are specified in the Architecture. To help with the description, functional blocks that are internal to the Controller and Network Element may be mentioned. However, not all implementations require these functions, and the interfaces to these blocks are usually not specified. The main emphasis when explaining the SDN Controller/Network Element's behavior is on factors that impact interoperability. The Architecture makes decisions about component partitioning and decides which interfaces are standardized and which are described, providing a justification for its decisions. While other working groups define details, such as specific interfaces, the emphasis is on principles. To minimize the efforts involved in standardization, implementation, integration, and validation, it is advised to use common models and mechanisms whenever feasible. To enable interoperability, a greater emphasis on these models and mechanisms is needed because SDN introduces a new ecosystem structure with more players of different kinds. The Architecture's specific goal is to provide a framework for the creation of information models.

REFERENCES

1. Al-Somaidai, M. B., & Yahya, E. (2014). Survey of software components to emulate OpenFlow protocol as an SDN implementation. *American Journal of Software Engineering and Applications, 3*(6), 74–82.
2. Ali, M., Hossain, M., & Pavez, M. (2015). Design and implementation of secure campus network. *International Journal of Emerging Technology and Advanced Engineering, 5*(7), 370–374.
3. Alsher, A. (2015). An overview of network virtualization and cloud network as a service. *International Journal of Network Management, 25*(1), 1–30. https://doi.org/10.1002/nem.1916.
4. Bernaille, L., Teixeira, R., Akodkenou, I., Soule, A., & Salamatian, K. (2011). Traffic classification on the fly. *ACM SIGCOMM Computer Communication Review, 36*(2), 23–26.
5. Channegowda, M. P., Nejabati, R., & Simeonidou, D. (2013). Software-defined optical networks technology and infrastructure: Enabling software-defined optical network operations. *IEEE/OSA Journal of Optical Communication and Networks, 5*(10), A274–A282. https://doi.org/10.1364/JOCN.5.000A274.
6. Chin, T., Rahouti, M., & Xiong, K. (2018). Applying software-defined networking to minimize the end-to-end delay of network services. *ACM SIGAPP Applied Computing Review, 18*(1), 30–40.
7. Christodoulopoulos, K., Tomkos, I., & Varvarigos, E. (2011). Elastic bandwidth allocation in flexible OFDM-based optical networks. *IEEE/OSA Journal of Lightwave Technology, 29*(9), 1354–1366. https://doi.org/10.1109/JLT.2011.2109194.
8. Curtis, A. R., Mogul, J. C., Tourrilhes, J., Yalagandula, P., Sharma, P., & Banerjee, S. (2011). Devoflow: Scaling flow management for high-performance networks. *SIGCOMM Computer Communication Review, 41*(4), 254–265.
9. Gosselin, S., et al. (2015). Fixed and mobile convergence: Which role for optical networks. *IEEE/OSA Journal of Optical Communication and Networks, 7*(11), 1705–1083. https://doi.org/10.1364/JOCN.7.001705.
10. Greenberg, A., Hjalmtysson, G., Maltz, D., Myers, A., Rexford, J., Xie, G., Yan, H., Zhan, J., & Zhang, H. (2005). A clean slate 4D approach to network control and management. *ACM Computer Communication Review, 35*(5), 41–54. https://doi.org/10.1145/1090191.1090196.
11. Hart, P., Nilsson, N., & Raphael, B. (1968). A formal basis for the heuristic determination of minimum cost paths. *IEEE Transactions on*

Systems Science and Cybernetics, 4(2), 100–107. https://doi.org/10.1109/TSSC.1968.300136.

12. John, W., & Tafvelin, S. (2007). Analysis of internet backbone traffic and header anomalies observed. In *Proceedings of the 7th ACM SIGCOMM conference on Internet measurement* (pp. 111–116). ACM.
13. Kutay, M., & Ercan, T. (2016). An overview of software-defined campus networks. *Selcuk University Digital Archive Systems, 4*(2), 155–164.
14. Martínez, R., et al. (2017). Integrated SDN/NFV orchestration for the dynamic deployment of mobile virtual backhaul networks over a multilayer (packet/optical) aggregation infrastructure. *IEEE/OSA Journal of Optical Communication and Networks, 9*(2), A135–A142. https://doi.org/10.1364/JOCN.9.000A135.
15. McKeown, N., Anderson, T., Balakrishnan, H., Parulkar, G., Peterson, L., Rexford, J., Shenker, S., & Turner, J. (2008). OpenFlow: Enabling innovation in campus networks. *ACM SIGCOMM Computer Communication Review, 38*(2), 69–74.
16. McKeown, N., Anderson, T., Balakrishnan, H., Parulkar, G., Peterson, L., Rexford, J., Shenker, S., & Turner, J. (2008). OpenFlow: Enabling innovation in campus networks. *ACM SIGCOMM Computer Communication Review, 38*(2), 69–74.
17. Mendonca, M., Nunes, B. A., Nguyen, X., Obraczka, K., & Turletti, T. (2014). A survey of software-defined networking: Past, present, and future of programmable networks. *IEEE Communications Surveys & Tutorials, 16*(3), 1617–1634. https://doi.org/10.1109/COMST.2014.2320098.
18. Murray, D., & Koziniec, T. (2012). The state of enterprise network traffic in 2012. In *Communications (APCC), 2012 18th Asia-Pacific Conference on* (pp. 179–184). IEEE.
19. Nunes, B., Mendonca, M., Nguyen, X., Obraczka, K., & Turletti, T. (2014). A survey of software-defined networks: Past, present, and future programmable networks. *IEEE Communications Surveys and Tutorials, 16*(3), 1617–1634. https://doi.org/10.1109/COMST.2014.2320098.
20. Rana, D., Dhondiyal, S., & Chamoli, S. (2019). Software-defined networking (SDN) challenges, issues, and solutions. *International Journal of Computer Sciences and Engineering, 7*(1), 884–889. https://doi.org/10.26438/ijcse/v7i1.884889.
21. Sahay, R., Meng, W., & Jensen, C. (2019). The application of software-defined networking on securing computer networks: A survey. *Journal of Network and Computer Applications, 131*, 89–108. https://doi.org/10.1016/j.jnca.2019.07.015.

22. Sama, M. R., et al. (2015). Software-defined control of the virtualization mobile packet core. *IEEE Communications Magazine, 53*(2), 107–115. https://doi.org/10.1109/MCOM.2015.7045607.
23. Schonwalder, J., Fouquet, M., Rodosek, G., & Hochstatter, I. (2009). Future internet: Content, services, and management. *IEEE Communications Magazine, 47*(7), 27–33. https://doi.org/10.1109/MCOM.2009.5182375.
24. Vilalta, R., et al. (2015). Multidomain network hypervisor for abstraction and control of OpenFlow-enabled multi-tenant multi-technology transport networks. *IEEE/OSA Journal of Optical Communication and Networks, 7*(11), B55–B61. https://doi.org/10.1364/JOCN.7.000B55.
25. Wickboldt, J., de Jesus, W., Isolani, P., Both, C., Rochol, J., & Granville, L. (2015). Software-defined networking: Management requirements and challenges. *IEEE Communications Magazine, 53*(1), 1–8. https://doi.org/10.1109/MCOM.2015.7045607.
26. Xia, W., Wen, Y., Foh, C., Niyato, D., & Xie, H. (2015). A survey on software-defined networking. *IEEE Communications Surveys and Tutorials, 17*(1), 27–51. https://doi.org/10.1109/COMST.2014.2320098.
27. Younis, O., & Fahmy, S. (2015). Flowmate: Scalable online flow clustering. *IEEE/ACM Transactions on Networking, 13*(2), 288–301. https://doi.org/10.1109/TNET.2004.827618.
28. Zhang, M., Dusi, M., John, W., & Chen, C. (2009). Analysis of UDP traffic usage on internet backbone links. In *Applications and the Internet, 2009. SAINT'09. Ninth Annual International Symposium on* (pp. 280–281). IEEE.

CHAPTER 9

BANDWIDTH SCHEDULING, MANIPULATION, AND CALENDARING

Contents

INTRODUCTION

A group of use cases known as bandwidth calendaring fundamentally represent the idea of time-based bandwidth manipulation. Under these circumstances, "manipulation" means adding, removing, or changing network bandwidth. The motivations behind bandwidth manipulation can take many different forms, but some common ones are service demands and disruptions, operational planning for capacity changes in the future, or changing bandwidth characteristics to better match traffic patterns.

The recurring pattern in all of these is that they usually involve a temporal cycle. Actually, not only is bandwidth manipulated according to a timed schedule, but the reasons for doing so are typically driven by the necessity to follow a schedule that would otherwise require manual labor.

9.1. BANDWIDTH SCHEDULING

Bandwidth scheduling refers to the process of managing and allocating available bandwidth resources within a network to ensure efficient and fair distribution among users, applications, or devices. This concept is crucial in both wired and wireless networks to optimize performance, prioritize critical traffic, and prevent congestion. Here's an overview of bandwidth scheduling:

9.1.1. Goals of Bandwidth Scheduling

1. **Resource Optimization:** Ensure that available bandwidth is utilized efficiently to meet the varying demands of different applications and users.
2. **Quality of Service (QoS) Management:** Prioritize and allocate bandwidth to critical applications or users to ensure they receive sufficient resources and meet performance requirements.
3. **Congestion Management:** Prevent network congestion by controlling the rate of data transmission and enforcing traffic policies to maintain stable network performance.
4. **Fairness:** Ensure fairness in bandwidth allocation among users or applications, preventing any single user or application from monopolizing network resources to the detriment of others.

9.1.2. Techniques Used in Bandwidth Scheduling

1. Traffic Shaping:

i. **Definition:** Traffic shaping regulates the flow of network traffic to smooth out bursts and control the rate of data transmission.

ii. **Purpose:** By shaping traffic, networks can enforce policies on bandwidth usage, prioritize certain types of traffic (e.g., real-time applications over bulk data transfers), and mitigate the impact of excessive traffic on network performance.

2. Quality of Service (QoS):

i. **Definition:** QoS mechanisms classify and prioritize traffic based on predefined criteria (such as application type, source/destination address, or packet contents).

ii. **Purpose:** QoS ensures that critical applications (e.g., VoIP, video conferencing) receive higher priority access to bandwidth resources to maintain performance levels, even during periods of network congestion.

3. Packet Scheduling Algorithms:

i. **Types:** Various algorithms, such as Weighted Fair Queuing (WFQ), Deficit Round Robin (DRR), and Token Bucket, are used to schedule packets for transmission based on priority, fairness, or other policies.

ii. **Purpose:** These algorithms manage the order and timing of packet transmission to optimize throughput, reduce latency, and enforce bandwidth limits as per network policies.

4. Bandwidth Reservation:

i. **Definition:** Reservation protocols allocate a guaranteed amount of bandwidth to specific users or applications in advance, ensuring they have dedicated resources available when needed.

ii. **Purpose:** This technique is critical for real-time applications requiring consistent performance (e.g., video streaming, online gaming) by preventing other traffic from impacting reserved bandwidth.

9.1.3. Implementation Considerations

1. **Network Architecture:** Bandwidth scheduling techniques vary depending on whether the network is centralized (e.g., SDN-controlled) or distributed (traditional network infrastructure).
2. **Scalability:** Effective bandwidth scheduling should scale with the size of the network and the number of connected devices or users to maintain optimal performance.
3. **Dynamic Adjustment:** Networks should be able to dynamically adjust bandwidth allocation based on real-time traffic conditions, user demands, and application priorities.

4. **Monitoring and Analytics:** Continuous monitoring and analysis of network traffic patterns and performance metrics are essential for optimizing bandwidth scheduling policies and identifying potential issues or bottlenecks.

9.1.4. Future Trends

1. **5G Networks:** With the advent of 5G, bandwidth scheduling will become even more critical to support diverse applications with varying performance requirements, such as IoT devices, autonomous vehicles, and augmented reality.
2. **AI and Automation:** Integration of artificial intelligence and machine learning algorithms will enhance bandwidth scheduling by predicting traffic patterns, optimizing resource allocation, and dynamically adjusting policies in real-time.
3. **Edge Computing:** Bandwidth scheduling will play a crucial role in managing distributed edge resources efficiently and ensuring low-latency communication for edge applications.

In conclusion, effective bandwidth scheduling is essential for ensuring network performance, reliability, and fairness in the allocation of resources. By implementing appropriate techniques and policies, organizations can optimize their network infrastructure to meet the diverse demands of modern applications and users.

9.2. BANDWIDTH MANIPULATION

According to the state of the art, bandwidth reservation is a crucial tool for network management that enables sufficient levels of real-time guarantees or quality of service. Ample performance is provided to real-time flows in both automotive and industrial communications, for instance, by the IEEE Audio-Video Bridging (AVB) set of standards, which can flexibly support multiple traffic classes even under heavy workloads because of bandwidth reservation. However, the need for flexible and efficient resource management raises new challenges, such as how to carry out dynamic network reconfiguration while maintaining the necessary Quality of Service (QoS). For both wired and wireless networks, SDN enables designers to quickly and simply implement dynamic and adaptive QoS control solutions. In particular, the work in Li, C., proposed resource management approaches suitable for a number of scenarios, including 5G SDN-based networks, Industrial Wireless Sensor Networks, data centers (Paliwal & Shrimankar, 2019), and IoT-enabled smart homes. In particular, the work in Li et al. (2016) proposed an architecture for software-defined Ethernet

Passive Optical Networks (EPONs) that allows the SDN controller to manage different dynamic bandwidth allocation algorithms based on the network status. Within Chang et al. (2019); and Jimson et al. (2017) works, two distinct methods that could reserve bandwidth for every software-defined network node were put forth. These mechanisms, in contrast to our approach, deal with flow-oriented node-oriented bandwidth management. According to Becker et al. (2019) suggests a resource provisioning scheme for network flows that is adaptive and based on ongoing monitoring of multiple transmission rate thresholds. Unlike our method, none of these earlier studies addresses virtual networks.

In 2012, Min et al. suggested a network hypervisor with an admission control. Nevertheless, it differs from our method in that it only determines whether there is adequate bandwidth when a request for establishing a network slice is received, rather than allocating bandwidth to the flows according to their priority. In 2019, Priyadarsini & Bera proposed an architecture for a secure virtual controller (SVC), which combines network function virtualization and SDN. But unlike our method, the goal of this kind of work is different because the SVC aims to balance traffic load and lower energy consumption.

Chen et al. (2016) proposed a FlowVisor-based network virtualization layer called EnterpriseVisor. To increase overall network resource utilization, EnterpriseVisor suggests a dynamic resource management scheme that controls how network resources are distributed among slices. Consequently, EnterpriseVisor is unable to guarantee high-priority flows with respect to Quality-of-Service (QoS). According to Mijumbi et al. (2014), put forth a plan to expand the Floodlight controller so that link and switch resources could be dynamically managed in a virtualized SDN environment. The controller adds, modifies, or removes flow rules from the switches to carry out path migrations based on the state of the network. An approach like this seeks to maximize the use of network resources, but the objective in this section is to prevent link overload in order to manage bandwidth constraints and manage flows with varying priorities.

The method by Aglianò et al. (2018), in particular, supports both high priority and low priority flows and suggests using static values to limit the bandwidth utilization of each slice. Nevertheless, this method is unable to respond to important occurrences that alter network traffic. Conversely, though, in 2019, Struhár et al. presented a dynamic framework for bandwidth distribution known as DART. It allows for the effective use of network resources by dynamically allocating network bandwidth among different services. To lessen congestion on the shared links, the SDN controllers in DART work together to divide up the bandwidth among the slices. The admission control completes a straightforward task and establishes a priority limit. A flow rule is sent to the switch each time a new flow with a priority higher than the priority limit requests bandwidth and is accepted for transmission. In the absence of such conditions, the flow cannot transmit. The PrioSDN_RM here proposed is different in several significant ways from DART. First, the suggested admission control makes choices based on network traffic as well as flow priority, i.e., low priority flows are not immediately eliminated because policies allow for their admission. Secondly, we set two distinct moving bandwidth thresholds that adjust in response to alarms. Third, to quickly handle important events, a portion of bandwidth in the PrioSDN_RM is set aside for alarm flows.

9.2.1. PrioSDN_RM: Bandwidth Management Strategy

The PrioSDN_RM's architecture and the reasoning behind the admission control are presented in this section. A generalized virtualized SDN network is included in the reference system description. The admission control is explained in great detail since it outlines the method that permits dynamic bandwidth management according to flow priority.

9.2.1.1. System Design

You can use the suggested resource management method on any virtualized SDN network. In Figure 9.1, the reference architecture is displayed. Our solution differs from a standard virtualized SDN network in that it incorporates a Priority-based Admission Control (PAC), an addition to a basic SDN controller that consists of a unique resource manager with bandwidth allocation policies. We anticipate that OpenFlow will be used to facilitate communication between the control layer and the infrastructure layer.

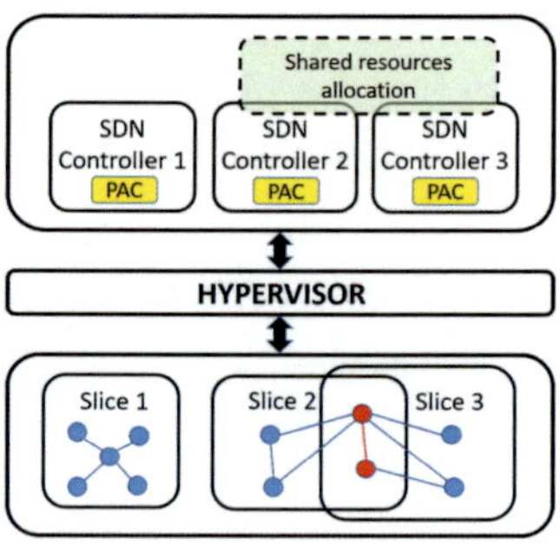

Figure 9.1. *The PrioSDN resource manager (PrioSDN_RM) architecture.*

Source: Leonardi, L., Lo Bello, L., & Aglianò, S., (2020) Priority-based bandwidth management in virtualized software-defined networks. Electronics, 9, 1009. https://doi.org/10.3390/electronics9061009.

Multiple slices of the physical network can be created (thanks to the use of a hypervisor). To improve the efficiency of resource utilization, the architecture can include both completely isolated slices and slices that share a portion of the physical network. On the other hand, the shared resource allocation module's job is to statically or dynamically negotiate the bandwidth allotted to each slice if a portion of the network is shared by two or more slices.

Specifically, Figure 9.1 shows three SDN controllers and a network segmented into three slices. Slice 1 in this network is isolated from the others, and slices 2 and 3 share a single network link (i.e., the one drawn in red in Figure 9.1). As such, SDN 1 and SDN 2 are able to use the shared link for operations.

9.2.1.2. Priority-Based Admission Control-Basic Concepts

The SDN controller's priority-based bandwidth management system revolves around admission control. In the case of a typical SDN controller, whenever the first message of a specific flow is sent by an end node or the flow rule (i.e., the routing rule for that flow) is not found in the flow table of the switch (i.e., a table-miss rule event occurs), the switch queries the SDN controller to obtain the relevant flow rule. Subsequently, the switch updates its routing table with the flow rule supplied by the SDN controller and forwards the message in accordance with it. Please note that the SDN controller does not perform any bandwidth consideration, e.g., it does not prevent overloading of the network links and therefore dropped messages (e.g., due to overflow of the network resources). As a result, the SDN controller is unable to ensure that the flows will receive a particular Quality of Service (QoS), such as a specific Packet Loss Ratio (PLR).

For this reason, we propose a priority-based admission control (PAC) for the SDN controllers. Please note that in our proposal we consider three different types of flows, i.e., low priority, high priority and alarms. In particular, we assume that an alarm is an event-driven flow (i.e., it is triggered by the occurrence of a specific event). Alarm flows are given the highest priority in the network according to our model. As seen in Figure 9.2, the PAC module consists of a compute module (CM) and a storage where data regarding the present state of the network (e.g., each network link's current bandwidth utilization) is preserved. Because of the OpenFlow functionality, which makes it possible to retrieve flows that are currently registered in the routing table and calculate bandwidth utilization, the data in the storage are constantly updated. In this manner, the SDN controller determines whether there is sufficient bandwidth on the links to assign a flow with a particular priority when the switch requests a flow rule. In the event that this flow requires no bandwidth, the flow rule is not created.

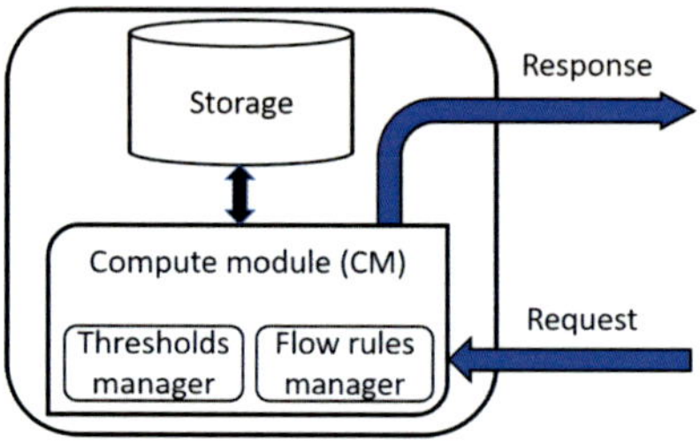

Figure 9.2. *The priority-based admission control.*
Source: Leonardi, L., Lo Bello, L., & Aglianò, S., (2020). Priority-based bandwidth management in virtualized software-defined networks. Electronics, 9, 1009. https://doi.org/10.3390/electronics9061009.

Specific criteria are used to make the bandwidth allocation decision. Every SDN controller maintains the bandwidth limit value for every network link that is pertinent to the slice that it oversees in the PAC storage. Because of this, the compute module has the ability to allot bandwidth for the slice's flows up to a given link's bandwidth limit. Additionally, as illustrated in Figure 9.3, the available bandwidth per link is divided into three segments using two moving thresholds, i.e., the high priority threshold (θ_{hp}) and the alarm threshold (θ_{alarm}). These thresholds define the bandwidth allotted to high priority flows and alarms, respectively.

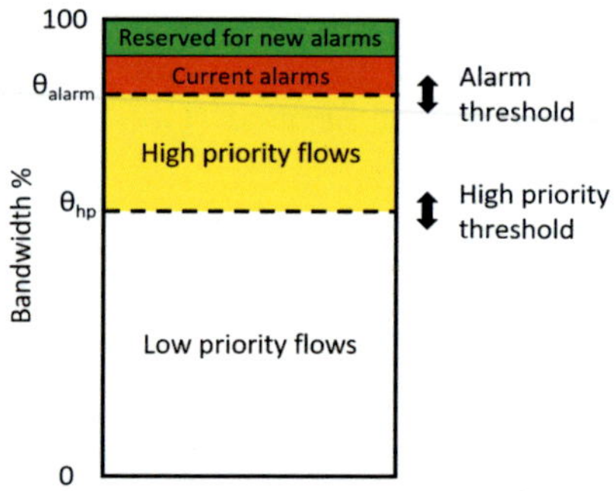

Figure 9.3. *The bandwidth subdivision.*

Source: Leonardi, L., Lo Bello, L., & Aglianò, S., (2020). Priority-based bandwidth management in virtualized software-defined networks. Electronics, 9, 1009. https://doi.org/10.3390/electronics9061009.

Specifically, a specific amount of bandwidth is reserved for alarm flows. These flows have the highest priority because they must meet strict timeliness and reliability standards. Because of this, a set quantity of bandwidth (a configurable value), i.e., Figure 9.3's green area is left "free" to be assigned to new alarm flows. As a result, each time an end node generates a new alarm flow, which the SDN controller then allocates, the thresholds manager module of the PAC moves the alarm threshold downward, increasing the amount of bandwidth set aside for alarm flows (i.e., the total of the sections that are red and green). In this manner, the red area in Figure 9.3 (i.e., when a new alarm flow is generated, the bandwidth that is being used by alarm flows) rises, but the green section stays unchanged. On the other hand, if an alarm flow is interrupted (i.e., the alarm ends), the alarm threshold is raised to decrease the amount of bandwidth allotted to alarm flows.

There is a small amount of bandwidth waste when alarm flows are reserved because some of the available resources (i.e., the green section) is not put to use. Nonetheless, this eliminates the need for delays brought on by insufficient bandwidth by enabling the prompt allocation of bandwidth to alarm flows and the commencement of their transmission. In this way, we give alarm flows the highest Quality of Service. It should be noted that the amount of bandwidth that remains "free" in PrioSDN_RM to be assigned to new alarm flows is a configurable parameter that varies depending on the application. Setting the alarm threshold to "free" the bandwidth portion required to support a single alarm flow alone will help minimize the possibility of bandwidth underutilization, i.e., the most demanding alarm that the application is capable of producing.

The section of bandwidth set aside for traffic with a high priority (i.e., the orange section in Figure 9.3), which is reserved for flows with a priority higher than a specific application-dependent value (kept in the PAC storage), is a fixed amount (a configurable value). The high priority threshold tracks changes in the alarm threshold because the orange bandwidth portion needs to be fixed, i.e., each time an alarm flow is generated or stopped, the two thresholds move in the same direction. This means that our method uses a runtime monitoring of the two thresholds to automatically start allocating resources to the flows according to priority.

Please take note that in Figure 9.3, θ_{alarm} denotes the maximum bandwidth that low priority flows can use, and θ_{hp} represents the maximum bandwidth that high priority flows can use. Stated differently, this method permits high priority flows to utilize bandwidth up to θ_{alarm}, i.e., they are able to utilize Figure 9.3's orange and white sections.

9.2.1.3. Priority-Based Admission Control-Bandwidth Allocation Procedure

It is assumed that the end nodes possess the ability to transmit multiple data flows, with varying levels of priority based on the significance of the data. Each end node can transmit flows with various priority levels as a result. The primary functions of the PAC are to assign bandwidth (if available) on the links that will be used for the transmission of the data flows and to verify the priority of the data flows.

An end node sends a request to the switch it is directly connected to whenever it creates a new flow. Both the necessary bandwidth and the flow priority are included in this request. Since the switch lacks a forwarding rule for the new flow's messages (i.e., the pertinent flow rule is absent), it sends the request to the SDN controller in charge of the slice that the switch and the end node are both a part of. The SDN controller oversees this kind of request, which is specifically assigned to the PAC module, which performs the following functions.

The flow parameters are extracted by the compute module, i.e., the bandwidth and priority requirements from the allocation request. Next, to find out the network slice's current state, the flow rules manager submodule sends a query to the PAC storage. The current bandwidth utilization and the threshold values of the links within the slice that the SDN controller is managing are specifically required.

The flow rules manager can allocate bandwidth for a flow using the suggested algorithm after determining whether there is sufficient bandwidth available on the links that the flow needs to be transmitted over. As the admission control algorithm operates on every SDN controller within the network, moving forward, we will make reference to a single SDN controller and, consequently, a particular network slice in order to streamline the explanation of the methodology presented here.

Three criteria are used by the flow rules manager to make decisions, i.e., bandwidth limit (BW_{lim}), thresholds (i.e., θ_{alarm} and θ_{hp}) as well as priority level ($prio_{lev}$). Every single one of these parameters is specified for every link in the network slice under consideration. The maximum bandwidth of link l that the network slice can use is defined by the BW^{l}_{lim}. Only a portion of the link's total bandwidth will be available if the link is shared by two or more slices. A request for bandwidth allocation is denied if it results in an increase in the bandwidth utilization of the link l above BW^{l}_{lim}.

In the event of limited bandwidth availability, the alarm threshold (θ_{alarm}) and the high priority threshold (θ_{hp}) enable bandwidth partitioning to provide distinct QoS levels. The high priority flows—and the alarm flows in particular—are given preference over the low priority flows in this situation. High priority flows are distinguished from low priority ones by a priority level defined by the DHS. Low priority flows are those that have a priority lower than $prio_{lev}$. A lower priority is indicated by a smaller priority value. As an example, suppose flows support eight distinct priority levels (i.e., from 0 to 7) and the link l's ($prio^{l}_{lev}$) priority level is 4, then the priority values between 0 and 3 are regarded as low priority (with 0 being the lowest priority). The maximum amount of bandwidth that low priority flows are permitted to use is specified by the θ_{hp} parameter. The bandwidth allotted to high priority flows is situated between θ_{hp} and θ_{alarm}. For alarm flows, the bandwidth above θ_{alarm} is set aside.

The flow rules manager rejects a request for a low priority flow to be transmitted on link l if it is sent to the SDN controller when the current bandwidth utilization surpasses the θ_{hp} threshold. If not, the request is approved by the manager of flow rules. Similarly, the flow rules manager rejects a request for a high priority flow if it is sent when the bandwidth utilization is greater than θ^{l}_{alarm}. Alarm flow requests, on the other hand, are always granted since a specific amount of bandwidth is set aside for them.

The SDN controller forwards the flow rule to the switch, which keeps it in the flow table, if the compute module responds positively to the request. If not, the flow rule is not recorded, and the flow's messages are not sent. A timer is set with a timeout value when a flow rule is added to a switch's flow table. The flow rule is removed from the flow table after the timeout period has passed. As a result, the switch would not find the pertinent flow rule in its flow table and would not be able to transmit a subsequent message of the flow directly. According to the PAC module mechanism, the switch will forward the request to the SDN controller, which either drops the flow or creates a new flow rule. The flow rule timeout value enables the selection of the preferred trade-off between the overall delay introduced by the admission control and the quality of service. As a result of the switch experiencing more table-miss rule events and having to repeat the admission control task, a lower timeout value actually causes a higher delay. However, by evaluating the network's current state more frequently, the admission control increases the proposed mechanism's ability to quickly adapt to changes in traffic flows. If not, a higher timeout value will have the opposite effect.

Please be aware that the timeout's value is per-flow and modifiable at runtime, i.e., every time the flow rule expires, the SDN controller has the ability to set the timeout with a different value (based on a particular algorithm). In this manner, distinct timeout values can be applied to high and low priority flows. In the event of traffic congestion, for example, it is anticipated that using a shorter timeout for low priority flows will improve the quality of service provided to high priority flows. Actually, we assume that high priority flows use a portion (percentage) of bandwidth equal to (θ_{alarm} – θ_{hp})%, while low priority flows use as much bandwidth as possible. A request for bandwidth made by a new, high priority flow will be denied, at least until the low priority flows release the necessary bandwidth, i.e., at least until a low priority flow's timeout expires. Consequently, improved management of the high priority flows is ensured by a lower timeout value for the low priority flows.

9.2.2. A Use Case for the PrioSDN_RM

The PrioSDN_RM can be used in a number of real-world situations, including the one covered by Struhár et al. (2019). In particular, the application type is somewhat different from Struhár et al. (2019), but the network topology remains the same, there aren't any alarm flows. In this instance, we're looking at a communication network that spans the entire factory and has a surveillance system integrated into it.

The bandwidth is dynamically assigned according to the flows' priorities. Divided into multiple slices, the network maintains distinct virtual network domains (e.g., the sales floor, the administrative office, the shop floor, etc.) and to distinguish between the various slices' QoS levels. However, resource sharing between slices must also be supported because some network services must be accessible for multiple slices at once.

Messages are sent by the end nodes in flows with varying priorities based on their quality-of-service demands. For example, end nodes in the surveillance system have cameras attached to them that send video streams (i.e., they routinely transmit a series of pictures) to a central station (i.e., the basin). While the video streams are processed centrally by the sink, which stores and processes the images, these end nodes are limited in their processing power and can only perform basic motion detection algorithms.

Such a sink may be located in a bandwidth-constrained shared network slice. Thus, in order to meet QoS requirements and avoid network congestion, priority-based bandwidth management should be used. The end node with cameras sends low priority or high priority flows based on the monitored area and the importance of the video stream. Furthermore, an alarm flow is generated each time an end node notices something suspicious.

9.2.3. Implementation

This section presents an implementation of the proposed PrioSDN_RM. For this purpose we used:

- **FloodLight:** A Java-based OpenFlow SDN controller that is freely available under an Apache license for research purposes. The FloodLight architecture consists of several easily adjustable modules.

- **FlowVisor:** An OpenFlow-based network hypervisor designed to virtualize software-defined networks. Network slice sharing and isolation are both supported by FlowVisor.
- **Zodiac FX:** An open-source firmware-powered little OpenFlow switch. The Zodiac FX is a great choice for research projects that involve experimentation because of its low cost and simple setup and configuration.
- **Raspberry Pi:** A low-cost single-board computer used as an end node.

9.2.3.1. Experimental Setup

A real testbed, shown in Figure 9.4, was implemented to show the feasibility of the proposed approach.

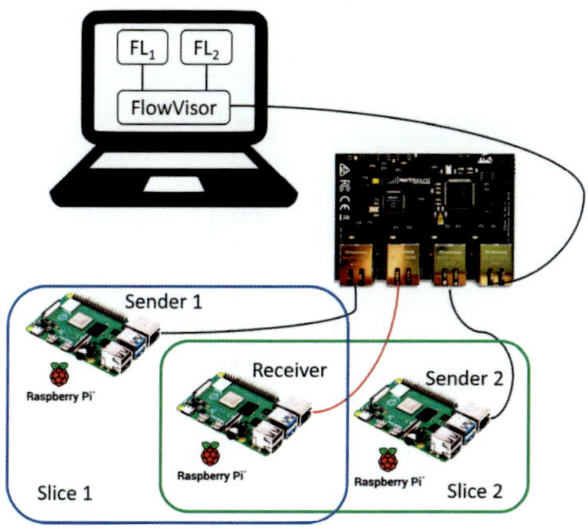

Figure 9.4. *The testbed setup.*

Source: Leonardi, L., Lo Bello, L., & Aglianò, S., (2020). Priority-based bandwidth management in virtualized software-defined networks. Electronics, 9, 1009. https://doi.org/10.3390/electronics9061009.

The three Raspberry PI nodes (nodes in the implemented topology) are, i.e., divided into two slices, with two senders and one receiver. Each slice shares the same link between the switch and the receiver node. A FloodLight controller (FL) is required for every slice. The four Ethernet ports on the Zodiac FX OpenFlow switch are well-equipped. One of them is linked to a laptop that runs the SDN controllers and the hypervisor, and the other three are connected to Raspberry PIs. Specifically, FloodLight controllers run on the host, while FlowVisor runs in a virtual machine. Through FlowVisor, the Zodiac FX switch and the FloodLight controllers exchange information.

FloodLight was extended with the implementation of the proposed priority-based admission control module, whose architecture is depicted in Figure 9.4. Floodlight's forwarding module was turned off because it handles flow rules automatically. In this manner, each time a switch receives a message about a new flow, the switch forwards the request to the SDN controller, which contains the PAC module. In accordance with the previously established policies, the latter evaluates the request and determines whether to approve or reject the flow transmission. A flow rule is added to the appropriate switch flow table in the event that the transmission is approved.

In the implemented testbed, communications were conducted using IEEE 802.1Q frames. Compared to the Ethernet frame format, the IEEE 802.1Q frame format, which is depicted in Figure 9.5, has four extra bytes. Specifically, it appends the Virtual Local Area Network (VLAN) tag, which designates the VLAN to which the frame belongs and is inserted between the Length/Type and Destination/Source MAC addresses of an Ethernet frame.

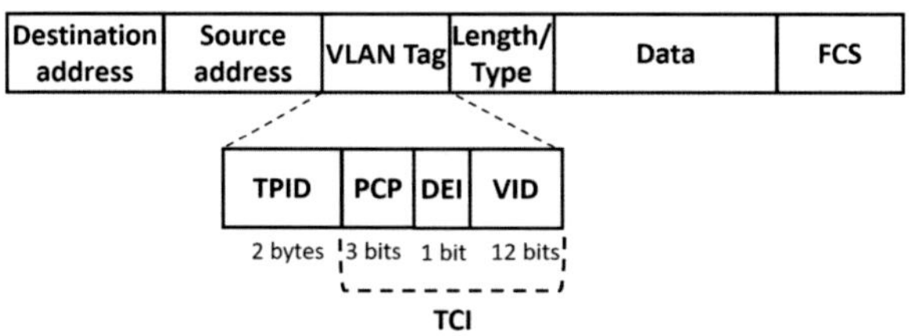

Figure 9.5. *IEEE 802.1Q frame.*

Source: Leonardi, L., Lo Bello, L., & Aglianò, S., (2020). Priority-based bandwidth management in virtualized software-defined networks. Electronics, 9, 1009. https://doi.org/10.3390/electronics9061009.

The first two bytes of the VLAN tag consists of the Tag Protocol Identifier (TPID) and indicates the frame type, e.g., the value 0 × 8100 indicates an IEEE 802.1Q frame. Two additional bytes are utilized for the Tag control information (TCI), which in turn houses the VLAN identifier (VID), Drop eligible indicator (DEI), and Priority code point (PCP). The PCP is a 3-bit field that maps to the frame priority level and indicates the class of service. Its value is between 0 and 7. It is possible to prioritize different traffic classes using different PCP values. A greater priority is indicated by a higher value. In the event of congestion, the DEI permits marking of the frames that are eligible for dropping. Lastly, the VID identifies the VLAN that a frame is assigned to.

Periodically, the senders create and send messages that are part of various flows, each with a distinct priority. Table 9.1 displays each sender's periodic flows. All messages sent to the FloodLight controller contain an encoding that indicates the bit rate and, consequently, the required bandwidth. Additionally, irregular alarm flows (i.e., senders can generate flows whose messages have PCP equal to 7). Multiple alarm flows can be generated simultaneously by a single sender. To document data regarding the messages they have received, the recipient keeps logs.

Table 9.1. *Network Slice Periodic Flows*

Flow ID	Bit Rate (Bit/s)	PCP
1	90	1
2	25	1
3	90	2
4	30	5
5	40	0
6	50	4

Source: Leonardi, L., Lo Bello, L., & Aglianò, S., (2020). Priority-based bandwidth management in virtualized software-defined networks. Electronics, 9, 1009. https://doi.org/10.3390/electronics9061009.

Considering that all of the slices have the same workload, we take into consideration a static bandwidth partitioning. The shared link's (sl) admission control parameters were configured as follows. Both slices' bandwidth limits (BW^{sl}_{lim}) were set at 200 bps, while the high priority (θ^{sl}_{hp}) and alarm (θ^{sl}_{alarm}) thresholds were initialized to 70% and 90% of the BW_{lim}, i.e., to 140 bps and 180 bps, respectively. The priority level ($prio_{lev}$) was set to 3.

9.2.4. Performance Evaluation

We assessed the performance of the implemented network using the shared link's Frame Drop Ratio (FDR) and throughput measurements. The fraction of dropped frame transmission requests relative to all requests is measured by the FDR. Equation (9.1) gives the percentage expression for it.

$$FDR = \left(\frac{n_{dropFrm}}{n_{totFrm}}\right) \times 100 = \left(1 - \frac{n_{accFrm}}{n_{totFrm}}\right) \times 100 \tag{9.1}$$

Where; n_{totFrm}, $n_{dropFrm}$ and n_{accFrm} are the number of totals, dropped and accepted frame transmission requests, respectively, measured on the shared port that connects the switch to the receiver.

We also evaluated the overhead introduced by the admission control.

9.2.4.1. Throughput

The receiver side is where the throughput was measured, i.e., taking into account the shared link between the switch and the receiver, both for slices 1 and 2 and with and without PrioSDN_RM. The SDN controllers supply flow rules regardless of the priority, bandwidth requirements, and bandwidth limitations of the flow in the event that the PAC module is deactivated. As a result, as illustrated in Figure 9.6, the throughput of the shared link increases to the bandwidth saturation (400 bps) in approximately 30 s if we add up the bandwidth utilized by both slice 1 and slice 2.

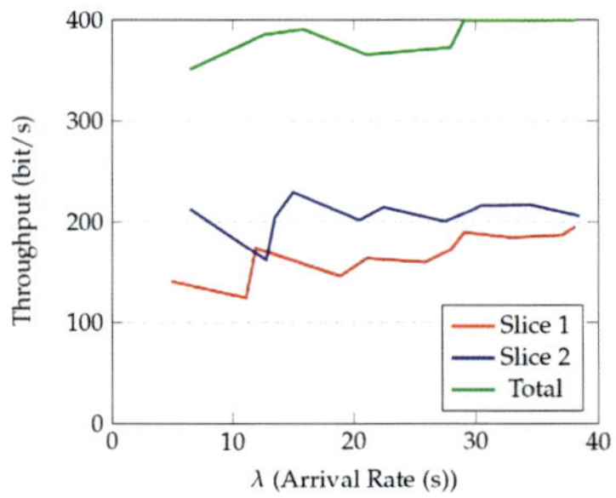

Figure 9.6. *Throughput of both slices without admission control.*

Source: Leonardi, L., Lo Bello, L., & Aglianò, S., (2020). Priority-based bandwidth management in virtualized software-defined networks. Electronics, 9, 1009. https://doi.org/10.3390/electronics9061009.

The PAC module was turned on for the same experiment. The findings are displayed in Figure 9.7, where horizontal lines are also used to represent the thresholds and bandwidth limit. The outcomes demonstrate that the PAC module effectively regulates bandwidth usage. In actuality, the throughput in both slices stays below the 200-bps bandwidth cap.

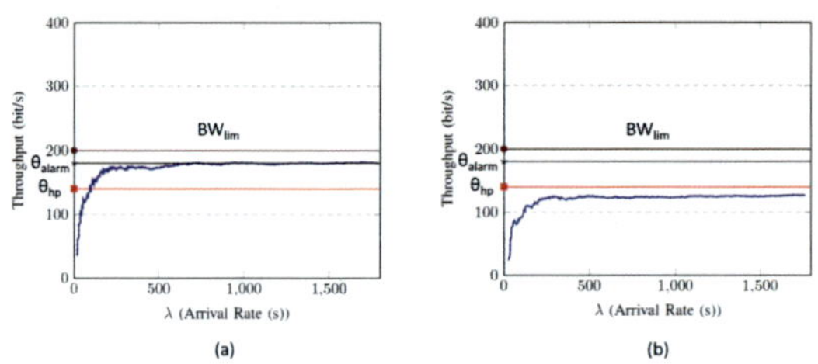

Figure 9.7. *Throughput with PrioSDN_RM – (a) slice 1; and (b) slice 2.*

Source: Leonardi, L., Lo Bello, L., & Aglianò, S., (2020). Priority-based bandwidth management in virtualized software-defined networks. Electronics, 9, 1009. https://doi.org/10.3390/electronics9061009.

Specifically, in slice 1, the throughput consistently remained below the bandwidth limit even though it occasionally exceeded the alarm and high priority thresholds. The throughput in slice 2 stayed below the bandwidth limit since it was below the high priority threshold. Please be aware that the internal scheduling of the flows in the sender nodes determines the disparate throughput values for slices 1 and 2.

The arrival times of the flow's transmission requests differ because the senders' application layers are actually not synchronized. As a result, different admission controls have different processing orders, which leads to different allocation decisions.

For example, the high priority flows arrive first and get all the bandwidth they need, which accounts for the throughput trend in Figure 9.7(b). Then the low priority flows come in, but some of them cannot be sent because doing so would mean going over the θ^{sl}_{hp}.

9.2.4.2. Frame Drop Ratio

After 20 minutes of experiments, the frame drop ratio (FDR) on the shared link was determined. Specifically, we assessed the FDR for slices 1 and 2 using a standard SDN controller (i.e., without admission control) as well as the PrioSDN_RM proposal.

Frames of any priority were lost when the simple SDN controller without admission control was used because of the network link overload. Since every flow was treated in the same manner, there was no discernible variation in the quantity of high priority frames that were dropped compared to low priority ones.

The FDR for slices 1 and 2, respectively, acquired with the PrioSDN_RM, is displayed in Tables 9.2 and 9.3. Two configurations in particular were assessed. The flow rule timeout (fr_{tout}) was configured in the first configuration (a) to be 40 s for each flow. The flow rule timeout in configuration (b) was adjusted to 40 seconds for high priority flows and 30 seconds for low priority flows.

Table 9.2. *PrioSDN_RM: Frame Drop Ratio-Slice 1*

PCP	Configuration a		Configuration b	
	FDR	Timeout (s)	FDR	Timeout (s)
1	64%	40	43%	30
1	33%	40	30%	30
2	70%	40	74%	30
5	28%	40	22%	40

0	89%	40	76%	30
4	35%	40	24%	40
7	0%	40	0%	40

Source: Leonardi, L., Lo Bello, L., & Aglianò, S., (2020). Priority-based bandwidth management in virtualized software-defined networks. Electronics, 9, 1009. https://doi.org/10.3390/electronics9061009.

Table 9.3. *PrioSDN_RM: Frame Drop Ratio-Slice 2*

PCP	Configuration a		Configuration b	
	FDR	Timeout (s)	FDR	Timeout (s)
1	52%	40	47%	30
1	58%	40	26%	30
2	84%	40	74%	30
5	29%	40	22%	40
0	100%	40	82%	30
4	60%	40	27%	40
7	0%	40	0%	40

Source: Leonardi, L., Lo Bello, L., & Aglianò, S., (2020). Priority-based bandwidth management in virtualized software-defined networks. Electronics, 9, 1009. https://doi.org/10.3390/electronics9061009.

When compared to the same scenario without admission control, where the drop ratio was between 44% and 47% for alarms and between 47% and 53% for high priority flows, respectively, the results show that using the PrioSDN_RM significantly improves the FDR of both alarm and high priority flows. On the other hand, compared to the results obtained without admission control, the FDRs obtained for the low priority flows are worse (i.e., PrioSDN_RM strongly favors alarm and high priority flows (between 49% and 55%). As anticipated, the alarm flow packet's frame drop ratio is 0% because a set amount of bandwidth is always set aside for incoming alarm flows. By lowering the flow rule timeout value for the low priority flows in configuration b, we are able to enhance the performance of the high priority flows, as demonstrated by the comparison of the FDR obtained in the two different configurations. Furthermore, a more equitable allocation of bandwidth among the low priority flows is made possible by the PAC module's more frequent assessment of the state of the network. The quality of service provided by the PAC module increases as predicted with decreasing flow rule timeout values.

9.2.4.3. Priority-Based Admission Control Overhead

The experimental evaluation of the delay caused by the suggested priority-based admission control, which is based on a virtualized SDN-based network, is presented in this section. This kind of latency was computed as the total delay brought about by the hypervisor (i.e., FlowVisor) as well as the SDN controller (i.e., FloodLight). Specifically, we evaluated the delay that occurs when a message is not able to be forwarded directly by the switch because it cannot locate the necessary flow rule in its flow table. In the alternative scenario, our method doesn't cause a noticeable delay. According to Chen et al. (2016), FlowVisor increases overhead for tasks involving both the control plane and the data plane, but it does not add overhead to the data plane itself. Specifically, when the OpenFlow port status is requested, FlowVisor causes an approximate 0.71 ms increase in port status response latency.

The overhead resulting from our method was measured as the difference in time between the instants at which the switch made the request for bandwidth allocation and when the switch received the pertinent admission control response. We conducted experiments for 20 minutes. The obtained results demonstrated that there is never a delay of more than 10 milliseconds.

Please be aware that the SDN controller only processes the initial message for each flow, along with any messages sent after the flow rule expires. Only the switch handles the other messages. Because the SDN controller will be handling the priority-based admission control task more frequently, lower flow rule timeout values will result in a greater delay, and vice versa, affecting the overall overhead introduced by the proposed mechanism.

9.3. BANDWIDTH CALENDARING

Bandwidth calendaring typically refers to the practice of scheduling and managing the allocation of network bandwidth resources over time. This can be crucial in environments where multiple users or applications compete for limited bandwidth, such as in corporate networks, internet service providers (ISPs), or data centers.

Here are a few key aspects and considerations related to bandwidth calendaring:

1. **Resource Allocation:** It involves allocating available bandwidth resources among different users or applications based on priorities, traffic patterns, or specific requirements. For example, critical applications like video conferencing or real-time data transfers might be given higher priority over non-essential tasks.

2. **Traffic Shaping:** Bandwidth calendaring often involves traffic shaping techniques, where network administrators enforce policies to control the flow of data. This can include rate limiting, prioritization of certain types of traffic, or even scheduling bandwidth availability during peak and off-peak hours.
3. **QoS (Quality of Service):** Implementing bandwidth calendaring usually ties into QoS strategies. QoS mechanisms ensure that critical applications receive the necessary bandwidth and latency requirements to function optimally, while less critical traffic may be limited to prevent congestion.
4. **Scheduling:** Networks may implement scheduling algorithms to dynamically allocate bandwidth based on real-time demands or pre-defined schedules. This helps in managing bandwidth spikes and ensuring fair distribution among users or applications.
5. **Monitoring and Adjustments:** Continuous monitoring of network traffic and bandwidth usage is essential for effective bandwidth calendaring. Administrators can analyze usage patterns, identify bottlenecks, and adjust bandwidth allocations accordingly to optimize performance.
6. **Tools and Technologies:** Various tools and technologies are available to assist in bandwidth management and calendaring, such as network management software, traffic shaping appliances, and routers with QoS capabilities.

In summary, bandwidth calendaring is about intelligently managing and scheduling network bandwidth to ensure optimal performance and fair distribution of resources across users and applications, aligning with organizational priorities and operational needs.

9.4. BIG DATA AND APPLICATION HYPER-VIRTUALIZATION FOR INSTANT CSPF

Thus far, the examples pertaining to the use case of bandwidth calendaring have necessitated a basic set of services that are supplied from the SDN controller/framework to the application.

These are mainly concerned with path computation, path provisioning, and topology. The required path computation is a relatively simple SPF (OpenFlow) or CSPF (PCE) with limited constraints (current network state, basic analytics in current flow stats and reservations, and a relatively simple, embedded policy). The topology is a layer 2 (OpenFlow) or layer 3/MPLS topology (PCE). The examples presented in the previous section are real-world and observable. Nonetheless, the ample can be expanded to a more intricate application, of which the bandwidth calendaring application's reservation system is a part. As seen in Figure 9.8, this is explained.

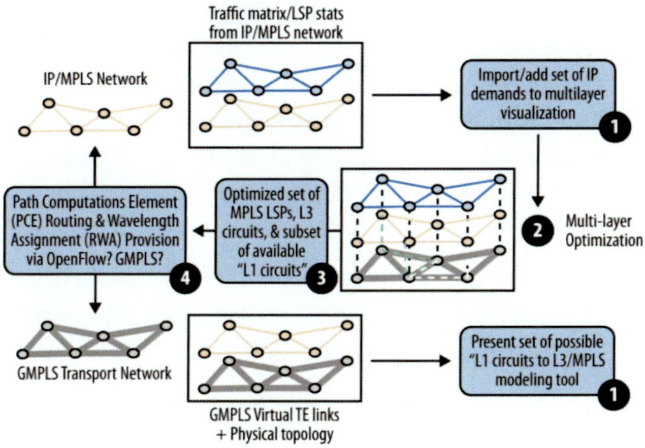

Figure 9.8. *A predictive, multilayer topology network optimization workflow.*

Source: Thomas, D. N., & Ken, G., (2013). SDN: Software Defined Networks, O'Reilly Media, Inc. ISBN: 9781449342302.

Nowadays, a lot of network operators use offline analytic and computation engines to optimize their networks (or portions of them) on a regular basis. The majority of these efforts are manual, though there is some room for automation. They are also constrained by the tools at our disposal and the static provisioning model (which we were attempting to work around in the bandwidth calendaring application). These operations typically use MPLSTE LSPs to steer traffic (with the same loading/on-ramping limitations mentioned in the earlier PCE example), as they predate the introduction of OpenFlow and SDN-driven overlay solutions.

Ingestion of a static topology (from element configurations or routing protocol database dumps, depending on the tool vendor) along with flow data and user-defined policies or constraints (e.g., optimize it for the most effective network utilization (typically in both an active and limited hypothetical failure scenarios), taking into account factors like maximum path delay or avoidance of Shared Risk Link Groups. An analytical run typically yields a recommendation that can be exported to a spreadsheet, which is subsequently transformed into the syntax and semantics of tunnel creation specific to a given vendor and provisioned during a maintenance window. Potential traffic rerouting during live operation presents challenges due to the time required by the static provisioning model and the inability of that pro-visioning model to orchestrate the changes in a nearly simultaneous fashion (which could result in undesired interim inefficiencies).

The complexity of the mathematical algorithms that these offline tools used to determine a result, along with the range of parameters and policies they can incorporate, are what make them strong. Yet, they can currently operate for a very long time, depending on the size and complexity of the network (or the flow data). Operators want to benefit from the network control SDN's provision-analyze-optimize cycle, which it promises to implement in a more dynamic and automated workflow. The path computation component in this workflow could optimize according to:

- Current utilization: Commonly from a flow data repository;
- Historical utilization: Generally a less specific graph of utilization based on historical flow data to indicate a diurnal pattern of network use (this diurnal pattern can be updated with a sliding window of historical data if there is a distinct variance in the trend);
- Future reservations: Managed by the Bandwidth Calendaring reservation system.

The combination of these inputs—which are most likely not mutually exclusive—provides the true predictive power in forecasting. The range of potential service demands between bandwidth calendaring, and this automated network optimization ("fly-by-wire") application highlights the need for modularity in components and (again) flexibility in the service APIs exposed. SDN and big data techniques may provide viable solutions for this network optimization application, though it is still only a potential application. Although the BCA application and its supporting controller(s)/framework offer a model for resolving this issue, a significant update is required for the path computation component. Furthermore, a more capable analytics module needs to be included in order to record, organize, and (possibly) compile pertinent flow data. Big data techniques, such as grid computing for customized distributed summarization of analytical data and Hadoop for farm the computational exercise, are being used by a number of commercial tool vendors to address the computational complexity of both the analytics management and path computation problems. Their results are then interfaced to a PCE server for provisioning.

REFERENCES

1. Aglianò, S., Ashjaei, M., Behnam, M., & Lo Bello, L. (2018). Resource management and control in virtualized SDN networks. In *Proceedings of the 2018 Real-Time and Embedded Systems and Technologies (RTEST)* (pp. 47–53). Tehran, Iran: IEEE. https://doi.org/10.1109/RTEST.2018.8397078.
2. Becker, M., Lu, Z., & Chen, D. (2019). An adaptive resource provisioning scheme for industrial SDN networks. In *Proceedings of the 2019 IEEE 17th International Conference on Industrial Informatics (INDIN)* (Vol. 1, pp. 877–880). Helsinki, Finland: IEEE. https://doi.org/10.1109/INDIN41052.2019.8972194.
3. Chang, Y., Chen, Y., Chen, T., Chen, J., Chiu, S., & Chang, W. (2019). Software-defined dynamic bandwidth management. In *Proceedings of the 2019 21st International Conference on Advanced Communication Technology (ICACT)* (pp. 201–205). PyeongChang, Korea: IEEE. https://doi.org/10.23919/ICACT.2019.8702052.
4. Chen, J., Ma, Y., Kuo, H., Yang, C., & Hung, W. (2016). Software-defined network virtualization platform for enterprise network resource management. *IEEE Transactions on Emerging Topics in Computing, 4*(1), 179–186. https://doi.org/10.1109/TETC.2015.2478757.
5. Jimson, E. R., Nisar, K., & bin Ahmad Hijazi, M. H. (2017). Bandwidth management using software defined network and comparison of the throughput performance with traditional network. In *Proceedings of the International Conference on Computer and Drone Applications (IConDA)* (pp. 71–76). Kuching, Malaysia: IEEE. https://doi.org/10.1109/ICONDA.2017.8270402.
6. Li, C., Guo, W., Wang, W., Hu, W., & Xia, M. (2016). Programmable bandwidth management in software-defined EPON architecture. *Optics Communications, 370*, 43–48. https://doi.org/10.1016/j.optcom.2016.02.070.
7. Mijumbi, R., Serrat, J., Rubio-Loyola, J., Bouten, N., Turck, F. D., & Latré, S. (2014). Dynamic resource management in SDN-based virtualized networks. In *Proceedings of the 10th International Conference on Network and Service Management (CNSM) and Workshop* (pp. 412–417). Rio de Janeiro, Brazil: IEEE.
8. Min, S., Kim, S., Lee, J., Kim, B., Hong, W., & Kong, J. (2012). Implementation of an OpenFlow network virtualization for multi-controller environment. In *Proceedings of the 2012 14th International*

Conference on Advanced Communication Technology (ICACT) (pp. 589–592). PyeongChang, Korea: IEEE. ISBN:978-1-4673-0150-3.

9. Paliwal, M., & Shrimankar, D. (2019). Effective resource management in SDN enabled data center network based on traffic demand. *IEEE Access, 7*, 69698–69706. https://doi.org/10.1109/ACCESS.2019.2919348.
10. Priyadarsini, M., & Bera, P. (2019). A secure virtual controller for traffic management in SDN. *IEEE Letters on Communications and Networking, 2*, 24–27. https://doi.org/10.1109/LOCS.2019.2933418.
11. Struhár, V., Ashjaei, M., Behnam, M., Craciunas, S. S., & Papadopoulos, A. V. (2019). DART: Dynamic bandwidth distribution framework for virtualized software defined networks. In *Proceedings of the 45th Annual Conference of the IEEE Industrial Electronics Society (IECON)* (Vol. 1, pp. 2934–2939). Lisbon, Portugal: IEEE. https://doi.org/10.1109/IECON.2019.8927780.

CHAPTER 10

USE CASES FOR DATA OVERLAYS AND NETWORK VIRTUALIZATION

Contents

INTRODUCTION

Data overlays and network virtualization are critical technologies in modern networking, providing significant flexibility, scalability, and efficiency. One prominent use case is multi-tenant data centers, where network virtualization allows multiple tenants to share the same physical infrastructure while maintaining isolated, secure, and customized virtual networks. This approach leads to efficient resource utilization, reduced capital expenditures, and the ability to quickly provision and de-provision virtual networks, exemplified by cloud service providers like AWS and Azure offering isolated virtual private clouds (VPCs) to different customers.

Another key use case is Network Function Virtualization (NFV), which involves virtualizing network functions such as firewalls, load balancers, and routers that traditionally ran on dedicated hardware, and moving them to general-purpose servers. This transition reduces hardware costs, increases flexibility, and speeds up the deployment of network services. Telecom operators, for instance, use NFV to virtualize their core network functions, resulting in more agile and scalable service offerings.

Enhanced network security is also a significant benefit of network virtualization. By segmenting virtual networks to isolate sensitive data and applications, organizations can reduce their attack surface and improve security. This approach, known as micro-segmentation, makes it easier to comply with security policies and reduces the risk of lateral movement by attackers. Financial institutions, for example, utilize virtualized networks to isolate different departments and ensure regulatory compliance.

Software-Defined WAN (SD-WAN) is another impactful application, where virtualization creates overlay networks connecting multiple sites over the internet or private networks. SD-WAN offers cost savings through the use of lower-cost internet connections, improved application performance, and enhanced network visibility and control. Enterprises adopt SD-WAN to connect branch offices, data centers, and cloud services, optimizing traffic flow and ensuring consistent performance.

In cloud interconnectivity, virtual networks enable seamless connectivity between on-premises data centers and multiple cloud providers, facilitating hybrid and multi-cloud environments. This flexibility allows businesses to leverage multiple cloud services, improve disaster recovery options, and burst workloads to the cloud during peak times. Organizations use network virtualization to create secure, high-performance connections between their data centers and public cloud providers like AWS, Azure, and Google Cloud.

10.1. OVERLAYING USE CASES

Cloud providers have embraced and widely deployed SDN; Google, Facebook, and Microsoft have been the most vocal about their adoption. Although the majority of their platforms and solutions remain proprietary, they have made individual components open sourced in an attempt to spur broader adoption. Second, major network providers like Comcast, DT, NTT, and AT&T have made public their intentions to implement SDN-based solutions, particularly in their access networks. However, they are moving slowly, with the majority of their projects either utilizing hybrid approaches or, in the case of pure play SDN, just beginning to enter production. Comcast deserves special recognition for implementing the open-source components. At last, businesses have started implementing SDN; however, there are two aspects of this scenario to consider. One is that, although pure play SDN is implemented in certain universities to foster research and innovation, enterprise adoption is generally slower. The most likely route for enterprises to adopt pure play SDN is through cloud providers' managed edge services. Connecting public clouds hosting scalable datacenter workloads with on-premises clusters running edge workloads is the idea. The second is that SDN products are widely available from enterprise vendors, with an emphasis on the advantages of logical control plane centralization over open interfaces to the data plane. As will be discussed below, network virtualization and software-defined wide area networks, or SD-WAN, have both seen significant success in the enterprise.

10.1.1. Network Virtualization

Virtualizing the network was SDN's first widely used use case. The Internet has long included virtual networks, such as Virtual Private Networks (VPNs) and Virtual Local Area Networks (VLANs). VLANs have shown to be beneficial in the past for separating various departments or lab groups within an organization, giving each the impression of having its own private LAN. These early virtualization techniques, however, lacked many of SDN's benefits and had a very narrow scope. They can be conceptualized as virtualizing a network's address space, but not its higher-level network functions like load balancing or firewall rules. Teemu Koponen and colleagues' NSDI paper describes the Nicira team's approach, which is widely credited with being the original idea behind using SDN to create virtual networks. The key realization was that in order to support modern clouds, networks needed to be built, maintained, and destroyed programmatically. This eliminated the need for a sysadmin to manually configure things like VLAN tags on numerous network switches. A single API entry point for the creation, modification, and deletion of virtual networks was made available by logically centralizing the control plane and separating it from the data plane. This meant that a virtual network could now be programmatically provisioned with the proper policies to connect those other resources, using the same automation systems that were being used to provision compute and storage capacity in a cloud (like OpenStack at the time).

The emergence of network virtualization was greatly facilitated by the rise of compute virtualization, which came a few years later. Compute virtualization eliminated the need for manual server provisioning and revealed the "long pole" in cloud service delivery to be the laborious, manual processes involved in network configuration. Further highlighting the shortcomings of manual network configuration was virtual machine migration, which allowed operating virtual machines (VMs) to relocate across different network locations while bringing their IP addresses with them. Although major cloud providers were the first to recognize the need for automated network provisioning, enterprise datacenters eventually adopted this practice. The requirements of these environments have led to further evolution in network virtualization as microservices and container-based systems like Kubernetes have grown in popularity. Numerous open-source network "plugins" are available, such as Calico, Flannel, Antrea, and others. that offer Kubernetes network virtualization services. Network virtualization's influence extended beyond the ease of use and automation of network provisioning, as its goal was to provide an entire suite of network services programmatically. A new method of network security was made possible when virtual networks evolved into lightweight, dynamic entities that could be created and destroyed as needed and provided a complete range of services (like deep packet inspection, stateful firewalling, and so forth). Security features could be built into the network from the beginning rather than being added after it has already been established. Moreover, the concept of microsegmentation gained traction since there was no restriction on the number of virtual networks that could be established. This means building isolated, fine-grained networks, or microsegments, tailored to the requirements of a particular distributed application, such as a collection of processes working together. Compared to earlier methods of network security, microsegmentation provides a clear advantage by significantly lowering the attack surface and the potential for attacks to propagate throughout a company or data center.

10.1.1.1. Bringing SDN to Life

Though the concepts underlying SDN had been developed for years, two connected incidents, when considered retrospectively, had a major influence in transforming the idea of programmable networks from theory to reality. The first was the establishment of Nicira Networks, a for-profit startup, in 2007. Three of the recognized SDN pioneers, Nick McKeown, Scott Shenker, and Martin

Casado, founded Nicira. Nicira was established with the intention of using SDN for business, but like many startups, it took some time to identify the right product for the market. Ultimately, Network Virtualization emerged as the first effective use of SDN in the industry. In 2011, Nicira's network virtualization platform made its debut, creating a category and ultimately opening the door for VMware to acquire the business and go on to develop VMware NSX. In order to accelerate the SDN revolution throughout the networking industry, McKeown and Shenker also founded three non-profit organizations around the same time: the Open Networking Foundation (ONF), which assumed responsibility for promoting network disaggregation and developing the OpenFlow standard; the Open Networking Laboratory (ON. The Open Networking Summit (ONS) was established as a conference platform to bring together academics and practitioners interested in SDN, while Lab was established to develop open source SDN-based solutions and platforms.

It is important to remember that in order to construct virtual networks in the manner that we have outlined, packets from the virtual networks must be encapsulated in a manner that permits them to pass through the underlying physical network. To put it simply, a virtual network can be isolated from the underlying physical address space and have its own private address space. Virtual networks have therefore employed a variety of encapsulation techniques, the most well-known of which is likely VXLAN. GENEVE, or Generic Network Virtualization Encapsulation, is a more adaptable encapsulation that has surfaced in recent years.

The typical architecture of a network virtualization system is shown in Figure 10.1. An SDN controller called the Network Virtualization Controller makes available a northbound API for the creation, monitoring, and modification of networks. It links to virtual switches that are operating on hosts, in this example, virtual machine-supporting hypervisors. By configuring the virtual switches to forward packets across the underlay network from host to host with the proper encapsulation, virtual networks are created. There have been valid discussions regarding the authenticity of SDN in relation to network virtualization. Undoubtedly, it exhibits a lot of the characteristics; in fact, OpenFlow was utilized by the original Nicira network virtualization platform to facilitate communication between the data plane elements and the central controller. And network virtualization was made possible by the centralization advantages of SDN, especially when it came to facilitating network automation. However, because the controllers and switches in a network virtualization system are usually very tightly integrated using proprietary signaling methods rather than an open interface, network virtualization has not really made it possible for networks to be disaggregated as intended by SDN. Furthermore, network virtualization is typically implemented as an overlay among the servers on which those computing abstractions are implemented, as its primary goal has been to connect virtual machines and containers. A physical network sits beneath that overlay, and network virtualization simply assumes that it exists (and that physical network need not implement SDN at all).

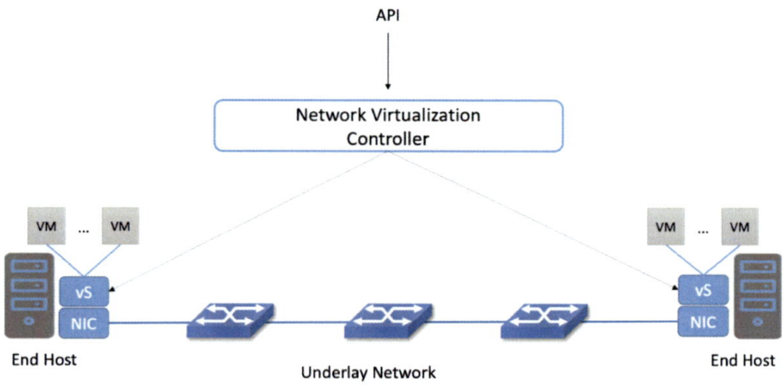

Figure 10.1. *An example network virtualization system.*

Source: https://sdn.systemsapproach.org/_images/Slide44.png.

10.1.2. Switching Fabrics

The most common application for pure play SDN is in cloud datacenters, where cloud providers have shifted away from proprietary switches (i.e., proprietary switches) in order to reduce costs and improve feature velocity (e.g., those typically offered by network vendors), in favor of bare-metal switches constructed with silicon switching chips from merchant vendors. The switching fabric, which connects all of these cloud providers' servers, is completely under software control. A network with a leaf-spine topology is called a datacenter switching fabric. Figure 10.2 shows a small 4-rack example to illustrate the basic idea. The servers within a rack are connected by a Top-of-Rack (ToR) switch, also known as the leaf switches of the fabric. For resilience, each rack normally has two of these ToR switches; however, for simplicity's sake, only one is shown in Figure 10.2. Next, each leaf switch links to a subset of the spine switches that are accessible. Two prerequisites must be met for this to happen: (i) there must be more than one path connecting any two racks; and (ii) every rack-to-rack path must consist of two hops, i.e., through a solitary spine switch in the middle). In leaf-spine designs such as the one displayed in Figure 10.2, each server-to-server path consists of two hops (server-leaf-server in the intra-rack scenario) or four hops (server-leaf-spine-leaf-server in the inter-rack scenario). Take note of this.

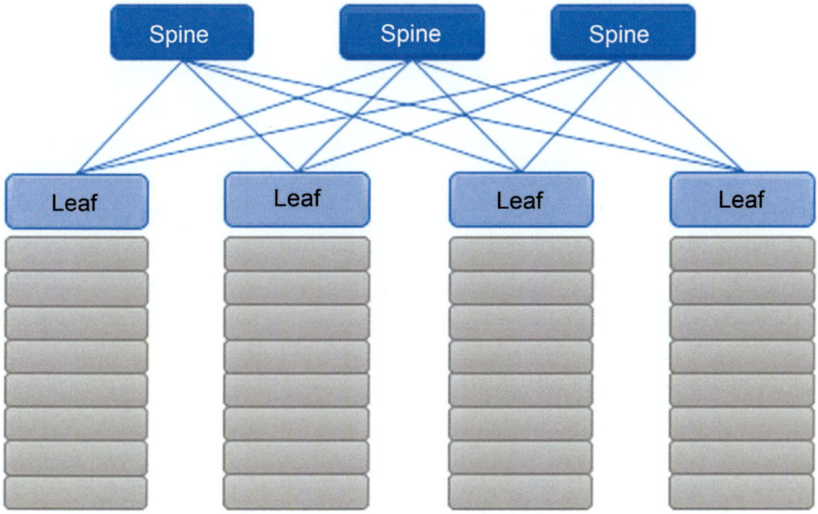

Figure 10.2. *Example of a leaf-spine switching fabric common to cloud datacenters and other clusters, such as on-premises edge clouds.*

Source: https://sdn.systemsapproach.org/_images/Slide20.png

L2 forwarding, or bridging, within a server rack and L3 forwarding, or routing, between racks are configured by the primary fabric-control software. Because L3 scales better than L2, it is a well-known concept in leaf-spine fabrics to use L3 down-to-the-ToR switches. Under such circumstances, Equal-Cost Multipath (ECMP) forwarding is used by the ToRs (leaves) to route traffic by hashing IP flows to various spines. There are numerous such equal-cost paths since each ToR is located two hops apart from each other. On the inside, the control software makes use of MPLS-like label switching principles. Because legacy workloads frequently require communication over an L2 network, the fabric control software must also support L2-bridging.

10.1.3. Traffic Engineering for WANs

Applying traffic engineering to the wide-area links connecting datacenters is another use case influenced by the cloud. For instance, Google has made their private backbone, known as B4, known to the public. It is constructed entirely of bare-metal switches and SDN. In a similar vein, Microsoft has detailed a method known as SWAN for connecting their data centers. A Traffic Engineering (TE) control program, which configures the network to meet the requirements of different application classes, is a key component of both B4 and SWAN. It is nearly as old as packet switching itself to consider traffic engineering for packet-switched networks; in fact, the Arpanet tried some traffic-aware routing concepts. However, the introduction of MPLS, which offers a set of tools to steer traffic to balance load across different paths, is largely responsible for the mainstreaming of traffic engineering for the Internet backbone. The fact that path calculation is a fully distributed process, just like traditional routing, is a significant drawback of MPLS-based TE. Although central planning tools are widely used, MPLS path real-time management is still entirely distributed. This implies that achieving any kind of global optimization is next to impossible since the path calculation algorithms, which activate whenever a link changes status or traffic loads fluctuate, are choosing what appears to be optimal locally.

Let's look at an example from Figure 10.3. Assume that we are attempting to find paths for three-unit flows of traffic and that all links have a unit capacity. Flow A is positioned first in the figure on the left and selects one of the two shortest paths available. Since Flow A has already occupied the single-hop path, Flow B is positioned next and follows the shortest path that is still available. Flow C must be placed last, leaving only the lengthy route as an option. However, the significantly less wasteful collection of paths seen on the right side of the figure would result from a central algorithm that examined all three flows simultaneously and attempted to arrange them optimally. Although this is a fictitious example, when there is no central view of traffic, suboptimal results like the ones on the left are inevitable.

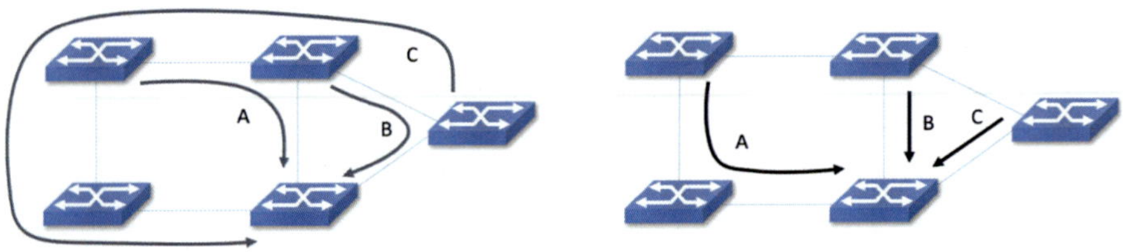

Figure 10.3. *Example of non-optimal traffic engineering (left); and optimal placement (right).*

Source: https://sdn.systemsapproach.org/_images/Slide53.png.

This weakness is acknowledged by B4 and SWAN, who transfer the path computation to a logically centralized SDN controller. The controller, for instance, determines a fresh mapping of traffic demands onto available links in the event of a link failure and sets up the switches to forward traffic flows so that no link is overloaded.

After many years of use, these strategies have advanced in sophistication. B4, for instance, changed from handling all traffic equally to accommodating a variety of traffic classes with varying degrees of availability and delay tolerance. Traffic class examples included the following: (i) copying user data; (ii) pushing large-scale data to synchronize state across multiple datacenters; (iii) accessing remote storage by computations that run over distributed data sources; and (iv) sending data (email, documents, audio/video, etc.) to remote datacenters for availability. User data is the highest priority, has the lowest volume on B4, and is the most sensitive to latency in this example. The group was able to significantly increase the network's efficiency while still satisfying the needs of the most demanding applications by segmenting traffic into these classes with distinct characteristics and executing a path calculation algorithm for each one. Google has reached almost 100% link utilization by combining programmatic rate limiting of traffic at the senders, traffic class differentiation, and centralizing the decision-making process. This is two to three times more efficient than the typical 30–40% average utilization for WAN links, which is required to enable those networks to handle both traffic spikes and link/switch failures. Microsoft also reported a similar experience with SWAN. These hyperscale SDN experiences demonstrate the usefulness of network customization as well as the ability of centralized control to modify networking abstractions.

10.1.4. Software-Defined WANs

Software-Defined Wide-Area Networks are another SDN use-case that has gained popularity among business users (SD-WAN). Businesses have been purchasing wide area network (WAN) services from telecommunications companies for many years, primarily to connect their numerous locations—main offices, branch offices, and corporate data centers—with dependable, private network services. The most popular technical method for creating these networks for the majority of the 21st century has been MPLS, with the use of a method called MPLS-BGP VPNs (virtual private networks). Another illustration of the effectiveness of centralized control is the quick ascent of SD-WAN as an MPLS substitute. Even though setting up a VPN with MPLS is simpler than with most previous methods, it still necessitates a considerable amount of local configuration on the Customer Edge (CE) router at each customer site and the Provider Edge (PE) router that the site is connected to. Furthermore, usually, the relevant Telco would need to provision a circuit from the customer site to the closest point of presence.

It was discovered that VPNs are well suited for centralized configuration with SD-WAN. An enterprise typically wants to apply a set of policies regarding security, traffic prioritization, access to shared services, and other things. It also wants its sites—and only its authorized sites—to be interconnected. These can be fed into a central controller, which can then send all the configuration that's required to a switch at the right office. It is possible to achieve "zero-touch" provisioning, which eliminates the need to manually configure a CE and a PE for each new site. An appliance is shipped to the new site with only a certificate and an address to contact, which it uses to get in touch with the central controller and acquire all the necessary configuration. Modifications to the policy that may impact numerous sites can be entered centrally and distributed to every site that is impacted. "Put YouTube traffic into the lowest priority traffic class" or "allow direct access to a given cloud service from all branch offices" are two examples of policies. The concept is shown in Figure 10.4.

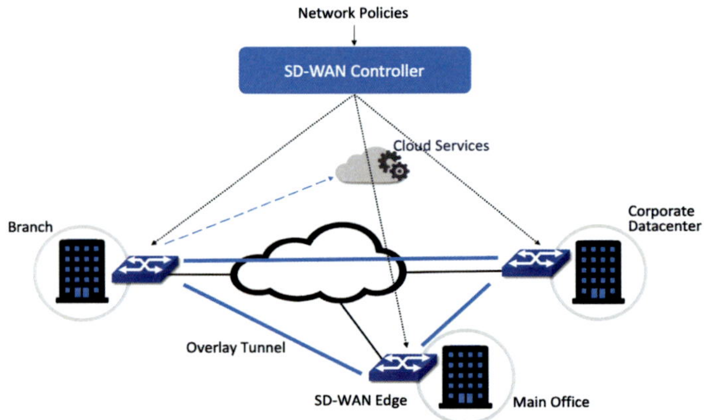

Figure 10.4. *An SD-WAN controller receives policies centrally and pushes them out to edge switches at various sites. The switches build an overlay of tunnels over the Internet or other physical networks and implement policies including allowing direct access to cloud services.*

Source: https://sdn.systemsapproach.org/_images/Slide43.png.

Keep in mind that the establishment of encrypted tunnels between locations is typically how the "private" portion of the VPN is accomplished. This is another instance of a task that is simple to accomplish when all switches receive their configuration from a central controller but is difficult to set up using traditional box-by-box configuration. To make SD-WAN a desirable choice, a number of external factors were taken into consideration. One of these was the widespread availability of broadband Internet access, which eliminates the need for a dedicated circuit and the associated installation time and expense when connecting a remote site.

However, before that could occur, the privacy issue needed to be resolved, and it was, by using centrally controlled, encrypted tunnels. An additional factor was the growing dependence on cloud services like Office365 and Salesforce.com, which have displaced on-premises software in business data centers. Although it makes sense that you would want to use an Internet-connected branch to access those services directly, traditional VPNs backhaul traffic to a central location before sending it out to the Internet, primarily so that security could be managed centrally. With SD-WAN, remote sites can connect to cloud services directly without the need for a backhaul because central control over security policy is achieved while the data plane is fully distributed. This is another illustration of how a new network architecture results from the separation of the control and data planes.

Similar to certain other use cases, SD-WAN may not fulfill all of the promises made by SDN. Similar to network virtualization, the control plane to data plane communication channel used by SD-WAN solutions is typically proprietary. These overlay networks are installed on top of conventional networks. However, because software is used to implement both the control planes and the edge devices, SD-WAN has created a space for innovation and centralization has brought fresh approaches to an age-old issue. In addition, the players in the SD-WAN market are fiercely competitive.

10.1.5. Access Networks

Another chance to use SDN principles is in access networks, which implement the last mile that connects residences, places of business, and mobile devices to the Internet. The Radio Access Network (RAN), which powers the core of the 4G/5G cellular network, and Passive Optical Networks (PON), also referred to as fiber-to-the-home, are two examples of access network technologies. These use cases are intriguing because, in contrast to all the others, which essentially allow programmable control over general-purpose switches, access networks are usually constructed using specialized hardware. Converting these specially designed devices into their merchant silicon/bare-metal equivalents so they can be managed by software is the difficult part. These devices are known as optical line terminals (OLT) and broadband network gateways (BNG) in the context of wired networks like PON. eNodeB, the RAN base station, and the Enhanced Packet Core (EPC) are two additional pertinent legacy elements in the context of the cellular network.

These devices seem to be worst-case scenarios for using SDN principles because they are proprietary, closed, and purpose-built. However, this also means that they offer the greatest potential for profit, and large network operators are actively pursuing software-defined PON and RAN networks for this exact reason. This project, which has been the focus of extensive business analysis, is sometimes referred to as CORD (Central Office Re-architected as a Datacenter). Disassembling the current legacy devices in order to separate the control plane from the data plane—the essential component of the data plane—is the main task of initiatives such as CORD. By doing this, it is feasible to implement the latter in software and package the former as commodity hardware. Disaggregating PON-based access networks is progressing pretty well; SEBA (SDN-Enabled Broadband Access) is one solution that's currently in production. Stated differently, the cluster consists of a variety of access and compute devices connected by a switching fabric. Additionally, the Open Compute Project (OCP) has certified bare-metal OLT devices in addition to bare-metal Ethernet switches. The code that implements a software-defined control plane runs on servers in the cluster, and it governs both the fabric switches and access devices. Furthermore, certain functionality originally offered by the legacy hardware can be programmed into the switches that make up the fabric when it is built using switches with programmable pipelines. For instance, BNG-equivalent functionality is programmed straight into a programmable switch rather than being packaged as a Virtual Network Function (VNF) that runs on a general-purpose processor. The packet processing is shifted from the compute servers to the switches in this technique, which is sometimes referred to as VNF off-loading. This is an excellent illustration of what happens when switch data planes are programmable: programmers create applications that can utilize the hardware in novel and unexpected ways (Figure 10.5).

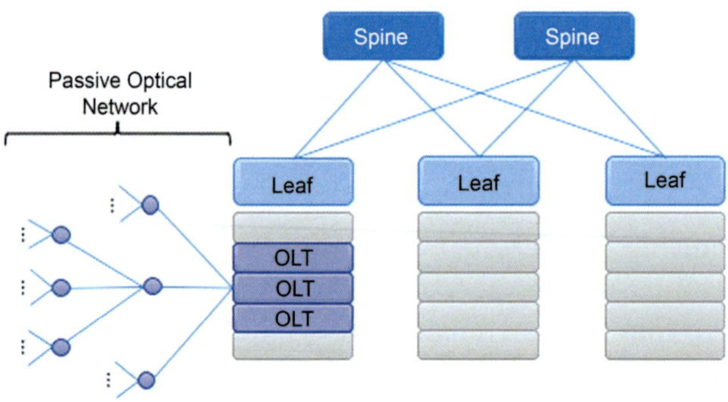

Figure 10.5. *General hardware architecture of SEBA: SDN-enabled broadband access.*

Source: https://sdn.systemsapproach.org/_images/Slide21.png.

Progress on software-defined radio access networks (SD-RAN) lags software-defined broadband, with early-stage systems starting to run in trial deployments. Disaggregating the RAN is a bigger challenge, but the payoff will likely be even larger, as it leads to a 5G-empowered edge cloud.

10.1.6. Network Telemetry

In-Band Network Telemetry (INT), a recent example made possible by the advent of programmable forwarding pipelines, brings this overview of SDN use cases to a close. The purpose of INT is to configure the forwarding pipeline to gather network information while packets are being handled, i.e., "in-band." This contrasts with the traditional monitoring carried out by the control plane, which involves reading different fixed counters (e.g., packets sent and received) or selecting specific subsets of packets (e.g., sFlow). Under the INT method, network switches process telemetry "instructions" as they pass through the forwarding pipeline after encoding them into packet header fields. These instructions specify what state to gather and how to write that state into the packet while it is being transmitted over the network by an INT-capable device. Sources of INT traffic (e.g., applications, hypervisors, and end-host networking stacks) have the option of embedding the instructions in either unique probe packets or regular data packets. Similar to this, INT traffic sinks gather and report the outcomes of these commands, enabling the traffic sinks to keep track of the precise data plane state that the packets saw (went through) during the forwarding process. Figure 10.6, which depicts an example packet traveling from source switch S1 to sink switch S5 via transit switch S2, exemplifies the concept. Every switch in the path adds INT metadata, which records the corresponding data for each switch and specifies what data needs to be collected for the packet.

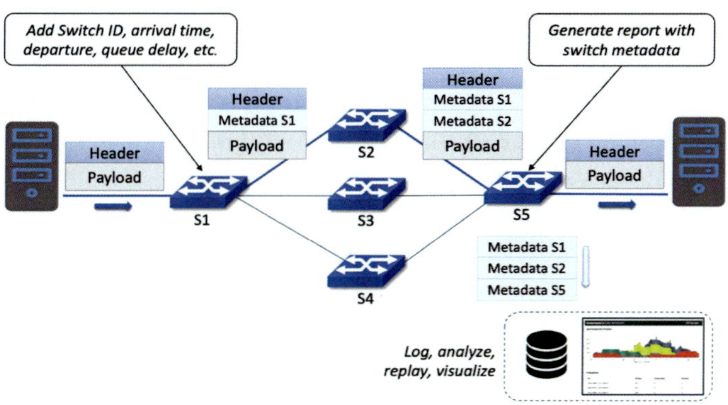

Figure 10.6. *Illustration of in-band network telemetry (INT), with each packet collecting measurement data as it traverses the network.*

Source: https://sdn.systemsapproach.org/_images/Slide38.png.

Although INT is still in its infancy, it has the potential to offer qualitatively deeper insights into network failure causes and traffic patterns. When a packet travels through a series of switches on an end-to-end path, for instance, INT can be used to measure and record the queuing delay it experiences. A packet such as the one in the figure reports: "I visited Switch 1 @780ns, Switch 2 @1.3μs, and Switch 5 @2.4μs." According to Xiaoqi Chen and colleagues, "this information can be used, for example, to detect microbursts—queuing delays measured over millisecond or even sub-millisecond time scales." This information can even be used to correlate packet flows that took different routes in order to identify the flows that shared buffer capacity at each switch. As with other decision-making processes, packets can also report how those decisions were made. For instance, a packet may report, "In Switch 1, I followed rules 75 and 250; in Switch 2, I followed rules 3 and 80." This makes it possible to confirm that the data plane is accurately carrying out the forwarding behavior that the network operator intended by using INT. This use case highlights another potential advantage of SDN: the capacity to test novel concepts that would not have been practical in the past. You would never have the opportunity to test a concept like INT to determine whether the advantages outweigh the costs when packet forwarding was handled by conventional fixed-function ASICs. Over time, SDN will yield enduring advantages due to its liberty to explore and create.

10.2. NETWORK VIRTUALIZATION

The first SDN use case to be successful commercially was network virtualization. Having said that, it is situated somewhat apart from SDN. This is due to the fact that servers can use network virtualization, usually without the switches in the actual network cooperating. The deployment process was greatly aided by the fact that network virtualization can be applied as an overlay on an already-existing network. However, because of its simplicity of deployment, it did not significantly affect the degree of innovation found in physical networks because it did not interfere with the physical network itself. In computer science, virtualization is a well-established idea that dates back many years. This also holds true for virtualization of networks. For instance, in the 1990s, virtual private networks (VPNs) were established through Frame Relay and ATM networks, and in the late 1990s, virtual LANs (VLANs) were incorporated into the Ethernet standards. These technologies were implemented using traditional networking technologies, and they shared very little with SDN. Crucially, they avoided dividing the control and data planes in the way that is thought to be essential to SDN.

10.2.1. Challenges

The evolution of modern datacenters, where a large number of commodity servers communicate with one another to solve computational tasks, is closely linked to network virtualization as it exists today. Large cloud providers (e.g., Amazon, Google) also share these datacenters (e.g., AWS, Azure, Google), in addition to numerous business establishments. A few of the difficulties in developing networks for these kinds of datacenters were outlined in the 2009

Microsoft Research VL2 paper. A significant portion of “east-west” traffic, or server-to-server traffic, as opposed to “north-south” traffic coming into or going out of the datacenter, is found in these types of datacenters.

Server virtualization gained popularity at the same period, which affected datacenter operations in a number of ways. Unlike the laborious and manual process of installing and configuring physical servers, provisioning virtual machines (VMs) can be done entirely through software. The “long pole”—the task that takes the longest to finish before a user can use their infrastructure—was revealed as the ease of provisioning a virtual machine (VM) reduced the time it took to obtain computational resources from days to minutes or seconds. Network virtualization was thus made possible by the realization that network configuration and provisioning needed to shift toward a model more akin to virtual compute. The ability to move virtual machines was one of server virtualization’s secondary effects. This presented some significant networking challenges for datacenters. The IP address of a virtual machine (VM) in the absence of network virtualization is derived from the physical network it is located on and needs to be unique to a subnet that links to the server hosting the VM. Therefore, in order for a virtual machine to migrate to a different server, it must either move to one where that subnet is also present or obtain a new IP address. The first option restricts its movement within the datacenter, which has an impact on how effectively resources are used. The latter option can be highly disruptive as it results in TCP connections being lost and may require restarting of applications. Additionally, some applications rely on a subnet of VMs remaining in that subnet while they move around the datacenter because they depend on layer-2 adjacency between communicating peers. Growing the size of layer-2 subnets within the physical network was one suggested solution to this problem, but it is not a very scalable approach. Layer-3 networking is a standard feature of large datacenters, used to link server racks.

The strategy put forth by Greenberg and colleagues is regarded as the initial stage of network virtualization. The mobility-related problems mentioned above were resolved when they built a Virtual Layer 2 (VL2) network in which the addresses used by virtual machines are separated from the addresses used in the physical network. A virtual machine (VM) obtains its IP address from a virtual layer 2 (VL2) network. As VMs move across physical networks, VL2 creates the necessary overlay to extend the virtual network wherever it needs to go. Network configuration is a slightly more complicated problem to solve. Networks are more than just plain subnets used to link servers; they have many other features that require configuration, such as firewall rules, network address translation (NAT) rules, VLANs, and other similar constructs to divide the network. Network configuration has become a barrier to datacenter configuration agility due to the complexity of these tasks. After addressing these configuration and provisioning-related problems, it was discovered that SDN offered a way to make virtual network creation and management as simple as physical network operation. The key finding is that the best way to define the desired behavior of a virtual network is to use a central API to an SDN controller. The controller will then handle determining how to implement the network using the resources at hand, like virtual switches in the servers' hypervisors in the datacenter. This method is based on the fundamental ideas of SDN, which include the separation of the data plane from the control plane and the centralization of the controller to oversee a large number of switching elements.

10.2.2. Architecture

Figure 10.7 depicts the most basic network virtualization system that is conceivable. Virtual machines are connected to virtual switches that are located at end hosts. An API that is exposed by the network virtualization controller allows it to receive inputs that specify the desired state of a virtual network. An API request might state, for instance, that "VM1 and VM2 should reside on the same virtual layer 2 subnet, network X." In order to create the necessary virtual network abstraction, the controller must first locate those virtual machines and then send control commands to the relevant virtual switches. Let's examine that abstraction in more detail.

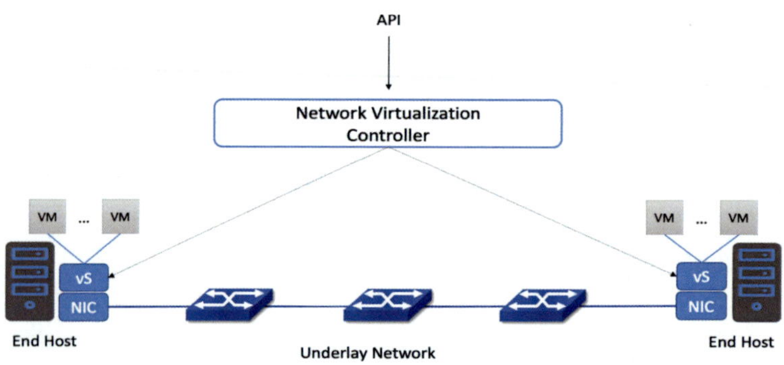

Figure 10.7. *A basic network virtualization system.*

Source: https://sdn.systemsapproach.org/_images/Slide44.png.

The IP addresses of the virtual machines (VMs) must be independent of the physical network topology, which is represented by the underlay network in the figure, so that they can roam freely within the datacenter. Specifically, we don't want the underlying physical network's subnet addressing to limit the location of a specific virtual machine. For this reason, overlay encapsulations like VXLAN or NVGRE are always used in network virtualization systems. A significant issue is resolved by encapsulation, a low-level technique that separates the virtual network's address space from the physical network's address space. It is important to remember that they are only one component of a larger network virtualization solution and should not be used as such.

One thing to note about virtual network encapsulation is that, as Figure 10.8 shows, there are a set of inner headers that are only relevant within the specific virtual network, and a set of outer headers that are used by the physical network to route the packet to the correct end host. Encapsulation separates the virtual network addressing from the physical network addressing in this way. This straightforward illustration also demonstrates one of the duties that the network virtualization controller must carry out. A virtual machine's (VM) current server location determines which outer header it needs to apply when it wants to communicate with one of its peers in a virtual network. It makes sense for the centralized controller to provide the mapping from the target virtual machine to the outer header. This is called a directory service in VL2. We need to take a closer look at the definition of a virtual network in order to gain a better understanding of the functions of the network virtualization controller.

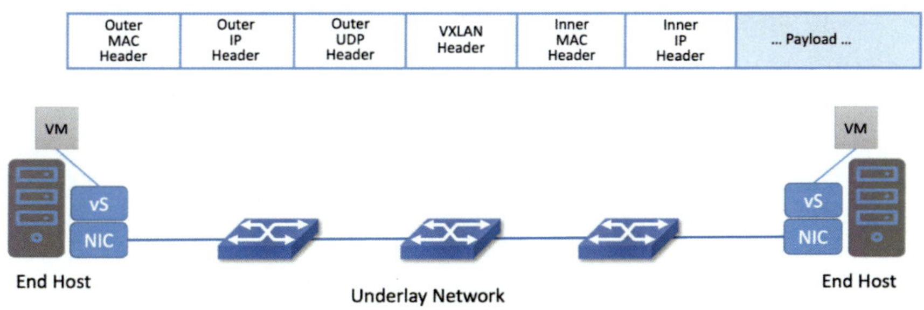

Figure 10.8. *Encapsulation decouples virtual network addresses from physical network.*

Source: https://sdn.systemsapproach.org/_images/Slide45.png.

10.2.2.1. Virtual Networks Defined

The concept of virtual networks is not new, as previously mentioned. Similar to how virtual memory enables processes to share physical memory, virtual LANs (VLANs) enable multiple LAN segments to coexist on a single physical LAN. But the Nicira team's vision for virtual networks, as outlined in the NSDI paper, is more like virtual machines. Virtual machines offer an accurate replication of a physical server's features, including its processor, memory, peripherals, and other components. Because of how thorough the replication is, a virtual machine can run an unmodified operating system precisely like a physical machine. In a similar vein, virtual networks have to mimic every feature of a physical network. Accordingly, higher layer functions like NAT, firewalling, and load balancing are included in virtual networks along with routing, switching, and addressing. An unmodified distributed application ought to be able to run on a virtual network in the same way that it would on a physical network, just as an unmodified operating system can run in a virtual machine. This is undoubtedly a more complex suggestion than a VLAN. Crucially, a virtual network must continue to function properly even when virtual machines (VMs) are moved. As a result, it's clear that a network virtualization controller's job is to take a specification of the desired virtual network and make sure it's implemented correctly on the right resources when circumstances change, and virtual machines migrate.

10.2.2.2. Management, Control, and Data Planes

This allows us to take a closer look at the fundamental design of a network virtualization system. A modern network virtualization system exposes a northbound API through which virtual networks can be created and managed, in contrast to earlier forms of virtual networks like VLANs and VPNs.

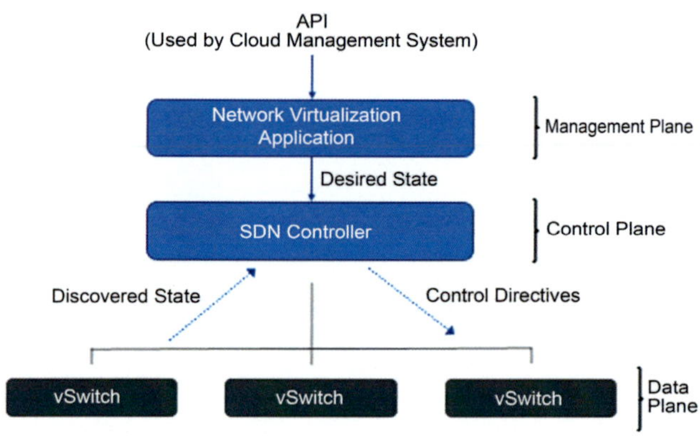

Figure 10.9. *The three planes of a network virtualization system.*

Source: https://sdn.systemsapproach.org/_images/Slide46.png.

The topology and services of a virtual network are defined by calls to this API, which can be made by a cloud automation platform or by a human user. "Create a layer 2 subnet," "Attach VM A to subnet X," or "Apply firewall policy P to traffic entering VM B" are examples of typical API requests. These API requests result in the creation of the desired state—the state in which the network ought to be—as seen in Figure 10.9. The management plane is the term used to describe the portion of the system that receives API requests and stores them in a database representing the desired state.

The data plane is located at the bottom of Figure 10.9. This is typically a collection of Virtual Switches (vSwitches) that operate on host hypervisors or containers. Virtual networks are implemented on the data plane. As demonstrated in the example, a virtual switch forwards packets between virtual machines (VMs) and the physical network; in order to do this, the packets must have the proper headers applied. The higher layers of the network virtualization system must take into consideration data from the data plane regarding the current state of the system, including the locations of virtual machines (VMs). The discovered state indicates this. The control plane is the central component of the system. It is positioned in between the system's desired and actual states. The data plane sends information about the discovered state to the control plane, which compares it to the desired state. The control plane determines the necessary adjustments and pushes them to the data plane, as shown by the control directives arrow, if the desired state and the actual state differ. In distributed systems, this paradigm of continuously balancing the desired state with the actual state is typical.

Whether made of software or bare-metal switches, a distributed data plane serves as the foundation upon which a centralized controller gathers operational state information and sends out control commands. This controller is referred to as a Network OS when it is implemented generally and is not case-specific. An early network operating system called Onix, created by the Nicira team, can be considered an ONOS forerunner. A management layer that comprehends the abstraction of a virtual network and responds to API requests sits at the top. You can think of this management layer as an OS application running on the network. Think of a basic illustration. In order to link two virtual machines, A and B, to a single L2 subnet, we need to build a virtual network. A series of API requests, such as create the subnet, connect A to the subnet, and connect B to the subnet, can be used to convey that intention. The management plane accepts these API requests and stores them in the desired state. The location of A and B as well as the IP addresses of the pertinent hypervisors must be ascertained by the control plane since it is observing changes in the desired state that are not yet reflected in the actual state. It uses this data to calculate the appropriate packet encapsulation for communication between A and B. This is used to calculate a set of control directives that must be added to the relevant vSwitches. These directives, which can be expressed as a set of OpenFlow rules, are pushed to the vSwitches. The control plane receives this information if one of the virtual machines (VMs) moves to a different hypervisor later on. It recognizes that the desired state has been replaced by the actual state. This starts a new calculation to find out what updates need to be pushed to the data plane, like new forwarding rules to the right set of vSwitches and data plane state deletion at the hypervisor that isn't hosting a virtual machine anymore. We can implement a wide range of virtual network features with this architecture. With enough richness in the data plane, one can now construct a network virtualization system that precisely replicates the characteristics of a physical network in software, including firewalls, load balancers, and other devices.

10.2.2.3. Distributed Services

Essential components of network virtualization are software implementations of network functions like load balancing, routing, and firewalling. However, it is not simply a matter of implementing a traditional network device in software. Think about the firewall as an example. When a traditional firewall is installed, it serves as a choke point because network traffic is designed to flow through it in order to move between different areas of the network.

Examine the illustration shown in Figure 10.10. Not always the shortest path from A to C, traffic sent from VM A to VM C must be routed over a path that passes through the firewall in order for it to be processed at a firewall in a traditional network. Traffic between virtual machines A and B that are hosted on the same host must be routed out of the host, across the network to the firewall, and back to B in the more severe scenario. This is obviously inefficient since it uses up NIC bandwidth for the hairpinned traffic in addition to network resources. Additionally, because all traffic that needs to be treated must pass through that one centralized device, the firewall itself may end up acting as a bottleneck.

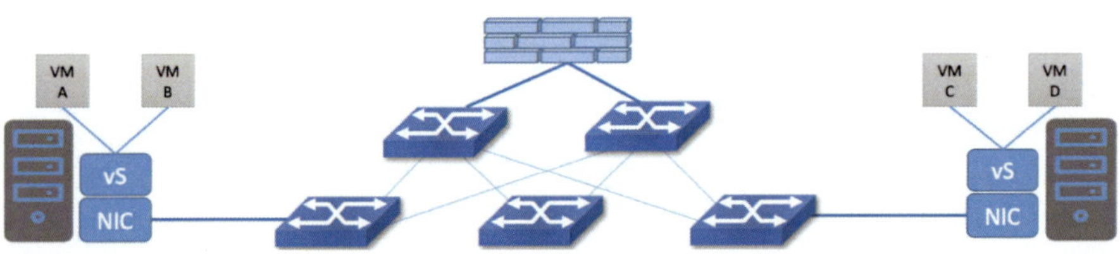

Figure 10.10. *A conventional firewall (not distributed).*

Source: https://sdn.systemsapproach.org/_images/Slide47.png.

Now look at Figure 10.11, which shows an implementation of a distributed firewall. In this instance, traffic sent between virtual machines A and C can be routed via the shortest path possible through the network underlay without hairpinning to an external firewall, provided that a firewall function processes it at one or both of the virtual switches it passes through. Moreover, traffic between VM A and VM B only needs to go through the virtual switch on that host in order to receive the required firewall treatment—it never even needs to leave the host where those two VMs are located. This method of service distribution has the important side effect of eliminating the central bottleneck. Virtual switches with the ability to perform some distributed service processing are created each time a new server is added to accommodate more virtual machines. This indicates that scaling up the quantity of firewalling—or whatever other service is being provided—in this manner is not too difficult. The same methodology can be used for many other services, such as intrusion detection, load balancing, routing, and others, which were previously possible to complete in a separate box. This is not to say that it is always easy to implement these services in a distributed fashion. However, we can provision and configure these services via an API (or a GUI) in a single location and implement them in a distributed fashion with the efficiency and performance benefits described here thanks to a centralized control plane.

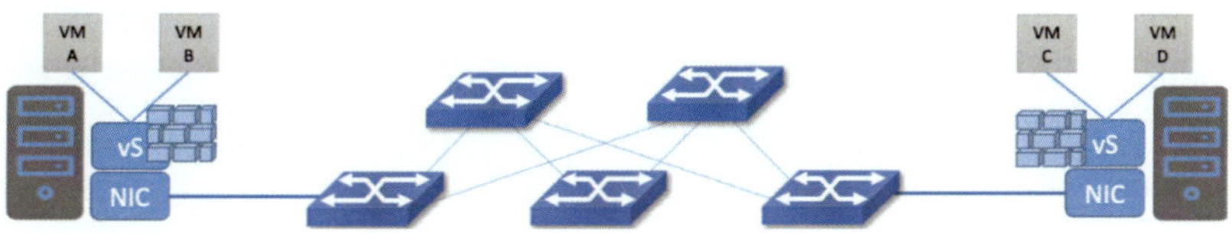

Figure 10.11. *A distributed firewall.*

Source: https://sdn.systemsapproach.org/_images/Slide48.png.

10.2.3. Building Blocks

Now that we understand the architecture of network virtualization systems, let's look at some of the building blocks used to construct such a system.

10.2.3.1. Virtual Network Encapsulation

As previously mentioned, network virtualization necessitates encapsulation of some kind in order to separate the addressing of the virtual network from that of the physical network. Network architects and engineers seem to enjoy coming up with new methods to encapsulate packets, and when network virtualization first emerged, there were already a few viable options. But none of them quite suited the bill, and in the past 10 years, a number more have been created. Even though VXLAN was first introduced in 2012 to a lot of attention, it was by no means the final solution for network virtualization encapsulation. Following many years of testing and cooperation between hardware and software providers as well as other IETF members, an encapsulation containing the majority of the required features was created and standardized. The requirements that GENEVE was created to satisfy are outlined in the accompanying RFC. The extensibility of GENEVE is a noteworthy feature. This constituted a compromise of sorts between those developing hardware endpoints intended to facilitate network virtualization and those developing software-based systems (like the one from Nicira). Hardware finds fixed headers to be convenient, but future expansion options are restricted. Ultimately, GENEVE contained an options scheme that provided the necessary extensibility and could be efficiently processed by hardware or ignored.

The main distinction between GENEVE and VXLAN, as illustrated in Figure 10.12, is the availability of a range of variable length options. A crucial component that built on past systems' experiences was the availability of options, which allowed for the transfer of virtual network metadata from one end of a tunnel to the other despite the VXLAN header's limited capacity. Giving a packet's logical source port so that it can be taken into account during further processing is one example of how to use such metadata. A general point to note is that, as virtual networks develop over time with more complex features implemented in software, it is crucial to avoid using excessively restrictive packet encapsulation to limit the amount of information that can be transferred inside a virtual network.

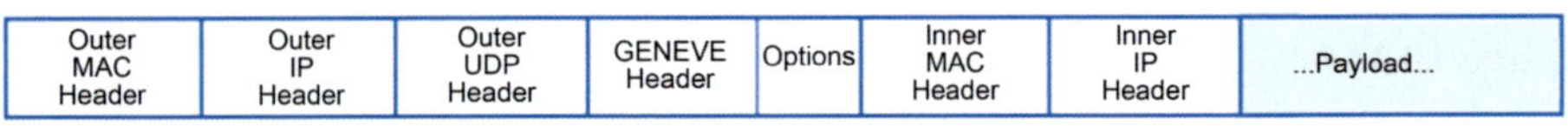

Figure 10.12. *GENEVE header format.*

Source: https://sdn.systemsapproach.org/_images/Slide49.png.

10.2.3.2. Virtual Switches

It is evident that the Virtual Switch is essential to network virtualization. It is the primary part of the data plane, and how well a network virtualization system can replicate the features of a physical network depends on how rich its feature set is. Open vSwitch (OVS) is the virtual switch that is most frequently used. Both open source and proprietary systems, including Open Virtual Network (OVN) and Nicira's Network Virtualization Platform and VMware NSX, have made use of Open vSwitch. It was made to be highly performant and have the flexibility required to satisfy network virtualization requirements.

Like many hardware switches, OVS is programmed by the control plane using OpenFlow, as shown in Figure 10.13. Additionally, it uses the Open vSwitch Database (OVSDB) protocol to receive configuration data over a different channel. In other words, OVSDB essentially performs the same function as gNMI/gNOI for a hardware-based data plane. Once more, the correspondence between these fundamental elements and their constituents, along with the variations in nomenclature and specifics, are predominantly ascribed to network virtualization's development as a custom-designed resolution. OVSDB can refer to either the protocol or the database; in the figure, it refers to the RPC protocol called OVSDB-server that is used to access the database. Consider OVSDB as the OVS equivalent of the OpenConfig schema, as it is a database. Similar to how gNMI uses protobufs, OVSDB uses a JSON-based message format as its protocol. It is also important to note that OVSDB has evolved into a distinct representation of network forwarding state that goes beyond the function depicted in Figure 10.13.

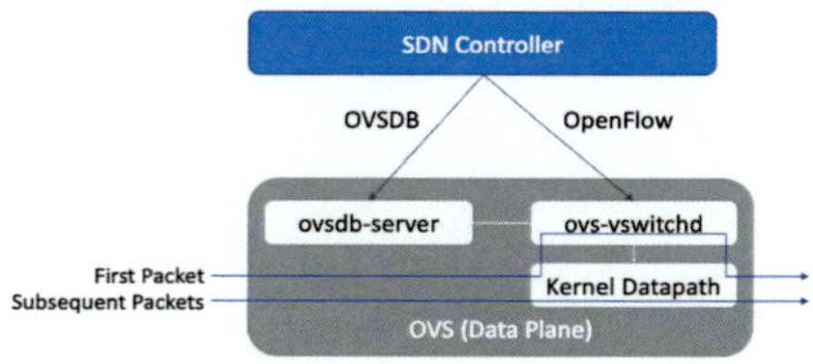

Figure 10.13. *Open vSwitch functional blocks.*

Source: https://sdn.systemsapproach.org/_images/Slide50.png.

Performance improvements in the OVS data plane have been made through a lengthy list of optimizations detailed in the Pfaff paper. One such improvement is a fast path in the kernel that utilizes a flow cache to forward every packet in a flow after the first. The userspace daemon OVS-vSwitchd receives the first packet in a flow and uses a set of tables to look up the flow. Unlike hardware implementations of OpenFlow switching, this set of tables can be practically infinite in number because it is implemented in software. This makes it possible for network virtualization to have the high level of flexibility that it needs. Concurrently, an endeavor is underway to integrate hardware- and software-based forwarding components, employing P4 as the standard language for developing packet forwarders. P4Runtime, the automatically generated interface for managing the data plane, is also included in this. It should be noted that OVS can be used in container environments to forward packets between containers on the same or different hosts, in addition to being used to forward packets between virtual machines and the outside world. As a result, a network virtualization system for containers can be constructed using many of the same parts as one for virtual machines (VMs), and mixed environments—where VMs and containers interact within a single virtual network—can also be achieved.

10.2.3.3. Performance Optimizations

The virtual switch's performance is vital because it is the first point of contact for all traffic entering and leaving virtual machines (VMs) and containers in a virtual network. Many performance optimizations over the years are covered in the OVS paper from 2015, but methods for enhancing vSwitch performance should be further explored. The first is the Data Plane Development Kit (DPDK), a collection of libraries designed to enhance the speed of virtual switching and other data-moving operations on the Intel x86 platform. Several of the ideas are simple (e.g., packets can be processed in batches, context switches can be avoided), but there is a wide range of optimizations that can be used effectively when done so. Depending on the specific operating environment, it has been successfully used to implement OVS with performance gains that can be substantial. When a virtual machine (VM) needs to communicate with something outside of the virtual network, one such scenario is using OVS to forward packets between a virtual and a non-virtual network. This could be, for instance, a publicly accessible device on the Internet or an unvirtualized server, like a mainframe or database. Known as a Virtual-to-Physical Gateway, this scenario is a good fit for DPDK since it primarily consists of forwarding packets (i.e., no additional CPU-bound processing is carried out). In this setting, experiments reported by RedHat Developer shows OVS-DPDK is able to forward over 16 Mpps on a high-end Intel processor. This is contrasted with a forwarding rate using OVS alone that is more or less 1 Mpps.).

Second, a hardware feature called Single Root IO Virtualization (SR-IOV) is intended to enhance IO performance between virtual machines (VMs) and the external environment. The fundamental concept is that a single physical network interface (NIC) appears to the hypervisor as a collection of virtual NICs, each with a unique set of resources. Performance might theoretically be enhanced if every virtual machine had its own virtual network interface and did not use the hypervisor at all. But since the virtual switch is omitted, this method of network virtualization isn't very helpful. Avoiding it goes against the grain of network virtualization because a programmable virtual switch's flexibility provides a large portion of its value. Nonetheless, it is important to acknowledge that the NIC is a part of the whole story. Certain functions have long been offloaded from the server to the network interface controller (NIC); one such function is TCP Segmentation Offload (TSO). With the popularity of SmartNICs, NICs have become more capable in recent years, and this presents an opportunity to transfer more vSwitch functionality to the NIC for possible performance gains. The difficulty lies in sacrificing performance for flexibility because SmartNICs still have less resources than general-purpose CPUs. The most recent generation of SmartNICs is becoming sophisticated enough that it might be useful to offload some or all of the vSwitch functions. It is important to remember that, even with excellent implementation, a software switch running on general-purpose hardware will not function as well as a switching hardware designed specifically for that purpose. Because of this, gateway implementations that utilize these bare-metal switches have also been made. One such instance made use of the VXLAN implementations found on numerous top-of-rack switches. There is a trade-off between the performance of less flexible, dedicated hardware and the flexibility of fully programmable devices, just like in many other networking environments. General purpose hardware has proven to be a more flexible solution in the majority of network virtualization deployments used for business purposes. In due course, the challenge will be to pinpoint the comparatively stable, yet broadly relevant, portion of that capability that yields the greatest efficiency gain when integrated into hardware.

10.2.4. Example System

Network virtualization systems have been implemented successfully in a number of cases, some of which we have already discussed. In this section, a well-documented open-source project called Open Virtual Network (OVN) is used as an illustration of a network virtualization system. Utilizing OVS for the data plane and a collection of databases (based on OVSDB) for the control and management planes, OVN is designed as an extension of OVS. Figure 10.14 displays the high-level architecture of OVN.

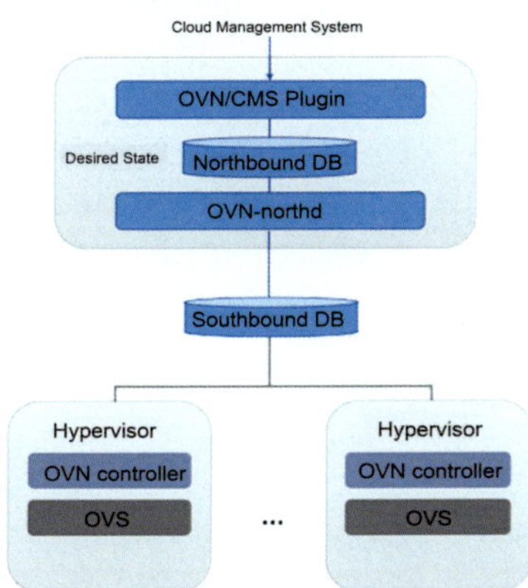

Figure 10.14. *OVN high-level architecture.*

Source: https://sdn.systemsapproach.org/_images/Slide51.png.

The fact that OVN stores state in two databases, known as Northbound and Southbound, is a crucial feature. OVSDB is used to implement these databases; it was first developed to store OVS configuration state. OVSDB plays a more significant role in OVN since it is utilized for both configuration state and control state. It is assumed that OVN functions in a setting where virtual networks are created by a Cloud Management System (CMS). Since OpenStack was the first CMS that OVN supported, it is most likely this. The mapping of CMS abstractions into generic virtual network abstractions that can be kept in the Northbound Database is the responsibility of the OVN/CMS plugin. In order to implement this database, OVN uses an instance of ovsdb-server. The Northbound DB can be thought of as the intended state repository, and the plugin as the management plane.

Comparing the OVN control plane to Figure 10.9's generic architecture, a noteworthy novel feature is evident. It is noteworthy that it is separated into two parts: the OVN controller, which is distributed and runs on each hypervisor, and the OVN-northd, which is centralized. The OVN team's experience working on previous systems that presented scalability challenges due to the centralized controller's full view of all flows led to the decision to split. While OVN distributes control functions related to physical information, like the location of virtual machines on particular servers, to each hypervisor, it maintains logically centralized control, allowing a single API entry point to be used for network creation, status queries, and other operations. The system's scalability increased significantly as a result of this. The logical network configuration is expressed in terms of traditional network concepts like switching and routing. A centralized component called OVN-northd translates this expression into logical datapath flows, which it then stores in the OVN Southbound Database. Figure 10.15 provides an example of how logical flows operate.

Logical_Switch

Name	Ports
LS1	LP1,LP2

Logical_Port

Name	MAC
LP1	AA
LP2	BB

Chassi (Physical Network)

Name	Encap	IP
HV1	Geneve	10.0.0.10
HV2	Geneve	10.0.0.11

Port_Binding

Name	Chassis
LP1	HV1
LP2	HV2

Logical_Flows

Datapath	Match	Action
LS1	eth.dst = AA	LP1
LS1	eth.dst = BB	LP2
LS1	eth.dst = <broadcast	LP1,LP2

Tables in ovn-sb

Physical Flows

Match	Enccap	Dest
eth.dst = AA	Geneve	10.0.0.10
eth.dst = BB	Geneve	10.0.0.11

Flows computed on individual hypervisors

Figure 10.15. *Logical and physical flows in OVN.*

Source: https://sdn.systemsapproach.org/_images/Slide52.png.

The forwarding rules that are filled in the data plane are represented abstractly by logical data path flows, which are specified without regard to the physical locations of the virtual machines. We have constructed a logical switch, LS1, with two ports, LP1 and LP2, in this example. Every port links to a virtual machine (VM), and the VMs' MAC addresses are AA and BB, as indicated in the Logical_Port table. The logical switch's packet forwarding strategy is illustrated in the Logical Flows table, which was constructed using data from the Logical

Switch and Logical Port tables. For instance, packets intended for a MAC address of AA must be sent to port LP1, according to the first row. However, since that depends on which hypervisors are currently hosting those virtual machines, there isn't enough information to actually forward packets in this flow. The OVN controller running on the relevant hypervisor is responsible for providing the binding of physical hypervisor nodes to virtual machines (VMs). In the sense that the hypervisors find the locations of the virtual machines and report them to the database, this is an example of discovered state. It is evident from the Chassis table that the controller on HV1 (hypervisor 1) has reported that it can be contacted at IP address 10.0 via the Geneve encapsulation.

Additionally, the hypervisor that is hosting the VM with LP1 has reported this information to the Port Binding table. Based on the virtual machines (VMs) that it presently hosts, the OVN controller for each hypervisor queries the OVN Southbound DB to determine which logical flows are pertinent to it in order to program the data plane. It is able to build the rules that must be programmed into the instance of OVS running locally on the relevant hypervisor by combining that information with the location data provided by other hypervisors for other VMs. Note that all of the elements depicted as part of the OVS data plane in Figure 10.13 are included in the OVS instances shown in Figure 10.14. Keeping with the previous example, in order for hypervisor 2 to forward packets from LP2 to LP1, OVS must have a flow rule. It can see this by examining the Logical_Flows in the OVN Southbound DB. With the help of data from the Port_Binding and Chassis tables, it can also ascertain the specifics of how to encapsulate packets and forward them to the appropriate destination server. The table at the bottom of the figure, which is a compilation of the flows computed at the two hypervisors rather than a component of the Southbound DB, shows the results for both hypervisors. Up until now, the conversation has presumed that virtual machines (VMs) serve as the endpoints for our virtual networks. However, the same principles that apply to VMs also apply to containers, albeit with some implementation details glossed over. A group of container hosts can be linked to the OVN Southbound Database, and they are able to establish virtual networks for the containers they are hosting by setting up flow rules for their OVS instances. In this instance, Kubernetes or another container management system is most likely the "cloud management system" that OVN interfaces with.

10.2.5. Microsegmentation

In the years since Nicira's initial product, network virtualization has undoubtedly had an impact on networking, especially in the datacenter. Network virtualization adoption rates are regularly released by VMware and Cisco, and the technology is currently widely used in Telcos and sizable enterprise datacenters. It is also widely used in the datacenters of big cloud providers, where it plays a crucial role in providing infrastructure as a service. The ability to alter the datacenter's security implementation is one of the intriguing side effects of network virtualization. As was already mentioned, network virtualization makes it possible to implement security features in software in a distributed fashion. Compared to the conventional method of manually configuring VLANs, it also makes the creation of numerous isolated networks fairly simple. The concept of microsegmentation was born out of these two factors working together. Compared to traditional network segmentation techniques, which involved connecting a sizable number of machines to a "zone" and using firewalls to filter traffic flowing between zones, microsegmentation involves fewer machines. This resulted in a relatively simple network configuration, but it also meant that many machines would be in the same zone even when communication between them wasn't necessary. Furthermore, as more and more rules were added to describe the traffic that could pass from one zone to another, the complexity of firewall rules would increase over time.

On the other hand, microsegments—which are specialized virtual networks that control which machines can communicate with one another and how—can be created thanks to network virtualization. For example, a three-tier application may have its own microsegmentation policy stating that web-facing machines may not communicate with each other, but that machines in the application tier may communicate with each other on a set of designated ports. Because every machine that was meant to be viewed by the internet would be located on the same network segment, it was challenging to implement this policy in the past. Before microsegmentation, machines from multiple applications would probably sit on the same segment due to the complexity of segment configuration, which made it possible for an attack to propagate from one application to another. It has long been known that one of the most important tactics used by successful cyberattacks is the lateral movement of attacks within datacenters. Examine how the firewall and virtual machines are arranged in Figure 10.10. Imagine that in the absence of network virtualization, we wished to divide VM A and VM B into separate segments and apply a firewall rule to traffic that originated in VM A and ended in VM B. In the physical network, we would need to set up two VLANs, link A to one, and B to the other. We would then need to set up the routing so that the path from the first VLAN to the second went via the firewall. We would need to confirm that the proper VLAN was reaching the new server, connect VM A to it, and confirm that the routing configuration was still driving traffic through the firewall if VM A were to be moved to a different server at some point. Although a little fabricated, this scenario shows why microsegmentation was practically unfeasible prior to the advent of network virtualization. As the foundation for "zero-trust" networking, microsegmentation has emerged as an acknowledged best practice for datacenter networking. This demonstrates how network virtualization has a wide-ranging effect.

10.2.6. Is Network Virtualization SDN?

The primary objection to Network Virtualization's inclusion in SDN is that physical network architecture remains unchanged. All it does is operate as an overlay over a typical L2/L3 network, which may be configured one box at a time using distributed routing protocols. Now that network virtualization is so widely used, this argument appears to be less common, but it is still incorrect. Put simply, Network Virtualization follows the fundamental architectural guidelines established by the creators of SDN. Control and data planes are clearly distinguished from one another, with a centralized controller in charge of a dispersed group of forwarding elements. OpenFlow is even employed as a potential control interface, albeit that was always an implementation detail rather than a core component of SDN. Lastly, network virtualization belongs firmly in the SDN realm since it makes use of an entirely programmable forwarding plane, as demonstrated by OVS. The reliance on software switches rather than hardware switches is crucial, and this is how Network Virtualization differs from the other use cases in terms of implementation. Although it came at the expense of being unable to demonstrate certain characteristics about how those functions operate and behave at runtime, the use of software-based switches sped up adoption and deployment and allowed for the development of more potent forwarding functions. Furthermore, these software-based implementations developed in a manner that was optimized for Network Virtualization rather than following the SDN software stack's general-purpose, use-case-agnostic approach.

All of this ought to be expected. SDN has always been a method for creating and managing networks in isolated areas where it is useful. The requirement of universality does not exist. One such domain is datacenter underlays, as leaf-spine switching fabrics demonstrate. Another example of this type of domain is virtual networking overlays. Without either knowing the other exists, they are even deployed concurrently in the same datacenters. It will be interesting to observe in the future how many mechanisms these two domains end up sharing (e.g., a common control interface generator (a common toolchain), a common network operating system, and a common language for coding forwarding functions. The boundary between the two domains will start to become less distinct as soon as an overlay-aware underlay or underlay-aware overlay is demonstrated to be valuable, so it will be interesting to watch if this happens.

10.3. BARE-METAL SWITCHES

The goal is not to give a detailed hardware schematic, but rather, to sketch enough of the design to appreciate the software stack that runs on top of it. Note that this stack is still evolving, with different implementation approaches taken over time and by different vendors.

10.3.1. Switch-Level Schematic

We begin by looking at a bare-metal switch in its entirety; the closest comparison is to picture a PC assembled from a variety of generic, off-the-shelf parts. In fact, the Open Compute Project (OCP) offers a complete architectural specification for switches that utilize these components online.

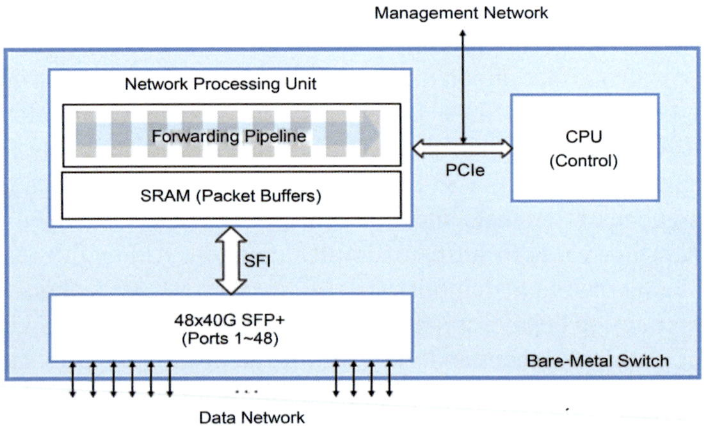

Figure 10.16. *High-level schematic of a bare-metal switch.*

Source: https://sdn.systemsapproach.org/_images/Slide10.png.

Similar to a home-built piece, this is the hardware equivalent of open-source software, enabling anyone to build a high-performance switch. However, just as the PC ecosystem includes commodity server vendors like Dell and HP, so too do bare-metal switch vendors like EdgeCore, Delta, and others offer pre-built (OCP-compliant) switches for purchase. A high-level schematic of a bare-metal switch is shown in Figure 10.16. The merchant silicon switching chip known as the Network Processing Unit (NPU) is designed with the purpose of parsing packet headers and deciding what to forward. With processing and forwarding speeds measured in Terabits-per-second (Tbps), NPUs can easily match 32×100-Gbps ports or the 48×40-Gbps ports depicted in the figure. The state-of-the-art for these chips at the time of writing is 25.6 Tbps with 400-Gbps ports.

Please take note that our usage of the term NPU may not be entirely conventional. In the past, network processing chips with more specific definitions—like those used to implement intelligent firewalls or deep packet inspection—were referred to as NPUs. Long-term trends, however, point to NPUs offering significantly more flexibility while matching fixed-function ASIC performance. It appears likely that the earlier generation of specially designed network processors will become obsolete due to the current merchant silicon switching chips. The terminology for NPUs used here is in line with the industry-wide movement toward the development of programmable processors tailored to specific domains, such as TPUs (Tensor Processing Units) for artificial intelligence and GPUs (Graphic Processing Units) for graphics.

The NPU is depicted in Figure 10.16 as an amalgam of an ASIC-based forwarding pipeline that implements a sequence of (Match, Action) pairs and SRAM-based memory that buffers packets while they are processed. The forwarding pipeline is explained. The NPU is managed by a general-purpose processor (GPC) in the switch, which is usually an x86 chip. For our purposes, this is where the Switch OS runs, exporting an API that enables an off-switch, Network OS to control the data plane. This is where BGP or OSPF would run if the switch is configured to support an on-switch control plane. Through a standard PCIe bus, this control processor connects to an external management network and communicates with the NPU. Additional commodity components that make this all feasible are also depicted in Figure 10.16. Specifically, it is possible to purchase pluggable transceiver modules that handle both the optics and all media access requirements, including 40-Gigabit Ethernet, 10-Gigabit PON, and SONET. All of these transceivers adhere to SFP+ and other standardized form factors, which allow them to be connected to other parts via a standardized bus (e.g., SFI). Once more, the important lesson is that the networking sector is about to enter the same commoditized environment that the computing sector has been living in for the past 20 years.

10.3.2. Forwarding Pipeline

A multi-stage pipeline is used by high-speed switches to process packets. It makes sense to use a multi-stage pipeline instead of a single-stage processor because sending a single packet probably requires examining several header fields. It is possible to program each step to examine a distinct set of fields. A multi-stage pipeline allows for the processing of multiple packets concurrently, but at the cost of slightly increasing each packet's end-to-end latency (measured in nanoseconds). For instance, while Stage 1 is performing an initial lookup on packet B, Stage 2 may be performing a second look up on packet A, and so forth. This indicates that the pipeline can handle the combined bandwidth of all of its input ports. Whether the stages in a given NPU's implementation of this pipeline are fixed function (i.e., every step is capable of processing headers for a specific protocol) or programmable (i.e., each step's programming is dynamic to determine which header fields to handle. The conversation that follows begins with the more general scenario—a programmable pipeline—and ends with a return to its fixed-function equivalent.

At an architectural level, the programmable pipeline is often referred to as a Protocol Independent Switching Architecture (PISA). A high-level overview of PISA, which consists of three main parts, is provided by Figure 10.17. The first is a Parser, which is designed to specify which header fields (as well as where in the packet they are located) should be identified and matched by subsequent phases. The second is a series of Match-Action Units, where each is designed to match one or more of the designated header fields and may take an action based on that matching. Before the packet is sent over the output link, the third component is the Deparser, which re-serializes the packet metadata into the packet.

Using all of the in-memory header fields that have been processed by previous stages, the deparser reconstructs the over-the-wire representation for every packet. A set of metadata pertaining to the packets moving through the pipeline is not displayed in the figure.

This includes flow-level state calculated over successive packets, like switch counters and queue depth, as well as per-packet state, like the input port and arrival timestamp. This metadata has an equivalent ASIC value (e.g., a register), is accessible for reading and writing at different stages. The Match-Action Unit may also make use of it, for instance when matching on the input port.

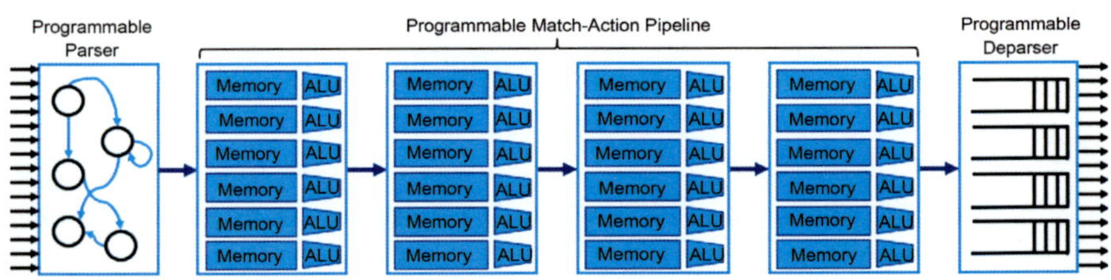

Figure 10.17. *High-level overview of PISA's multi-stage pipeline.*

Source: https://sdn.systemsapproach.org/_images/Slide11.png.

A closer examination of each of the Match-Action Units in Figure 10.17 is warranted. The memory depicted in the figure is commonly constructed by combining SRAM and TCAM. It functions as a table, storing bit patterns that must match in the packets that are being processed. The particular combination of memories is relevant because, although TCAM can support wildcard matches, it is more expensive and power-hungry than SRAM. To be more precise, the term "CAM" in TCAM refers to "Content Addressable Memory," indicating that the key you wish to search through in a table can actually be used as the memory address to access the table itself.

Technically speaking, the letter "T" stands for "Ternary," which means that the key you wish to look up may contain wildcards (e.g., both 1001 and 1011 are matched by key 10*1). The primary lesson from the software point of view is that wildcard matches cost more than exact matches and ought to be steered clear of whenever feasible. The action and matching pattern are then put into practice by the ALU depicted in the figure. Among the options are changing particular header fields (e.g., reducing a TTL), ejecting or pushing tags, etc., e.g., VLAN, MPLS), increasing or deleting different switch internal counters (e.g., packets handled), as well as configuring internal and user metadata (e.g., the routing table's VRF ID to be used).

It would be laborious to write microprocessor assembly code to directly program the parser, match-action units, and deparser; instead, we use a high-level language such as P4 to express the desired behavior and rely on a compiler to produce the corresponding low-level program. For the time being, we will use a graphic representation of the ideal forwarding pipeline that is even more abstract—Figure 10.18. We will discuss the specifics of P4 later.

In keeping with previous instances, we refer to this program as forward. Page 4. This sample program matches either IPv4 or IPv6 header fields first, then L2 header fields, and lastly applies some ACL rules to the packets before permitting them to pass. Consider the latter as rules for a firewall filter. The P4 compiler is in charge of allocating the available PISA resources in addition to translating the high-level representation of the pipeline onto the underlying PISA stages.

As in Figure 10.17, there are four slots (rows) for the available Match-Action Units in this instance. The P4/PISA equivalent of register allocation for a traditional programming language operating on a general-purpose microprocessor is assigning slots in the available Match-Action units. The compiler distributes entries in the available Match-Action Units in accordance with our assumption that there are significantly more IPv4 Match-Action rules than IPv6 or ACL rules.

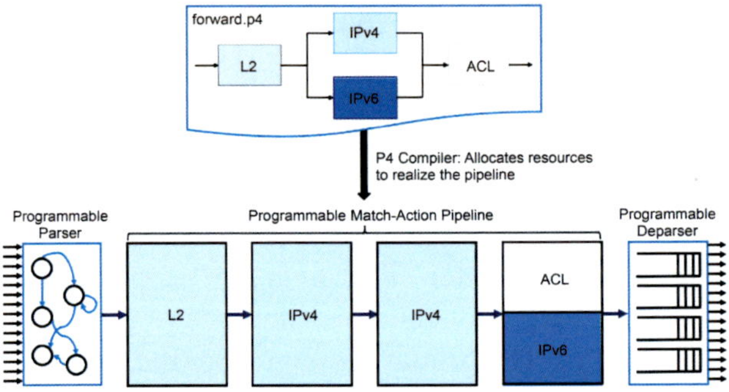

Figure 10.18. *Depiction of the desired forwarding behavior (as specified by a pictorial representation of a P4 program) mapped onto PISA.*

Source: https://sdn.systemsapproach.org/_images/Slide12.png.

REFERENCES

1. Benzekki, K., El Fergougui, A., & Elbelrhiti Elalaoui, A. (2016). Software-defined networking (SDN): A survey. *Security and Communication Networks, 9*(18), 5803–5833. https://doi.org/10.1002/sec.1737.
2. Casado, M., Freedman, M. J., Pettit, J., Luo, J., & McKeown, N. (2007). Ethane: Taking control of the enterprise. Stanford University.
3. Farrel, J., Vasseur, J., & Ash, J. (2006). A Path Computation Element (PCE)-based architecture. *Internet Engineering Task Force*. https://doi.org/10.17487/RFC4655.
4. Gude, N., Koponen, T., Pettit, J., Pfaff, B., M. C. (2011). OpenFlow Switch Specification.
5. Lakshman, T. V., Nandagopal, T., Ramjee, R., Sabnani, K., & Woo, T. (2004). The Soft Router architecture.
6. McKeown, N., Anderson, T., Balakrishnan, H., Parulkar, G., Peterson, L., Rexford, J., Shenker, S., & Turner, J. (2008). OpenFlow: Enabling innovation in campus networks.
7. Montazerolghaem, A. (2020). Software-defined load-balanced data center: Design, implementation and performance analysis. *Cluster Computing, 24*(2), 591–610. https://doi.org/10.1007/s10586-020-03134-x.
8. Montazerolghaem, A. (2021). Software-defined Internet of Multimedia Things: Energy-efficient and load-balanced resource management. *IEEE Internet of Things Journal, 9*(3), 2432–2442. https://doi.org/10.1109/JIOT.2021.3095237.
9. Salim, J., Khosravi, H., Kleen, A., & Kuznetsov, A. (2003). Linux Netlink as an IP services protocol. *Internet Engineering Task Force*. https://doi.org/10.17487/RFC3549.
10. Yang, L., Dantu, R., Anderson, T., & Gopal, R. (2004). Forwarding and control element separation (ForCES) framework. *Internet Engineering Task Force*. https://doi.org/10.17487/RFC3746.

INDEX

D

E

F

G

H

I

Q

R

S

U

V

W

X

MIX
Papier | Fördert gute Waldnutzung
FSC® C083411

Kolibri 360 GmbH
Ferdinand-Jühlke-Straße 7
99095 Erfurt, Deutschland
produktsicherheit@kolibri360.de